D0435678

Women in Hispanic Literature

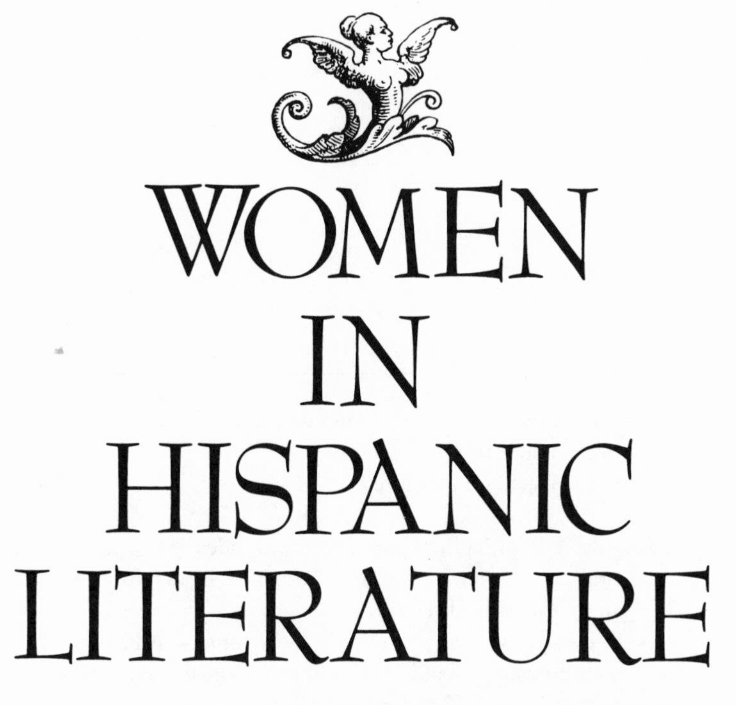

WOMEN IN HISPANIC LITERATURE

Icons and Fallen Idols

Edited by
Beth Miller

University of California Press
Berkeley · Los Angeles · London

Library of Congress Cataloging in Publication Data
Main entry under title:
Women in Hispanic Literature.

Includes bibliographical references and index. 1. Spanish literature—History and criticism—Addresses, essays, lectures. 2. Spanish American literature—History and criticism—Addresses, essays, lectures. 3. Women in literature—Addresses, essays, lectures. 4. Spanish literature—Women authors—History and criticism—Addresses, essays, lectures. 5. Spanish American literature—Women authors—History and criticism—Addresses, essays, lectures. I. Miller, Beth Kurti.
PQ6048.W6I26 860′.9 81-14663
ISBN 0-520-04291-3 AACR2
ISBN 0-520-04367-7 (pbk.)

University of California Press
Berkeley and Los Angeles, California
University of California Press, Ltd.
London, England

Printed in the United States of America

1 2 3 4 5 6 7 8 9

Y tú sonríes, misteriosamente
como es tu obligación. Pero yo te interpreto.

Rosario Castellanos
("Mirando a la Gioconda")

You don't hear their silence.

Thomas Pynchon
(*Gravity's Rainbow*)

Contents

Acknowledgments ix

Introduction: Some Theoretical Considerations 1

Spain's First Women Writers
Alan Deyermond 27

Echoes of the Amazon Myth in Medieval Spanish Literature
Estelle Irizarry 53

Sexual Humor in Misogynist Medieval Exempla
Harriet Goldberg 67

Women in the *Book of Good Love*
Rosalie Gimeno 84

Marina/Malinche: Masks and Shadows
Rachel Phillips 97

Women Against Wedlock: The Reluctant Brides of Golden Age Drama
Melveena McKendrick 115

The Convent as Catalyst for Autonomy: Two Hispanic Nuns of the Seventeenth Century
Electa Arenal 147

A School for Wives: Women in Eighteenth-Century Spanish Theater
Kathleen Kish 184

Gertrude the Great: Avellaneda, Nineteenth-Century Feminist
Beth Miller 201

Notes Toward a Definition of Gabriela Mistral's Ideology
Fernando Alegría 215

Female Archetypes in Mexican Literature
Luis Leal 227

Sara de Etcheverts: The Contradictions of Literary Feminism
Francine Masiello 243

The Greatest Punishment: Female and Male in Lorca's Tragedies
Julianne Burton 259

The Changing Face of Woman in Latin American Fiction
Marcia L. Welles 280

The Censored Sex: Woman as Author and Character in Franco's Spain
Linda Gould Levine 289

Sexual Politics and the Theme of Sexuality in Chicana Poetry
Elizabeth Ordóñez 316

From Mistress to Murderess: The Metamorphosis of Buñuel's Tristana
Beth Miller 340

Contributors 361

Index 365

Acknowledgments

My sincere thanks to the Del Amo Foundation for a grant that helped to pay for some of the expenses involved in the preparation of this volume and to the deans of humanities and of the graduate school, University of Southern California, for additional support.

Thanks to all those who read portions of the manuscript and offered suggestions to the contributors: Doris Kretschmer of the University of California Press; Mark Cramer of the University of Southern California; John H. R. Polt and John Walsh of the University of California, Berkeley; Kathryn Newman, editor of *Melus*; and especially to Alan Deyermond of the University of London. For her help in the preparation of the manuscript, I would like to express my gratitude to Mary Greco, bibliographer at the UCLA Research Library.

Introduction
Some Theoretical Considerations

A comprehensive series of essays on the women writers of Spain and Latin America would fill several volumes. Serrano y Sanz's catalogue, which covers Spanish women writers up to the early nineteenth century, occupies two substantial tomes, and Kathleen O'Quinn's work in progress, a bio-bibliography of Latin American women authors, lists some five thousand writers.[1] Obviously a thorough study of female characters in Hispanic literature—if it attempted to deal with ten centuries of literary production and, in the modern period, the national literatures of some twenty Spanish-speaking countries—would be far more extensive still. The present volume, therefore, does not aim at a complete coverage. The editor and contributors have sought to deal with writers and topics that are important and interesting in their own right. The articles included here represent varied scholarly and critical approaches and range in time from the eleventh century to the 1970s, from the Old World to the New (Argentina, Chile, Mexico). The literary genres treated include the novel, short story, drama, lyric poetry, history, didactic prose, and autobiography, and the volume ends with an essay on a film. The women characters studied are equally diverse: nuns and prostitutes, city dwellers and cowherds, aristocrats and peasants. The women writers, not by accident, include some obscure and overlooked, some lesser-known, and some quite famous literary figures.

These essays on women writers and characters represent the interests of a diverse group of scholars. The great majority of the articles

1. Manuel Serrano y Sanz, *Apuntes para una biblioteca de escritoras españolas desde el año 1401 al 1833* (Madrid: Tipografía de la Revista de Archivos, 1903 and 1905; facsimile ed., Madrid, 1975).

were written especially for this volume and are here published for the first time. The few that were published before have been substantially revised. Each article has a double aim: to present its subject in a way that interests and informs the general reader, and to offer an original contribution to scholarship. This is, then, a book for all readers interested in Hispanic culture or in women in literature.

The poet Muriel Rukeyser writes:

What would happen if one woman told the truth about her life?
The world would split open.[2]

It is a powerful image, but I think many women writers *have* told the truth about their lives, and it is generally they who split open, break down, biodegrade, while the world goes on much as before. Not heard, the woman chooses silence or death. Or not accepted on her own terms, she adopts masks, speaks in code, tries to conform apologetically. In the novel, anger and frustration often lead to defeat (or self-defeat) expressed by the comeuppance, downfall, death, or marriage of the fictional heroine after her initial rebellion against social norms. In poetry, a woman writer's anxiety or depression may be expressed as sadness, suffering, guilt, or morbidity, if not turned into archness and irony, as in the lines of Sor Juana Inés de la Cruz:

Hombres necios, que acusáis
a la mujer sin razón
sin ver que sois la ocasión
de lo mismo que culpáis.[3]

Foolish men who berate
Woman unjustly,
Not seeing that you create
The very image you denigrate.

Despite the high cost, many women writers through the centuries have been heroically rebellious and iconoclastic, usually with great effort and inner resistance, although a few are sometimes propelled by gusty winds of circumstance or fate or conviction. Alfonsina Storni, born in Argentina in 1892, was an unmarried mother, who lived and wrote in the important cultural center of Buenos Aires during a wave of feminism in the 1920s and 1930s. Storni sought her identity as a

2. Muriel Rukeyser, from "Käthe Kollwitz," *The Collected Poems of Muriel Rukeyser* (New York: McGraw-Hill, 1978), p. 482.

3. Sor Juana Inés de la Cruz, *Poesía, teatro y prosa*, ed. Antonio Castro Leal (7th ed., Mexico: Editorial Porrúa, 1976), pp. 34–37.

woman and a writer through her poetry, and many of her poems offer testimony of her struggle against cultural prejudices transmitted from generation to generation. One poem bears the title "La que comprende" (She Who Understands), a signifier of the social and historical message in the text:

> Con la cabeza negra caída hacia adelante
> Está la mujer bella, la de mediana edad,
> Postrada de rodillas, y un Cristo agonizante
> Desde su duro leño la mira con piedad.
> En los ojos la carga de una enorme tristeza,
> En el seno la carga del hijo por nacer,
> Al pie del blanco Cristo que está sangrando reza:
> —¡Señor, el hijo mío que no nazca mujer![4]
>
> With her dark head fallen forward
> The beautiful woman, not young
> On her knees before a dying Christ
> Who looks at her with pity from his hard cross.
> In her eyes the weight of an enormous sadness,
> In her belly the weight of an unborn child;
> At the foot of the white bleeding Christ she prays:
> "Oh Lord, my child, may it not be a girl!"

I believe that even the reference to the white Christ and the apostrophe to "Señor" are bitterly ironic signs of Storni's view of the male-dominated world at large of which the male-dominated literary world is a part. As Gertrude Stein wrote in a fairly obscure poem called "Patriarchal Poetry," published in 1927, thirteen years after *Tender Buttons* had brought her the title "The Mama of Dada," "Patriarchal poetry might be what they wanted." Although Stein is one who did not give them what they wanted, it is what most women poets, although not all, and some only sometimes, were taught to cherish and therefore sought to provide. In Stein's explanation, "Patriarchal Poetry is the same as Patriotic poetry is the same as Patriarchal poetry is the same as Patriotic poetry is the same as patriarchal poetry is the same."[5] This theme and the word itself recur in poetry by women and

---

4. Alfonsina Storni, *Languidez* (Buenos Aires: Cooperativa Editorial Buenos Aires, 1920), p. 96. See Rachel Phillips, *Alfonsina Storni: From Poetess to Poet* (London: Tamesis, 1975), pp. 1–11.

5. Gertrude Stein, "Patriarchal Poetry," *The World Split Open: Four Centuries of Women Poets in England and America, 1552–1950*, ed. Louise Bernikow (New York: Vintage, 1974), pp. 232, 235.

recently in feminist literary criticism.[6] Storni laments the burden of patriarchal social strictures in antipatriarchal poems such as "Peso ancestral" (Ancestral Weight) and "Veinte siglos" (Twenty Centuries).

Because patriarchy is so ancient—it actually dates much further back than a mere twenty centuries—women's literary production in Spanish is relatively meager until modern times. There are only three women writers of late medieval Spain to have left any substantial work—Leonor López de Córdoba, Teresa de Cartagena, and Florencia Pinar—and ninety-nine of one hundred Hispanists have never heard their names. Most women writers, at least from the time of María de Zayas Sotomayor in the sixteenth century and Aphra Behn in the seventeenth, but especially since the early thirties of this century, have been aware that literary history chronicles the doings and attitudes of dominant male literati. Even in the seventeenth and eighteenth centuries few women in the Spanish empire wrote, and we have very few analyses of women's literature from these periods. We ask where women writers and scholars have been for two thousand years and examine the works of the few who have survived (such as Saint Teresa) or been disinterred (such as the Venerable Madre Isabel de Jesús). Knowing that as a group women in the seventeenth century fell below unskilled male laborers in their rate of literacy, we marvel at those extraordinary women writers and scholars of whose achievements we have any notice.[7]

Clearly, there is a great deal to be learned about women writers from history itself. Feminist historians, both male and female, are currently involved in scholarship on the history of feminism and on

---

6. See Annette Kolodny, "Some Notes on Defining a 'Feminist Literary Criticism,'" *Critical Inquiry*, 2 (1975–1976), 75–92; also the ensuing discussion and debate: the exchange between Kolodny and William W. Morgan in *Critical Inquiry*, 2, 807–32, and Josephine Donovan's response in *Critical Inquiry*, 3 (1976–1977), 605–08.

7. See the introductory comments in *The Female Spectator: English Women Writers Before 1800*, ed. Mary R. Mahl and Helen Koon (Bloomington: Indiana University Press; Old Westbury, N.Y.: Feminist Press, 1977), pp. 1–11. Dorothy Gies McGuigan, in "To Be a Woman and a Scholar" (paper presented at the Center for Continuing Education for Women, University of Michigan, 20 April 1978) on the Venetian scholar Elena Cornaro, the first woman in the world to receive a doctoral degree (in 1648), points out that before 1650 barely 10 percent of women in the city of London could sign their names and that in the seventeenth century the average woman's life expectancy had risen only to thirty-two years. Not until one hundred fifty years later did American universities admit women for degrees, and two centuries were to pass before Oxford and Cambridge conferred degrees on women. Today women earn over half the doctorates in Spanish.

women's history which is scarcely mentioned in the standard histories. There exists, for instance, a sizable body of scholarship by American and British scholars on the experiences of women through the centuries as recorded in letters, diaries, autobiographies, and memoirs, but Hispanists have so far shown little corresponding interest in these materials. Similarly, although many researchers in England and the United States (Florence Howe and others) have studied the correlations between women's history and the literary production of women, there has been a notable absence of comparable scholarship on Spanish and Latin American writers. Referring to the psychological significance of foremothers, Doris Lessing, in *The Golden Notebook*, writes: "Are you saying there haven't been artist-women before? There haven't been women who are independent? There haven't been women who insisted on sexual freedom? I tell you, there are a great line of women stretching out behind you into the past, and you have to seek them out and find them in yourself and be conscious of them."[8]

We can, if we seek them out, find thousands of Hispanic artist-women who have participated in and sought a literature of their own.[9] The poets in particular are aware that they are *women* writers, but, nevertheless, they yearn at the same time, for obvious practical reasons, to be recognized by male critics and poets and in literary history written by men. This ambivalence, although natural, constitutes one of the most difficult contradictions encountered in the study of women writers; it is part of an old and ongoing dialectic that is pertinent to an understanding of women's writing and has posed a major theoretical

---

8. Doris Lessing, *The Golden Notebook* (New York: Simon & Schuster, 1962), p. 472. Also see Sheila Rowbotham, *Hidden from History: Rediscovering Women in History from the Seventeenth Century to the Present* (New York: Vintage, 1976).

9. In the last decade many feminist writers have quoted Virginia Woolf's now-famous diagnosis and prescription for women writers. In a 1928 paper she said:

> Intellectual freedom depends upon material things. Poetry depends upon intellectual freedom. And women have always been poor, not for two hundred years merely, but from the beginning of time. Women have had less intellectual freedom than the sons of Athenian slaves. Women, then, have not had a dog's chance of writing poetry. That is why I have laid so much stress on money and a room of one's own.

Reprinted in *A Room of One's Own* (New York: Harcourt, Brace & World, 1957), p. 112; Spanish version, *Un cuarto propio* (Buenos Aires: Ediciones Sur, 1936). Also see Elaine Showalter, *A Literature of Their Own: British Women Novelists from Brontë to Lessing* (Princeton, N.J.: Princeton University Press, 1977), pp. 3–36.

problem for scholars. Much fiction as well as poetry by women is structured upon another not unrelated dialectic, one we may term things-as-they-are versus things-as-they-might-be. Recognizing this tension and its source in the contexts of women's writing enables us to understand the texts better. Sara de Etcheverts, for example, in her later novels, explores alienation and the historical factors that produce it, integrating history and fiction through characters who engage in despairing ideological formulations. As Annis Pratt has pointed out: "The world of woman's art is not the aesthetic other-world of the new critics, self-existent, with no reference to historical and cultural context."[10] This consideration is not new; it is reflected in the narrative techniques and characterization by Latin American women novelists as different from each other as María Luisa Bombal, Elisa Serrana, Silvina Bullrich, Marta Lynch, and Elena Poniatowska, and in the anxiety of these lines by Alfonsina Storni:

> Pudiera ser que todo lo que aquí he recogido
> no fuera más que aquello que nunca pudo ser,
> no fuera más que algo vedado y reprimido
> de familia en familia, de mujer en mujer.[11]
>
> It could be that all I have recovered here
> is nothing more than what could never have been,
> merely something suppressed, kept hidden,
> from family to family, from woman to woman.

In 1938, the year that Storni committed suicide, Gabriela Mistral (born in Chile in 1889) published in her volume *Tala* a poem entitled "Todas íbamos a ser reinas" (Yes, We All Were Going to Be Queens) that analyzes young women's romantic fantasies, limited aspirations, and inevitable disillusion, all of which derive from a common sociohistorical and cultural context. In "La extranjera" (The Stranger) she paints a poignant portrait of an aging, marginal, isolated woman. This

---

10. Annis Pratt, "The New Feminist Criticisms: Exploring the History of the New Space," in *Beyond Intellectual Sexism: A New Woman, A New Reality*, ed. Joan I. Roberts (New York: David McKay, 1976), p. 193.

11. The poetry quotation is the first quatrain of Storni's sonnet "Bien pudiera ser." I have chosen the version which appears in *Antología femenina: Los mejores versos de las mejores poetisas*, ed. F. Santelso (Mexico: Ediciones Lux, n.d.), p. 59, rather than the widely reprinted earlier version found in the standard anthologies and in Ramón J. Ruggero's compilation of Storni's poetry.

kind of poem, organized around a central female-feminist figure, carries a tenor that concerns class as well as sex discrimination.[12] Such figures recur in poetry by Latin American women. Rosario Castellanos (born in Mexico in 1922), in a long dramatic monologue that combines social reality and myth, transmits the solitude and pain of an Indian woman, giving voice to her silence:

> Vine de lejos. Olvidé mi patria.
> Ya no entiendo el idioma
> que allá usan de moneda o de herramienta.
> Alcancé la mudez mineral de la estatua.[13]
>
> I came from far away. I forgot my country.
> I no longer understand the language
> used there as coin and tool.
> I have attained the mineral muteness of a statue.

Although Gabriela Mistral was the first Latin American writer to win a Nobel Prize in literature (in 1945), her reputation, based on her poetry, has declined shockingly. Like Gertrudis Gómez de Avellaneda, Mistral received a great deal of critical attention for a time, but it resulted in a lopsided view of her achievement. She is praised for gaining international recognition but blamed for her sentimentality as a poet and her lack of formal experimentation in avant-garde techniques. For Fernando Alegría, however, Mistral's charismatic force is contained in her prose writings from which her doctrine of human rights emerges with clarity and courage. For this scholar, Mistral's thought—as revealed in her extemporaneous speeches, newspaper articles and interviews, and thousands of letters—provides the key to understanding her following and influence and will in time be considered "the most profound and valuable expression of her creative genius" (see below, p. 215). This attempt to alter the stereotype of a woman author in or-

---

12. See my essays "The Poetry of Rosario Castellanos: Tone and Tenor," in *Homenaje a Rosario Castellanos*, ed. Maureen Ahern and Mary Seale Vázquez (Valencia: Albatros-Ediciones Hispanófila, 1980); and "Women and Feminism in the Works of Rosario Castellanos," in *Feminist Criticism: Essays on Theory, Poetry, and Prose*, ed. Cheryl L. Brown and Karen Olson (Metuchen, N.J.: Scarecrow Press, 1978), pp. 198–210; Spanish version, "El feminismo mexicano de Rosario Castellanos," in Beth Miller, *Mujeres en la literatura* (Mexico: Fleischer, 1978), pp. 9–19.

13. "Monólogo de la extranjera," most accessible in the volume of Castellanos' collected poetry, *Poesía no eres tú* (Mexico: Fondo de Cultura Económica, 1972), pp. 112–14.

der to permit new readings of her works represents a radical practice in Hispanic literary criticism, one which necessitates the rearrangement of the shards of a fallen idol.

Far more common is scholarship that attempts new interpretations, including feminist perspectives, in the study of women characters in mainstream Hispanic literary texts. The majority of such studies to date have been devoted to female characterization in narrative and dramatic works by peninsular Spanish male authors. Even in this area, diverse approaches may be complementary, and each may yield distinctive insights. In general, there is a consensus that misogyny and idealization have been two aspects of a single tendency through centuries of literary production in Spanish. From the medieval exempla and the *Libro de Buen Amor* (*Book of Good Love*) of the fourteenth century through Golden Age dramas of the baroque period female characters reflect a limited stock of stereotypes. These are generally dichotomized, in moral terms, as either "good" or "bad," icons worthy of veneration or more sexual fallen idols deserving of ridicule and contempt. At the same time, these characters reflect the nature of social institutions, the predominant influence of the Catholic church, and the internalized cultural concepts designated by the terms "female" and "feminine." When virtually all writers are men, female literary characters appear to be full of "otherness," embodying projections of male authors' attitudes toward women. This is the case in the eighteenth-century *sainetes* of Ramón de la Cruz as also in the images of women in nineteenth-century Romantic dramas such as *Don Juan Tenorio* or *Don Alvaro* and in the Romantic novel par excellence, *María* by the Colombian author Jorge Isaacs. Even in modern classics, examples of the persistent good woman/bad woman dichotomy abound. We think of *Marianela* by Benito Pérez Galdós, a Spaniard, or *Doña Bárbara* by Rómulo Gallegos, a Venezuelan. And Luis Leal, a cautious gentleman scholar, is able to affirm without hesitation: "The characterization of women throughout Mexican literature has been profoundly influenced by two archetypes present in the Mexican psyche: that of the woman who has kept her virginity and that of the one who has lost it" (see below, p. 227).

Although it is demonstrably possible, then, to arrive at generalizations about women characters in Hispanic literature (see the essay below on Tristana, pp. 340–59), the assumption that it is possible to generalize about women writers, or even about Latin American women writers, is sexist since no specialist would presume to encompass in a single category Latin American or Hispanic men writers.

There are obviously differences among them, some of which depend on time and place, others on individual style and talent. Still, as the fourteen graduate students in my seminar on Hispanic women writers in 1978 were quick to discern, in academia, the expression "Spanish (or Latin American) writers" has in practice meant men. It is perhaps slightly easier to discuss women's writing in the various genres. Poetry is the most controversial area in women's literature. Women poets seem to have had a more difficult time gaining recognition than prose writers have mainly because of the very nature of poetry. Poems are more subject to changing tastes, more easily forgotten, and certainly more easily misinterpreted. In Latin America in the last fifty years, some women poets have gained acceptance in a token way, especially if they have appeared to conform to the tastes and canon of a particular place and period and if they were fortunate enough to have powerful male friends or relatives who were literary critics or editors of prestigious journals.

Some Hispanic women poets, usually dead ones, have been considered first rate, but these are rare instances. Nearly all women poets in Spanish and Spanish-American literature are considered minor—the very word *poetisa* ("poetess," still used in Spanish) is condescending, as is the widespread Hispanic convention of referring to women writers by their first names. And although it has been claimed by leading Latin Americanists that after the First World War poetry became a "feminine art," the anthologies and histories reflect a deep conviction that it is men who excel in this so-called feminine art (*The Penguin Book of Latin American Verse*, for example, includes four females and seventy-nine males). It appears not only that "woman" and "poet" have been believed incompatible but that women poets, because of the hypothetical limitations of their sex, are by definition "minor."

Yet there are possible approaches to the history of women's writing, as well as to the study and appreciation of the texts, that have no recourse to the terms major and minor. Such an assertion is by no means a self-evident truth, and it draws us into a still quite uncharted territory—a controversial area that calls for recognition of the subjectivity of judgments and analysis of unstated or unexamined assumptions. We assume that we share, as scholars, certain assumptions about literature. And we do. We do not share, I do not share, the assumption of a monolithic theory and a set of objective standards for judging quality. Also, it seems obvious to me that just as those who have decided on the greatness and importance of poets have been men, so too those who have decided which poems, if any, by women to include in anthologies of Hispanic literature have been men.[14] Generally, these anthologists have tended to choose—perhaps not consciously or with malevolence—those poems by women which suited their ideas of what women's poetry should be like and often of what women should be like.

A few feminist critics are suggesting different frames of reference that question both literary history and traditional ways of valuing literature. Nearly all the North American women scholars who have rebelled against these fundamental aspects of their training have become aware that it is in their professional interest, if they wish to succeed or perhaps to survive, not to go too far in this direction, for their male colleagues will judge their scholarship to be superficial, irrelevant, or politically contaminated; ergo, their critical faculties are judged inferior. Nevertheless, particularly in the past ten years, a number of women scholars in a variety of disciplines have been laying the groundwork for widely applicable critical theories and approaches. In studying the role of gender in literary history, they question standard methodologies such as formalism. The majority of the pioneers in this field in literature have been from English-speaking countries—Josephine Donovan, Mary Ellmann, Shulamith Firestone, Kate Millett, Ellen Moers, Lillian S. Robinson, and others.[15] Many of the essays in this volume similarly challenge canons. Linda Levine, for example, combines literary criticism with sociohistorical research to explain the ambiguities and conflicts expressed in the fiction of writers such as Ana María Matute, Carmen Martín Gaite, and Anna María Moix, whose feminist critiques and vision emerged within the repressive censorship of the Franco period in Spain (see below, pp. 289–315).

A central problem for those working in Latin American literature is that many Latin American feminists do not fully accept the tenets of North American radical feminism, since feminists in Latin America

---

14. See Beth Miller, "A Random Survey of the Ratio of Female Poets to Male in Anthologies: Less-Than-Tokenism as a Mexican Tradition," in *Latin American Women Writers: Yesterday and Today*, ed. Yvette E. Miller and Charles M. Tatum (Pittsburgh, Pa.: Latin American Literary Review Press, 1977), pp. 11–17. Especially since 1975 there has been some improvement in some anthologies and a corresponding increase in women's studies publications.

15. For a fuller listing, see Cheri Register, "American Feminist Literary Criticism: A Bibliographical Introduction," in *Feminist Literary Criticism*, ed. Josephine Donovan (Lexington: University Press of Kentucky, 1975), pp. 1–28; and Jane Williamson, *New Feminist Scholarship: A Guide to Bibliographies* (Old Westbury, N.Y.: Feminist Press, 1979).

(although there are differences according to country) tend to endorse socialist feminism, which they believe to be more appropriate ideologically to the history and status of their nations: once colonies of the Spanish Empire and now, they believe, dependent or Third World countries, under the domination of an imperialist outside world, which some call "the United States" and some identify as multinational hegemony. The ideological position of these women, then, is that in their countries females are no more oppressed than their jobless or economically exploited male counterparts and that the only solution to social problems lies in changing the political and economic systems, not in seeking equality for women.[16] This position has largely prevented the development of a substantial body of theoretical work applying feminist perspectives in the field of Latin American literature, even though other women scholars in Latin America have produced significant research on women in anthropology, history, and political science.[17]

Yet there is strong evidence of an interest in contemporary feminist

---

16. Varieties of this ideological position may be found, e.g., in Arlene Eisen Bergman, *Women of Vietnam* (San Francisco: People's Press, 1974), Spanish version *Las mujeres de Vietnam* (Mexico: Era, 1977); Gisèle Halimi, *La cause des femmes* (Paris: Editions Grasset et Fasquelle), Spanish version *La causa de las mujeres* (Mexico: Era, 1976); Alejandra Kollontay, *El marxismo y la nueva moral sexual* (Mexico: Grijalbo, 1977); Julia Kristeva, *Des Chinoises* (Paris: Editions des Femmes, 1974); Isabel Larguía and John Dumoulin, *Hacia una ciencia de la liberación de la mujer* (Caracas: Universidad Central de Venezuela, 1975); Michèle Mattelart, *La cultura de la opresión femenina* (Mexico: Era, 1977); Margaret Randall, *Cuban Women Now* (Toronto: Women's Press and Dumont, 1974); Evelyn Reed, *Problems of Women's Liberation*, (1969; 5th ed., New York: Pathfinder, 1970); Sheila Rowbotham, *Women, Resistance, and Revolution* (London: Penguin, 1972); Anon., *La liberación de la mujer* (Mexico: Folletos Bandera Socialista, no. 14 [1975?]). The few histories of the women's movement published in Spain and Latin America to date tend to be nationalistic rather than to employ a broadly international perspective which would shed light on contacts and connections across national boundaries. These works are useful, nevertheless; see, for example, Amparo Moreno, *Mujeres en lucha: El movimiento feminista en España* (Barcelona: Anagrama, 1977).

17. There is still, however, relatively little scholarship which attempts to relate the literary production by women to the history of the feminist movement or to women's history, as studied in such articles as Johanna S. R. Mendelson's "The Feminine Press: The View of Women in the Colonial Journals of Spanish America, 1790–1810," or June E. Hahner's "The Nineteenth-Century Feminist Press and Women's Rights in Brazil," or Ana Macías' "Felipe Carrillo Puerto and Women's Liberation in Mexico," all in *Latin American Women: Historical Perspectives*, ed. Asunción Lavrín (Westport, Conn.: Greenwood Press, 1978). Michael H. Handelsman attempts such an approach in his two-

writings on the part of women writers in Latin America as well as feminist intellectuals and academics, even in their frequent references to Virginia Woolf and Simone de Beauvoir. Books by bourgeois North American and European feminist critics such as Germaine Greer (published in Spanish) appear in increasing numbers on bookstore shelves alongside a wide variety of works by women writers from non-Spanish-speaking countries: Djuna Barnes, Colette, Doris Lessing, Clarice Lispector, Katherine Mansfield, Jean Rhys, and others. Erica Jong's *Fear of Flying* was on the best-seller list in Spain for over two years, as it had been previously in Mexico.[18]

It is a curious footnote to literary history that the important Mexican literary group of the mid-twenties to mid-thirties, the Contemporáneos, included no women and paid scant attention to Mexican women writers (except for the seventeenth-century nun Sor Juana). It may seem paradoxical at first glance that the poet-critics in the Contemporáneos circle published in their journal, from 1928 to 1931, translations of Marianne Moore (by Salvador Novo) and H. D. (by Xavier Villaurrutia), and examined foreign women writers in their

---

volume *Amazones y artistas: Un estudio de la prosa de la mujer ecuatoriana* (Guayaquil: Casa de la Cultura Ecuatoriana, 1978), a work along the same lines as José Macedonio Urquidi's *Bolivianas ilustres* (La Paz: Escuela Tipográfica Salesiana, 1918). A number of scholars are, however, producing good spadework on Hispanic women writers in their sociohistorical contexts and presenting the products of their research at conferences or in journals; see, for example, Iris M. Zavala, "Dos mujeres contra el mundo: Flora Tristán (1803–1844) y Louise Michel (1830–1905)," *Sin Nombre*, 7(3) (1976), 37–45; or the work on women writers in Peru by Cecilia Bustamante, Lucía Fox-Lockert, and Daniel Reedy. Additional bibliography appears in Meri Knaster, "Women in Latin America: The State of Research, 1975," *Latin American Research Review*, 11(1) (1976), 3–74; Ann Pescatello, *Power and Pawn: The Female in Iberian Families, Societies, and Cultures* (Westport, Conn.: Greenwood Press, 1976); and Meri Knaster, *Women in Spanish America: An Annotated Bibliography from Pre-Conquest to Contemporary Times* (Boston: G. K. Hall, 1977).

18. My remark is based on an assessment of the situation derived in conversations and during a trip to Mexico City in early December 1978 to deliver a series of lectures on the Mexican writer Rosario Castellanos. I found the response at the National University (UNAM) favorable and the questions sophisticated, and I was encouraged to perform feminist analyses. Some of the students accused me of being a tepid bourgeois feminist. A few questioned my scholarly interest in Mexican women writers, so marginal in terms of the international scene and in contrast to the more important writers they were reading, such as Jane Austen, Rita Mae Brown, Susan Sontag, and—in the pages of the prestigious magazine, *Vuelta*—Spanish translations of Sylvia Plath.

critical articles (Jaime Torres Bodet, for example, wrote with perspicacity of Alfonsina Storni and Norah Lange, among others). The explanation of this paradox involves another problem encountered in research on Latin American women writers, one which has to do with the Latin Americans' insecurities about their own literature. This issue was much discussed, of course, even before the "Boom" of the Latin American novel in the sixties, when a number of writers from different countries began to achieve an international readership and reputation and began to be read in translation and reviewed in other languages. In this connection, it is interesting that Rosario Castellanos' first novel, *Balún-Canán*, published in 1958 and immediately translated into English by Irene Nicholson (*The Nine Guardians*), is to an extent a precursor of the Boom novels, also that Elena Garro's *Los recuerdos del porvenir* (*Recollections of Things to Come*) is thought by some scholars to have had a significant influence on *Cien años de soledad* (*One Hundred Years of Solitude*) by Gabriel García Márquez, who read Garro's manuscript.[19]

Although Latin American writers actively seek recognition abroad, many Latin American critics and intellectuals, including feminists, tend to resent the quantity of recent scholarship by foreigners on their literature, which some view as further evidence of cultural imperialism. This is especially true in Mexico.[20] Gabriel Zaid has an essay in his collection *Cómo leer en bicicleta* (*How to Read While Bicycling*) in which he sarcastically proposes a Malthusian model to explain the phenomenon of the "geometric" proliferation of North American scholars hovering threateningly over Mexican writers whose number augments only arithmetically.[21] It is well known among most Latin Americanists at institutions outside Latin America that Spanish-American writers since the time of the independence have longed for a literature of their own and, more recently, a literary criticism of their own, that is, not Spanish or French or Anglo-American in origin. The desire to avoid the old models and influences, highly respected in ear-

---

19. The information about Garro is from Gabriela Mora, "Exploración temática en la obra de Elena Garro," a paper presented at the Conference on Women Writers from Latin America (Pittsburgh, Pa.: Carnegie-Mellon University, 15 March 1975). *Los recuerdos del porvenir* (Mexico: Joaquín Mortiz, 1963) has been translated into English by Ruth L. C. Simms: *Recollections of Things to Come* (Austin: University of Texas Press, 1969).

20. See, for example, José Luis Martínez, "Los estudios norteamericanos sobre México," *Diálogos*, 15(2) (1979), 12–14.

21. Gabriel Zaid, "La nueva ley de Malthus," *Cómo leer en bicicleta* (Mexico: Joaquín Mortiz, 1975), pp. 11–12.

lier periods, is one explanation for the surprising number of translations into Spanish of works written in languages spoken in the Communist countries, and vice versa. At the same time, since the old influences are still strong, although often unacknowledged, it is helpful to take into account another ongoing dialectic, one which has continued from the last century: nationalism versus elitist cosmopolitanism. In short, the unresolved problems and the political elements in scholarship and criticism relating to Hispanic literature in general further complicate the controversial area of feminist criticism and research on women writers.

Many questions spring forth in the study of women's literature in any language. One fascinating issue concerns the degree to which feminist scholars are warranted in speaking of a separate literary tradition, a specifically female heritage or line. Griselda Alvarez, for example, in a volume she edited in 1973, *Diez mujeres en la poesía mexicana del siglo XX* (Ten Women in Mexican Poetry of the Twentieth Century), finds it imperative to state a position (that literature has no gender) in her Introduction: "We have intentionally avoided the title *Anthology of Feminine Poetry* because . . . we have never believed in the existence of feminine and masculine poetry, that is, hormonal poetry, whether it inclines more to estrogen or to testosterone."[22] It is interesting to note that seventeen years earlier, Julieta Carrera, a Cuban writer, had taken an opposite position, less common in Latin America, in defending her anthology *La mujer en América escribe* (Women Writing in the Americas): "One perceives, in different tones, the same desire, a central theme, a unifying force."[23] A recent North American anthologist, Emily Stipes Watts, in the Introduction to her book *The Poetry of American Women from 1632 to 1943*, like Alvarez, espouses the unisex stance: "In following this course of investigation, I do not mean to imply that poetry by American men and poetry by American women are two separate kinds of poetry, although they have at times been so treated in the past."[24] Needless to say, women poets are affected by men as well as by women writers, by what is called the poetic tradition, as well as by artistic developments, intellectual currents, and the writer's time, place, and circumstances, but this does not deny the pos-

---

22. Griselda Alvarez, *Diez mujeres en la poesía mexicana del siglo veinte* (Mexico: Colección Metropolitana, 1974), p. 7.

23. Julieta Carrera, *La mujer en América escribe* (Mexico: Ediciones Alonso, 1956), p. 4.

24. Emily Stipes Watts, *The Poetry of American Women from 1632 to 1945* (Austin: University of Texas Press, 1977), p. 3.

sibility of feminist writings or of women's consciousness and/or experience as women.

The question of whether there is a separate female literary tradition differs from the less subtle one concerning an identifiable female style. Although both fit into the examination of the relationship between gender and creativity, the latter has to do with gender and style, that is, the hidden assumptions of a "feminine" style which can be praised or blamed for its degree or lack of "femininity." The answer to the first question would seem to be yes and no, a political and strategic matter, while the latter question could be approached empirically, for example, by a procedure similar to I. A. Richards' experiment at Cambridge, as described in his *Practical Criticism.*[25] It seems to me that men and women use much the same language in poetry and that gender-linked differences, when they occur, are mainly in the tenor—to use Richards' term—not significantly in the syntax or versification or other formal elements. Of course, there is nothing to be lost by continued exploration of this question, an enterprise currently occupying a number of scholars in the fields of linguistics, communication, behavioral psychology, and semiotics. I think, however, that we are on more defensible ground when we focus on content, even on elements such as theme and attitude, thought and statement, persona, poetic (or narrative) stance, and the use of allusion.

It does appear that certain strong women writers have been able to pass on a special kind of consciousness, a vague term, by which I do not mean to suggest a militant commitment to women's rights or the Equal Rights Amendment, not anything that leads necessarily to overtly or intentionally feminist poetry, but rather, perhaps, a willingness to write out of one's own experience as a woman, even in defiance of the prevailing canon, and to value other women's writing. Louise Bernikow tries to define this quality in the preface to her anthology of women poets in England and the United States:

> I have tried in this book to uncover a lost tradition in English and American poetry. My desire is to bring out into the open many poets now lost to our eyes, and also to bring some specific kinds of content, things that have been shaped into various po-

---

25. I. A. Richards, *Practical Criticism: A Study of Literary Judgment* (1929; rpt. New York: Harcourt, Brace & World, 1956), pp. 3–16. Josephine Donovan examines this question more controversially in "Feminist Style Criticism," in *Images of Women in Fiction: Feminist Perspectives*, ed. Susan Koppelman Cornillon (Bowling Green, Ohio: University Popular Press, 1972), pp. 341–54.

> etic forms now lost to our ears. I do not think the loss has been an accident, but rather a result of the patriarchal structure of literary life and work in both countries.

A feminist critic, Bernikow is anxious to find "poems that are not often printed, the poems on being a woman, the poems on traditionally 'unfeminine' subjects, the poems that sometimes don't quite make it on purely esthetic grounds, whatever those grounds are, but make attempts that are interesting and often revolutionary."[26]

Adrienne Rich is a poet-critic who defends a related thesis: that there exists a common and detectible sensibility in women's poetry. Like Tillie Olsen, Armonía Somers, and Cristina Peri Rossi, Rich understands both women's objectification and their silences. She writes of her

> sense that women of whatever class, nation, or race share a common sensibility—a sensibility that is complex, subversive, and heterodox. . . . For none of these poets could it be simple to be a poet in a woman's body, that object perceived alternately as sacred and filthy, necessary and loathsome, that chattel of civilization, that machine for reproduction. For a woman to detach herself from prescribed relationships long enough to close a door behind her and sit down to write is still a pressing challenge. The mere sense of identity required has had to be fought for in patriarchal culture, and has been won, if at all, at great cost.[27]

This is a radical-feminist view, one that may be considered liberal and would need to be changed to be able to include Domitila and Concha Michel.

Mainly because Anglo critics cannot read Spanish and have been far more ignorant of Hispanic literature than vice versa, one thing that has scarcely been done but needs doing is the comparison of Hispanic women writers with women writers from other cultures. In poetry by Spanish-speaking women, as in poetry written by women who speak other languages, there is a familiar history of having to deal with obstructions, of having to be presumptuous in facing male convention and ridding oneself of internalized masculinist norms and expectations. Anne Finch, the Countess of Winchilsea, in the late seventeenth century, understood the sociohistorical source of many women writers' self-deprecation:

---

26. Louise Bernikow, *The World Split Open*, p. xii.

27. Adrienne Rich, "Foreword," in *The Other Voice: Twentieth-Century Women's Poetry in Translation*, ed. Joanna Bankier et al. (New York: Norton, 1976), p. xviii.

Alas! a woman that attempts the pen,
Such an intruder on the rights of men,
Such a presumptuous Creature, is esteem'd,
The fault can by no virtue be redeem'd . . .
How are we fal'n, fal'n by mistaken rules?
And Education's, more than Nature's fools,
Debarr'd from all improvements of the mind,
And to be dull, expected and designed. . . .[28]

And so we see the same theme in Anne Finch and Anne Bradstreet, in Sor Juana and Storni and Castellanos, falling by "mistaken rules," as much as though they were characters in novels or plays.

Ultimately, the question of a women's tradition in poetry may be considered to be as open to interpretation as any question of influence or intention, particularly if one limits the admissible evidence to analyses of the texts alone. Even on the basis of the texts, however, we can discern at the very least an "intertextuality" (to appropriate Derrida's expression) among very different women writers. But there is no real reason to ignore other important evidence of this "female line" available in dedications, epigraphs, and quotations in poems, as well as in many authors' autobiographical writings, letters, and published or broadcast literary interviews.[29] If we look at these sources it becomes evident that many women writers explain their vocation, sometimes also their political or social consciousness, and often their sense of a connectedness between personal experience and historical realities as having been discovered through the works of other women authors with whose experiences they identified or sympathized.

Thus, although we may raise objections on several grounds to the practice of mentioning Sor Juana Inés de la Cruz, a traditional baroque poet, in discussions of contemporary women writers who seem to have nothing in common with her apart from gender, it is nevertheless true that a large number of Spanish and Spanish-American women writers continue to acknowledge a debt to the seventeenth-century nun, a powerful muse, an icon destroyed and then resurrected and reconstructed (or deconstructed). Yet it is not Juana de Asbaje's celebrated long poem, "Primero Sueño" (First Dream), nor the much-

28. Anne Finch, "The Introduction," in *The Poems of Anne Finch, Countess of Winchilsea*, ed. Myra Reynolds (Chicago: University of Chicago Press, 1903), pp. 4–5.

29. Studies of such sources are beginning to increase in number in Hispanic letters. One example, published during the International Women's Year, is Isaac Rojas Rosillo's edition of the letters of Antonieta Rivas Mercado, *Cartas a Manuel Rodríguez Lozano (1927–1930)* (Mexico: SepSetentas, 1975).

anthologized *redondillas*, nor the magnificent sonnets, but rather her autobiographical writing (particularly the letter known as "Respuesta a Sor Filotea") that have provided spiritual energy and an early example of a woman writer's moral courage and determination in response to formidable institutional obstacles. Women writers in Spain and Latin America are able to identify with Sor Juana's intellectual obsession and suffering as well as with her vicissitudes at the hands of arrogant male critics and literary historians. Nearly three centuries after her death (in 1695), she alone among Hispanic women poets has been securely canonized in literature, that is, labeled a "great poet" and not only "the greatest woman poet."

There are things then—attitudes, the questioning of traditional canon—to be picked up from reading other women. Beyond this we can detect, I suggest, a way of handling certain literary allusions, female figures, and provincial images (relating, for example, to illiterate Indians or rural schoolteachers or the boredom and frustration of old-fashioned spinsters) that characterizes the literature of women. We may also find a tendency toward deflated language and understatement and attempts at the decoding of male-poet clichés. Many women writers have explored ways to "de-create," rejecting and/or reinterpreting myths and images of women and men in literature. The delightful poem "Caballero" by the forgotten Lázara Meldiú is an example of early twentieth-century underground women's poetry in Latin America. The poem is traditional in form but not in its statement, which is elegantly defiant and devastatingly ironic and witty about patriarchy and, by extension, patriarchal poetry. In a discourse quite different from that of Gertrude Stein quoted above, Meldiú criticizes, gracefully and unstridently, not only sex discrimination, but racial prejudice as well (for example, line 2), and comments explicitly on class privilege, viewed as a historical and cultural inheritance from the Spaniards at the time of the conquest. Like Rosario Castellanos and Marge Piercy, Meldiú seizes on the connection between patriarchy and ideological hegemony:

CABALLERO

Por tu gesto que marca la grandeza
singular y elegante de tu raza;
por tu perfil que tiene la serena
línea de envejecida aristocracia.

Por la callada plenitud que lleva
la señorial sonrisa de tu hidalga

estirpe, que jugó aventuras
y es regia y monástica y pirata.

Por tu ademán que tiene la magnífica
tranquilidad del fraile y del monarca,
por esa rancia lírica que forma
la flor de los escudos de tu heráldica;

Abro mi canto en madrigal de seda
bajo la luna en madrigal de plata,
y llego a tus deseos en ofrenda
con un trino de alondras en el alma.[30]

GENTLEMAN

In honor of your look that marks
the singular elegant greatness of your race,
of your profile's serene line
of aged aristocracy.

In honor of your quiet plentitude
that carries the seignorial smile
of your privileged pedigree and playful adventures,
and is regal, monastic, and piratical.

In honor of your gesture with its magnificent
tranquility of friar and monarch;
in honor of that rancid lyricism
that flowers in your heraldic scutcheons;

I open my song in a madrigal of silk
under the moon in a madrigal of silver,
and I come to your desires, an offering,
with a lilt of larks in my soul.

Neither the arbitrary, distorting stereotypes routinely imposed on a woman writer by the dominant critics of her day nor her predictable decline from "major" to "minor" or, more commonly, from "minor" to oblivion, is of primary importance in the context of this hypothetical female writer kinship and heritage. What matters here, rather, is the possibility of influence; for example, in the process by which another woman writer, as reader of her predecessor's work, comes to a self-discovery, finding the impetus to write and the temerity to publish her own work. Storni began writing poetry inspired by the verses and example of Delmira Agustini, an already established writer and a pop-

---

30. *Antología femenina*, p. 118.

ular one, a rare contemporaneous role model in Spanish-American poetry.[31] Thirty years after Storni's suicide and near eclipse, Castellanos writes that it was from Storni she learned to use irony in self-defense.[32] And all of the older, largely unknown, Mexican women writers, such as Caridad Bravo Adams, Amalia Castillo Ledón, and Esperanza Zambrano, that I interviewed between 1973 and 1976, mentioned the example of the South American *poetisas* (Agustini, Ibarbourou, Mistral, Storni), who served as prototypes, partly through contact with the heritage of women poets, in the struggle against the patriarchal past.[33] It is for similar motives that contemporary women write poems to Emily Dickinson, and Amy Lowell wrote about Elizabeth Barrett Browning, Barrett Browning about George Sand, Elizabeth Bishop about Marianne Moore. Chilean writer Mistral addresses long poems to female contemporaries,[34] and Claudia Lars of El Salvador writes admiringly to Mistral. The Cuban writer Gertrudis Gómez de Avellaneda dedicated poems to obscure women poets one hundred and fifty years before Adrienne Rich, in the same spirit, accepted the National Book Award for poetry (1974) in the United States on behalf of centuries of forgotten women poets. The message is one of mutual appreciation and support, of valuing, as in the literary exchanges between

---

31. Storni admitted as much in an interview in *El Pueblo* of Montevideo (23 February 1935); quoted in Sonia Jones, *Alfonsina Storni* (Boston: Twayne, 1979), p. 40. Storni addressed a sonnet to Agustini in her volume *Ocre* (Buenos Aires: Babel, 1925).

32. Castellanos speaks of her debts to Delmira Agustini, Juana de Ibarbourou, and Alfonsina Storni in an autobiographical essay in *Los narradores ante el público* (Mexico: Joaquín Mortiz, 1966), I, 93. She writes of the important influence of Gabriela Mistral's poetry on her own early work, in *Mujer que sabe latín* (Mexico: SepSetentas, 1973), p. 206.

33. See the interviews in Beth Miller and Alfonso González, *26 autoras del México actual* (Mexico: Costa-Amic, 1978), pp. 43–61, 139–52, 441–52.

34. See, for example, her "Recado a Victoria Ocampo en la Argentina," in *Antología de Gabriela Mistral*, ed. Emma Godoy (Mexico: Costa-Amic, 1967), pp. 118–20. Mistral also wrote articles about women in literature and the arts. A recently published volume of her prose, *Materias*, ed. Alfonso Calderón (Santiago: Editorial Universitaria, 1978), includes articles on Norah Borges, Emily Brontë, Isadora Duncan, Sor Juana Inés de la Cruz, Selma Lagerlöf, and Teresa de la Parra. Castellanos wrote a number of articles on women writers; her *Mujer que sabe latín* includes essays on María Luisa Bombal, Agatha Christie, Ivy Compton-Burnett, Isak Dinesen, Betty Friedan, Penelope Gilliatt, Natalie Ginzburg, Lillian Hellman, Violette Leduc, Doris Lessing, Clarice Lispector, Mary McCarthy, María Luisa Mendoza, Silvina Ocampo, Flannery O'Connor, Mercedes Rodoreda, Corín Tellado, Elsa Triolet, Simone Weil, and Eudora Welty.

Anne Sexton and Erica Jong and the innumerable homages to Sappho throughout the centuries.

What is perhaps most vital to the women poets as women, cut off from the grand literary world and the prestigious journals, may often be different from their significance as defined by the brilliant male historians who are not interested in women's consciousness and prefer, or used to prefer, women to write about their love of men or God, not about politics or poverty or "machismo." Although Gertrudis Gómez de Avellaneda is probably the most important Hispanic woman writer between Sor Juana Inés de la Cruz in the seventeenth century and Castellanos in the 1970s, her major importance is defined by many traditional historians in terms of the canon; that is, her importance in literary history is reduced to the premodernist experimentation in her later verse. Storni's achievement is similarly misunderstood; she receives lukewarm praise for the vanguardist techniques in the last volume she published during her lifetime and for the antisonnets of *Mascarilla y trébol* (Mask and Trefoil), published posthumously. These two examples suggest why it is not surprising that poems chosen by mainstream anthologists may differ from those that appear in collections of women's poetry compiled by feminist anthologists.

This leads us, again, to the question of gender-linked differences. Some women writers subscribe to the Virginia Woolf position that a writer's mind is androgynous (generally these writers tend to reject or pretend to reject feminism).[35] Others say women's literature differs from men's not because of biologically determined traits but because a woman's experience of life differs from a man's in nearly every known society. It is the latter position that is found appropriate by political activists. A clear statement of this position—one which traces an evolution in thought—may be found in Simone de Beauvoir:

> The reason why I have taken part in demonstrations and committed myself to specifically feminist activities is that my attitude with regard to the state of woman has evolved. . . .
>
> As I have already said [in *Force of Circumstance*], if I were to

35. Since about 1975 (International Women's Year) more Latin-American writers than in the past are willing to endorse feminist positions. See, for example, Elena Castedo-Ellerman, "¿Feminismo o femineidad?: Seis escritoras opinan," *Américas*, 30(10) (October 1978): 19–24. This article contains brief interviews with six of the women writers who attended the Tercer Congreso Interamericano de Escritoras, held in Ottawa in May 1978: Cecilia Bustamante, Griselda Gambaro, Alicia Jurado, María Luisa Mendoza, Carlota O'Neill, and Luisa Valenzuela.

write *The Second Sex* today I should provide a materialistic, not an idealistic, theoretical foundation for the opposition between the Same and the Other. I should base the rejection and oppression of the Other not on antagonistic awareness but upon the economic explanation of scarcity. As I have also said, this would not modify the argument of the book—that all male ideologies are directed at justifying the oppression of women, and that women are so conditioned by society that they consent to this oppression.

"You are not born a woman; you become one." . . . Of course there are genetic, glandular and anatomical differences between the human female and the male; but they are not an adequate definition of femininity, which is a cultural formation, not a natural datum.[36]

There are, in addition to the newer critical questions to be addressed, some quite traditional problems of literary scholarship involved in the study of Hispanic women writers. Since, with very few exceptions, even the most interesting of these writers are scarcely studied until after their deaths, when one approaches their works and reviews the scholarly research and criticism on them, one is appalled to find that generally they have not been read carefully enough to note striking variants in the texts or to get straight the most basic biographical and bibliographical facts. The problem of getting to the bottom of repeated critical errors is often arduous, but the reason for them is fairly evident: the writings were not deemed worthy of sustained attention. This is just as true in the case of contemporary writers such as Magda Portal, Guadalupe Amor, or Isabel Fraire, as it is of Avellaneda scholarship, and until very recently the situation was even worse for women writers before 1800.[37]

Castellanos is the most famous Mexican woman writer since Sor Juana. Some anthologies omit mention of all others, and it is interesting to pose the question about those excluded and why, in which periods, and to search out and reread some of the forgotten texts. One might think that such scholarship on relatively recent writers, of the

36. Simone de Beauvoir, *All Said and Done* (New York: Warner, 1975), pp. 462–63; this is a translation of *Tout Compte Fait* (Paris: Gallimard, 1972).

37. In the 1970s there has been an increase in scholarship on Hispanic women writers; also in bibliographies and catalogues such as *La mujer en las letras venezolanas* (Caracas: Imprenta del Congreso de la República, 1976); and anthologies of women's literature, such as *Poetisas mexicanas, Siglo XX*, ed. Héctor Valdés (Mexico: UNAM, 1976), and *Cuentistas mexicanas, Siglo XX*, ed. Aurora M. Ocampo (Mexico: UNAM, 1976).

late nineteenth and early twentieth centuries, would seem not a difficult task compared with the archival research and archeology performed by colonialists or medievalists. Yet, many women writers published their works in small private editions, in short-lived journals, in uncirculated anthologies of women's poetry edited by obscure, well-meaning, feminist-leaning admirers, or sometimes failed to publish their manuscripts at all. The reason-for-being of anthologies of women's writings should be obvious: during most periods, in most Latin-American countries, women writers had difficulty finding outlets for their work. Very few have enjoyed the advantage of participating in writers' groups such as the Bloomsbury circle or have been at the core of highly regarded literary magazines, as Victoria Ocampo was in *Sur* of Argentina, and Marianne Moore in *The Dial* of the United States. One strategy was the formation of women's literary circles (possible mainly in metropolitan centers) or, recently, feminist groups and the undertaking of several types of magazines by women. These publications, however, tend to be poorly distributed and are always considered separate but not equal by contemporaneous male writers, and their purpose has always been a subject of controversy among conservative scholars.

Hispanic women writers have written largely in isolation, with less writerly contact and less assurance of an eventual audience than their male counterparts. Unfortunately, most Hispanic women writers who achieve fame, even posthumously, undergo a rapid transformation from cliché to archetype (to borrow McLuhan's term, by which he meant something else), and in due course a further progression from icons to fallen idols. Nevertheless, a careful study of the fluctuating merit ratings of representative women authors, one that takes into account women's history and literary history, reveals that even when a writer's style has passed out of fashion or when she falls into disgrace because of some aspect of her personal life (a political or romantic association, for example) that adversely affects her reputation and alters her public image, she may continue to exert particular sorts of influence on other women poets in her own time as well as after her death. Therefore, even though feminist scholars and students of literature may find it offensive and misguided for male critics to group together such stylistically, thematically, and intellectually dissimilar poets as Gabriela Mistral (Chile, 1889–1957), Delmira Agustini (Uruguay, 1890–1914), Alfonsina Storni (Argentina, 1892–1938), and Juana de Ibarbourou (Uruguay, 1895?–1979) in most standard works of literary history, these writers indeed have in common that they individually and together influenced several generations of women poets in many parts of Central and South America, especially in the first half of this century, and spawned hundreds, perhaps thousands, of imitators.[38] Part of their power came from the achievement of a selfhood, a voice, and a literary persona; part derived from their various messages of rebellion—about daring to be unconventional in terms of sexual mores, of poetic themes, daring to enter the male-dominated literary terrain and to write subjectively, as women, from their own experience, of their perceptions, imaginative visions, joys and disappointments. These women writers, and others like them, in early times as well as in our own century, have been iconoclastic in a number of ways. Obviously, by creating divergent iconic images of women in their literary texts and by gaining public recognition as writers, they helped to correct and enrich the limited stock of stereotypical images of women prevalent in literary works by male authors, as well as in the minds and fantasies of their contemporaries.

The present volume as originally conceived was to focus solely on female characters in peninsular Spanish literature. Julianne Burton, then a graduate student at the University of Texas at Austin, circulated a call for papers for an anthology of critical articles, tentatively titled *The Image of Woman in Spain: Ten Centuries of Literary and Artistic Achievement*, which she worked on from 1973 to 1975. Her essay on Lorca and my own on the Buñuel film were written for that collection. I began working on the present volume at Burton's request when she left the project in 1976.

---

38. There are numerous examples of reputable works which discuss these poets together, for example: *La poesía hispanoamericana desde el modernismo*, ed. Eugenio Florit and José Olivio Jiménez (New York: Appleton-Century-Crofts, 1968), p. 178; *Literatura hispanoamericana*, ed. Enrique Anderson-Imbert and Eugenio Florit (New York: Holt, Rinehart and Winston, 1967), p. 571. Earlier, Arturo Torres-Ríoseco gave a plausible rationale in *The Epic of Latin American Literature* (Berkeley: University of California Press, 1959):

> One of the most interesting single events in this contemporary period is the emergence of women in the realm of Spanish American letters. Formerly relegated to a role of unimportance in intellectual life, women are today coming to the fore in journalism, lecturing, editing, teaching, writing, and more particularly in the field of poetry. Some of this change is due to the growing material prosperity of countries like Argentina, Brazil, and Chile, where men are too busy with practical tasks in the pampas, the mines, the rubber plantations, the factories, to pay much attention to poetry—which is thus permitted to become a feminine art. Be this as it may, Spanish America boasts a good number of distinguished twentieth-century poetesses. . . . (p. 120)

In the last four years the scope of the volume has broadened while the focus has become more specific. It was impossible in 1976 to find substantial articles in print applying new feminist perspectives in our field, and even the papers submitted in response to published announcements were not appropriate for the sort of volume envisioned. The present collection includes a number of essays on women writers and several which deal with the literature of Spanish America. As regards the focus, all the essays attempt, by and large, to reread or reevaluate aspects of Hispanic literature. Some of the essayists analyze the women characters in standard works by men (Harriet Goldberg, Luis Leal, Melveena McKendrick, Estelle Irizarry, Rachel Phillips), some in works by women (Linda Levine, Elizabeth Ordóñez, Marcia Welles); some shed light on women authors forgotten by history (Alan Deyermond, Francine Masiello), others provide new critical perspectives, focusing on fairly well-known works (Julianne Burton, Kathleen Kish) or a major woman author (Fernando Alegría). Some of the essays present polemical feminist arguments (Electa Arenal, my own essays), others are more traditional (Rosalie Gimeno). Most if not all the scholars whose essays are included in this collection pose new questions and/or take stands on old controversies.

It should not be necessary to make a case for the need for this work. Hispanists have lagged behind other scholars in recognizing the existence of women's studies. Even at the present time, course syllabi in college and university Spanish departments include even fewer women authors than those in English departments. Few academic critics in the Hispanic field have perceived that formalist criticism can be enriched by feminist criticism, and few in the past decade have been willing to accept the validity of Lillian Robinson's statement that "the literary mistreatment of women has been compounded by the critical mistreatment of women's literature."[39] New (and older) brands of feminist criticism are generally considered to be marginal and frivolous. For these reasons, there does not exist an extensive body of scholarship of the sort that comprises *Icons and Fallen Idols*, and it is hoped that more work will be stimulated by this publication.

Beth Miller
Santa Monica, 1978

39. Lillian Robinson, "Dwelling in Decencies: Radical Criticism and the Feminist Perspective" (1970), in Robinson's *Sex, Class, and Culture* (Bloomington: Indiana University Press, 1978), p. 12.

Spain's First Women Writers

Alan Deyermond

The earliest surviving literary text in Spanish, a lyric of four short lines, expresses a woman's love. It is one of the *kharjas* or final lines of Arabic or Hebrew poems from medieval Spain, and like the others it is difficult to transcribe and interpret accurately.[1] In the best-known (though controversial) modern reconstruction, it reads:

Tant' amare, tant' amare,
ḥabib, tant' amare;
enfermiron welyoš nidioš
e dolen tan male.[2]

This article owes much to the kind assistance recorded in various footnotes. I am also deeply indebted to friends in England and America who read a final draft of the article: Reinaldo Ayerbe, David Hook, and Dorothy Severin. Their help provided me with additional material and saved me from a number of errors. Special thanks are due to Beth Miller, who read two drafts, encouraged me to correct an unconscious bias, and gave invaluable help in the reshaping of the article for the present volume.

1. For some of the difficulties, see Richard Hitchcock, "Some Doubts About the Reconstruction of the *Kharjas*," *Bulletin of Hispanic Studies*, 50 (1973): 109–19. There is now disagreement even as to whether some *kharjas* are in Spanish or in Vulgar Arabic: Hitchcock, "Sobre la *mamá* en las jarchas," *Journal of Hispanic Philology*, 2 (1977–1978): 1–10.

2. Emilio García Gómez, *Las jarchas romances de la serie árabe en su marco* (Madrid: Sociedad de Estudios y Publicaciones, 1965), appendix, no. 18. For other readings, see S. M. Stern, *Les Chansons mozarabes: Les vers finaux (kharjas) en espagnol dans les muwashshahs arabes et hébreux* (Palermo: Manfredi, 1953); and J. M. Sola-Solé, *Corpus de poesía mozárabe (las ḫarǧa-s andalusíes)* (Barcelona: Hispam, 1974). English translations here and throughout this article are mine.

So much loving, so much loving,
my lover, so much loving;
healthy eyes became sick,
and hurt so badly.

This quatrain cannot be later than 1042 and may well be much earlier. It seems likely that the *kharjas* of Andalusia, the *cantigas de amigo* of Galicia, the *villancicos* of Castile, the *refrains* of northern France, and perhaps some other lyric traditions descend from Vulgar Latin women's love songs, widely diffused in the Roman empire but never written down.[3] The surviving texts are transmitted, and no doubt often reworked or even composed, by men. All of the *cantigas de amigo*, for instance, are attributed in the manuscripts to male poets, who probably took the popular love songs and filtered them through a cultured masculine sensibility. I find it hard to believe, however, that these lyrics have a purely mimetic ancestry, that they merely represent man's view of how woman should feel and speak. It seems far more probable that the popular oral poets with whom the tradition began were women.

It is disconcerting to find, after what seems to be such an early beginning of women's literature in the Iberian Peninsula, that works actually attributed to women writers are few and late; the first text of this kind is the *Memorias* of Leonor López de Córdoba, early in the fifteenth century. It is perhaps even more disconcerting that López de Córdoba and two other women writers of that century—all well worth reading for their literary quality even apart from their historical interest—have been largely neglected by critics and literary historians. It would be pointless as well as invidious to single out offending histories of literature other than my own. Writing in 1970, I gave half a page to López de Córdoba, seven lines to Florencia Pinar, and three lines of a footnote to Teresa de Cartagena.[4] Yet this inadequate coverage is a good deal more than these authors receive in any other recent history of literature (most do not mention them at all), and it was indeed condemned as excessive by a Spanish reviewer.[5] And although

3. James T. Monroe, "Formulaic Diction and the Common Origins of Romance Lyric Traditions," *Hispanic Review*, 43 (1975), 341–50.

4. Alan Deyermond, *A Literary History of Spain: The Middle Ages* (London: Ernest Benn; New York: Barnes and Noble, 1971), pp. 154–55, 200, 172.

5. Antonio Antelo, "La literatura española medieval y su historia (a propósito de un manual reciente)," *Anuario de Estudios Medievales*, 8 (1972–1973): 627–66, at 658. I should add that over a hundred years ago, José Amador de los Ríos gave substantial coverage to Cartagena and Pinar (*Historia crítica de la literatura española*, vol. 7 [1865; rpt. Madrid: Gredos, 1969], 176–78, 237–38).

Cartagena and Pinar are to be found in the standard bibliography of Spanish literature, López de Córdoba is not.[6]

When I first tried to deal with these writers at some length (in a lecture given in 1972 and, more extensively, in a paper read to the Association of Hispanists of Great Britain and Ireland in 1974), I was not surprised to find that their names as well as their works were, in general, unknown. It was, however, more surprising to discover that, even in the changed climate of 1977, a leading Hispanist with a special interest in women's writing (not to put too fine a point on it, the editor of the present volume) had no idea who the three writers might be. A brief description of them, of their circumstances, and of the special qualities of their works may therefore be of interest to others besides medievalists. To take account of neglected authors is to rewrite literary history to some extent. When those authors have a common feature which is lacking in their better-known contemporaries—whether that feature be their sex, their race, or some purely literary characteristic[7]—the rewriting goes further. I do not suggest that literature by women can always be clearly distinguished from that by men of the same time and country. Nevertheless, the literary map of fifteenth-century Spain takes on a different aspect if these three writers are given their due place, just as the overall picture of women's writing in Spanish changes if late medieval authors are included.

It is perhaps stretching a point to call Leonor López de Córdoba the first of our women writers since she seems to have dictated her reminiscences to a notary. It is a statement made on oath:

> Sepan quantos esta esscriptura vieren, como yo Doña Leonor López de Córdoba . . . juro por esta significancia de † en que yo

---

6. José Simón Díaz, *Bibliografía de la literatura hispánica*, vol. 3, pt. 2, 2nd ed. (Madrid: CSIC, 1965). There are now more encouraging signs; two of the three writers have been edited in a thorough and scholarly way (see notes 8 and 16, below). Failure to take due account of women writers is not confined to early or even to Peninsular literature. See Beth Miller, "A Random Survey of the Ratio of Female Poets to Male in Anthologies: Less-Than-Tokenism as a Mexican Tradition," in *Latin American Women Writers: Yesterday and Today*, ed. Yvette E. Miller and Charles M. Tatum (Pittsburgh, Pa.: Latin American Literary Review, 1977), pp. 11–17; and "El sexismo en las antologías," in Beth Miller, *Mujeres en la literatura* (Mexico: Fleischer Editora, 1978), pp. 32–38.

7. An example of the last type is the neglect by Spanish literary historians of one of the major medieval genres, the romance. See my "The Lost Genre of Medieval Spanish Literature," *Hispanic Review*, 43 (1975): 231–59.

adoro, como todo esto que aquí es escrito, es verdad que lo vi y pasó por mí. . . .[8]

Let all those who read this document know that I . . . swear by this sign of the cross which I adore that everything written here is what I truly saw and what happened to me.

Its length and content, however, justify its common title of *Memorias* and justify us in treating it as a literary work. So does its style. Once López de Córdoba is launched on her tale, the notarial formulas drop away, to be replaced by what sounds remarkably like her own style of conversation:

Así que yo soy fija del dicho Maestre [Don Martín López de Córdoba], que fue de Calatrava, enel tiempo del Señor Rey Don Pedro, y el dicho Señor Rey le hizo merced de darle la Encomienda de Alcántara, que es en la Ciudad de Sevilla; y luego le hizo Maestre de Alcántara, y a la postre de Calatrava; y el dicho Maestre mi padre era deszendiente dela Casa de Aguilar, y sobrino de Don Juan Manuel, fijo de una sobrina suya fija de dos hermanos; y subió a tan grande estado, como se hallará en las Corónicas de España; e como dicho tengo soy fija de Doña Sancha Carrillo, sobrina e criada del Señor Rey Don Alfonso, de mui esclarezida memoria (que Dios dé Santo Paraýso), padre del dicho Señor Rey Don Pedro, y mi madre falleció mui temprano. . . . (pp. 16–17)

So I am the daughter of the aforesaid former Master of Calatrava, in the time of King Peter, and that King did him the favor of granting him the lordship of Alcántara, which is in the city of Seville; and then he made him Master of Alcántara, and finally of Calatrava; and the aforesaid Master, my father, was descended from the House of Aguilar, and a nephew of Don Juan Manuel, son of a niece of his who was daughter of two brothers;[9] and he rose to as high an estate as can be found in the Chronicles of Spain; and as I was saying I am the daughter of Doña Sancha

8. Reinaldo Ayerbe-Chaux, ed., *Journal of Hispanic Philology*, 2 (1977–1978), 11–33. The passage quoted is on p. 16. All subsequent references are to this edition, the only accurate one; it contains details of all previous editions. I am grateful to Professor Ayerbe-Chaux for allowing me to consult the typescript of his edition and for supplying page references. Here and elsewhere in the present article, I supply accents and punctuation and regularize capitalization and the use of *i* and *j*, *u* and *v*, where necessary.

9. As Ayerbe-Chaux notes, this is a copyist's error for "daughter of his brother."

> Carrillo, niece and servant of King Alfonso of noble memory (may God grant him Heaven), father of the aforesaid King Pedro, and my mother died very early. . . .

I have a clear vision of the unfortunate notary, trying desperately to keep everything on a proper level of legal phraseology, being overwhelmed by Leonor López' flood of words, and realizing with a sigh that he had better reconcile himself to writing the story just as she told it.

This memoir is, she says, written so that those in trouble may learn how the Virgin Mary favored her and will help others if they believe in her. It is, in other words, a piece of devotional exemplary literature—as well as a memoir and a self-justification. The story covers two periods of the author's life, with some flashbacks; and because of her family's prominence and her own political importance in later life, we are able to fill the gaps by reference to chronicles.

Leonor López was born in Calatayud, in December 1362 or January 1363. Her experience as a helpless and bewildered victim of high politics in a violent and treacherous age began early, when in 1366 she and her family were left in Navarre as hostages for the fulfillment of a treaty with Pedro I of Castile. She was married at the age of seven to Ruy Fernández de Hinestrosa, son of King Pedro's Chancellor of the Secret Seal, Juan Fernández, who had died in battle against the supporters of Pedro's illegitimate half-brother, Enrique de Trastámara. This early marriage may have been due, as she suggests in the *Memorias*, to her mother's death; it may also reflect her father's sense of the storm, which had already swept away his king, gathering strength to sweep him away in turn, and his wish to see his daughter allied before it was too late to another powerful loyalist family. The civil war did not end with Pedro's murder at Montiel in 1369; López' father held the South for the loyalists, making a last stand in 1371 in the fortress of Carmona, between Córdoba and Seville.

The *Memorias* include an eyewitness narrative of the siege of Carmona, with a strange episode, in which the moral comment that might have been expected is strikingly absent:

> Y acaso haviendo salido mi padre fuera de [Carmona], y sabiéndolo los del real del Rey [Enrique de Trastámara] cómo era salido dela dicha villa, y que no quedaría tan buen cobro en ella, ofreciéronse doze cavalleros a escalar la villa, y subidos a ella a la muralla, fueron presos, y luego fue avisado mi padre de tal echo, y vino luego, y por el atrevimiento les mandó cortar las cavezas. . . . (pp. 17–18)

> And my father having by chance left Carmona, and those of the King's camp knowing this, and knowing that the town would not be as well guarded as before, twelve knights volunteered to scale the town walls, and when they were at the top of the wall they were captured, and then my father was informed of what had happened, and he came at once, and for their temerity he ordered that their heads be cut off.

We should not, I think, judge López too harshly here. She was speaking long after events which had happened in her childhood; she had been buffeted by fate for thirty years; all her will power had been concentrated on survival for herself and her immediate family; and only a threat to that survival was by now capable of rousing her to moral judgment. Thus, when she deals with the violation of the safe conduct under which her father surrendered Carmona and with his execution by the victorious Trastámarans, she does not hesitate:

> El Señor Rey mandó que le cortasen la cabeza a mi padre en la Plaza de San Francisco de Sevilla . . . y yéndole a cortar la cabeza encontró con Mosén Beltrán de Clequín, cavallero franzés, que fue el cavallero que el Rey Don Pedro se havía fiado dél, que lo ponía en salvo estando cercado en el castillo de Montiel, y no cumpliendo lo que le prometió, antes le entregó al Rey Don Enrrique para que lo matase, y como encontró a el Maestre [mi padre] díjole: "Señor Maestre, ¿no os decía yo que vuestras andanzas havían de parar en esto?" Y él le respondió: "Más vale morir como leal, como yo lo he echo, que no vivir como vós vivís, haviendo sido traydor." (p. 18)

> The King ordered that my father be beheaded in the Plaza de San Francisco in Seville . . . and when they were taking him to execution he met Monsieur Bertrand Du Guesclin, a French knight, who was the knight whom King Pedro had trusted to take him to safety when he was besieged in the castle of Montiel, and he [Du Guesclin] did not keep his promise, but rather handed him over to King Enrique to be killed; and as he met my father he said to him: "Master, did I not tell you that your deeds would end in this?" And my father replied: "Better to die loyal, as I do, than live like you, as a traitor."

The French mercenary concerned was probably not Du Guesclin,[10] but this lapse of memory in no way impairs the vigor and drama of the narrative or the scathing condemnation of treachery.

---

10. P. E. Russell, *The English Intervention in Spain and Portugal in the Time of Edward III and Richard II* (Oxford: Clarendon, 1955), p. 164n.

An equal triumph of narrative art, with pathos replacing the dramatic tension of the previous episode, is the account of the family's imprisonment:

> Y estubimos los demás que quedamos presos nueve años hasta que el Señor Rey Don Henrrique falleció; y nuestros maridos tenían sesenta libras de hierro cada uno en los pies, y mi hermano Don Lope López tenía una cadena encima delos hierros en que havía setenta eslabones: él era niño de treze años, la más hermosa criatura que havía enel mundo, e a mi marido en especial poníanlo en el algive dela hambre, e teníanlo seis, o siete días que nunca comía, ni vebía por que era primo delas Señoras Ynfantas, hijas del Señor Rey Don Pedro: en esto vino una pestilencia, e murieron todos mis dos hermanos e mis cuñados, e treze cavalleros dela casa de mi padre . . . e a todos los sacaban a desherrar al desherradero como moros. . . . (p. 18)

> And the rest of us remained prisoners for nine years, until King Enrique died, and our husbands had irons weighing sixty pounds on their feet, and my brother Lope López had a chain of seventy links on top of the irons; he was a child of only thirteen years, the most beautiful child in the world. And they singled out my husband for the starvation dungeon, and kept him on several occasions for six or seven days without food or water, because he was the cousin of the princesses, King Pedro's daughters. At this point there came a pestilence, and my two brothers and my brothers-in-law all died, as did thirteen knights of my father's house . . . and they were all taken out to have the chains struck from their dead bodies, as if they were Moors. . . .

The last words of this account refer to the practice of unchaining a dying Christian prisoner as a symbol of the freedom of his redeemed soul whereas Moorish prisoners were allowed to die in their chains as a symbol of the eternal condemnation of the infidel. Thus, López' apparently callous and dismissive words do not necessarily, given the conventions of the time, reveal a severe limitation of her human sympathies. In any case, it would be hard to blame her in the light of her bitter struggle for survival.

The prisoners were released by the belatedly contrite provisions of King Enrique's will, but the dying king's order that their property be restored was not carried out because "los derechos ya sabéis cómo dependen a los lugares que han conque se demandar" (p. 20) (You know that rights depend on the position of those who claim them)—one of the few generalizations that López permits herself, and one cannot maintain that, in the moral climate which prevailed after the Trastámaran victory, she was exaggerating. Therefore, "perdióse mi marido, e andubo siete años por el mundo, como desbenturado, y nunca halló pariente, ni amigo que bien le hiziese, ni huvise piedad de él" (p. 20) (My husband wandered forlornly about the world for seven years, like one persecuted by fate, without finding any relative or friend who would help him or take pity on him); and López had to fend for herself.

At this point the chronological basis of the narrative is replaced by something very like free association. López tells us of a successful appeal to an aunt, one of a family who had switched their support to the Trastámaran side. This consideration of her ancestry reminds her of the circumstances of her birth and of her mother's early death, after which she passes without any transition to her husband's return from his fruitless seven years' wanderings (p. 20). Her narrative method gives some support to Zimmermann's contention that "it is the sense of organization and purpose which distinguishes true autobiography from garrulous recollections."[11] Purpose is clearly present in the *Memorias*, but organization is not. Of course, López' life had scarcely conduced to serene reflection, and it may not be wholly coincidental that when Nadezhda Mandelstam, the widow of the poet Osip Mandelstam, one of Stalin's victims, published her memoirs a few years ago the reviewers praised most aspects of her work but found the structure rambling and disjointed. In both cases, a woman caught up in great events and surveying them from the wreckage of her personal life prefers the vividness and authenticity of recollection to the requirements of formal structure.

We learn of López' difficulties while dependent on her aunt, her wish to have a direct entrance from the house she was using into her aunt's—a wish granted and then withheld because "criadas suyas le havían buelto su corazón, que no lo hiziese, y fui tan desconsolada, que perdí la paciencia, e la que me hizo más contradición con la señora mi tía se murió en mis manos, comiéndose la lengua" (p. 21) (Her servants had turned her heart against me, that she should not do what she had promised, and I was so disconsolate at this that I lost all patience; and the servant who had caused most trouble for me with my aunt died in my arms, choking on her own tongue). She clearly regards this

---

11. T. C. Price Zimmermann, "Confession and Autobiography in the Early Renaissance," in *Renaissance Studies in Honour of Hans Baron*, Biblioteca Storica Sansoni, new series, 49 (Firenze: Sansoni, 1971), pp. 119–40. See also Marcus Billson, "The Memoir: New Perspectives on a Forgotten Genre," *Genre*, 10 (1977): 259–82.

death as divine retribution. Soon afterwards, when she had been praying to the Virgin Mary for a house of her own,[12] she saw in a dream the ideal site, "e que entraba yo por allí, y cojía flores dela sierra, y veía mui gran cielo" (p. 21) (And I entered there, and gathered wild mountain flowers, and saw the heavens open)—the kind of dream frequent in saints' lives and probably in this case inspired by her reading of such works.

At this point López mentions the Córdoba pogrom of 1392, part of the first serious and sustained persecution of the Jews in Christian Spain, but she does so only because she adopted a Jewish boy, presumably orphaned in the riots; as before, great national events enter the *Memorias* when they impinge on the author's life and not otherwise. Her prayers and her good deed in adopting the orphan lead, she is convinced, to her aunt's willingness to buy the site of her dream and to finance the building of houses there. Just as all seemed happily settled, however, the plague drove the author, her aunt, and their households from Córdoba (there has been some foreshortening here: four years separate the 1392 pogrom and the purchase of the site, and another four elapse before the plague, but the events are presented as an uninterrupted sequence). They move to Santaella, where a familiar pattern of quarrels, based on supposed jealousies, reasserts itself, and then on to Aguilar, hoping to avoid the plague, but López' adopted son, the Jewish orphan, follows them, already infected. She shames one of her father's old servants into taking the sick youth and looking after him, "e por mis pecados treze personas, que de noche lo velaban, todos murieron" (p. 23) (And for my sins thirteen people who watched by his sickbed at night all died). López prays that she and her children may be spared but that if any has to die, it may be her eldest son since he is a sickly child anyway. When there is nobody else left to watch by the sickbed, she tells this luckless son, who is only twelve and a half, to take over the duty. The boy's wholly reasonable expostulation is overborne by the force of López' formidable personality. He does as he is told, and it kills him. Then a touch of black farce: "y el emfermo vivió

12. Part of the text of her prayer is given not, as one might expect, at this point but later as a flashback (p. 22). It is in verse and linguistically older than the rest of the *Memorias*; it may well be a traditional prayer of some antiquity. A male contemporary of López' also included a verse prayer in a prose work; see Rafael Lapesa, "Un ejemplo de prosa retórica a fines del siglo XIV: Los *Soliloquios* de Fray Pedro Fernández Pecha," in *Studies in Honor of Lloyd A. Kasten* (Madison, Wisc.: Hispanic Seminary of Medieval Studies, 1975), pp. 117–28, reprinted in *Poetas y prosistas de ayer y de hoy: Veinte estudios de historia y crítica literarias* (Madrid: Gredos, 1977), pp. 9–24.

después haviendo muerto todos los dichos" (p. 24) (And after all those who watched over him had died, the sick man recovered). This episode brings on another quarrel with a cousin, which proves to be the breaking point. The aunt's family bring irresistible pressure to bear, and López is sent packing to Córdoba.

Here, in 1400, the *Memorias* end, but we are able to trace the subsequent course of López' life in other works, principally Álvar García de Santa María's *Crónica de Juan II*. The reason is that not long after the break with her aunt, she attracted the attention of Queen Catalina, wife of Enrique III and granddaughter of the murdered King Pedro. By the time of Enrique III's death (1406), López is comfortably ensconced at court, as a senior officer of the queen's household. Both chronicles and private letters make it clear that she was, moreover, Catalina's favorite, addressed by her as "my most beloved mother." The queen's series of favorites is the subject of acid comment by Fernán Pérez de Guzmán in his volume of biographical sketches, *Generaciones y semblanzas*.[13] Pérez de Guzmán alleges that López imposed other favorites, who were an equally bad influence, on the queen, and he describes López as "una liviana e pobre muger" (p. 34) (a wretched and flighty woman). He was not alone in his hostility: the *Cancionero de Baena*, an anthology compiled in the second quarter of the fifteenth century, includes two poems that, according to their rubrics, are satires directed against her.[14] It is not surprising that trouble gathered around her at court, just as it had in her aunt's household. The Trastámaran courtiers were presumably suspicious of her influence; to see a former political prisoner, the daughter of a leading loyalist, as the queen's favorite must have made them uneasy. No doubt, also, she made matters worse by a series of gaffes, which can easily be imagined by readers of the *Memorias*. Eventually, Catalina broke with her and banished her from court. In 1412 she tried to regain her position, but, in a confused atmosphere of intrigue and recrimination, Catalina sent messengers who ordered her to turn back on the road and warned that she would be burned alive if she showed her face at court again. With

13. R. B. Tate, ed. (London: Tamesis, 1965), p. 9.

14. They are by Gómez Pérez Patiño. *Cancionero de Baena*, ed. José María Azáceta (Madrid: Clásicos Hispánicos, 1966), III, 799–803. If they are indeed satirical, they are worded with remarkable indirectness, and López de Córdoba's name is not mentioned in the texts of the poems; but the fact that Juan Alfonso de Baena, the compiler, included such rubrics suggests a hostile atmosphere.

that, López disappears from sight. We do not know when she died, but it is generally assumed that she did not long survive this final humiliation.[15]

The *Memorias* deal, as we have seen, with only two segments of López' life, probably those at which she felt most ill used. She has a severely limited outlook, is self-centered (ruthlessly so when necessary), garrulous, and inconsequential. Yet her story is moving despite that—or because of it? She is as hurt and bewildered and defiant over family quarrels as over the horrors of the Atarazanas prison. And it rings true. We cannot rely on López as an accurate witness to factual detail, but she tells us about herself without any barriers of artifice (although with an artist's instinct for the telling phrase). When we read the *Memorias*, we share in a life.

Our second author, Teresa de Cartagena, comes from a very different and even more illustrious background: a *converso* family (converted from Judaism) that achieved prominence in literature and in the church. Her grandfather, Pablo de Santa María, successively chief rabbi and bishop of Burgos, was a poet (author of a 2,660-line *Edades del mundo* [The Ages of the World]). Her uncle, Alfonso de Cartagena, also bishop of Burgos, was a translator of, among others, Cicero and Seneca, and a writer of didactic prose in Latin and the vernacular. Her nephew Pedro was a poet with a varied production of courtly verse. And among her other relatives was the chronicler Álvar García de Santa María, to whom we owe much of our knowledge of Leonor López de Córdoba's life. Her literary connections were not confined to her family; she was urged to write her second book by the wife of the famous poet Gómez Manrique.[16] She was probably born

15. Much information, with quotation from primary sources, is given by Adolfo de Castro, "Memorias de una dama del siglo XIV y XV (de 1363 a 1412), Doña Leonor López de Córdoba, comentadas ahora y proseguidas," *La España Moderna*, no. 163, July 1902, pp. 120–46, and no. 164, August 1902, pp. 116–33. Castro's edition of the *Memorias* is wholly superseded by Ayerbe-Chaux's, but his supplementary information is still valuable. Interesting comments on López de Córdoba are also to be found in Manuel Serrano y Sanz, *Apuntes para una biblioteca de escritoras españolas* (hereafter cited as *Apuntes*) (1903–1905; rpt. in Biblioteca de Autores Españoles [hereafter cited as BAE], vols. 268–71, Madrid: Atlas, 1975), vol. 2, pt. 1 (BAE, 270), 16–18.

16. *Arboleda de los enfermos: Admiraçión operum Dey*, ed. Lewis J. Hutton, *Boletín de la Real Academia Española*, supp. 16 (Madrid: RAE, 1967), p. 111, ll. 4–6. All references to Teresa de Cartagena's works are to this excellent edition; I give page numbers in parentheses.

between 1420 and 1425, studied at Salamanca (p. 103), became a nun (probably a Franciscan), and at an early age was afflicted by deafness.[17]

The first of her two works, *Arboleda de los enfermos* (The Grove of the Sick), was composed in the third quarter of the fifteenth century, perhaps soon after 1450. The title, with its allegorical use of an ideal landscape, follows a fairly common late medieval practice; contemporary works in Spanish and Portuguese are entitled *Vergel* (Glade) *de consolación*, *Orto* (Garden) *do Esposo*, *Jardín* (Garden) *de nobles donzellas*, and *Vergel de príncipes*. The *Arboleda's* theme is the spiritual benefits of illness and specifically of the author's deafness, which had begun twenty years before and was a torment to her:

> E no syn razón me enojan algunas personas quando me ruegan y dizen: "Yd a fulanos qu'os quieren ver e aunque vós no lo oygaes, oyrán ellos a vós." E bien conosco que se me dize con buena amistat e synpleza apartada de toda maliçia, mas ni por esto dexo de me enojar, conosçiendo claramente qu'el ablar es prolixo sin el oýr . . . el fablar syn el oýr no vale nada nin faze otro bien sino acreçentar tormento a su dueño. (pp. 41–42)

> And I have reason to be irritated when people say to me: "Go and visit so-and-so, for they want to see you, and even though you can't hear them, they'll be able to hear you." And I know well that they say it in simple friendship, without any malice, but it still annoys me, for I know very well that speech is pointless without hearing . . . the gift of speech if one cannot hear is worthless and does nothing but increase its owner's torment.

Cartagena's intellectual awareness of her affliction's beneficial effects, in isolating her from worldly distractions, is as acute as her emotional awareness of the affliction itself. Her deafness and her life as a

17. For information on her life and background, see Hutton's introduction to his edition (note 16, above) and also Francisco Cantera Burgos, *Álvar García de Santa María y su familia de conversos* (Madrid: CSIC, 1952), pp. 536–58. For important comments on her works, see also Amador de los Ríos (note 5, above); Serrano y Sanz, *Apuntes*, vol. 1, pt. 1 (BAE, 268), 218–33; Américo Castro, *The Structure of Spanish History*, trans. Edmund L. King (Princeton, N.J.: Princeton University Press, 1954), p. 346n.; and Juan Marichal, *La voluntad de estilo: Teoría e historia del ensayismo hispánico*, 2nd ed. (Madrid: *Revista de Occidente*, 1971), pp. 42–45. This section of the present article is an abridged and revised version of my "'El convento de dolençias': The Works of Teresa de Cartagena," *Journal of Hispanic Philology*, 1 (1976–1977): 19–29; I am grateful to the editor for permission to make use of the material here.

nun blend in her imagery, just as they do in her daily experience: "aquellos que en el convento de dolençias tenemos hecha profesyón" (p. 58) (those of us who have made our profession in the convent of afflictions); "los enfermos con quien tengo hecha carta de hermandad" (p. 61) (the sick with whom I have signed a pledge of sisterhood); "las claustras de mis orejas" (p. 44) (the cloisters of my ears). She distinguishes between physical and spiritual hearing and emphasizes that physical deafness can be a defense against spiritual blindness (p. 47; this is repeated in her second work, *Admiraçión operum Dey*, p. 136, and p. 137). The *Arboleda* is, then, to some extent a work of autoconsolation, a variant of the widespread fifteenth-century genre of the consolatory treatise which derives ultimately from Boethius' *De consolatione Philosophiae*.[18]

Cartagena's imagery is rich and varied and would merit a separate study. In general, it follows the lines one would expect: biblical images, especially those drawn from landscape and from the pastoral life, and images from family relationships and from a domestic setting. There is a more elaborate set piece at the beginning of the *Arboleda*:

> Grand tienpo ha, virtuosa señora, que la niebla de tristeza tenporal e humana cubrió los términos de mi bevir e con un espeso torvellino de angustiosas pasyones me llevó a una ýnsula que se llama "Oprobrium hominum et abiecio plebis" donde tantos años ha que en ella bivo, si vida llamar se puede, jamás pude yo ver persona que endereçase mis pies por la carrera de paz, nin me mostrase camino por donde pudiese llegar a poblado de plazeres. Asý que en este exillyo e tenebroso destierro, más sepultada que morada me sintiendo, plogo a la misericordia del muy Altýsimo alunbrarme con la luçerna de su piadosa graçia. . . . (p. 37)
>
> Long ago, virtuous lady, the cloud of temporal and human sadness covered the frontiers of my life, and with a dense whirlwind of anguished suffering bore me off to an island which is called "The scorn of men and the outcast of the people," where I have lived for so many years, if it can be called life, without ever having been able to see anyone who could guide my feet into the way of peace, nor show me a road by which I could reach the town of pleasures. Thus in this exile and gloomy banishment, where I feel buried rather than in a dwelling place, it pleased the compassion of the Highest to enlighten me with the lamp of his merciful grace. . . .

---

18. I owe this observation to Gerry Ashton. Cartagena quotes Boethius on p. 58.

This chain of images runs on for another dozen lines. I suspect that Cartagena was determined to show at the outset that she was capable of stylistic virtuosity if she chose to display it. Some of the images may show the influence of secular reading, and it is probably significant that the rhythm of *arte mayor*, one of the dominant verse forms of the time, may be detected in her prose.

Structurally the *Arboleda* is an amplification on the theme of suffering, and among the techniques of amplification are the etymologizing of *paçiencia* (*paz*, "peace," plus *çiençia*, "knowledge"), the parable of the five talents, the seven deadly sins, and the six roots of pride which are cured by suffering.[19] Suffering leads to the fear of God, and there are two types of fear. The place of patience between the cardinal and theological virtues is discussed. And all these devices of amplification branch out and interlace in the manner that Eugène Vinaver has demonstrated for the structure of medieval romances.[20] For example, the image of suffering as pay leads to the parable of the five talents, but this is not developed until twenty pages later.

Among Cartagena's sources, the Bible is explicitly cited, as are Boethius, St. Jerome, St. Augustine, Gregory the Great, and St. Bernard, though it is possible that her knowledge of some of these may have come from compendia rather than from direct reading of the texts. There are other sources, but not many. She is intelligent, moderately well read, but not a prodigy of learning. The *Arboleda* is valuable for other reasons: for its authenticity both as a record of suffering and as a record of religious experience, and for the integration of these two areas, both on the level of theme and on that of imagery. It is probably true that, as Juan Marichal says, Cartagena lacks the rhetorical techniques that would have enabled her to reveal her personality fully, though his conclusion that, on those grounds, she cannot be considered a real writer[21] suggests an unusual definition of "writer." However, there is no reason to suppose that she wished to display her personality. She has little self-deception, and her awareness of her own motives and weaknesses is trained and systematic, but there is no evidence that she was interested in her personality as distinct from her moral character. Indeed, she may well not have been aware that she

19. The last three classifications are of the type prescribed by confessors' manuals and developed in catechisms. See Zimmermann, "Confession and Autobiography," and Derek W. Lomax, "The Lateran Reforms and Spanish Literature," *Iberoromania*, 1 (1969): 299–313.

20. Eugène Vinaver, *The Rise of Romance* (Oxford: Clarendon, 1971), Chap. 5.

21. Marichal, *La voluntad de estilo*, p. 44.

had a personality. Her aim was to teach others a moral lesson that she had painfully learned and to forge for herself a weapon against adversity.

Cartagena's authorship of the *Arboleda* seems to have caused surprise and even indignation in some quarters, as she tells us in her second work, *Admiraçión operum Dey* (Wonder at the Works of God). She quotes her adversaries as asking: "¿Qué palabra buena ni obra devota devéys esperar de muger tan enferma en la persona e tan bulnerada en el ánima?" (p. 112) (What good word or devout work can be expected from a woman so frail in body and wounded in soul?). And, she says, those who do not object are almost worse in their insulting bewilderment (the *admiraçión* of the title); and some flatly refuse to believe that she wrote the book. This surprise is itself surprising, at least in a European rather than a merely Hispanic context; from the twelfth century onward, nuns in England, France, Germany, and Italy contributed significantly to the literature of devotion, mysticism, and autobiography. In Spain, however, Cartagena's achievement was more of a novelty and clearly came as something of a shock. Her Jewish origin may well have made things worse since the intellectual life of the *conversos* was viewed with considerable suspicion by many fifteenth-century Spaniards.[22]

The *Admiraçión*, whose sources and imagery are similar to those of the *Arboleda*, is an answer to Cartagena's critics. There are plenty of modesty *topoi* in both works (for example, "la baxeza e grosería de mi mugeril yngenio," [p. 38] [the lowliness and crudity of my woman's intellect]), and she explicitly disclaims any wish to make feminist propaganda. She does not intend to "ofender al estado superior e onorable de los prudentes varones" (p. 118) (offend against the superior and honorable status of prudent men)—but is there a hint of irony in the use of *prudentes*? Be that as it may, Cartagena will not give ground on the main issue: God can endow women with strength and martial valor, as in the story of Judith and Holofernes, so He can certainly give them intellectual power; it is easier to wield the pen than the sword (p. 120). The inspiration for the *Arboleda*, she asserts, came from God, not from a human source, and she did not copy her work from the books of others, as has been alleged (p. 131). It may be significant that, at a time when such concepts as plagiarism and copy-

22. Nicholas G. Round, "Renaissance Culture and Its Opponents in Fifteenth-Century Castile," *Modern Language Review*, 57 (1962): 204–15; and "Five Magicians, or the Uses of Literacy," *Modern Language Review*, 64 (1969): 793–805.

right were unknown, when the incorporation of material from established authorities was considered an enhancement of a literary work, a woman writer should be accused of dependence on the works of others. It may be, in other words, that in literature as in sex, a double standard prevailed.[23]

It is interesting to find the same accusations, some two and a half centuries later, made against one of the earliest of North American poets, Anne Bradstreet:

> I am obnoxious to each carping tongue
> Who says my hand a needle better fits,
> A poet's pen all scorn I should thus wrong,
> For such despite they cast on female wits:
> If what I do prove well, it won't advance,
> They'll say it's stol'n, or else it was by chance.[24]

The demure tone of Bradstreet's reply will also seem familiar to readers of Cartagena:

> Men can do best, and women know it well.
> Preeminence in all and each is yours;
> Yet grant some small acknowledgment of ours.

Only the more insensitive male readers of either work can have felt wholly content with such a tribute in such a context. Cartagena's protest and her unflinching defense of a woman's right to literary activity make the *Admiraçión*—despite her modest disclaimers—the first extant piece of feminist writing in Spanish.

Cartagena's indignant words have a second and equally important implication. Here and at other points in the *Admiraçión* (for example, p. 111 and p. 112, on the effects of illness on the writer, and p. 115, on the scarcity of women writers), we have what at that period was still unusual in Spanish literature: a writer's reflections on the creative process, an indication of how it feels to be a writer. Even apart from the intense human interest evoked by Cartagena's solitary and beleaguered position, the *Admiraçión* deserves the attention of anyone who undertakes the daunting task of writing a history of Spanish literary criticism.

---

23. This assumes that what Cartagena says of her detractors is correct. It is probably substantially true—her work exhibits little sign of paranoia—but it is easy for a deaf person to misunderstand what is said, so we should perhaps allow for some margin of error.

24. "The Prologue," stanza 7, in *The Works of Anne Bradstreet*, ed. Jeannine Hensley (Cambridge, Mass.: Belknap Press of Harvard University Press, 1967), p. 16.

Though Cartagena shows herself to be intellectually adventurous, as one of her background was likely to be, there is no suggestion of religious unorthodoxy in her writings; Hutton looked carefully for such evidence and found none.[25] This is not surprising since the family's conversion took place a full generation before her birth. However, as Hutton points out (p. 35), Cartagena's awareness of the *conversos'* position in society affects her choice of one image: "Bien asý por qualquier cobdiçia tenporal que contra nuestra ánima se levante, es fecho grand ruido en la çibdat de nuestra conçençia; e sy todo este maldito pueblo se levanta contra el ánima nuestra . . ." (p. 46) (Just so any worldly desire that rises up against our souls makes a great noise in the city of our conscience; and if all this accursed people rises up against our souls . . .). This was, as Hutton says, written at a time when anti-Jewish and anti-*converso* riots were common, and he could have added that the worst of these, the Toledo rising of late 1449, came immediately before the date most commonly accepted for the composition of the *Arboleda*, and, in any case, at an impressionable period of the author's life. Nor is that all; the rising was the direct cause of two important works by *conversos*, Fernán Díaz de Toledo's *Instrucción del Relator*[26] and the *Defensorium unitatis christianae* (The Armor of Christian Unity) of Teresa de Cartagena's uncle Alfonso. It is reasonable to suppose that the Toledo rising was the specific inspiration for the image just quoted from the *Arboleda*; this point has some historical and biographical interest, but its literary implications are even more notable. First, the traditional Christian image of the city as a settled and secure place under the rule of God (Augustine's *De civitate Dei*: "God . . . hath prepared for them a city," Hebrews 11:16; "For here we have no continuing city, but we seek one to come," Hebrews 13:14) is transformed so that "la çibdat de nuestra conçiençia" (the phrase is used several times) becomes a place of danger. Thus Cartagena expresses the sense of the secure and the familiar giving way beneath her, not as existential anguish but as a local and concrete fear; possibly, too, she associates her position with that of the apostles when cities were roused against them (for example, Acts 17:5). This

25. See pp. 26–27 of his edition. I should, however, add that Américo Castro detected a *converso* flavor in Cartagena's works before her background was conclusively documented (see note 17, above).

26. The post of *relator*, which Fernán Díaz held, was one of the highest in the royal administration. See Nicholas G. Round, "Politics, Style, and Group Attitudes in the *Instrucción del Relator*," *Bulletin of Hispanic Studies*, 46 (1969): 289–319. For the historical background, see Nicholas G. Round, "La rebelión toledana de 1449," *Archivum*, 16 (1966): 385–446.

fusion of traditional image with contemporary danger does not stand alone; Cartagena also fuses her isolation caused by deafness with the fear of isolation which beset her family and others of their class in the aftermath of the Toledo rising.

We know a good deal about the backgrounds and lives of Teresa de Cartagena and Leonor López de Córdoba, but the third author whom I wish to discuss, Florencia Pinar, is so far only a name attached to a few poems. This is a fairly frequent occurrence among *cancionero* (late medieval songbook) poets, though recent investigations have established the basic biographical facts about several hitherto shadowy figures, and it is to be hoped that eventually Pinar's life will also be documented.

The extraordinary outburst of poetic activity in Spain at the close of the Middle Ages—the work of some seven hundred poets survives as a whole or in part—seems to have been an almost entirely male activity.[27] The *cancioneros* include the work of only half a dozen named and two anonymous women poets, and all but one of these are represented by only a few lines.[28] Florencia Pinar is the exception. In her case we possess adequate, though not abundant, material for study. Her poems appear in three *cancioneros* from the late fifteenth and early sixteenth centuries, the most readily accessible being the *Cancionero general* published by Hernando del Castillo in 1511. Of only

27. I take the number of poets from Brian Dutton's forthcoming catalogue of fifteenth-century Spanish poetry; it covers poets included in all *cancioneros* compiled before 1520. I am grateful to Professor Dutton for allowing me to draw on his work. The number is much higher than for the corresponding period in any other European country and probably exceeds the combined figure for poets writing in English, French, and German at that time. If one takes into account poets whose work is lost, the number is, of course, even higher. The causes of this phenomenon are now being discussed by scholars; see especially Roger Boase, *The Troubadour Revival: A Study of Traditionalism and Social Change in Late Medieval Spain* (London: Routledge & Kegan Paul, 1978).

28. The *Cancionero general*, one of the late medieval collections of Spanish poetry, contains a *mote* (a verse epigram) by Doña Marina Manuel (known chiefly for her influence on Diego de San Pedro's prose style). The *mote*, beginning "Esfuerce Dios el sofrir," is glossed by the poet Cartagena, who died in 1486, so it must have been composed before then. See Keith Whinnom, "The Mysterious Marina Manuel ("Prologue," *Cárcel de Amor*)," in *Studia iberica: Festschrift für Hans Flasche* (Bern: Francke, 1973), pp. 689–95. Also in the *Cancionero general*, Cartagena glosses a *mote* by Doña Catalina Manrique ("Nunca mucho costó poco"); and a Latin *mote* ("Transeat a me calix iste"), attributed only to "Una dama," is glossed by the poet Soria. Another attribution to an anonymous woman in the same *cancionero* is the "Pregunta de una dama a Diego Núñez." See Mary Mosley, "Women in Fifteenth-Century *Can-*

three poems can we say with anything approaching certainty that they are by Florencia Pinar. A few more are attributed to her in one *cancionero* but not in others, and confusion is inevitably caused by the existence of another and more prolific poet, known only as Pinar (without a first name), who seems to have been Florencia's brother.[29]

It would be an error to suppose that Florencia Pinar has only a scarcity value. Her poems are, it is true, dismissed by Serrano y Sanz as weak and insubstantial,[30] but most modern readers have rightly been much more enthusiastic. Part of the reason is no doubt Pinar's preference for concrete imagery over the abstractions which dominate the *cancioneros*; as Keith Whinnom observes, the *cancionero* poems most often included in modern anthologies are in general those with images of animals, plants, and other tangible objects.[31] There are, however, additional reasons for giving close attention to Pinar's poetry.

One of the three poems which are definitely hers, "¡Ay!, que ay

---

cioneros," dissertation, University of Missouri at Columbia, 1976, pp. 3–4, 101–02; I am grateful to Harold G. Jones for drawing my attention to this dissertation. An earlier poem—perhaps the earliest known *cancionero* poem by a woman—is a religious piece by María Sarmiento, entitled *Otras* [*coplas*], *quando alzaren la ostia y el cáliz y a los agnus*. It was no. 40 in the *Cancionero de Martínez de Burgos*, which was compiled in the 1460s, and Sarmiento may have written her poem many years before that (a document of 1428 seems to refer to her). Only the first two lines and the last stanza survive, in a transcription by the eighteenth-century bibliophile Rafael Floranes. See the edition of the surviving part of the *Cancionero* by Dorothy S. Severin, Exeter Hispanic Texts, 12 (Exeter: University of Exeter, 1976), pp. xvii, 59; and Serrano y Sanz, *Apuntes*, vol. 2, pt. 1 (BAE, 270), 391. The *Cancionero de Herberay des Essarts* contains a *pregunta* (a poem asking a question) by Diego de Sevilla, about the Navarrese princess Leonor de Foix; the *respuesta* (a poem in reply) is by a poet identified only as Vayona. The *Cancionero*'s modern editor concludes that these two poems date from the period 1457–1461, and he suggests that Vayona was a Frenchwoman and a member of the princess's retinue. See *Le Chansonnier espagnol d'Herberay des Essarts (XVᵉ siècle)*, ed. Charles V. Aubrun, Bibliothèque de l'Ecole des Hautes Etudes, 25 (Bordeaux: Féret, 1951), lix–lxiii, 37. Poems are also attributed in *cancioneros* of this period, though on dubious authority, to Juana de Portugal, wife of King Enrique IV of Castile, and to a female court dwarf, but Pinar, Manuel, Manrique, Vayona, and Sarmiento are the only names of which we can be certain.

29. It may be possible, by the application of computer techniques, to resolve this confusion. I hope to deal with the question elsewhere.

30. "Bien flojas e insustanciales," *Apuntes*, vol. 2, 1, 129. For a more recent discussion, see Mosley, "Women," pp. 103–4.

31. "Hacia una interpretación y apreciación de las canciones del *Cancionero general* de 1511," *Filología*, 13 (1968–1969): 361–81, at 369.

quien más no bive"[32] (Alas, there is one who no longer lives), seems to me to have no merit beyond that of a moderately difficult puzzle and need not detain us further. The other two are of a very different type.

Otra canción de la misma señora a unas perdizes que le embiaron bivas

> Destas aves su nación
> es cantar con alegría,
> y de vellas en prisión
> siento yo grave passión,
> sin sentir nadie la mía.
>
> Ellas lloran, que se vieron
> sin temor de ser cativas,
> y a quien eran más esquivas,
> essos mismos las prendieron.
> Sus nombres mi vida son,
> que va perdiendo alegría,
> y de vellas en prisión
> siento yo grave passión,
> sin sentir nadie la mía.[33]

Another song by the same lady, to some live partridges that were sent to her

> The nature of these birds is to sing happily, and seeing them caged, I feel acute suffering without anybody's sympathizing with me. They weep because they had no fear of being imprisoned, and they were caught by those from whom they were most aloof. Their names are my life, which is losing its happiness, and seeing them caged. . . .

This poem has long been known and liked for its vivid picture of imprisoned birds and for Pinar's unequivocal linking of her feelings with theirs, of their predicament with her own. However, there has, I think, been some misunderstanding of the nature of those feelings and of that predicament. Pinar is fairly obviously in love, hence the rele-

---

32. It is only fair to add that some readers take a different view. For the text of the poem and a very brief discussion, see my "The Worm and the Partridge: Reflections on the Poetry of Florencia Pinar," *Mester* (Los Angeles), 7 (1978): 3–8. This section of the present article is a revised version of that contributed to *Mester*, and I am grateful to the editor for permission to make use of the material here.

33. In *Cancionero general recopilado por Hernando del Castillo* (Valencia, 1511), facsimile ed. by Antonio Rodríguez-Moñino (Madrid: Real Academia Española, 1958), folio cxxv^{v}.

vance of the betrayal and trapping of the partridges in the second stanza.[34] The hunt is a frequent image for love,[35] and Pinar's adaptation of the image seems to reflect a traditional Spanish method of trapping female partridges. A male partridge is placed in a cage and taken to the area where the birds live. The females are attracted to the cage by his mating calls and are captured. Thus the fate of the partridges represents that of a woman who, long immune to love, is overcome by it and then betrayed, and the parallel is reinforced by the play on words, *perdiz/perder*.[36]

I have no wish to query the relevance of Pinar's image of the trapped partridges, the success of her identification of her feelings with those of the unfortunate birds, or the high quality of her poem. At the same time, it seems to me that the full meaning of the poem escapes modern readers who are unfamiliar with the medieval bestiary, a moralized account of the origins and habits of real and mythical beasts. I have found, in the course of another study, ample evidence that medieval Spanish authors and their public were thoroughly familiar with at least some parts of the bestiary, despite the apparent lack of any Castilian bestiary text.[37] If we turn to the appropriate section, we find it said of partridges: "Frequent intercourse tires them out. The males fight each other for their mate, and it is believed that the conquered male submits to venery like a female. Desire torments the females so much that even if a wind blows toward them from the males they become pregnant by the smell."[38] Other Spanish writers of the period, and their readers, were fairly obviously aware of the bestiary account

---

34. The birds are identified as partridges only in the heading to the poem (in both the *cancioneros* that contain it), and the heading may have been supplied by a *cancionero* compiler, though I think it highly probable that it formed part of the original poem. I am grateful to Ian Macpherson for drawing my attention to the importance of this point.

35. For varieties of this image, see Dámaso Alonso, "La caza de amor es de altanería (Sobre los precedentes de una poesía de San Juan de la Cruz)," in *De los siglos oscuros al de oro (Notas y artículos a través de 700 años de letras españolas)* (Madrid: Gredos, 1958), pp. 254–73; and Marcelle Thiébaux, *The Stag of Love: The Chase in Medieval Literature* (Ithaca, N.Y.: Cornell University Press, 1974).

36. These three sentences summarize an analysis which Joaquín Gimeno Casalduero kindly sent to me after reading a draft of the article referred to in note 32, above; the full analysis is quoted in that article.

37. A forthcoming book by Néstor A. Lugones will add greatly to our knowledge of the bestiary in Spain.

38. T. H. White, *The Book of Beasts, Being a Translation from a Latin Bestiary of the Twelfth Century* (London: Jonathan Cape, 1954), p. 137.

of the partridge, and it seems reasonable to suppose that the same is true of Pinar. Indeed, I think one must conclude that even if the bestiary description was not primarily responsible for Pinar's choice of image, it reinforced that choice and that she wished not only to associate her plight with that of the trapped birds but also to identify her instincts with those that the bestiary, especially in the last sentence quoted, so graphically describes.

If any doubt existed on this score, it would be dispelled by a consideration of the third poem:

Canción de Florencia Pinar

Ell amor ha tales mañas
que quien no se guarda dellas,
si se l'entra en las entrañas,
no puede salir sin ellas.

Ell amor es un gusano
bien mirada su figura;
es un cáncer de natura,
que come todo lo sano.
Por sus burlas, por sus sañas,
d'él se dan tales querellas
que si entra en las entrañas
no puede salir sin ellas. (folio clxxxv[v])

Song by Florencia Pinar

Love has such crafty ways that whoever is not on guard against them will find that once love has entered one's entrails he can leave only by tearing them out. Love, if you look closely at his appearance, is a worm; he is a cancer of nature who devours all the healthy flesh. By his deceits and by his cruelty he arouses such complaints that if he enters one's entrails he can leave only by tearing them out.

Here, as in the previous poem, there is a play on words (*entra/ entrañas*).[39] Pinar uses the common late medieval image of love as a fatal illness ("es un cáncer de natura").[40] The most striking image is, however, that of the worm. Its implications in this poem are, I think,

39. There may be another: *querellas*, as well as bearing the meaning that I have given in the translation, is an archaic form of the infinitive plus the pronoun, *quererlas*, "to desire them."

40. This is not only an image; late medieval and Renaissance medical treatises devote considerable attention to love melancholy, its dangerous consequences, and its possible remedies. See J. Livingston Lowes, "The Loveres Maladye of Hereos," *Modern Philology*, 11 (1913–1914): 491–546; and

different from those of the worm image in the medieval Spanish dance of death, the *Dança general de la Muerte*, where death warns the two damsels of the waiting "gusanos rroyentes, que coman de dentro su carne podrida" (gnawing worms, who [will] devour the rotten flesh from within). In Pinar's poem the worm, representing love and penetrating the live woman's entrails, seems to be a phallic symbol, even if only at the unconscious level. The obvious objection—that the invertebrate worm's limpness makes it a poor representation of the phallus—need not apply here: although Old Spanish *gusano* normally means a worm in the modern sense, it can sometimes (like Middle English "worm") mean a snake.[41] The repeated statement that love, once lodged in his victim's entrails, can leave only by tearing them out seems to be an allusion to the supposed reproductive habits of the viper; the bestiary tells us that when the young are ready to be born, they break out through their mother's side, killing her.[42] The implied image of the viper (if my identification is correct) thus serves as a bridge between the two explicit images of the poem: a snake is visually

---

Diego de San Pedro, *Obras completas*, ed. Keith Whinnom, vol. 2, *Cárcel de Amor* (Madrid: Clásicos Castalia, 1972), pp. 13–15. It is possible, but very far from certain, that *natura* in this poem also has a secondary meaning: "the sexual organs." This meaning occurs from time to time in medieval texts in Latin, the Romance languages, and English, and it is also found in modern Spanish.

41. In the *Libro de los gatos*, the "gujano hydrus" is a snake, as may be seen by reference to the hydrus section of the bestiary: *El libro de los gatos*, ed. John Esten Keller (Madrid: Clásicos Hispánicos, 1958), p. 54; cf. *The Book of Beasts*, pp. 178–79. However, as Colbert Nepaulsingh has pointed out to me, a worm may be phallic without being explicitly vertebrate, as in William Blake's "The Sick Rose":

> O Rose, thou art sick!
> The invisible worm,
> That flies in the night,
> In the howling storm,
>
> Has found out thy bed
> Of crimson joy;
> And his dark secret love
> Does thy life destroy.

42. This piece of zoological misinformation is incorporated in the "Prologue" to one of the best-known works of Pinar's time, *La Celestina*:

> La víbora, reptilia o serpiente enconada, al tiempo del concebir, por la boca de la hembra metida la cabeza del macho y ella con el gran dulzor apriétale tanto que le mata y, quedando preñada, el primer hijo rompe las ijares de madre, por do todos salen y ella muerta queda y él casi como vengador de la paterna muerte. ¿Qué mayor lid, qué mayor conquista ni guerra que engendrar en su cuerpo quien coma sus entrañas?" (ed. Dorothy S. Severin [Madrid: Alianza, 1969], p. 41)

similar to a worm and is often a phallic symbol;[43] and the death of the mother viper is (like "un cáncer de natura") an assertion of the fatal consequences of love.

Pinar's use of animal imagery, then, makes her poetry strongly sexual in tone, and I am sure that this was consciously intended in at least one poem.[44] What is more, the imagery enables her to say about herself indirectly but very clearly things which the conventions of the time prevented her from saying explicitly. I am not, of course, suggesting that this is an admission of sexual promiscuity. What Pinar is telling us is that she feels strong sexual desire for the man she loves. It is dangerous to reconstruct a poet's life from his works, as the examples of Jaufre Rudel, François Villon, and Macías show us. We cannot know anything of Pinar's life until the necessary archival research has been carried out, but by studying her poems we can reconstruct her temperament.

López de Córdoba, Cartagena, and Pinar are not the only Spanish women writers of the fifteenth century, but they are the best. Not merely, I believe, the best of the very small number of contemporary women authors, but—for reasons I have tried to illustrate—good and

---

> The viper, reptile or poisonous snake, at the moment of conception, the head of the male being inserted in the mouth of the female, she, because of the intensity of pleasure, squeezes him so much that she kills him; and, she being left pregnant, the first of her young breaks through her flank, so that the others follow through the gap torn in her, she dies, and the first born is the virtual avenger of his father's death. What greater struggle, conquest or war can there be than to engender in one's own body someone who will eat one's entrails?

Despite the similarities, the use made of the viper story by Pinar seems to be independent of that by Fernando de Rojas since Pinar's poem occurs in a fifteenth-century *cancionero* (the *Celestina* prologue was composed around 1502), and Rojas took his material from one of the Latin works of Petrarch. For other varieties of the viper story, see Florence McCulloch, *Mediaeval Latin and French Bestiaries*, 3rd ed. (Chapel Hill: University of North Carolina Studies in the Romance Languages and Literatures, 33, 1970), pp. 183–84.

43. This, of course, depends on the context, and it is easy to find nonphallic snakes in literature. For a clearly phallic snake in medieval Spanish, see Gonzalo de Berceo, *Vida de Santo Domingo de Silos*, stanzas 327–28, and my "Berceo, el diablo y los animales," in *Homenaje al Instituto de Filología y Literaturas Hispánicas: Dr. Amado Alonso en su cincuentenario 1923–1973* (Buenos Aires, 1975), pp. 82–90.

44. Some readers will think me guilty of the intentional fallacy, but it seems to me that any attempt to discuss the meaning of a poem must involve some discussion of the poet's intentions even if only to discover what was meant by the words used.

interesting writers by any standard, writers who deserve much more attention than they have so far received. It is perhaps worth asking one question in conclusion. Why did these three write when almost all other women of their time did not? It is easy enough to see the reasons for the near-universal silence. Even apart from technical limitations (how many women had learned to write or, failing that, had access to a notary who could take down their words?), the social and cultural assumptions of the time were unfavorable to any serious female commitment to literature.[45] The reaction to Cartagena's first book shows us the psychological obstacles that confronted a woman author. It seems likely that only some powerful impulse would have enabled these three to surmount the obstacles, and here—in the tentative way proper to one who speculates on the basis of very slender evidence—I suggest that we may receive some help from the theory that illness, abnormality, or suffering may set the creative process in motion. It is not necessary to adopt the theory—popularly but mistakenly attributed to Freud[46]—of art as neurosis in order to recognize that there may be, and often is, some kind of connection between abnormal physical or mental states and artistic creation. Edmund Wilson, in *The Wound and the Bow*, takes the myth of Philoctetes as the starting point for his association of psychological injury with literary genius in some modern authors.[47] W. H. Auden puts this in a characteristically wry and throwaway style in his poem on Rimbaud:

> The nights, the railway-arches, the bad sky,
> His horrible companions did not know it,
> But in that child the rhetorician's lie
> Burst like a pipe: the cold had made a poet.[48]

---

45. The obstacles to women's literary and artistic achievement have been frequently discussed in recent years. An especially useful treatment of the technical and social obstacles is given by Linda Nochlin, "Why Have There Been No Great Women Artists?" in *Art and Sexual Politics: Women's Liberation, Women Artists, and Art History*, ed. Thomas B. Hess and Elizabeth C. Baker (New York: Collier Books, 1973), pp. 1–39.

46. Richard Wollheim, "Neurosis and the Artist," *Times Literary Supplement*, 1 March 1974, pp. 203–04, shows that Freud explicitly rejected the theory.

47. Edmund Wilson, *The Wound and the Bow: Seven Studies in Literature* (Cambridge, Mass.: Houghton Mifflin, 1941). Wilson's most memorable formulation of the theory is that "genius and disease, like strength and mutilation, may be inextricably bound up together" (p. 289).

48. W. H. Auden, "Rimbaud," in *Collected Shorter Poems 1927–1957* (London: Faber, 1966), p. 126.

López de Córdoba, Cartagena, and Pinar are very different in background, experience, and temperament. Perhaps one of the most striking differences is in their level of self-awareness and capacity for self-analysis: systematic and trained in Cartagena, instinctive and symbolic in Pinar, virtually nonexistent in López de Córdoba, who possesses to a high degree the human talent for self-deception. Is it possible to find a common factor that might explain their exceptional achievement in the face of all the difficulties? I do not think it glib to suggest imprisonment as a unifying factor. We are all, to some degree, imprisoned by our heredity and our environment, but these three women seem to have suffered to an acute degree. López de Córdoba experienced, at a formative period of her life, the literal prison of the Atarazanas; Cartagena suffered the confining effects of deafness; Pinar suffered the restraints imposed by fifteenth-century society on her sexual impulses. We have explicit textual evidence that López de Córdoba and Cartagena chafed under their restraints, and an analysis of Pinar's imagery shows that the same is true of her. I do not suppose that in happier circumstances these three women would have been incapable of literary creativity, but I think it likely that without their different kinds of imprisonment, they would not have produced some of the most interesting and moving literature of the fifteenth century.[49]

---

49. Compare what Adrienne Rich, one of the greatest contemporary poets of America, says of one of the earliest:

> To have written poems, the first good poems in America, while rearing eight children, lying frequently sick, keeping house at the edge of wilderness, was to have managed a poet's range and extension within confines as severe as any American poet has confronted. If the severity of these confines left its mark on the poetry of Anne Bradstreet, it also forced into concentration and permanence a gifted energy that might, in another context, have spent itself in other, less enduring directions.

(*The Works of Anne Bradstreet* [see note 24, above], p. 42).

Echoes of the Amazon Myth in Medieval Spanish Literature

Estelle Irizarry

A considerable number of female characters in medieval Spanish literature fall into the category of essentially passive creatures, who, secluded in convents or guarded in their homes by male relatives fearful of injury to their honor, receive the homage of knights or the songs of troubadors. To some, women were worthy of reverence whereas others saw them as a mortal danger to man's salvation. As King Alfonso X, the Sage, aptly expressed it in a thirteenth-century *cantiga* or troubadour song: "Entre Ave Eva / gran departiment'á" (Between Ave [Maria, i.e., the Virgin Mary] and Eve there is a great difference).[1] The poem refers to the fact that *Ave* is the Spanish name *Eva* spelled backwards, which allows for the poet's contention that between the saintliness of the Virgin Mary (traditionally saluted in the *Ave Maria*) and the imperfect Eve (seen as man's perdition) "there is a great difference." Naturally the image of woman varied greatly between these two extremes of idealization and contempt, but essentially women were praised or criticized for their moral qualities and admired for their physical beauty.

It is difficult to imagine that among the stiff feminine figures we often see in medieval illustrations, persons attired in fancy headdresses and long skirts, there were women capable of feats of physical strength

1. Antonio G. Solalinde, *Antología de Alfonso X el Sabio* (Madrid: Espasa-Calpe, 1966), Cantiga 60, p. 33. This English translation and those hereafter are mine.

or violence reminiscent of the classical amazon myth. The role assigned to women in medieval Spanish society is exemplified in its most representative epic poem (ca. 1207), in which the Cid's wife Doña Jimena waits patiently in a monastery for years while he battles against Moorish enemies to regain his monarch's favor. In the *Poema de Mío Cid*, the hero's daughters, mistreated by their husbands, are avenged by King Alfonso VI's court trial and by combat between the Cid's chosen warriors and the offending Infantes of Carrión and their brother.

There are, however, a number of female characters in major medieval Spanish works who stand out because of their strength and audacity in physical attack, exhibiting qualities traditionally reserved for men, whose domain was that of waging war and bearing arms. Particularly interesting is the fact that these aggressive women warriors depicted in literature come from all walks of life, from queens and countesses to humble mountain dwellers, and that they do not retreat from bellicose encounter. They take an active role in seeking men but insist on dealing with them on their own terms. They are, I believe, inspired by the amazons, who, as the legend goes, fascinated and terrified men. One branch of amazons, which resided in Libya, conserved the family unit, but women were the rulers, serving as soldiers and masters, who conquered Atlantis until they were annihilated by Heracles. Perhaps the most famous amazons were those of Asia Minor, extraordinary horsewomen and archers, who were permitted to mate with their neighbors, the Gargarian men, only during two spring months after qualifying by having killed a man in battle. Girls were kept and reared as soldiers schooled in female ascendancy whereas male children were returned to the Gargarians. A few males were crippled by the amazons in order to serve as slaves, incapacitated for rebellion. Greek sculptures represent them as beautiful women, armed for battle, mounted on fiery horses and trampling on their defeated foes.[2]

According to Donald Sobol, who has compiled and organized information on the amazons from numerous sources, there is no incontrovertible proof that such martial maids actually existed. Nevertheless, the persistence of these legends attests to the attraction of such an image of warrior women, neither fearful of men nor desirous of

2. The most complete and up-to-date source of information about the amazons I have found is Donald J. Sobol's *The Amazons of Greek Mythology* (New York: A. S. Barnes, 1973), which includes a bibliography on the subject, pp. 163–65.

their constant company, using them essentially as sex objects and as a means of continuing the species. Since medieval Spanish literature drew heavily on classical sources, it is not surprising that variations of this fascinating myth appear in important works of the time.

This paper will discuss outstanding variations of the amazon type which appear in medieval Spanish writings as representations of amazons from the ancient world and as Spanish counterparts in the Middle Ages. While not necessarily retaining all the characteristics associated with the classical model, they are self-willed women who dictate the terms of their relationships with men, behave as dominant partners, and are capable of exercising physical violence or of carrying out feats of great strength.

The early thirteenth-century *Libro de Alexandre*[3] (Book of Alexander), the longest known poem of the *mester de clerecía* or scholarly form, deals with the life of Alexander of Macedon and devotes twenty-six quatrains (quatrains 1701–26) to the visit of Thalestris, queen of the amazons, who, among other notables, came to pay homage to the great conqueror. She appears in the poem accompanied by three hundred maidens on very swift horses. The amazons in this collective appearance are very imposing:

> todas eran maestras | de far golpes certeros
> de tirar de balestas | e ferir escuderos (quatrain 1702 cd)
>
> All were experts in dealing precise blows,
> Wounding shield-bearers and shooting crossbows.

The anonymous Spanish poet gives a detailed description of their customs, drawing upon *Historia de Proeliis*, a tenth-century version of earlier classical sources, and the twelfth-century Latin poem *Alexandreis*, by Gautier de Châtillon. The poet explains that three times a year the amazons lie with their husbands, keeping only the female babies resulting from the union. He describes the amazons' arms, battle dress and physical prowess, stating that "semeian bien uarones | en toda su fechura" (quatrain 1708 d) (they look like men in every respect). According to Ian Michael's study of the treatment of classical material in the poem, the Spanish author is responsible for the original

3. *El libro de Alexandre*, ed. Raymond S. Willis, Jr. (Princeton, N.J.: Princeton University Press, 1934) (Madrid manuscript); I have regularized the forms of some letters. See also Harvey L. Sharrer, "Evidence of a Fifteenth-Century *Libro del Infante don Pedro* and Its Relationship to the Alexander Cycle," *Journal of Hispanic Philology*, 1 (1976–1977): 85–98, 94–97.

contribution of a portrait of Queen Thalestris, which endows her with great beauty in conformity with "the medieval rhetorical prescription for descriptions of women."[4] She is described with great delicacy and Christian modesty so as not to arouse sinful thoughts. Her beauty is such that "nunca fue en el mundo | cara meior taiada" (quatrain 1711 c) (never was there in the world a face more fairly formed). The poem recounts Thalestris' interview with Alexander, in which she reveals the motive of her visit. Because of his famed wisdom, strength, and character, she wishes to have a child by him. Alexander accedes, and the amazon queen later returns to her country.

The poet's elaboration of Thalestris' visit to Alexander is evidently directed toward enhancing the king's stature since Thalestris considers him the only man of his time worthy of fathering a future amazon princess. The image of the amazon woman, allowing for the medieval prescription for beauty, is in accordance with the classical legend in that she is depicted as extremely fair, warlike, and desirous of male contact only to mate.

Interest in the amazons in the thirteenth century is again evidenced in another treatment of the myth in stories about Alexander the Great, this time in the fourth part of the *General e grand estoria* (Great and General History), a history of the world begun under the direction of King Alfonso X, the Sage in the 1270s but left unfinished.[5] First, King Alexander comes to a land where no man is to be seen, and there he observes beautiful women bearing golden arms, dressed in fearsome raiment and mounted on fine horses. In another Indian jungle, he comes upon strange women with large bodies, long beards, and flat heads. They wear animal skins, are excellent hunters and riders, and use savage beasts trained by them. Later he enters another fantastic land in which the Lamias dwell. They are beautiful women with ankle-length hair and horses' feet, who reach a height of seven feet. The first group described is closest to the classical amazon type because of their general beauty whereas the other tribes are evidently corruptions of the original myth that incorporate fantastic details. They all have in common the ability to live successfully without the company of men

4. Ian Michael, *The Treatment of Classical Material in the "Libro de Alexandre"* (Manchester, England: Manchester University Press, 1970), p. 208.

5. *General e grand estoria*, vol. 1, ed. Antonio G. Solalinde (Madrid: Centro de Estudios Históricos, 1930); vol. 2, ed. Solalinde, Lloyd A. Kasten, and Victor R. B. Oelschläger (Madrid: Consejo Superior de Investigaciones Científicas, 1957–1961), 2 vols. Parts 1 and 4 are included in the microfiche edition of the texts from Alfonso's royal scriptorium, by Lloyd Kasten and John Nitti (Madison, Wisc.: Hispanic Seminary of Medieval Studies, 1978).

and their physical prowess. No attempt is made to individualize any of their number.

It may be noted, as an aside, that this fourth part of the Alphonsine work contains a rather lengthy version of the story of Judith and Holofernes, in which Judith may be considered an ancient biblical heroine akin to the previously described amazon types that Alexander encountered. The chronicle tells how she beheaded the enemy with only two blows and was paid the highest compliment conceivable in a man's world: being the pride of Israel and an honor to her people for having acted like a man.

The fifteenth-century writer and defender of women Juan Rodríguez del Padrón presents a portrait of a classical amazon queen in a poem entitled *El planto que hizo Pantasilea* (The Lament of Pantasilea).[6] By showing the amazon queen crying over Hector's body, Rodríguez del Padrón changes the traditional amazon image to that of a veritable lady of the court, perhaps a reversion to the Galician-Portuguese *pastorela* portraits of women. The queen laments that, always triumphant in war, she was defeated by love for Hector but found him only after he had been killed by Achilles. By depicting Pantasilea in a typical medieval *planto*, overflowing with sentiment, the poet debilitates the full enormity of the classical amazon image.

One of the most extraordinary women of medieval Spanish literature is Doña Sancha, the Infanta who married Fernán González, the heroic count who is credited with founding Castile by uniting several provinces and liberating them from the domination of León and Navarre.

The story is told in the *Poema de Fernán González* (Poem of Fernán González), believed to have been written by a monk of San Pedro de Arlanza in the mid-thirteenth century.[7] Although the protagonist Fernán González is imbued with Cid-like qualities, obviously inspired by that epic hero, the poem employs *mester de clerecía* or scholars' poetry, as did *El libro de Alexandre*, rather than the traditional epic meter. The Castilian count is depicted as a formidable enemy of the Moors, victorious warrior, clever diplomat, and model of generosity and equanimity. Though few historical details about his life can be

---

6. Martin S. Gilderman, *Juan Rodríguez de la Cámara*, Twayne's World Authors Series, 423 (Boston: Twayne, 1977), p. 69, cites articles by Alessandra Bartolini and Charles H. Leighton in agreeing that the "Planto" was erroneously attributed to the Marqués de Santillana until recently.

7. *Poema de Fernán González*, ed. Alonso Zamora Vicente, Clásicos Castellanos, 128, 2nd ed. (Madrid: Espasa-Calpe, 1963), p. xix.

proved from existing chronicles, Alonso Zamora Vicente gives his probable date of birth as between 890 and 895 and that of his marriage to Doña Sancha as sometime before 912. The Infanta's marriage to him was her third. It is generally conceded that the episodes in which Doña Sancha intercedes to help the count are novelesque and legendary. Scholars have pointed out and documented abundant points of contact between *El libro de Alexandre* and the *Poema de Fernán González*, but among the many curious stylistic and thematic analogies, it has not been noticed that the characterization of Doña Sancha bears striking similarity to the amazon type described collectively and individually in *El libro de Alexandre*. The elevation of the Infanta to legendary status would seem directed toward providing the hero with a wife worthy of such a man, just as the amazon queen, Thalestris, sought the most outstanding man of her time.

In the *Poema de Fernán González*, the Castilian count, tricked by the queen of León into seeking alliance with Don García, king of Navarre, finds himself imprisoned by the latter. The visiting count of Lombardy informs the Infanta, García's daughter, that Fernán González had gone to Navarre to seek her hand in marriage as a means of establishing an alliance and that if she does not help the Castilian count, she will be responsible for his death, the loss of all Castile, and the triumph of the Moors. He convinces her of the advantages of marriage to such a fine man, and the Infanta enters the prison, presenting Fernán González with a rather terse ultimatum: if he does not marry her, he will die in prison. Needless to say, the count readily accepts her proposal and is led from prison. According to the poem:

> El conde don Fernando non podia andar,
> ouol'ella vn poco a cuestas a llevar. (stanza 636 cd)
>
> The Count Don Fernando was unable to walk;
> She had to carry him awhile on her back.

Interestingly enough, when the poem was prosified in the *Estoria de España* (History of Spain)[8] of King Alfonso the Sage, there was significant exaggeration of these details:

> Et porque el conde non podie andar por los fierros que eran muy pesados, ouole la infant a leuar a cuestas una grand pieça; y andidieron assi toda la noche fasta otro dia mannana. (p. 190)

---

8. *Estoria de España* has been edited, under the title of *Primera crónica general*, by Ramón Menéndez Pidal, 2nd ed., 2 vols. (Madrid: Gredos, 1955).

> And because the count could not walk, due to the chains, which were very heavy, the Infanta had to carry him on her back *a good way*; and they walked in this fashion *all night until the next day.*[9]

Although it is true that the theme of princesses who help imprisoned foreigners is common in Germanic and Frankish epics (and more recently, in the Pocahontas story in the United States), Doña Sancha's prodigious physical stamina can best be explained in light of the amazon myth. It should be duly noted that the count could not walk because of the weight of the chains, but the Infanta carried not only the weight of the man, which in itself would be an extraordinary feat, but also that of the chains.

Doña Sancha's remarkable strength is further exhibited in the following section, in which the couple, lost in the woods, is discovered by a lecherous archpriest who threatens to turn them over to King García. Unimpressed by the count's offer of one of Castile's finest cities, he demands the lady's favors. Doña Sancha pretends to agree, but when the archpriest least expects, she deals him a blow to the head and, throwing him to the ground, maneuvers him so that she and the count are able to finish him off with his own knife. They continue traveling and run into the Castilian warriors who have been searching for their leader. The great fright Doña Sancha experiences in the uncertainty of whether the approaching group is that of friend or foe contrasts with the intrepid calm and fearlessness she has shown in single-handed combat, but this is understandable in view of the fact that she and her husband would have been greatly outnumbered had the approaching warriors been enemies.

The episode of the count's liberation apparently was so successful and popular that, according to reconstructions of a lost part of the poem, it is repeated again, with some variations, in León, where the Infanta persuades her husband's captors to allow her to spend the night in his cell. This scheme makes it possible for him to escape in her clothes. Despite Doña Sancha's devotion, we can see in this early Spanish heroine many of the classical qualities of the amazon woman, in her extraordinary beauty, her intrepid character, her physical strength, and her attitude toward the male, preferring to be the chooser rather than the chosen, the rescuer rather than the rescued.

Lucy Sponsler, in a book on women in the epic and the lyric, refers to additional cases of "aggressive women," such as Lambra, central figure in the *Cantar de los Siete Infantes de Lara* (Song of the Seven

9. Emphasis mine, as are this and all other translations.

Infantes of Lara) and Doña Urraca of the *Cantar del cerco de Zamora* (Song of the Siege of Zamora), but they do not conform to the amazon type because they do not exhibit unusual physical strength as Doña Sancha does, even though they are strong-minded, revengeful characters.[10] They prefer to incite others to carry out the vengeance they initiate but are devoid of the muscle power that accompanies amazon athleticism.

In his excellent article "Medieval Spanish Epic Cycles," Alan Deyermond dedicates a section to "dominant women," in which he points out the significant association of vengeance with women who play an active and sometimes dominant role in every epic of the Counts cycle.[11] While treating at length these violent, treacherous, and even savage females, he mentions Sancha, wife of Fernán González, only briefly as a woman of courage, resourcefulness, and daring; it is obvious that Deyermond does not consider her in the same category as the bloodthirsty female characters. Doubting Sponsler's notion that these aggressive women reflect the rigor of life in those times, Deyermond suggests that they stem from universal folk tradition, as do many other characters and motifs found in the Spanish epic. My speculation would thus be in line with Deyermond's theory of the dominant woman as a folk motif. This Sancha is a different breed of dominant woman from Lambra, from Sancha *la condesa traidora* ("treacherous countess"), and from the Sancha of the *Romanz del infant García*. She is strong, frank, and courageous, rooted in a particular myth, that of the amazons.

Not all amazon figures are queens and countesses, however, as we find in the mountain girls depicted in two *serranillas*, parodies of the *pastourelle*, in the *Libro de buen amor* (Book of Good Love) (1330), by Juan Ruiz, the archpriest of Hita.[12] The *serranilla*, cultivated by a

---

10. Lucy A. Sponsler, *Women in the Medieval Spanish Epic and Lyric Traditions*, Studies in Romance Languages, 13 (Lexington: University Press of Kentucky, 1975), pp. 13–17. The two epics cited are lost. We know their content only through prose versions in medieval chronicles. For those prose versions, plus commentary, see: Ramón Menéndez Pidal, *Le leyenda de los Infantes de Lara*, 3rd ed. (Madrid: Espasa-Calpe, 1971); Carola Reig, *Cantar de Sancho II o Cerco de Zamora*, *Revista de filología española*, supplement 37 (Madrid: Consejo Superior de Investigaciones Científicas, 1947).

11. Alan Deyermond, "Medieval Spanish Epic Cycles: Observations on Their Formation and Development," *Kentucky Romance Quarterly*, 23 (1976): 281–303.

12. Juan Ruiz, Arcipreste de Hita, *Libro de buen amor*, ed. Manuel Criado de Val and Eric W. Naylor (Madrid: Consejo Superior de Investigaciones Científicas, 1972).

number of medieval Spanish poets, frequently describes in autobiographical form the adventures of gentlemen who try to compliment and please lovely mountain girls (*serranas*) in exchange for guiding them through the passes or providing them with food, shelter, or other solace. These isolated mountain dwellers who waylay male travelers, consider wrestling an appropriate prelude to love-making, and intimidate men with their brutality seem related to two mythological heroines, Cyrene and Atalanta, upon whom rests the theory that the amazon myth in its earliest version began with single individuals. Cyrene, a huntress-athlete who wrestled lions for sport, was, according to legend, carried off by Apollo to Libya where, it will be remembered, one branch of the amazons lived. Atalanta was reared in the mountains, living among inaccessible trails and caves. She was later the only woman to join the Argonauts in Jason's quest for the Golden Fleece and to participate in the Calydon boar hunt. She defeated the hero Peleus at wrestling and outran all her potential suitors until Hippomenes won with the help of Aphrodite. Both figures, Sobol tells us, were huntresses, and Cyrene a shepherdess besides: "Whenever seen, the huntress and shepherdess, living apart from the paths of men, beautiful, self-sufficient, and protecting flocks or hunting wild beasts, have magnetized the artist" (p. 134).

Courtship as an athletic contest is common in the mythology of various lands (like Brunhilde, heroine of the early thirteenth-century German *Nibelungenlied*, for example) and is very much in consonance with the warrior-huntresses of amazonian folklore whose motive is to depreciate men, much like Ruiz' first two *serranas*. Later versions depict the girls as robbers and extortionists. Ruiz, however, endows two of his mountain maids with familiar amazon attributes as he displays cowardice and terror before them.

He first describes in *cuaderna vía* form his encounter with the *Chata* ("Pug nose") of Malangosto, who confronts him and blocks his way, demanding jewels. The archpriest promises her gifts, and the Chata lifts him bodily, flings him around her neck, and carries him over streams and hills. This incident is further parodied in a shorter-versed troubadour poem he says he composed about the encounter. In this lyric version, which provides an ironic contrast, the bedeviled and infuriated Chata throws her staff at him, aims her slingshot, and demands payment, which the narrator, sufficiently intimidated, promises in return for shelter. She grabs the "wretch" by one hand, flings him around her neck "like a light purse," and after feeding him, subjects him by the wrist and obliges him to do her will. With his usual good humor, the archpriest comments succinctly: "creet que fis buen varato" (p. 280, 971 d) (Believe me, I got a good deal). In a departure from the traditional amazon image, the girl is not particularly attractive although the archpriest's ironic lyrical version calls her "beautiful." A negative indication about her physiognomy is contained in her name because the ideal woman should have a fine nose. As in the encounters with amazons, it is the man who submits to her invitations to tarry after the meal, and apparently she was not as ugly as another *serrana* the poet describes in a later adventure—and from whom he flees—because the Chata does seem acceptable enough for him to consider that the experience was worthwhile after all.

Following the episode with the Chata, we find another meeting of the same type when the cowgirl of Riofrío confronts him when he has lost his way while traveling to Segovia. When the poet invites himself into her company, she is angered by his forwardness and attacks:

> proue me por llegar a la gaha maldita.
> dio me con la cayada tras la oreja fita. (stanza 977 cd)
>
> When to that accursed wretch I came near,
> A blow fom her staff left me with a wounded ear.

The cowgirl pushes him downhill, leaving him stunned but, then, grabbing him by the hand, leads him to her hut where he eats and pays, but refusing to tarry, awakens her anger again.

R. B. Tate notes that in these first two adventures, in which there is general correspondence between the narrative and lyrical versions, we have the traditional *serrana*: "the protagonist plays a sad second fiddle and violence and bawdy brutality is the substance" whereas in the following two episodes the girls are not fearsome and marriage is mentioned.[13] It is not improbable that what Tate calls the "caricaturesque wild woman of the sierra," portrayed in the Chata of Malangosto and the cowgirl of Riofrío, is also an echo of the amazon myth, one of the many classical influences apparent in the *Libro de buen amor*.

The female bullies who waylay the traveler in the *Libro de buen amor* are very different from the rustic heroines of Iñigo López de Mendoza, the marquis of Santillana, who, a century later, represents the *serranas* as delightful creatures. His *serranillas* contain playful dialogues between the country girls and the poet, who is captivated by their beauty and treats them as though they were ladies of the court.

The fearsome image of the archpriest of Hita's mountain girls reap-

13. R. B. Tate, "Adventures in the *sierra*," in *"Libro de buen amor" Studies*, ed. G. B. Gybbon-Monypenny (London: Tamesis, 1970), p. 223.

pears in the famous ballad of "La serrana de la Vera," whose legend also inspired plays of the same title by the Golden Age dramatists Lope de Vega and Vélez de Guevara. The mountain girl of the Vera is a latter-day Circe, surrounded by the bones (in some versions, tombs) of the men she has enticed into her cave. In the ballad, the narrator manages to escape when the *serrana* falls asleep, but she awakens and, armed with her slingshot, follows her escaping prey in hot pursuit of the would-be victim.

Another medieval figure reminiscent of the amazon is presented in the *romance* or ballad "La doncella guerrera" (The Maiden Warrior), one of the most widely sung ballads of the sixteenth century but composed well before then, according to Menéndez Pidal.[14] It is still repeated in Portugal, the Azores, and among Spanish-speaking Jews in the Mediterranean region; and there are Italian, French, Greek, and Albanian versions.

The ballad generally begins with the lament of a count who, with seven daughters, has no son to send to the recently proclaimed wars between France and Aragon. The number seven recalls the famous seven Infantes of Lara, whose tragic story is told in a cycle of early ballads, and it becomes obvious by the implied contrast that the father of seven daughters must have felt extremely frustrated. The youngest daughter decides to go to the wars, concealing her femaleness in order to fight, disguised as Don Martin of Aragon, or in some versions as Oliveros and in others as Don Martinos. During the years she serves the king as a valiant soldier (for two, three, or seven years, in different versions), the prince becomes enamored of her beautiful eyes and suspects the soldier is really a woman. His mother suggests various tests, such as throwing rings into the soldier's lap to see if he joins his legs to catch them, as a man, accustomed to wearing pants, would do. In all the tests, the maiden warrior proves herself more clever than the prince, but when faced with the final test, swimming, she asks leave to visit her dying father. The prince pursues her, but she outrides him: "Reventó siete caballos y no la fue de alcanzar"[15] (He ran seven horses to death and still could not overtake her). In a composite version given by Menéndez Pidal, the maiden not only outrides the prince, but also chides him complacently:

14. Ramón Menéndez Pidal, *Flor nueva de romances viejos* (Madrid: Espasa-Calpe, 1969), p. 203.

15. Manuel Alvar, *El romancero viejo y tradicional* (Mexico: Porrúa, 1971), p. 266.

Corre, corre, hijo del rey,
que no me habrás de alcanzar
hasta en casa de mi padre
si quieres irme a buscar.

Faster, faster, good king's son,
I'll leave you far behind me,
until I'm in my father's house,
where, if you wish, you'll find me.

Upon arriving home, she is ready to turn in her arms for a distaff to spin as the prince arrives.

The immense popularity of this ballad attests to the fascination which such a theme exerted through the centuries. The heroine, despite her prowess at arms and on horseback, in true amazon style, is still attractive as a woman. So successfully did she conceal her identity during her years in battle that only a king's son suspected the truth. Exhibiting a typical amazon attitude, even after "retiring" from war to return to her father's house she will accept the royal suitor only on her own terms. The prince, who could choose any woman in the court, is taken with this beautiful warrior, and her father has no doubt learned that a valiant daughter can be a consolation for not having sons who could emulate the seven Infantes of Lara.

The confusion as to Don Martin's true sex, generated by the disguise and valor in battle, has an interesting counterpart in one theory about the origins of the amazon myth: that they were really clean-shaven men. According to this theory, the warriors of the Hittite empire, which flourished between 2000 and 1200 B.C., the same period during which the amazonian empire was reputed to be at its height, were clean-shaven and were mistaken for women by the bearded Greeks who associated beardlessness with women.[16] The first Greeks who confronted the beardless warriors in combat may well have been as confused as the ballad prince with regard to their being men or women.

In contrast to the ballad "La doncella guerrera," with its attractive maiden warrior, the famous *Corbacho* or *Arcipreste de Talavera*[17] (Archpriest of Talavera) (1438) by Alfonso Martínez de Toledo is full of misogynistic satire. His delightful sermons accuse women of every possible defect, with very graphic details and novelesque dialogue. At

16. Sobol, *Amazons*, pp. 120–23.

17. Alfonso Martínez de Toledo, *Arcipreste de Talavera o Corbacho*, ed. J. González Muela (Madrid: Castalia, 1970).

the end, however, we find a sort of retraction whose seriousness has long been questioned by scholars. This palinode announces that "el auctor faze fin a la presente obra e demanda perdón si en algo de lo que ha dicho ha enojado o no bien dicho" (p. 280) (the author ends the present work and asks forgiveness if, in anything he has said, he has offended or stated badly).

The vision evoked in the retraction is that of amazonic vengeance. The author states that he dreamed that a thousand women of extreme beauty, fame, and gentle appearance attacked him with fists, clogs, and hair-pulling to punish him for what he wrote. They warn him not to consider himself immune, for even old men are vulnerable to women's attractions. The scene which follows is truly an antifeminist's nightmare. One woman pulls his hair, dragging him to the ground; another places her foot on his neck, making his tongue hang out; and still others beat him with distaffs and clogs as if he were a hired servant. Finally, more dead than alive, he awakens and, reflecting on the dangers of sleeping alone, considers himself duly chastised for his writings by these irate assailants whose description is, in fact, as uncomplimentary as that of the other women in the *Corbacho*.

As we have seen, the aggressive female who exhibits physical strength and who refuses to accept a passive role in her relationship toward men is a persistent motif in medieval Spanish literature, in notable contrast to the subservient role expected of medieval women. Sponsler offers the explanation that aggressive female characters in early Spanish epics and lyrical traditions "became the subject of stories precisely because they were such exceptions to the general norm."[18] It is a matter for conjecture whether the amazonlike figures represented in medieval Spanish works are grounded in historical reality or are picturesque inventions. Such fabulous females as the original amazons or later counterparts may have existed in reality from remote antiquity to our times, but there is no proof that they did. Sobol, who provides a number of theories regarding the truth or fiction of the classical amazons, concedes that despite existing historical explanations, the myth "may be nothing more than a primeval edition of the modern feminist rebelling against male tyranny—or merely the antipathy of the sexes expressed in story form."[19]

The archpriest of Talavera's nightmare may suggest that part of the literary representation of amazon types is an imaginative projection of repressed fear. The conqueror fears the possible rebellion of those

18. Sponsler, *Women*, p. 22.
19. Sobol, *Amazons*, p. 140.

he dominates. Man, firmly in control of his world, fears rebellious women, like those of the archpriest's nightmare, who cry:

> Loco atrevido, ¿do te vino osar de escribir ni hablar
> de aquellas que merescen del mundo la victoria? (p. 280)
>
> Impudent madman, how dare you write or talk
> about those who deserve victory in the world?

These are angry words we might expect of aggressive women reminiscent of the amazons, whose myth was very much alive in medieval Spanish literature.

Sexual Humor in Misogynist Medieval Exempla

Harriet Goldberg

The term "antifeminist" has been applied widely and indiscriminately to any story in which, even superficially, it appears that a woman is being criticized.[1] Many such stories occur in exempla—short tales, usually with a moral, which form an important part of medieval fiction and popular preaching in Castile as in the rest of Western Europe. These tales vary in theme and in tone, some being jocular, others serious.

Leading the field among the overtly hostile instances of undisguised aggression directed toward women is the story of the Duchess Rosinalda, who suffered sexual mutilation at the hands of Cacavo, the Hungarian invader of her land. Instead of marrying her as she had expected, Cacavo turned her over to his lieutenants for their use, order-

1. The feminist debate as it pertains to medieval Castilian literature has been summarized by Jacob Ornstein, "La misoginía y el profeminismo en la literatura castellana," *Revista de filología española*, 3 (1941): 219–32; and in Ornstein's edition of Luis de Lucena, *Repetición de amores* (Chapel Hill: University of North Carolina Studies in Romance Languages and Literatures, 23, 1954). See also María del Pilar Oñate, *El feminismo en la literatura española* (Madrid: Espasa-Calpe, 1938); Barbara Matulka, *An Antifeminist Treatise of Fifteenth-Century Spain: La repetición de amores* (New York: Institute of French Studies, Comparative Literature Series, 1931); Father Fernando Rubio Álvarez, "Desfavorable concepto moral de la mujer en algunas obras de origen oriental," *Ciudad de Dios*, 177 (1964): 267–87; and my article, "Two Parallel Medieval Commonplaces: Antifeminism and Antisemitism in the Hispanic Literary Tradition," in *Aspects of Jewish Culture in the Middle Ages*, ed. Paul E. Szarmach (Albany: SUNY Press, 1979), pp. 85–119; Lucy Sponsler,

ing that after three days she be discarded with "un palo por la natura fasta la garganta"[2] (a stick up her private parts up to her throat)—the ultimate husband she merited. Another theme indicating real hatred and dread of woman is found in the stories that deal with her as the witting or unwitting bearer of death in the form of a contact poison in her sweat.[3] In the *Poridat de las poridades*, a work of guidance supposedly written by Aristotle for Alexander the Great, the "author" claims to have saved the life of the young Alexander by warning him against such a maiden sent to him by an Indian prince.[4] Perhaps the most concise expression of serious misogyny is found in a work of wisdom literature—a genre related to the exemplum but which conveys its moral not by stories but by citing the real or apocryphal sayings of famous philosophers and sages. In the late thirteenth-century *Libro de los buenos proverbios*, the imagined Diogenes, on seeing the burned corpse of a woman hanging from a tree, remarked: "Oxalá

Women in the Medieval Spanish Epic and Lyric Traditions (Lexington, Ky.: Series in Romance Literature, 13, 1975). In my edition of *Jardín de nobles donzellas*, a profeminist work written in 1468 by Fray Martín de Córdoba (Chapel Hill: University of North Carolina Series in Romance Languages and Literatures, 137, 1974), I point out the relationship of the misogynist debate to the advice-to-princes (*de regimine principum*) tradition in this work, which is dedicated to the instruction of the young Princess Isabel (pp. 95–126).

2. Clemente Sánchez de Vercial (died ca. 1434) includes this tale in his compilation of exempla prepared in the fifteenth century for the use and the pleasure of his fellow preachers (*El libro de los exenplos por a.b.c.*, ed. John Esten Keller [Madrid: Consejo Superior de Investigaciones Científicas, 1961]), Ex. 246, p. 192. All translations are mine.

3. Norman Penzer, *Poison Damsels and Other Essays in Folklore and Anthropology* (London: Privately Printed for C. J. Sawyer, 1952), pp. 16–17.

4. Pseudo-Aristotle, *Poridat de las poridades*, ed. Lloyd A. Kasten (Madrid: 1957), p. 8. Aristotle said: "Et uenga uos emiente del presente que uos enuió el rey de Yndia, et enbió uos en el una muy fermosa manceba que fue criada a uegambre fasta que se tornó de natura de las bíuoras, et sy non fuesse por mí que lo entendí en su uista et de miedo que auié de los sabios desa tierra pudiera uos matar; et después fue prouado que mataua con so sodor a quantos se llegaua." (And recall the present that the king of India sent you; he sent you a beautiful young woman who had been raised on poisonous matter until she took on the nature of a viper herself, and if it had not been for me and the fear I had of the wise men of that land, she might have killed you; and afterward it was proven that she was able to kill anyone who approached her by means of her sweat). In the twelfth century, Johannes Hispalensis translated this work from Arabic into Latin as the *Secretum Secretorum*. In the thirteenth century a translation from Arabic was made into Castilian, and in the same period a Hebrew version appeared.

llevasen todos los árboles tal fructo"[5] (Would that all trees might bear such fruit). Consonant with the dread of the devil and his demonic powers is the tale in which the devil takes the form of a woman to harm good men.[6] In these cases, women are inextricably linked with the terrible powers of Satan.

On the other hand, the jocular tales, the subject of this study, are perplexing if we choose to consider them as tales aimed at attacking women. Even a casual reading suggests that the real target is either the complaisant husband, who is so expertly cuckolded, or the naïvely unaware ascetic, who is tempted sexually by the supposedly wicked woman. Peter Berger, in his study of how the comic can be used to understand the human condition, notes: "The essence of the comic is discrepancy." He calls attention to Freud's assertion that wit consists of unmasking the reality of a situation.[7] Certainly, the reader who sees through the deceitfulness of the woman in her artful confusion of her husband is amused by his own recognition of the discrepancy between the reality of the situation and that other reality, the version offered by the woman to her credulous husband. The question must be asked, nevertheless, Is the man the object of derision, or is the woman the

---

5. Hermann Knust, *Mittheilungen aus dem Eskurial* (Tübingen: Litterarisches verein Eskurial, 1879), p. 24. See also the edition by Harlan Sturm, *Libro de los buenos proverbios* (Lexington: University of Kentucky Press, 1970), p. 138. Father Fernando Rubio Alvarez cites the *Libro de los buenos proverbios*, the *Poridat de las poridades*, *El libro de los engaños y assayamientos de las mugeres*, and *Bocados de oro* as works of Eastern origin, in which women were regarded unfavorably, with the apparent intention of showing that they were ennobled in the Christian tradition and denigrated in the non-Christian Eastern sources ("Desfavorable concepto," pp. 277–87). In contrast to Rubio Alvarez' contention, John Walsh's study of the *Libro de los buenos proverbios* shows that much of the antifeminist material in it that is attributed to Socrates was uttered by Seneca in later versions that may have been Christianized ("Versiones peninsulares del 'Kitāb Ādāb Al-Falāsifa' de Ḥunayn Ibn Isḥāq: Hacia una reconstrucción del 'Libro de los buenos proverbios,'" *Al Andalus*, 41 (1976): 355–84). The later compilations of wisdom to which Walsh refers are *Floresta de philósophos*, ed. R. Foulché Delbosc, *Revue Hispanique*, 11 (1904): 5–154; and an unedited Pseudo-Seneca, *Los proverbios de Séneca llamados vicios y virtudes* (Biblioteca de El Escorial, ms. S-II-13).

6. Sánchez de Vercial, *El libro de los exenplos*, Ex. 115, p. 105. The *refrán* reads: "El diablo toma forma de mugier por que a los buenos enpesçer" (The devil takes the form of a woman to harm good people).

7. Peter Berger, "Christian Faith and the Social Comedy," in *Holy Laughter: Essays on Religion in the Comic Perspective*, ed. M. Conrad Hyers (New York: Seabury Press, 1969), pp. 123–33.

ridiculous figure? In this connection we must consider what Martin Grotjahn has to say. Basing his discussion of laughter on Freud's *Jokes and Their Relation to the Unconscious*, he identifies as central the aggressive nature of humor. In Grotjahn's scheme, wit is a repressed form of aggression—we laugh because we are relieved of feeling an uncomfortable level of anger, which we disguise as humor.[8] Although it might be said that we disapprove of the wily woman, we reserve our derision for her credulous husband. Although disapproval could be regarded as a sign of antifeminist bias, the ridicule directed at the cuckold is the risible element in the story and, therefore, is the reflection of our repressed aggressive feelings.[9] At least in part, our task here is the examination of the underlying feelings in these tales.

As a preliminary step, the stories themselves must be identified. Insofar as it is possible to ascertain, exempla entered the European tradition by way of Hispanic translations from the Arabic into either Latin or Spanish. That they were a part of the Arabic literary tradition also seems clear. Gustave von Grünebaum gives a list of the ten qualities of *adab* (an ideal of graceful and pleasing erudition in medieval Islam), the tenth of which is superior to all the rest and is "the knowledge of stories which people put forward in their literary gatherings."[10] The use of humorous stories to enliven Christian sermons was a device which served to attract the attention of the listener.[11] The popular nature of these humorous stories, even their salacious content, has long been evident in the Christian tradition. Robert Detweiler explains that they served as a relief from the repressive moral system and yet their comic tone did not deny or abandon that tradition.[12]

An enthusiastic advocate of humor in didactic literature was Juan Ruiz, archpriest of Hita, who cited the authority of the *Distichs of*

---

8. Martin Grotjahn, *Beyond Laughter: Humor and the Subconscious* (New York: McGraw-Hill, 1957), pp. 10–16; Grotjahn offers the summary, "Wit begins with an intention to injure, which our culture requires us to repress" (p. 14).

9. G. R. Owst identifies the most prevalent stories among the exempla: "tales which relate how the weaker partner manages to score off her unwitting spouse" (*Literature and Pulpit in Medieval England: A Neglected Chapter in the History of English Letters and of the English People* [Cambridge: Cambridge University Press, 1933], p. 163).

10. Gustave E. von Grünebaum, *Medieval Islam* (1954; rpt. Chicago: Phoenix Press, 1962), p. 254.

11. Owst, *Literature and Pulpit*, pp. 167–68, describes this usage as "early pulpit realism and feeling for raw humanity."

12. Robert Detweiler, "The Jesus Jokes: Religious Humor in the Age of Excess," *Cross Currents*, 24 (1974): 55–74.

Cato as his justification for the use of comic tales of questionable taste. Even further he averred that sadness can lead to sin whereas pleasure can improve the mind.[13] Obviously, because of the fine line between the comic and the tasteless, the medieval Church was concerned with the didactic application of ribald stories. Hugo Rahner, in his investigation of *eutrapelia* (the upholding of the mean in recreational play and joking), points out that although Aristotle had praised a moderate use of the playful, the inclusion of frivolous matter in sermons had been condemned for centuries until St. Thomas Aquinas praised a moderate use of the comic.[14] Even after Aquinas, succeeding Church councils continued to condemn the use of this material in sermons.[15] Some priests, however, defended the practice by referring to Jesus' use of parables to teach.[16] Most probably, the use of these tales was condemned because of their sexual content and not because they were comic. In fact, a wise man in the *Disciplina clericalis*, a Hispano-Latin exemplum collection written in the early twelfth century by the converted Jew Pedro Alfonso, expresses his reluctance to tell his pupil about the wiles of women because of his fear that such instruction will cause him to be regarded as an immoral man. His pupil reassures him that Solomon had told similar stories in the Bible and that he had not suffered for having done so.[17]

Bearing in mind Ruiz' conviction that the introduction of humor in his work would impart wisdom to his readers, we can then proceed to try to decide what is funny in the exempla that have hitherto been

---

13. Juan Ruiz, *Libro de buen amor*, ed. and trans. Raymond S. Willis (Princeton, N.J.: Princeton University Press, 1972), stanza 44.

14. Hugo Rahner, "*Eutrapelia*: A Forgotten Virtue," in *Holy Laughter*, pp. 185–97.

15. María Rosa Lida de Malkiel, "Tres notas sobre D. Juan Manuel," *Romance Philology* 4 (1950–1951): 155–94; see also Owst, *Literature and Pulpit*, p. 161.

16. J. Th. Welter, *L'exemplum dans la littérature réligieuse et didactique du moyen âge* (Paris: 1927; rpt. New York: AMS, 1973), p. 33.

17. *The Scholar's Guide*, trans. and ed. Joseph Ramon Jones and John Esten Keller (Toronto: Pontifical Institute of Medieval Studies, 1969), p. 55. The *Disciplina clericalis* has been edited and translated into Spanish by Angel González Palencia (Petrus Alphonsi, *Disciplina clericalis, edición y traducción del texto latino* [Madrid: Consejo Superior de Investigaciones Científicas, 1948]). See also the four-part study by Haim Schwarzbaum, "International Folklore Motifs in Petrus Alphonsi's 'Disciplina clericalis,'" *Sefarad*, 21 (1961): 267–99; *Sefarad*, 22 (1962, Fasc. 1): 17–59; *Sefarad*, 22 (1962, Fasc. 2): 321–44; and *Sefarad*, 23 (1963): 54–73. See also the new English edition, *The "Disciplina clericalis" of Petrus Alfonsi*, ed. Eberhard Hermes, trans. P. R. Quarrie (Berkeley and Los Angeles: University of California Press, 1977).

identified as antifeminist. From a psychological viewpoint, Grotjahn describes the nature of aggressive humor by saying that the first teller of the tale disguises his aggressive feelings, hoping to release them when the person to whom he tells the anecdote laughs; it is only then that the initiator of the story is free to laugh.[18] As to the content of the story, it is useful to note that laughter must respond to the exigencies or standards of society.[19] Clearly, the humor that arises from the temptation of a celibate or from the tricking of a foolishly gullible husband is a reaction to a recognizable social institution or a moral system. Because this system has not changed substantially, it is reasonable to assume that this kind of humor is able to traverse boundaries of time and space. A striking example is the reappearance in today's popular sexual humor of a version of the story of D. Pitas Payas.[20]

The basic comic situation to which Bergson refers is that of a man defeated by mechanical forces beyond his control: the body is a mindless machine whose demands make him ridiculous.[21] Walter Kerr, the drama critic, calls attention to the comic moment when a man loses control over his own body. Further, he suggests that sex itself is funny because it is essentially a mechanical force. He writes that although we may choose to be celibate, we are not free to be or not to be sexual.[22]

A most common comic situation in exempla which is directly related to sexual humor is that of the woman who displays unusual skill in deceiving her husband so that she may satisfy her excessive sexual appetites. We laugh for several reasons. Bergson explains that laughter's natural milieu is indifference, referring to the relative disengagement of the reader. In a discussion of the sacred and the comic, M.

---

18. Grotjahn, *Beyond Laughter*, pp. 255–57.

19. Henri Bergson, *Le Rire: Essai sur la signification du comique* (Paris: F. Alcan, 1930), pp. 7–8.

20. Juan Ruiz, *Libro de buen amor*, stanzas 474–84, tells the story of a husband who paints a picture of a lamb on his wife's body before leaving her at home alone, the purpose of which is to ensure her chastity since any contact will erase the picture. After an extended absence, the woman's lover restores the picture, erring in portraying not a lamb but a mature animal. The comic explanation offered to the cuckolded husband is that the animal had grown during his absence. A twentieth-century story (reported in New York City in 1939) tells of an animal originally painted on the inner thigh of the woman but repainted by her lover on the wrong thigh. The comic explanation is that the animal had crossed from one thigh to the other by swimming across the stream of urine.

21. Bergson, *Le Rire*, p. 51.

22. Walter Kerr, *Tragedy and Comedy* (New York: Simon & Schuster, 1967), pp. 116, 154.

Conrad Hyers writes, "On the one hand, humor is a mechanism of withdrawal and objectification; it is an act of separation, distancing and detachment."[23] Detweiler emphasizes the noncommitment involved in the telling of a sick joke so that we can "draw back from the abyss before it overwhelms."[24] From the safe distance of the comic, we can mock the moral system without putting ourselves in jeopardy. Why the reader is not engaged by the plight of the cuckold can be explained by another comment of Bergson's. "Un personnage comique est généralement comique dans l'exact mésure où il s'ignore lui même"[25] (A comic figure is generally funny to the exact point where he is unaware of himself). Grotjahn, writing from a psychoanalytic viewpoint, says, 'The naïve is a good illustration of the special aspects of the comic. Naïveté occurs when a person puts himself outside and beyond inhibition. The naïve person will not feel guilty and will cause no guilt feelings in the onlooker because the effect is unintentional."[26] If we think of the comic figure as the butt of the aggression of others, we can add the comment of Jan Huizinga: "The category of the comic is closely connected with *folly* in the highest and lowest sense of that word."[27]

After considering the comic aspects of a person helpless in the grip of mechanical forces and the unaware victim of his wife's deceitful behavior, we can also recognize another comic element in exempla. We can see what might be called an interchange of normal societal roles or values, which Bergson calls "inversion."[28] This is the comic inversion which Barry Ulanov sees as the explanation of why a fantasy like Shakespeare's *Midsummer Night's Dream* is not a frightening nightmare of magic and enchantment. "Everything is turned upside down. . . . That is the nature of this comedy of inversion. An ass's head really belongs atop Bottom."[29] In this sense, humor is the protective device of which Gerson Legman speaks in his extensive study of sexual humor.[30]

23. M. Conrad Hyers, "The Dialectic of the Sacred and the Comic," in *Holy Laughter*, pp. 208–40.

24. Detweiler, "The Jesus Jokes," p. 63.

25. Bergson, *Le Rire*, p. 17.

26. Grotjahn, *Beyond Laughter*, p. 16.

27. Jan Huizinga, *Homo Ludens: A Study of the Play Element in Culture* (Boston: Doubleday Anchor, 1950), p. 6.

28. Bergson, *Le Rire*, pp. 94–97.

29. Barry Ulanov, "The Rhetoric of Christian Comedy," in *Holy Laughter*, pp. 103–22.

30. Gerson Legman, *The Rationale of the Dirty Joke: An Analysis of Sexual Humor* (New York: Grove Press, 1968), pp. 664–737.

Having thought about what causes these tales to be funny, we need to turn our attention to the principal collections of exempla in which we find these apparently misogynist anecdotes, in the hope of identifying the comic elements we have discussed. The first collection that can properly be called Spanish—in nationality, even though not in language—is *Disciplina clericalis.* Although Jacob Ornstein, in his penetrating study of peninsular antifeminism, chose to exclude this and other works of apparently Oriental origin, stating that the first Spanish antifeminist material was not written until the fifteenth century, it seems to me that these works, composed or translated by Spaniards for a Spanish public, are important evidence for literary attitudes in twelfth- and thirteenth-century Spain.[31]

The stories in *Disciplina clericalis* are arranged in a rudimentary frame—a young boy receives instruction from his father; a teacher counsels his pupil. The stories are linked by admonitions that the youth not commit the same errors as the personages in the next tale or by a general observation to be illustrated in the succeeding example. Jones and Keller recognize "a pseudo-didactic overtone . . . a kind of tongue-in-cheek seriousness,"[32] which is undeniable. In his prologue, Pedro Alfonso declares his intention to instruct but explains that man's temperament is delicate: "it must be instructed by being led, as it were, little by little, so that it will not become bored" (p. 34). In a section on table manners, the boy laughs and tells a joke of his own and then is anxious to hear more about Maimundus, the slave, because everything about him is funny (pp. 99–100). A pupil asks for enlightenment about the wiles of women and is understandably aroused by the three tales that concern the evil ways of women: a man returns from his vineyard with a wounded eye and his wife covers his good eye, thereby permitting her lover to escape unseen (Ex. 9); a wife and her mother hold up a sheet for inspection so that a lover may slip out of the house unnoticed (Ex. 10); a lover is told by the wife's mother to pretend that he was seeking refuge from dangerous street bullies by hiding in her house (Ex. 11).

The pupil begs for more stories about women since he is dazzled by their "presumptuous audaciousness" (p. 59). He complains that his master has only told three short tales. Now he wants a more satisfying long one. The master teasingly warns him that long stories can be used as delaying tactics and tells the folkloric tale without end of the peasant who had to ferry his sheep across the river, two by two (Ex. 12).

31. See note 1 above.
32. Jones and Keller, *The Scholar's Guide*, p. 18.

Invoking the affection between them, the pupil begs for more, and the master accedes with the story of the weeping bitch (Ex. 13), in which a wily go-between deceives a virtuous woman in order to procure her favors for her client. With very little urging, the master continues with the story of the man whose excessive measures to guard the virtue of his wife are of no avail; he is eventually locked out of his well-guarded house (Ex. 14). Although the ostensible purpose of these exempla as a part of the young pupil's curriculum is to instruct him about the dangers that face him in dealing with women, all five of them deal with a clever woman and a foolish, gullible victim (in only one is the victim a young woman). The butt of the joke is the comically naïve figure described by Grotjahn who suffers from the comic unawareness described by Bergson.

Clearly, the reader's emotions are not engaged; he feels no pity for the deceived husband. Humor has served to create the social distance, the protective shield of which Legman writes. J. P. S. Tatlock recognizes this detachment or disengagement with the comment that the characters in the *Disciplina clericalis* are like the stock characters in the Sunday supplement of a modern newspaper.[33] Worthy of mention is the fact that this collection does not contain the other kind of antifeminist story, which is a part of this study—the comic temptation of a ridiculously naïve ascetic. In this connection it is appropriate to remember von Grünebaum's observation: "The Prophet's injunction against celibacy, in part, perhaps, provoked by the influence of Nestorian Christianity, removed virginity from the ascetic ideals, and the community was not prepared to countenance the development of organized monasticism on Christian lines."[34]

In *El libro de Calila e Digna*, a collection of apologues said to have been translated from Arabic in 1251, we find the story of the woman, who, having had her nostrils cut off in questionable circumstances, returns home and convinces her husband that he must have cut them off himself. She has saved herself from the necessity of having to explain her complicity in the sexual misconduct of another.[35] This remarkable

33. J. S. P. Tatlock, "Mediaeval Laughter," *Speculum*, 21 (1946): 289–94.

34. Von Grünebaum, *Medieval Islam*, p. 125.

35. *El libro de Calila e Digna*, ed. John Esten Keller and Robert White Linker (Madrid: Consejo Superior de Investigaciones Científicas, 1967), pp. 62–67. The common source for this collection of tales is the Indian Panchatantra, written in Sanskrit, passing later into Persia, in *pehlavi*, and from there into Arabic (pp. xvi–xix). The Castilian translation is thought to have been made in 1251 by order of the *infante* Alfonso before he succeeded to the throne (pp. xxi–xxii).

credulity on the part of the husband is surpassed by another example. A carpenter, hiding under a bed occupied by his wife and her lover, overhears his wife declare to her lover that she really loves her husband best of all. So touched is this ludicrously naïve husband by what he considers to be his wife's devotion to him that he remains under the bed the whole night, joining his wife in bed only after the departure of her lover. He says to her, "Por Dios, amiga, dormid ca mucho velaste esta noche, e mucho lazraste. E por buena fe synon que me temí te fazer pesar, yo matara aquel omne por lo que te fizo"[36] (For God's sake, my dear, sleep because you were awake a lot tonight, and you suffered much. In fact, if I were not afraid of causing you pain, I would kill the man who did it to you). Can anyone doubt that the reader is expected to laugh at the comic unawareness of the husband? His exaggerated concern for her feelings is a reflection of a comic inversion of the values of his society since his expressed tenderness is for a woman who is cynically violating her marriage vows. As in other exempla from the Arabic tradition, the evil nature of the woman is defined in terms of her deception of her husband, not as a tempter of the celibate.

Another work in the Islamic tradition, contemporary with *Calila e Digna*, is the *Libro de los engaños y assayamientos de las mugeres*, in which the frame story is quite elaborate.[37] A wicked woman (in this case, the stepmother of the young prince) attempts to seduce him for what one suspects are political motives rather than sensual ones. Although the commonly accepted title of the book makes use of the word *engaños* ("deceits"), Keller, in his edition, notes that on the first page of the only surviving manuscript, it is clear that initially the word had been written *engañados* ("deceived ones") (pp. xi–xii). Does the scribal confusion between "the deceived ones" (masculine plural) and the "deceits" reflect the copyist's perception of the work as one in

---

36. *Calila e Digna*, pp. 221–30. For a curious miniature that appears to be illustrating this tale in spite of a caption identifying it in another manner, see Gustave Le Bon, *The World of Islamic Civilization* (Geneva: Ed. Minerva, 1974), p. 18.

37. The *Libro de los engaños y assayamientos de las mugeres* was translated under the patronage of the *infante* Fadrique in 1253. A version of the Sindbad stories, once thought to be Indian in origin but now thought to be Persian, it has been edited by John Esten Keller (Chapel Hill: University of North Carolina Series in Romance Languages and Literatures, 20, 2nd ed., 1959). Angel González Palencia edited *Versiones castellanas del "Sendebar"* (Madrid: Consejo Superior de Investigaciones Científicas, 1946), in which he includes later versions dating from the fifteenth and sixteenth centuries along with the thirteenth-century version.

which the victims of deceit were an important comic element and not only the deceits themselves?

The comic pattern is the alternate narration of exempla designed to convince the king that he ought to kill his son or that he ought not to. The youth's stepmother, who had accused him of trying to rape her, tries to convince the king that children are a peril, and the king's seven counselors try to convince the king that precipitate action is often regretted and that women are often evil. In a sense, the king is as much a gullible credulous fool as any of the cuckolded husbands in the exempla since each tale apparently convinces him either to kill the youth or to spare his life. Each story ends with: "E el rey mandó matar su fijo" (The king ordered that his son be killed), or "El rey mandó que non matasen su fijo" (The king ordered that they not kill his son).

Another comic element is evident here—comic repetition—of which Bergson writes, "Il ne s'agit plus, comme tout à l'heure, d'un mot ou d'une phrase qu'un personnage repétè, mais d'une situation, c'est-à-dire d'une combinaison de circonstances, qui revient telle quelle à plusieurs reprises, tranchant ainsi sur le cours changeant de la vie"[38] (It is not a question of a word or a phrase that a character repeats, but rather of a situation, that is to say, a combination of circumstances that return repeatedly, interrupting the changing course of life). Each repetition of a mildly humorous situation conditions the reader so that a point is reached when a new occurrence provokes real laughter. In *Libro de los engaños* the wicked stepmother queen uses her stories to convince her gullible husband that children bring harm (p. 17) or that he ought not to rely on the bad advice of wicked counselors (pp. 22–23). The privy counselors tell two kinds of stories: six tales counsel against precipitate action which might be repented later, and five are directly sexual in content with the woman as the deceiver of a man. These include the story of the parrot who is tricked by the wife into being an unreliable witness to her infidelities (pp. 15–16); the story of the sword, in which the lover pretends to have taken refuge from street bullies (pp. 20–21);[39] the vendor of cloth and the confusion of identity to deceive the husband (pp. 35–37); the story of the weeping bitch (pp. 29–31);[40] and the tale of the young man who would not marry until he knew the evils of women and who received first-hand instruction from the wife of a foolishly complaisant husband (pp. 46–48). One story, that of the bathhouse keeper who of-

38. Bergson, *Le Rire*, pp. 90–91.

39. *Disciplina clericalis*, Ex. 11.

40. *Engaños*, pp. 29–31. See also *Disciplina clericalis*, Ex. 13, and *Libro de los exenplos*, pp. 235–36.

fers his wife to the uninitiated young prince, is used by the *privados* ("counselors") to counsel against precipitate action, but certainly the wife is really betraying her foolish husband when she refuses to leave the side of the young prince, saying, "¿Cómmo yré? ca le fizo pleyto que dormiría con él toda esta noche" (pp. 27–28) (How can I go home? I promised him I would sleep with him all night long). It certainly sounds as though she were enjoying herself. This is a case of another kind of inversion—the cheater cheated.

The most extensive collection of exempla is *El libro de los exenplos por a.b.c.* compiled by Clemente Sánchez de Vercial in the first quarter of the fifteenth century, in which 438 exempla are arranged alphabetically according to the first word of the Latin moralization.[41] Although the stories cover a wide range of ethical and moral problems, we find a fair number which clearly belong to the group of tales that deal with the wily woman and her ridiculous husband. It is in this collection, in which the Oriental material has been assimilated into the Christian tradition, that we encounter that other group of stories dealing with the temptation of the comically helpless celibate.

Among the stories of the woman as deceiver of her husband in *El libro de los exenplos*, we find tales familiar from other sources: the man who returns from the vineyard with a wounded eye (Ex. 161, p. 133);[42] the deceitful woman whose mother aids her in hiding her lover by means of an outstretched sheet (Ex. 162, p. 134);[43] the weeping bitch (Ex. 234, pp. 235–36),[44] which here is used to illustrate the double message: "Del engaño de muger te deves bien guardar, que ahun a las castas induze a pecar" (Beware of woman's deceitfulness, because she can cause even chaste women to sin). The theme of the husband whose excessive precautions are insufficient to guard his young wife (they result in his downfall) also appears in this collection (Ex. 303, pp. 237–38).[45] An unwanted husband is disposed of neatly by an ingenious woman who delivers him drugged and apparently moribund to a monastery, saying that it was her husband's last wish that he die as a member of the religious order. The next morning the husband awakens to find himself irrevocably enrolled in a celibate order and unable to return home (Ex. 304, pp. 238–39). There are

41. See note 2.

42. *Libro de los exenplos*, Ex. 161, p. 133. Cf. *Disciplina clericalis*, Ex. 9.

43. *Libro de los exenplos*, Ex. 162, p. 134. Cf. *Disciplina clericalis*, Ex. 10.

44. *Libro de los exenplos*, Ex. 234, pp. 235–36. Cf. *Disciplina clericalis*, Ex. 13, and *Engaños*, pp. 29–31.

45. *Libro de los exenplos*, Ex. 303, pp. 237–38. Cf. *Disciplina clericalis*, Ex. 14.

other tales of the wiliness of women, but the ones cited are those with an explicitly humorous content. With the exception of the weeping bitch story, the common factor is the naïve unawareness of the credulous husband. He has slipped on a sexual banana peel; his fall makes us laugh. As Bergson says, it is not the fall itself that we find funny, it is the involuntary nature of the fall—the "maladresse."[46] If we remember Grotjahn's observation that humor represents a kind of emotionally acceptable disguise for our aggressive feelings, then we must wonder whether these stories are indeed antifeminist.

In the other kind of sexual jokes in *El libro de los exenplos por a.b.c.*, the woman tempts a celibate either intentionally or unintentionally. The comic figure is the rigorously chaste man whose exaggerated innocence sets him apart from other men in the sense that he is the perfect fool.[47] He is in the power of his own body, which is behaving mechanically. Two tales deal with monks who have been forced to pass the night under the same roof with an attractive woman; these tales appear to be two versions of the same story (Ex. 253, 254, pp. 196–97). That these tales were considered to be funny can be deduced from the circumstances in the more complete version. Some young men, *mancebos*, have arranged for a prostitute to pretend to need shelter for the night in the house of a hermit. The story teller does not call them instruments of the devil, nor does he give any reason for their plan. By not assigning to them any sort of motivation, he is acknowledging that this is the kind of thing that young men might do to a hermit. In other words, this is a practical joke which the public for whom it was intended might be expected to recognize. It is only after the woman is in the house that the devil begins to act "començó a mover el coraçón del" (began to move his heart). The hermit lights a candle because light can vanquish the devil's darkness. He passes the night putting his fingers one by one in the flame to distract himself from the temptation under his roof—a physical counterirritant as a remedy for a physical difficulty. However, even in the choice of the distraction, a certain sly humor is evident. Could we not expect the public to be as aware as we are of the conjuror's trick of passing one's fingers through the cool area of a candle's flame? As a logical conclusion to their trick, the young men come to the hermit's house in the morning to inquire if a young woman had come there the night before. They are told that she

46. Bergson, *Le Rire*, p. 9.

47. In *Rationale of the Dirty Joke*, Legman identifies a category of stories in which the fool is a clergyman whose chastity or innocence is the element that makes him the foolish butt of the joke (pp. 122–24).

is sleeping, but when they enter, they find her dead. They pray for her, and the hermit querulously shows them his fingers saying, "Vet que me fizo esta fija del diablo" (See what this daughter of Satan did to me), an apparently trivial complaint when compared with the death of the woman. If we ask ourselves why this tale is comic, we can answer first that the butt of the joke, the hermit, is the naïve, unaware figure made ridiculous by his helplessness against the mechanical nature of his body. Second, we can recognize a comic discrepancy or what Detweiler calls incongruity when he refers to Arthur Koestler's explanation of a comic situation that results from the "collision of matrices" within a moral and social system.[48] Finally, the explanation of why such a practical joke should be thought of as funny can be sought in Grotjahn's identification of the aggressive nature of joking.

Two other stories set up an elderly woman as a source of temptation, another instance of comic discrepancy. In one, a monk is preparing to carry his aged mother across a stream. He finds it necessary to envelop his hands in some clothing to protect himself from the temptation that his mother's body represents. She asks him why he is doing this and he replies, "Porque el cuerpo de la mugier es fuego, e llegando a ti, acordavasseme de las otras mugieres" (Ex. 306, p. 240) (Because a woman's body is fire, and touching you reminded me of other women). In another, an elderly cleric, with his last breath reproves his wife who has placed her ear near his nostrils to determine if he is still breathing: "Tírate allá, mugier, que aun el fuego pequeño vive e quema la paja" (Ex. 396, p. 307) (Get away from here, woman, because even a small fire is alive and burns straw). Is it the incongruity of a man's fearing sexual arousal while fording a river or the exaggeration of the power of the sexual reaction that makes these tales amusing? Why is it ridiculous that a man should not be giving his last thoughts to his salvation but rather that he be concerned with controlling his sexual appetite? Is it possible that a situation is comic when there is disharmony between the cause and the effect?[49]

In another exemplum in Sánchez de Vercial's compilation, two celibates who are seated at a window of their cell see an attractive, well-dressed woman pass by. One of them, who had apparently never seen a woman before, asks his companion what she is. His having to ask this absurd question marks him as a person of exaggeratedly comic

---

48. Detweiler, "The Jesus Jokes," p. 58. The reference to Koestler is to *The Act of Creation* (New York: Dell Publishing, 1967), pp. 32–42.

49. See Bergson, *Le Rire*, appendix to the 32nd ed. (Paris: F. Alcan, 1930), p. 205.

naïveté. His companion answers that she is a goat. The poor innocent is so lovestruck that he cannot eat. However, when his friend asks him why he is not eating, he answers, "que tanta piedat avia de aquella cabra que non podia comer" (Ex. 300, p. 234) (he had such compassion for that goat that he was unable to eat). Did the innocent brother really believe that the woman was a goat? Was the meal he refused roast goat? Obviously, the amusing element in the story is the unawareness of the troubled man who is disturbed by physical forces he does not understand which he chooses to explain as pity. His companion's unawareness is open to question.

Although the *Arcipreste de Talavera* (1438) of Alfonso Martínez de Toledo is not a collection of exempla as such, he has certainly drawn extensively on the exemplary tradition.[50] He introduces his anecdotes with such expressions as, "Contarte he un enxienplo, e mill te contaría" (I will tell you a tale, and a thousand more I would tell you) or "Otro enxienplo te diré" (Another tale I will tell you), showing his recognition of the custom of using exemplary material to add interest to instructional discourses. He makes use of the familiar theme of the blinding of the gullible husband so that the lover may escape. However, instead of the outstretched sheet or the wounded eye, his cuckolds are fooled differently. A woman blinds her husband by squirting milk from her breasts into her husband's eyes; another shampoos her husband's hair so that the friar she has hidden under the bed can leave the house unseen. A clever woman sends her husband for a new candle while her lover departs; a pot in need of mending is held up to obscure the husband's vision (pp. 162–65).

Martínez de Toledo adds enough lively dialogue to create the effect of a real anecdote. In one instance the husband is convinced that the sound he hears is the noise of cats, and another poor foolish cuckold is put on the defensive by the suggestion that it is he who is returning from an amorous encounter. Obviously, such an original and irrepressible spirit as Martínez de Toledo would not have been content with simply making use of traditional material. Nevertheless, the narrative elements remain the same. A clever woman creates a comic diversion so that her lover can escape; her gullible, credulous husband

50. Alfonso Martínez de Toledo, *Arcipreste de Talavera*, ed. Joaquín González Muela and Mario Penna (Madrid: Clásicos Castalia, 1970), pp. 162–65. Jacob Ornstein sees this work as a part of the courtly debate (see *Repetición de amores*). See also Christine J. Whitbourn, *The "Arcipreste de Talavera" and the Literature of Love* (Hull: University of Hull, 1970); and E. Michael Gerli, *Alfonso Martínez de Toledo* (Boston: Twayne, 1976).

does not recognize the deception. Although the stated purpose is to show the wickedness of women, the butt of the jokes is the unaware man. If we consider Grotjahn's assertion that some jokes are psychically safe ways of expressing hostility, might we not suspect that the hostility is directed at the cuckolds and not at their patently cleverer wives?

Martínez de Toledo continues his condemnation of worldly love, telling the story of the queen whose price for acceding to the sexual advances of a lover is complete sway over the entire world. The story deals with a man who has insulted a woman by suggesting that she is sexually available. She rebuffs him, vowing that she wouldn't accept him for a million dollars (the contemporary equivalent of complete sway over the world), ending with an indignant, "What do you think I am?" His answer suggests that he is taking the question literally. "We have established what you are; now we are haggling over the price." According to Grotjahn's analysis of the sense of humor in relation to sex, the men in these tales experience discomfort "because it is so difficult for their unconscious to accept the fact that women seem to them simultaneously inferior and superior. . . ."[51] We laugh at the discomfort and at the emotionally safe aggressive feelings which are expressed in jest.

Another reaction to feminine superiority is the medieval commonplace that even wise men have been blind victims of wicked women who have ruined them. The Archpriest of Talavera cites Virgil and Aristotle as a part of the list which usually includes Samson, Solomon, and David.[52] Ruiz, the other archpriest, who could hardly have been called antifeminist, used the exemplum about Virgil in the basket in which the poet is the ridiculous victim of the woman whom he had been pursuing.[53] The *Arcipreste de Talavera* refers to the humiliation of Aristotle by a woman who rode astride his back, whipping him on.[54] This story is a reflection of the societal inversion to which we

51. Grotjahn, *Beyond Laughter*, p. 58.

52. *Arcipreste de Talavera*, pp. 76–81.

53. Juan Ruiz, *Libro de amor*, stanzas 262–68. A woman pursued by Virgil, the necromancer, lowers a large basket from her window so that he may be pulled up. She halts the raising of the basket so that the next day all Rome sees him dangling in it. His revenge is remarkably inventive. He extinguishes magically all flame in Rome, telling the populace that the only way to rekindle any flames in the city is to ignite torches or candles by contact with the haughty woman's private parts.

54. The story of Aristotle is embellished by the fact that he was found in this humiliating position by his young pupil, Alexander. See the *Arcipreste de Talavera*, p. 76 and accompanying illustration.

have referred, and we laugh just as much as we do at the thought of Virgil, the great poet and necromancer, exposed to ridicule suspended in the basket.[55] It would be difficult, indeed, to maintain that either the woman who is astride the philosopher or the woman who has arranged for the poet to be trapped in that laughable position is the object of hostility in these stories. We are amused by the humiliation of the great men.

The conclusion is inescapable: these stories traditionally designated as antifeminist do not really reflect hostility toward women as much as a kind of amused disdain of their supposed victims. It is not the comic nature of the tales that precludes their being antifeminist; rather it is the consistency of the pattern of humorous scorn that makes their nature evident. Granted that there were truly misogynist stories in the folkloric tradition, like that of Rosinalda, it is evident that the stories of the skillful adulteress, or the temptress, of the otherwise chaste man, or the woman whose power causes even the wise and the mighty to be demeaned are in a different class. The cuckold is the naïve, unaware, comic figure described by Bergson and Grotjahn. The celibate man is the victim of his own body as machine, to which both Bergson and Kerr refer. The great men made ridiculous by a woman are products of a societal inversion or role reversal. If we remember the psychologically based observation that humor can be an expression of aggressive feelings couched in a socially safe form, then we can assume that the storytellers were directing hostility toward the comic figures in their stories, none of whom was a woman. Instead of hostility, perhaps we can say that at most they reflect a certain mistrust of women or men's uneasiness about their own competence.[56]

---

55. See the discussion of the medieval catalogues of great men betrayed by women in Domenico Comparetti, *Vergil in the Middle Ages*, trans. E. F. M. Benecke (1929; rpt. Hamden, Conn.: Shoe String Press, 1966), pp. 327–28. See also George Sarton, "Aristotle and Phyllis," *Isis*, 14 (1930): 8–19.

56. See my treatment of this material in *Jardín de nobles donzellas, Fray Martín de Córdoba: A Critical Edition and Study* (Chapel Hill: University of North Carolina Studies in Romance Languages and Literatures, 137, 1974), pp. 121–23. See also Joseph H. Chorpenning, "Rhetoric and Feminism in the *Cárcel de amor*," *Bulletin of Hispanic Studies*, 54 (1977): 1–8; he suggests that profeminism was a means of making a new statement about the interior development of man (p. 8).

Women in the *Book of Good Love*

Rosalie Gimeno

During the first half of the fourteenth century, in Castile, Juan Ruiz, archpriest of Hita, composed a masterful poem known as the *Libro de buen amor*. One of two reasons he gave for writing it was "por muchos males e daños / que fazen muchos e muchas a otras con sus engaños"[1] (for many evils and wrongs that many men and women do to other women with their deceits). Through the *Book of Good Love*, he undertook to "reduzir a toda persona a memoria buena de bien obrar" (pp. 10–11) (to guide everyone back to good memory of good deeds). In an entertaining and edifying way, he exposed the "muchas engañosas maneras . . . para pecar e engañar las mugeres . . . porque sean todos apercebidos e se puedan mejor guardar de tantas maestrías como algunos usan por el loco amor" (pp. 10–13) (many deceitful measures . . . for sinning and for deceiving women . . . so that all might be alerted and be on guard against the many tricks that certain people practice for the sake of mad and heedless love).

The archpriest of Hita treats men and women equally when he dis-

---

I am grateful to Alan Deyermond for his valuable help in the preparation of this essay.

1. Juan Ruiz, *Libro de buen amor*, ed. Raymond S. Willis (Princeton, N.J.: Princeton University Press, 1972), stanza 1634 of the revised text dated 1343. In the 1330 version, the sinful acts were done *a otros* ("to others"). Spanish quotations of the archpriest's book are from Willis' edition, as are excerpts of his English paraphrase. Page numbers refer to the prologue in prose; stanza numbers, to poetic passages.

cusses in orthodox Christian terms the human condition. He defines people as composites of finite, material bodies and infinite, spiritual souls. Initially, time, he says, destroys youth, beauty, strength, health, boldness, and honor, attributes that permit a sense of physical well-being and of pride as well as enjoyment of life on earth. Time ultimately destroys the fragile body itself; after death, it disintegrates into ashes. The body tends to procure immediate gratification through the five senses whereas the soul tends to seek a permanent home outside the body through the manipulation of its three faculties. Understanding allows one to distinguish the good from the bad. Memory serves as a repository of the knowledge the understanding acquires. The will enables one to desire virtue or vice.

An individual with perfect understanding, memory, and will knows God and his laws, remembers them, and desires to perform virtuous deeds. The perfect soul rules over the body and directs physical activity toward the accomplishment of meritorious acts on earth in order to earn the beatitude of heaven as well as the corporal and spiritual glory Christ promised to the elect on Judgment Day. However, Ruiz reports, human beings by nature are imperfect. Consequently, the soul and its faculties can falter. Characterized as creatures more inclined toward sin than toward virtue, men and women must struggle with their innate imperfection in this life, a dramatic and dynamic battle of the sinner in search of salvation.

People are influenced by powerful beings. With respect to these powers who exert pressures that are positive (Christ, the Virgin Mary, Dame Lent) or negative (Sir Love, Lady Venus, Sir Carnal) upon the human characters, male and female forces are balanced. Distributed in pairs by the poet, the members of the twosomes either complement each other (Christ and Mary, Sir Love and Lady Venus) or oppose each other (Sir Carnal and Dame Lent). One masculine and two feminine figures cultivate desire for eternal bliss, and two masculine and one feminine figures foster interest in temporal pleasures. In the poem, neither sex monopolizes virtue or sin. Good and evil rise above gender; they are universal constants.

Ruiz portrays men, in general, as materialistic, imperfect creatures. He attributes this axiom to Aristotle: "el mundo por dos cosas trabaja: la primera / por aver mantenencia, la otra cosa era / por aver juntamiento con fembra plazentera" (stanza 71) (the whole world exerts itself for two things: the first is to find sustenance, the other thing is to couple with a pleasant female). To substantiate this statement empirically, the poet observes that "omnes, aves, animalias, toda bestia de cueva, / quieren segund natura compaña siempre nueva" (stanza

73) (men, birds, animals, all beasts in caves, by nature constantly crave a new mate). The author then focuses on the mad love men pursue: "e mucho más el omne que toda cosa que s' mueva" (stanza 73) (and much more so does man than all things that move).[2] Potency and a compelling interest in venery especially characterize youthful males. The predicament of young, urban women arises from the "costumbre de mancebos usada / querer siempre tener alguna enamorada" (stanza 167) (custom practiced by young men always to try to have some paramour).

The protagonist, a young, urban male with the same name and profession as the author, introduces himself as a sinner who has been in love (stanza 76). He narrates adventures with the opposite sex, in which he often tries "to couple with a pleasant female" and sometimes concerns himself principally with his "sustenance." At first an advocate of courtly love, he soon finds himself overpowered by his libidinous desires. No longer content to perfect himself in the service of superior ladies, he seeks physical correspondence instead of spiritual recompense. As an apprentice of Sir Love and Lady Venus, he seeks to learn the art of seduction and pursues sensual love with little success to become finally a distinguished theoretical, if unsuccessful practical, disciple of his counselors.[3] Nevertheless, he manifests another preoccupation: the eternal salvation of his soul and his body. During reflective moments, he attempts to reject sensual love to embrace "good love" by serving Christ and Mary for the sake of future, unending happiness. A weak human being, he never succeeds in making one commitment. On the contrary, he oscillates between licentious and pious behavior. Portrayed with neither the profligate foolhardiness of the wicked nor the infallible wisdom of the saint, he typifies the average young Christian male: imperfect man, the sinner, fumbling intermittently for a woman, for sustenance, and for salvation.

On the whole, the other male characters fare worse than the fea-

---

2. The archpriest of Hita amplifies this idea in the next stanza of the poem as follows: "Digo muy más el omne que toda criatura: / todas a tiempo cierto se juntan, con natura; / el omne de mal seso, todo tiempo, sin mesura, / cada que puede quier' fazer esta locura" (stanza 74) (Man, I say, much more than any other creature: they all at certain times couple together naturally; the man of bad sense, at all times, without moderation, whenever he can, wants to perform this act of madness).

3. At the request of Sir Love, an advocate of medium-sized women, the cleric expounds on the virtues of little women (stanzas 1608–17). There he outshines his teacher, for instance, in his exposition of the role of females; cf. stanzas 446 and 1609.

tured man; for they lack his concern with being saved. Sir Melon is confused with the protagonist at the beginning of the longest episode of the book. As the lay marriageable counterpart of the cleric bound by celibacy, he represents also the deceptive seducer like "todos los omnes" (stanza 881) (all men). An opportunist, he manages to obtain both sustenance and sex by seducing a rich widow, who then marries him. Ferrand García, the archpriest's messenger to a baker girl, demonstrates his lust by usurping his employer's role as lover. Master Ferret, the last procurer, although young, already has distinguished himself as a scoundrel on fourteen counts, which the author conscientiously lists. Sir Carnal and Sir Love, personifications who direct, respectively, sustenance and coupling with a pleasant female, each personifies a single vice—gluttony and lechery—and both are also associated with the gamut of mortal sins (stanzas 1163–69, 217–19).[4]

Ruiz concentrates on one male figure to represent young men in general; in contrast, he introduces thirteen females to represent young women. They not only form a varied catalogue of types—the refined and courtly lady, the maiden, the attractive widow, the Moorish girl, the nun, the baker girl, and the rural lass—they also vary with respect to their intellectual and spiritual faculties. For instance, some have "buen entendemiento" (pp. 10–11) (good understanding), some have "poco entendimiento" (pp. 10–11) (little understanding), and some have no understanding at all and are classified as "non cuerdo" (pp. 10–11) (unwise). They parallel the people the archpriest of Hita supposed would make up his audience. The prudent and wise lady of the third adventure who "todo saber de dueña sabe con sotileza" (stanza 168) (knew all woman's wisdom with great subtlety) typifies the female of good understanding. Immediately refusing illicit love, "bien fuxo de avoleza" (stanza 172) (she wisely fled from wickedness), saying that "'Non muestran pereza / los omnes en dar poco por tomar grand riqueza'" (stanza 172) ('Men show no sluggishness in giving trifles in order to receive great wealth'). She distinguishes between sin and virtue and loves God above all: "'Non perderé yo a Dios nin al su paraíso / por pecado del mundo . . . / non só yo tan sin seso'" (stanza 173) ('I will not deprive myself of God or His paradise for the sake of worldly sin . . . I am not so witless'). The desire to be saved takes priority in her life and determines her responses to temporal stimuli. Lady Sloe, from the exemplary vignette based on the twelfth-century

4. For the connection between gluttony and lust, see Janet A. Chapman, "A Suggested Interpretation of Stanzas 528 to 549a of the *Libro de buen amor*," *Romanische Forschungen*, 73 (1961): 38–39.

Latin comedy *Pamphilus*, illustrates the female of little understanding. Concerned less about "God or His paradise" than about her own reputation, torn between personal honor and love of the heart, she accedes to what her heart favors (stanzas 852–54). She repeatedly meets with the go-between, visits the messenger's house, remains there alone with Sir Melon, and is seduced. Only after losing her honor does she fully ponder the deceits practiced by "todos los omnes" (stanza 881) (all men) and their old go-betweens as well as the consequences (stanzas 882–85). The prudent and wise lady has foresight; Lady Sloe, hindsight. The foolish baker girl (stanza 112), in contrast, has no sight at all. Blinded by mad and heedless love, she incarnates the female without understanding of virtue. So zealous an advocate of corporal gratification is she that instead of becoming the paramour of the cleric, she couples with the male retainer sent to intercede on behalf of the protagonist.

The above are but three of the thirteen female types in the poem. A breakdown of the women characters demonstrates a balance in the number of those whose spiritual faculties are keen and dull. The wisdom to foresake false love characterizes five solicited women: the prudent lady, the good and highly educated lady, the widow who rejects the go-between, the beautiful widow who remarries, and the sensible, terse Moorish girl. Three female characters falter by consenting to negotiate with the expert intermediary and are enchanted and deceived by her: Lady Sloe (stanzas 716, 868), the young maiden (stanzas 916, 918), and the nun Lady Bride-of-the-Lord (stanzas 1490, 1494). The Lady Sloe episode, based on a known source, ends in the marriage of the seducer and the seduced; however, the deaths of the youthful girl and the nun terminate the protagonist's relationship with them. Five foolish women (the baker girl and four *serranas*, or wild mountain women) counterbalance the five wise ones.[5] Unrestrained desire for the things of the world—sexual pleasure in the cases of the baker girl, the pug-nosed cowgirl, and the mountain lass Gadea or material possessions in the cases of the mountain maid by the Cornejo inn and the rustic Alda—rules these witless females who never question the rectitude of their acts.

The wise females provide "ensiemplo de buenas costumbres" (pp. 10–

5. These ten women remind one of a much older story, the parable of the ten virgins in Matthew 25:1–13. In Christian exegesis, the five wise virgins represent the elect and the five forms of the contemplative life; the five foolish virgins, those who are lost and the five senses.

11) (examples of good conduct) and illustrate the archpriest's prescription for desirable feminine responses to the things of this world. The wavering women who are victimized underscore this lesson of the book: ladies, targets of deceit, beware of false suitors and their evil go-betweens! The foolish women of "mal entendimiento" (pp. 8–9) (depraved understanding) incarnate negative examples of womanhood. Ruiz discourages the profligacy they represent by ridiculing these figures with light-hearted parody.[6]

As a group, these women reinforce the vision of people in the book. In his portrait of the typical male, the poet shows the protagonist to be occasionally wise and virtuous, often wavering, and usually foolish and sinful. By using two techniques in his sketch of young people, Ruiz creates the illusion that the overall spiritual portrait of women is more positive than that of men, for we catch a glimpse of five wise females without ever finding a steadfast male. Both sexes are shown to be capable of sin and virtue since eight women also demonstrate human imperfection and since the cleric proves to be endowed with excellent understanding on several occasions.

Female characters can be grouped for analysis into three categories: (1) authority figures, (2) the go-between, and (3) the urban and rural young women. Let us examine now some features of their presentation. Dame Lent, the Virgin Mary, and Lady Venus constitute the catalogue of female authorities. A messenger of God sent annually to all sinners, Dame Lent enforces the law for "las almas que se an de salvar" (stanza 1075) (all souls that shall be saved). This peacemaker, who prescribes abstinence and acts of contrition, preaches austerity and spiritual fortification. The slim lady prevails annually for just forty days; during the rest of the year her gluttonous and self-indulgent adversary, Sir Carnal, governs. The Virgin Mary as the queen of heaven reigns there with her son; and as the advocate of Christians, the mother of sinners, she mediates between Christ and the transgressors of His law so that they might be saved. Lady Venus represents the female teacher of seduction. Although she teaches illicit love, she is portrayed as the wife of Sir Love. Like so many pedagogues, she does not practice what she teaches. An outspoken proponent of deceiving young women, she betrays her sex.

Ruiz makes parallels in his characterizations of Mary and Lady

6. For the nature of this parody, consult Alan D. Deyermond, "Some Aspects of Parody in the *Libro de buen amor*," in "*Libro de buen amor*" *Studies*, ed. G. B. Gybbon-Monypenny (London: Tamesis, 1970), pp. 62–64.

Venus.[7] While Mary is "comienço e fin del bien" (stanza 1626) (the beginning and the end of all good), including good love, Lady Venus is "comienço e fin" (stanza 583) (the beginning and the end) of the illicit love quest. The cleric affirms he cannot seduce the woman he wants without Venus: "sin vos yo non la puedo començar ni acabar" (stanza 587) (without you I can neither start nor finish it). Just as the sinner in search of salvation relies on the Virgin Mary, so the sinner in search of carnal pleasure relies on Lady Venus, the theoretician who informs the lustful man how to possess the female flesh he desires. Lady Venus exercises her power over those motivated by lechery. The protagonist states that "Ella es nuestra vida e ella es nuestra muerte; / enflaquece e mata al rezio e al fuerte; / por todo el mundo tiene grand poder e suerte; / todo por su consejo se fará ado apuerte" (stanza 584) (She is our life and she is our death; she weakens and kills the robust man and the strong; the whole world over she has great power and fortune; all things will be done at her instruction wherever she makes her appearance). The contrastive parallel with the Virgin peaks here; for while Mary blesses, helps, and guides her servants toward beatitude, Venus weakens and kills hers, even the heartiest ones. In any case, the protagonist calls her "noble dueña" (stanza 585) (noble lady), just as he calls the Virgin (stanza 1045). He identifies himself to Venus as he does to Mary, as her servant (stanzas 585, 1058). The goddess's sovereignty exceeds that of Christ and his mother, for Lady Venus, along with Sir Love, is the sovereign of all beings, obeyed by all men, who fear and serve the couple as their creations (stanzas 585–86). Her jurisdiction outreaches the Christian community and extends throughout the living world.

The go-between represents the human, female manifestation of wickedness.[8] Too old to enjoy sexual activity, she earns her living by joining young, urban couples in carnal love. She incorporates many of the aspects of Mary and Lady Venus as well as those of Sir Carnal and Sir Love. As an intermediary, her role approximates the roles of the two feminine authorities. The panderess mediates between the unscrupulous male and his target of seduction. The sophisticated se-

---

7. José J. Labrador pointed out some of these parallels in "El mito de Venus: Un descubrimiento de los poetas castellanos medievales," in *Studies in Language and Literature: The Proceedings of the 23rd Mountain Interstate Foreign Language Conference*, ed. Charles L. Nelson (Richmond: Eastern Kentucky University, 1976), p. 320.

8. In connection with the go-betweens, see Raymond S. Willis, "Two Trotaconventos," *Romance Philology*, 17 (1962–1963): 353–62.

ducer regards an expert message-bearer as indispensable: "'Madre señora, tan bien seades venida; / en vuestras manos está mi salud e mi vida: / si vos non me acorredes mi vida es perdida'" (stanza 701) ('Mother, my lady, be welcome here; I am putting my well-being and my life in your hands: if you don't help me, my life is lost'). The courteous nouns of address are the same ones used to salute Mary and Venus; the nature of the alliance equals that made with the two female authorities. The go-between also counts as the beginning of a quest, as the "comienço para el santo passaje" (stanza 912) (start of the holy pilgrimage). Neither the journey nor the messenger is holy; in fact, the deceitful hag shares unholy denominators with Sir Carnal and Sir Love. Like them, she represents evil ("artera e maestra e de mucho mal saber" [stanza 698] [wily and expert, and full of wicked wisdom]) and the devil ("'Tal eres . . . vieja, como el diablo, / que dio a su amigo mal consejo e mal cabo'" [stanza 1453] ['You, old woman . . . are like the Devil, who gave bad counsel and a bad end to his friend']). Lady Venus indirectly betrays her sex by educating men in the art of seduction, but the false go-between deceives women directly with hypocritical righteousness; "'Es maldad e falsía mugeres engañar; / grand pecado e desonra en las assí dañar'" (stanza 848) ('It is wicked and false . . . to deceive women; it is a great sin and disgrace to harm them by such means'), she says. Neither Venus nor the old mediator practices what she preaches. Ladies, therefore, should be wary about suspect old women (stanzas 908–09) since "estas viejas croyas, / éstas dan la maçada" (stanza 937) (these wicked old bawds, these are the ones who bludgeon).

Through the protagonist's and the go-between's words and deeds, the author portrays the faults of young men and evil old women. To point out the failings of young women, he has the proponents of false love reveal what they consider to be the vulnerable areas of the female personality. The unbecoming composite portrays the ideal woman to seduce. Of the thirteen young female characters, most, perhaps all, do not fit the model. Let us review the paradigm.

The middle-class father raises his daughter with care and devotion. Brought up in luxury and comfort, kept at home and guarded, she has many eager suitors if she is pretty and spirited (stanza 394). When she reaches marriageable age, her parents make arrangements to marry her off well "porque se onren d'ella su padre e sus parientes" (stanza 395) (so that she will bring honor to her father and her kindred). However, the plan fails, for "do cuida tener algo en ella, non tiene nada" (stanza 394) (just when the man expects to have a treasure in her, he has nothing at all).

What goes wrong? When the girl reaches sexual maturity, her mother, who once was young and knows the pitfalls of youth, guards her virginity. With an iron hand, the mother enforces chastity by scolding, shaming, beating, and abusing her daughter (stanza 521). At this upbringing the daughter rebels (stanza 395) because what her parents forbid—sexual relations with men—is what she most desires since all women desire the prohibited (stanza 523). The physical and mental coercion used by the protective mother proves not only useless but also counterproductive; it motivates the precise response it was designed to thwart (stanza 522).

Once the false suitor surmounts the obstacle of the anxious mother by employing an expert go-between, he can arrange to be alone with the girl. Seduction, then, becomes relatively easy; for "non solas las vacas / mas que todas las fembras son de coraçón flacas" (stanza 1201) (not only cows but all female creatures are faint-hearted). Women respond to gifts and money (stanza 489), praise (stanza 560), music and song (stanza 515), nimble and daring feats (stanza 518), refined manners, dress, and conversation, complaints (stanza 616) as well as sighs (stanza 627). Above all, constant service conquers women (stanza 612); "muger mucho seguida olvida la cordura" (stanza 526) (a woman who is long pursued ends up by losing her prudence). Images of the hunt correlate with the seduction of women (stanza 866);[9] men dedicated to venery artfully trap their prey, be it a wild animal or a lady.

Since women are raised to react to male advances with fear and embarrassment, they often do not do what they really would like to do (stanza 634). They manifest not lack of desire but socially learned apprehension (stanza 634). The go-between and seducer must overcome this obstruction by coaxing the lady, through cunning, from a posture of refusal to one of hesitation because "la muger que está dubdando ligera es de aver" (stanza 642) (a woman who is hesitating is easy to get). If the suitor can make the female lose her sense of shame just one time, she will be his (stanzas 468, 471).

Women also have these inborn reactions to sexual activity: "al co-

---

9. For a study of this imagery, consult Gail Ann Phillips, "The Imagery of the *Libro de buen amor* by Juan Ruiz, Archpriest of Hita," dissertation, Westfield College, London, 1973, pp. 125, 128, 142, 159, 172, 251–52; see also Gail Ann Phillips' study of the female characters, pp. 154–74. To even the score, Ruiz has a rustic lass call the male protagonist a "res muda" (stanza 990) (dumb beast) in need of taming who does not know the rural ways of domestication.

mienço del fecho siempre son referteras; / muestran que tienen saña, e son regateras; / menazan mas non fieren; en celo son arteras" (stanza 632) (at the beginning of the act they are always contrary; they appear to be angry, and they like to make a bargain; they threaten, but they don't strike you; they are crafty when they are feeling passionate). An untame woman can be subdued thorugh courtship (stanza 633); even "la dueña mucho brava usando se faz' mansa" (stanza 524) (a lady who is very fierce becomes tame with constant attendance). Upon being aroused, she will advocate false love (stanza 469).

This is the composite portrait of the vulnerable female, the ideal candidate for seduction. She starts out protected, fearful, embarrassed; licentious young men and dissolute old bawds convert her into a libertine like themselves. In the process, she lets her "alma e cuerpo e fama" (stanza 469) (body and soul and their reputation) all go to ruin.

In fact, few, if any, of the females in the amorous adventures exactly match the model. Five urban women, many of them beautiful, reject illicit love; therefore, they lack vulnerability. Five working women (the baker girl and the peasants), some of them ugly, do not demonstrate the socially learned inhibitions of the middle-class daughter, nor do they possess her refinement. With them a go-between is either impractical or unnecessary.[10] The remaining three come closest; they are pretty and vulnerable. Lady Sloe typifies the urban widow who vacillates between honor and carnal pleasure; the maiden, the offspring of a middle-class family who guards her virginity without success; Lady Bride-of-the-Lord, the timorous nun who struggles with her spiritual matrimony and her infatuation with the protagonist. Because Ladies Sloe and Bride are not daughters still attached to their families, they do not meet all specifications of the model. Only the maiden somewhat fits the pattern. She is beautiful, vivacious, quite young, rich, virtuous, and well born. Her mother and duenna watch over her (stanzas 923, 936) and require her to stay at home so that she seldom leaves her house (stanza 912). The panderess emphasizes her shyness and ignorance of worldly matters (stanza 917). By bewitching this bashful maiden, the retainer "mucho aína la sopo de su seso sacar" (stanza 941) (managed to drive her out of her mind very quickly). The girl dies just a few days after having succumbed to mad love (stanza 943). To fit the stereotype, however, she must be rebellious. Was she?

10. Joaquín Casalduero, "El sentimiento de la naturaleza en la Edad Media española," in *Estudios de literatura española*, 3rd ed. (Madrid: Gredos, 1973), pp. 15–16.

The text does not explicitly answer this question. Portrayed as innocent, inexperienced, and delicate, she falters possibly because she does not recognize the dangers of a concupiscent world.

From the outset, Ruiz informs us that false love always speaks falsely (stanza 161). The proponents of lasciviousness err as expected in their portrait of women. The diversity in the types of young females[11] and the variety of their responses to carnal love (rejection, hesitation, acceptance) prove that indeed the portraitists were wrong. Women are neither all attractive nor all assailable.

In addition to dispelling the notion that all women correspond to the vision wanton individuals harbor of them, the archpriest addresses the plight of young females in the urban society of his time. He takes the male protagonist to the unfamiliar mountains where he turns the tables on him[12] so that he can experience the trials and tribulations of women in the city. An overdose of his own medicine awaits the cleric there.

Without adequate provisions, transportation, and lodging, he ventures alone into the country and gets caught in a spell of wintry weather. No protective family sustains him; no expert accomplice assists him. He turns out to be even more dependent than young women in the city. He must now look to the rustic girls he encounters for his sustenance, and they prove more aggressive with the traveler than he proves to be with females in the city. They follow no refined social conventions like courtly love and artful seduction. Friendly persuasion is alien to them; no sophisticated rules and regulations bind them. The harsh rural life has taught them how to get what they want, by brute force and barter. Covetousness, the sin from which all others derive, according to the author, be it in the direction of avarice or lust, characterizes them.[13] Using their strength and business sense, they try to

---

11. María Rosa Lida de Malkiel notes that this catalogue of female types is far superior to any other in Spanish medieval literature. See *Juan Ruiz: Selección del "Libro de buen amor" y estudios críticos* (Buenos Aires: Editorial Universitaria de Buenos Aires, 1973), p. 24.

12. Deyermond, "Some Aspects of Parody," p. 63.

13. Joaquín Casalduero suggests that the mountain girls incarnate sin. See "Sentido y forma del *Libro* del Arcipreste de Hita," in *El Arcipreste de Hita: El libro, el autor, la tierra, la época*, Actas del I Congreso Internacional sobre el Arcipreste de Hita (Barcelona: S.E.R.E.S.A., 1973), p. 28. Thomas R. Hart suggests that the *serranas* represent the devil and sensuality. See *La alegoría en el "Libro de buen amor"* (Madrid: Revista de Occidente, 1959), pp. 67–92, especially p. 90.

exact their cravings (money, presents, sex, marriage) from the cleric. For him, a warm hut and a substantial meal now take priority over sexual pleasure. Realizing his perilous situation, the rustics drive a ruthless bargain. In exchange for their food, shelter, and orientation, they make demands upon the protagonist's few possessions, his life, and his body.

The four mountain lasses are burlesque figures who parody "el amor loco del pecado del mundo" (pp. 8–9) (the mad and heedless love of the sin of the world). By exaggerating the cleric's dependence upon them and by portraying the four as self-centered backwoods girls unworthy of the urban male's attention under normal circumstances, Ruiz shows him what it is like to be treated as an object from which others derive personal benefit. The beleaguered male, like the besieged Ladies Sloe and Bride, reacts with anxiety, fear, and confusion. He, as they, has trouble interpreting his experiences; under pressure, his spiritual faculties falter. Consequently, he sometimes provides conflicting interpretations of his rural adventures, each told twice, once in narrative, once in lyric verse,[14] just as the two women's perceptions of the go-between and the suitor change. The confounded protagonist resorts to soliciting the help of God to deliver him from the ordeal (stanzas 984, 1007, 1043) that young urban women usually experience in the fourteenth century according to the author.

Although this work corresponds to the middle-class milieu of the city (not the court) and addresses an urban audience, it lacks the misogyny characteristic of the traditional middle-class literary attitude.[15] Ruiz seems much less biased in favor of or against women—or, for that matter, men—than in favor of the good deeds (pp. 10–11) and against the evils and wrongs they do (stanza 1634). As Roger Walker remarked, "the dynamic is what interests the Archpriest."[16] A Christian, he defined life in terms of action and taught that neither sex is served by debasing, sinful activity. In the *Book of Good Love* he showed that both the seduced female and the male seducer jeopardize their futures, temporal and eternal, by engaging in false love. For this reason Ruiz interrupts his tale to counsel at different times women (stanzas 161–62, 311, 892, 904), men (stanzas 1531, 1579), and men

14. With respect to the twice-told rural episodes, consult R. B. Tate, "Adventures in the *sierra*," in "*Libro de buen amor*" *Studies*, pp. 219–29.

15. Lida de Malkiel, *Juan Ruiz*, p. 181.

16. Roger M. Walker, "A Note on the Female Portraits in the *Libro de buen amor*," *Romanische Forschungen*, 77 (1965): 120.

and women together (stanzas 1580, 1628). He viewed human beings as the privileged creatures of the earth put here to work separately or together in a harmonious, orderly fashion to merit the salvation offered by their Creator, who provided them with the New Law as their guide. By loving God above all and by loving other people as His children, the Christian of good will, he believed, could, with divine providence and grace, triumph body and soul over the world, the devil, and the flesh.

Marina/Malinche

Masks and Shadows

Rachel Phillips

In Mexico there is a term *malinchista*, which Octavio Paz in his *Labyrinth of Solitude* describes as a "contemptuous adjective . . . recently put into circulation by the newspapers to denounce all those who have been corrupted by foreign influences."[1] The word derives from Malinche, the Indian name for Marina, the woman whom Cortés used as interpreter and mistress during the early stages of the conquest of Mexico. In the same context Paz discusses the attitude of the Mexican to the triad of archetypes: God the Father, God the Son, and the Great Mother. For the figure of the Mother, he says, the Mexican has a double representation—the Virgin of Guadalupe, refuge of the oppressed, and *La Chingada*, the violated one, victim of the *macho*, the stranger. And he continues thus:

> If the *Chingada* is a representation of the violated Mother, it is appropriate to associate her with the Conquest, which was also a

---

This article diverges in a number of ways from the norms established for the volume; for example, it gives many quotations only in translation, without giving the original Spanish text. The author's commitments have unfortunately made it impossible for her to revise the article to conform to the general style of this book.

1. Octavio Paz, *El laberinto de la soledad* (Mexico: Fondo de Cultura Económica, 1959), p. 72; English translation by Lysander Kemp (New York: Grove Press, 1961), p. 86. The name Malinche derives from *Malinali*, the twelfth day of the month in the pre-Columbian Mexican calendar, which was apparently Malinche's birthday. See F. Gómez de Orozco, *Doña Marina la dama de la Conquista* (Mexico: Fondo de Cultura Económica, 1942).

> violation, not only in the historical sense but also in the very flesh of Indian women. The symbol of this violation is doña Malinche, the mistress of Cortés. It is true that she gave herself voluntarily to the conquistador, but he forgot her as soon as her usefulness was over. Doña Marina becomes a figure representing the Indian women who were fascinated, violated or seduced by the Spaniards. And as a small boy will not forgive his mother if she abandons him to search for his father, the Mexican people have not forgiven La Malinche for her betrayal.[2]

The significance of Malinche's persistent presence in the Mexican consciousness can only be touched on in this chapter;[3] space allows for little more than a sample presentation of the texts in which her story is recorded. She can be found in the earliest eyewitness accounts both of Spaniards and Indians, in the chronicles and in the history books down through the centuries to the present. There are drawings of her, interpretations of her behavior, judgments for and against her. Later, biographies appeared; historical novels, including two by Paz's own grandfather, Ireneo Paz, *Amor y suplicio* (n.d.) and its sequel, *Doña Marina* (1883); and, most recently, a play by Carlos Fuentes, *Todos los gatos son pardos* (1970).[4] And from all this material, one fact consistently emerges: little is really known about her. Thus, most of the written portraits turn out on closer examination not to be portraits at all but mirrors in which are reflected the faces of the writers themselves.

Everyone who touches on the subject of Marina reveals an evocation of a historical being. Marina escapes description and categorization because of the centuries which separate us from her and the paucity of evidence about her which has survived. She also escapes us perhaps, because, though she lived by language, for us she has no language and no words. Or it may be because she is a woman, and therefore she is Other to the men who, by trying to capture her essence, have succeeded only in defining themselves. She has been exploited without apology by writers of all disciplines and ideologies—historians, sociologists, novelists, dramatists, imperialists and antiimperialists, right-

2. Paz, *El laberinto*, p. 86.

3. For a criticism of Paz's interpretation of La Malinche, see Beth Miller, "Seducción y literatura" in her *Mujeres en la literatura* (Mexico: Fleischer, 1978), pp. 39–45, and Jorge Aguilar Mora, *La divina pareja: Historia y mito en Octavio Paz* (Mexico: Era, 1978).

4. Published in Mexico by Siglo Veintiuno Editores. For a more complete listing of biographies based on the life of Marina in recent times, see note 20 below.

ists and leftists, all of whom have thought of her as an empty vessel ready to be filled by their formulations.

Since the person who brought her into history was Hernán Cortés, his dispatches and letters are the earliest and in some ways the most interesting sources of information about Marina, interesting as well for what he does not say as for what he does. Cortés first refers to Marina in the dispatch of 1520 written after the retreat from Tenochtitlán on the so-called *Noche triste* ("Sad Night").[5] Cortés was then mustering his forces for a counterattack on the Aztec capital and had sought help from the chiefs of Cholula, a neighboring city-state. Sensing his vulnerability, these chiefs prepared a surprise attack of sufficient magnitude to wipe out Cortés and his Indian allies had Cortés not been warned of the plot by Malinche. We gather from other accounts that Marina was indispensable to all Cortés' exchanges with Indian chieftains and that she did, in fact, alert him on many occasions to dangers which he might otherwise not have perceived or perceived too late. Fortunately, other descriptions of the Cholula episode exist, for Cortés gives scant mention to the woman who apparently saved the entire Spanish force from destruction:

> In the three days I was there, they [the Cholulans] provided poorly for us, and worse each day, and the lords and important people of the city came to see and talk to me only rarely. And while I was puzzling over this state of affairs one of the women of this city confided in my interpreter, who is an Indian of this region whom I got in Putunchan, the big river which I mentioned in the first letter to Your Majesty. The Cholulan told her that a large force of Moctezuma's warriors was nearby, and that the Cholulans had evacuated their women and children and were about to fall on us and kill us all. The Cholulan tried to persuade her to save herself and leave with her, promising to provide for her. And all this she told to Jeronimo de Aguilar, the interpreter I acquired in Yucatan . . . and he told it to me. . . . (p. 58)

However, this mention of Cholula was made at a time when Cortés was in an aggressive and confident mood and his star was in the ascendancy. His only other reference to Marina occurs in a different, personal context and sheds quite another light on both protagonists. It appears in the fifth dispatch, written in 1526 after the failure of

5. Hernán Cortés, *Cartas de relación* (Buenos Aires: Austral, 1954); hereafter, page numbers refer to this edition. This and all other translations are my own.

Cortés' expedition to Honduras, an expedition which Cortés undertook in desperation, it would seem, partly to punish the rebellion of his lieutenant Cristóbal de Olid and partly to rehabilitate himself in the emperor's eyes. Most unwisely, given the jungles of the interior and the almost impassable swamps, Cortés took with him a majestic force of soldiers and servants and was then helpless to prevent their gradual decimation by disease and starvation. The dispatch of 1526 is a disconsolate memorial of travails and hardships which defy the writer's powers of description. It shows Cortés on the verge of disintegration, almost unrecognizable as the resolute commander of earlier years.

In this sad state, incredulous at his calamities, and unable to alleviate the sufferings of his starving army, Cortés mentions Marina by name. The moment occurs relatively early in the letter, soon after the execution of Cuauhtémoc and Tetepanquetzal, lord of Tacuba. These were the supposed ringleaders of an Indian conspiracy which was to overthrow first Cortés, then the Spanish forces throughout Mexico. Whatever the truth may have been about the alleged conspiracy, we do know that Cortés was greatly affected by the need to carry out such a cold-blooded execution, though clearly he did not hesitate to do so, having judged it inevitable. But other sources as well as his own letter to Charles indicate that he was preoccupied and seemed unusually anxious, not to say erratic, in his daily conduct.

At this juncture the Spaniards' overland route had brought them with enormous difficulty to Tabasco. Here a local chief whose good offices were essential to the survival of the Spaniards mentioned an earlier expedition of invincible white lords about whom he had heard many stories. These lords had won great victories, he said, obviously contrasting them to Cortés' shattered troops. Cortés replied that he had been the captain of those lords also,

> if he wanted to be sure it was true, he should ask the interpreter, who is Marina, whom I have always brought with me, because she had been given to me there with twenty other women. And she talked to him and assured him that I had conquered Mexico, and told him of all the lands which I have subjugated and which I hold in the name of Your Majesty's empire. (pp. 317–18)

No more is said, but there is a heartfelt and unusually confessional quality about the phrase, "que es Marina, la que yo siempre conmigo he traído" (who is Marina, whom I have always brought with me). We sense a personal reliance upon her which only a moment of great emotional weakness could have forced Cortés to admit to so spontaneously.

Although Cortés makes little or no reference to Marina's importance in his communication with the Indian tribes, the few surviving indigenous accounts present her as indispensable. The iconography of several codices and some written texts survive as evidence of the different ways the conquered peoples reacted to the destruction of their civilization. One of Cortés' most useful traits was his ability to take advantage of the hostility and resentment felt by one tribe toward another—most notably by the states which the Aztecs had subjugated toward Moctezuma and his empire. The Tlaxcalans, for instance, were eager to ally themselves with any enemy of the Tenochas (Moctezuma's capital was Tenochtitlán), and it was partly through the resources of the Tlaxcalans that Cortés was able to pull together his shattered forces after the Aztecs had all but wiped them out before the retreat of the *Noche triste*.

An artist or group of artists in Tlaxcala painted on a huge strip of linen cloth, now referred to as the *Lienzo de Tlaxcala*, the homegrown version of the conquest. The original *Lienzo* has been lost, but copies are extant,[6] and these represent very clearly the exploits of the brave Tlaxcalans who make possible the victory of the armed men on horses and thereby bring about the defeat of the wicked Aztecs. In the scenes painted on this canvas Marina is pictured always at Cortés' side or slightly behind him. She is dressed in Mayan costume, as she would have been when she was presented to the Spaniards, and to the Tlaxcalan mind at least, she was inseparable from the great white lord or *teul* ("god"), as Cortés was called even after the Indians had realized that he was not Quetzalcoatl incarnate. The true hero of the *Lienzo de Tlaxcala* is a collective one—the Tlaxcalan people. Yet among their Spanish allies they clearly granted to Cortés *and* Marina the places of greatest importance in all their representations of scenes of the conquest, and they short-sightedly saw the Spaniards' victory as salvation for themselves from the tyranny of Moctezuma and his tribesmen.

But other Indian sources give the viewpoint of the vanquished. Father Sahagún was one of the most devoted students and preservers of indigenous cultures, and he encouraged the Indians under his tutelage to compile a large body of texts written in Nahuatl and accompanied by painted codices. These provide an ethnographic and anthropologi-

6. One copy, owned by Alfredo Chavero and authorized by Porfirio Díaz, was reproduced and published in Mexico in 1892 in honor of the four-hundredth anniversary of the discovery of America, *Homenaje a Cristóbal Colón: Antigüedades Mexicanas* (Mexico: Oficina Tipográfico de la Secretaría de Fomento, 1892); this is the copy referred to in this chapter. Malinche appears in 22 of the 48 plates of Part 1.

cal treasure house of information about preconquest Mexico and also of the events of the conquest itself.[7] Marina appears in several of the scenes represented in the drawings, usually as a large, imposing figure standing in a position of strategic importance between Spaniards and Indians. Often little speech balloons go out from her in both directions, showing that she was in fact a linguistic bridge between cultures. In the written texts we gather that Moctezuma was greatly affected when he learned that Cortés had penetrated the secrets of his language. The passage in question is laconic but poignant:

> And it was told, discovered, shown, set forth, announced, and given as assurance to Moctezuma that a woman of our people here was bringing them here and interpreted for them. Her name was Marina; Teticpac was her home. There at the coast they had first come upon her and taken her. (Chap. 9 and pl. 22)

Another scene occurring a little later on shows the growing resistance of native to invader and Marina's importance as a mouthpiece:

> And when . . . all the gold had been gathered, then Marina summoned all the noblemen. She got up on the rooftop, on a parapet. She said: "O Mexicans come hither! The Spaniards have suffered great fatigue. Bring here food, fresh water, and all which is needed. For they are already tired and exhausted; they are in need; they are spent and in want. Why do you not wish to come? It appeareth that you are angered?"
>
> But the Mexicans no longer dared go there. They were very much frightened; they were weak with fear; they were terrified. Great awe spread; dread reigned. No longer did one dare do anything. It was as if a fierce beast were there; as if the land lay dead. . ." (Chap. 18 and Pl. 51)

There remain two eyewitness accounts by Spaniards, both captains in Cortés' army and both eager to present a version of the conquest which would support their particular bias. One is the *Relación* of Andrés de Tapia,[8] whom other sources mention as a brave, reliable officer. From the *Relación* Tapia emerges as an unskilled, humorless, but sincere author who suffered greatly from hero worship. He constantly refers to Cortés as "el Marqués," a title which Don Hernán acquired

7. Fray Bernardino de Sahagún, *Florentine Codex*, Aztec-English edition by Arthur Anderson and Charles Dibble (Sante Fe, N.M.: School of American Research, 1950). See Part 12, especially Chaps. 9, 16, and 18 and Plates 22, 44, and 51.

8. Andrés de Tapia, "Relación," published in *Crónicas de la Conquista*, ed. A. Yáñez (Mexico: Universidad Nacional Autónoma de México, 1963), p. 35.

only in later years but which distances both Tapia the writer and ourselves the readers from the general of the troops. The tone of Tapia's account casts Cortés as a sober, high-principled, and invincible leader; little or no attention is paid either to his foibles or to the more human side of his personality. Thus, Marina gets scant mention, even though Tapia was apparently close at hand when her value as an interpreter was first discovered.[9] He makes no personal comments about her, and communicates only the following, matter-of-fact information:

> And having brought some maize, which is their staple grain, and some fruit, and having sent it all to the ships, the lords of that land gave the Marquis twenty of the women they keep as slaves so that they could knead bread. . . . The Marquis had shared out among some of the gentlemen some of the twenty Indians who I have said were in the same group as the present author; and as some Indians went past, one of the women spoke to them, so that we saw she knew two languages, and our Spanish interpreter understood her, and she told us that when she was a child some merchants had stolen her and taken her to be sold in that region which was where she had grown up; and so we had an interpreter again. (p. 35)

In his inimitable fashion Bernal Díaz del Castillo redresses the balance. A born raconteur, where Tapia was not, Díaz del Castillo was far from feeling an inferiority complex vis-à-vis his general. He began his *Historia verdadera de la conquista de la Nueva España* (True History of the Conquest of New Spain)[10] in his old age, but the vividness

---

9. Marina was born in Painala in the province of Oluta and had been brought up speaking Nahuatl. She had been sold or given away as a child to some merchants from Xicalango, who had in turn sold or traded her to the people of Tabasco where Cortés acquired her. In Tabasco she had learned Mayan, the language spoken by Jerónimo de Aguilar, a Spaniard whom Cortés had found stranded in Yucatan and subsequently used as his interpreter. Moctezuma's envoys, however, who came as far as Tabasco to intercept and examine the supposed "teules," spoke only Nahuatl, which Aguilar did not know. Malinche greeted the Aztec emissaries whom she heard talking in her native language, and a triangular system of communication was established—Nahuatl to Mayan to Spanish—though it appears that Malinche learned Spanish in a relatively short time, and then Aguilar was no longer needed as an intermediary.

10. Bernal Díaz del Castillo, *Historia verdadera de la conquista de la Nueva España . . . por uno de sus conquistadores*, ed. Enrique de Vedia (Madrid: M. Rivadeneyra, 1862), vol. 26, 312; page numbers refer to the Biblioteca de Autores Españoles edition (hereafter BAE). The *Historia* was begun before 1552 and concluded in 1568 (see note 11 below).

of his descriptions and the pace of his prose are in themselves convincing signs of an accurate memory. Furthermore, all the events he relates and the large majority of the details are corroborated in other accounts, such as Cortés' own dispatches and Tapia's *Relación*. His *True History* is an objectively reliable record of the period, even though subjectively it approaches the realm of the polemic. The author undertook his task with one clear intention, and this he emphasizes time and again throughout the work. He wished to protect the reputations of those who had participated in the conquest yet whom traditional historians were most likely to overlook—namely, himself and his comrades-in-arms. Díaz del Castillo knows, his text tells us, that the names of Cortés and his commanders will survive gloriously—and when Francisco López de Gómara's *Crónica general* (General Chronicle) appeared,[11] this assertion proved to be correct. However, like Tolstoy, Díaz del Castillo insists that history is the work of many small men and the sum of insignificant events; it is not directed only by the great, who themselves are less great to those who know them intimately. Consequently, on his scale of values, Cortés' personal achievements weigh relatively less but those of his soldiers, helpers, and advisers correspondingly more.

Another fact must be remembered about Díaz del Castillo since it affects the tone of his chronicle. For him, the conquest of Mexico was a living chivalric novel,[12] and he and each of his companions could play out his fantasy role of hero, Amadís, Olivero, Esplandián, and so on. But adventures of chivalry require a heroine, and there were few likely candidates other than Doña Marina. Therefore, probably unconsciously, the author allows his portrayal of her to take on a very special and somewhat idealized coloration, which deeply influenced many of the later versions of Malinche's life.

Marina occupies a relatively large place in Díaz del Castillo's text, of which a few key passages deserve quotation. First, the description of the gifts—which included Marina—given to Cortés in Tabasco. Unlike Tapia, he indicates the surprise of the Spaniards at what must have seemed to them odd presents indeed:

---

11. Francisco López de Gómara, *Crónica general de las Indias*, Part 2, *La Conquista de Méjico* (BAE, vol. 22). Díaz del Castillo had already begun his *Historia verdadera* when López Gómara's *Crónica general* appeared; the latter was written in 1551 and published in Madrid in 1552. In Chapter 18 of Díaz del Castillo's work he mentions that he has seen López de Gómara's version and gives free rein to his indignation at his glorification of Cortés at the expense of his soldiers.

12. See, for example, Chap. 31.

> The next morning, which was at the end of March 1519, many chieftains and elders of that town and neighboring regions came to us all with signs of great esteem, and brought offerings of gold, four diadems and some figurines of lizards, and something like little dogs, and earrings and five ducks, and masks of Indian faces, and two gold soles like those they have on their sandals, and some other things of little value which I don't remember, nor what they were worth. And they brought cloaks like those they made and wore, which are of very coarse cloth; and this offering was nothing compared with a gift of twenty women, and among them a very excellent woman who was called Doña Marina, this being her name after she was baptized. (p. 30)

Another important section recounts Marina's station in life and personal charms:

> And the friar with our interpreter Aguilar preached to the twenty Indian women who had been given to us, telling them many good things about our holy faith . . . and then they were baptized and the name of Doña Marina was given to that Indian lady whom they had given us. Indeed she was a princess and daughter of great chieftains, and a lady over vassals, and she showed it in her person; and later on I shall tell how and by what means she had been brought there. I cannot remember all the other women's names, and naming a few makes no sense, but these were the first Christian women in New Spain. And Cortés shared them out each to a captain, and this Doña Marina, being of pleasing appearance and sharp-witted and outward-going he gave to Alonso Hernández Puertocarrero, whom I have already said was a noble gentleman, cousin of the count of Medellín. After Puertocarrero went to Castille, Doña Marina was with Cortés, who had a son by her called Don Martín Cortés, later a knight of Santiago. (p. 31)

For Díaz del Castillo she is brave:

> Let us tell how Doña Marina who was a woman of those parts, resisted manfully even though she was hearing daily that they would kill us and eat our flesh, and had seen us hard pressed in battle. And though now she saw us wounded and in pain, she never let us see any weakness in her, rather a strength far surpassing that of a woman. (p. 59)

She is also intelligent:

> And Moctezuma saw our captains in anger, and asked Doña Marina what they were saying with those heated words; and as Doña Marina was very intelligent, she said to him, "Lord Moc-

> tezuma, what I advise you is to go with them to your chamber with no fuss or bother. . . ." (p. 95)

And so closely associated with Cortés is she that the Indians referred to him by her name:

> And the reason they [the Indians] gave him [Cortés] that name is that, as Doña Marina our interpreter was always in his company, especially when ambassadors or messengers came from the chieftains and she turned everything into the Mexican language, they therefore called Cortés Marina's captain, or Malinche for short. (p. 66)

The Cholula episode already mentioned gave the author an opportunity to spread his storytelling wings and present a scene of espionage and deception. As a result, later authors who were looking for evidence to support the image of a "Quisling" Marina found grist for their mill here, though Díaz del Castillo himself intended Marina's astuteness to arouse only admiration in his readers.

He describes the exchange between Marina and the old Cholulan woman who has taken a liking to her and is trying to save her from the holocaust to come. The old woman was the wife of a Cholula chieftain involved in the conspiracy, and she was offering Marina her son as a husband. Then the author's inspiration runs away with him, and he begins to put words into Marina's mouth. The rest of the scene is as follows:

> And when Doña Marina heard this, as she was very shrewd, she said: "Oh mother, how grateful I am to you for telling me this! I would go with you now, except that there is no one whom I trust to bring me my robes and gold jewels, of which I have many. For heaven's sake, Mother, wait a little, you and your son, and we will leave tonight; for now you see that these Teules are awake and will hear us." And the old woman believed her and stayed there chatting to her, and Donã Marina asked her how they were to kill us and how and when the plan had been made. And the old woman told her neither more nor less than what the two priests had already stated [to Cortés], and Doña Marina said, "Well, if this affair was so secret, how did you get to know about it?" The old woman said her husband, who was chief of one of the parties in the city, had told her, and that he was at that moment with the people who were in his charge, ordering them to assemble in the canyons with the squadrons of the great Moctezuma, and that she thought they would all be waiting together when we left, and would kill us then. And she had known about the plan for three days, since the Mexicans had sent her husband

> a golden drum, and to some other chieftains they had sent rich mantles and gold jewels for delivering us up to their lord Moctezuma. And Doña Marina, hearing it, deceived the old woman, saying, "Oh, how happy I am to know that the son you want me to marry is a person of rank! We have been talking for a long time. I didn't want them to hear us, so wait for me here, Mother. I will start getting my belongings, because I can't take everything at once, and you and your son, my brother, will take care of my things, and then we shall be able to go." And the old woman believed it all, and she and her son sat resting; and Doña Marina quickly went to Captain Cortés and told him all that had happened with the Indian woman. . . . (p. 76)

The scene clearly takes little resetting for Marina to emerge as villainess not heroine, as happens for instance in Gustavo Rodríguez' *Doña Marina.*[13]

Díaz del Castillo's *True History* presents another theme that later authors have developed and embroidered. Before the arrival of Cortés, Moctezuma was distressed by a series of evil omens which were interpreted to him by his wise men as portents of doom—a doom which might well be the return of Quetzalcoatl since that event would spell the end of the present era of mankind. One such omen was the constant reappearance of Cihuacoatl, who was the goddess of women who had died in childbirth and was, consequently, regarded as fatal to children. She was said to wander the streets in the dead of night, sobbing and moaning, and dressed in long white robes. Cihuacoatl disappeared officially with the whole Aztec pantheon, but she lingered on in popular legend as *La Llorona*, the weeping woman, who appeared to haunt naughty children, sometimes carrying a cradle with nothing in it but a bloody dagger. Gustavo Rodríguez asserts directly, "Our weeping woman is the Malinche of the conquest," and continues with a melodramatic rendering of Marina's sins and guilt-stricken remorse.[14] Here we again see the black legend—attaching itself to the Indian version of her name—which grew up in opposition to the sweetheart-of-the-troops Marina of Díaz del Castillo; yet this identification of Marina with *La Llorona* can be traced back to Díaz del Castillo's own work.

While Cortés was away on the fateful Honduras expedition which so diminished both his personal and political strength, his enemies in

---

13. Gustavo Rodríguez, *Doña Marina* (Mexico: Imprenta de la Secretaría de Relaciones Exteriores, 1935).

14. Ibid.; see Chap. 5, "Doña Marina y la leyenda."

Mexico City spread the rumor that he and all his army were dead and proceeded to take control over the colony. To support this rumor a ghost story was invented, and from this ghost story seems to have sprung the confusion of the legend of Cihuacoatl with the real Doña Marina. Díaz del Castillo tells the tale as follows:

> And as there are also traitors and flatterers in this world, one of them turned out to be a man who had been regarded as a man of honor (and I shall not name him here so as not to dishonor him further). This man told the *factor* [in] the presence of many other people that he was sick with fright because one night as he was passing near Tatelulco, which is where the idol called Huichilobos used to be and where the church of Our Lord St. James now stands, he saw in the courtyard the souls of Cortés and Doña Marina and Captain Sandoval all burning. He had become very ill from the scare it had given him. Another man whom I won't name because he was well regarded also came to tell the *factor* that evil beings were haunting the courtyards of Tezcuco, and the Indians said they were the souls of Doña Marina and Cortés. And the whole thing was a pack of treacherous lies told to the *factor* so that those men could ingratiate themselves with him. Or else the *factor* had ordered them to say all these things. (pp. 264–65)

As the author makes clear, the so-called ghosts were still alive, and the whole affair was a malicious invention. Yet the idea of a phantasmal Malinche had taken root in the popular mind, and in an odd fusion of folklore and fact Marina became confused with the pre-Hispanic goddess Cihuacoatl.

With Díaz del Castillo the eyewitness accounts end, and as these few examples show, they have been either neutral or highly complimentary. After his *Historia* but still in the sixteenth century, the images of Marina reflected in current historiography begin to diverge, and we can see the origins of the different archetypal Marinas—traitress or romantic princess—propagated in history, polemics, and fictionalized accounts from then on. A few quotations from early texts will show how the written word acts to blur the always vague outlines of the actual Marina and then to re-form her according to each writer's preferred dogmatism.

First, there is Francisco López de Gómara, another hero-worshipper of Cortés and a puritan where relations between the sexes were concerned. He seems to have sensed what few other chroniclers did, namely, that Marina's position could have served admirably for counterespionage had her loyalties in fact been with the Indians.

Clearly, however, she remained loyal to Cortés and his Spaniards, for which she should not be blamed, having been given away or sold by her mother out of one Indian tribe into another, growing up a slave to people speaking a language which, though indigenous, was to her still foreign. López de Gómara downplays Marina's importance and deals harshly with the matter of her marriage, which Díaz del Castillo had handled gently and tactfully.[15] On the Honduras expedition Cortés had apparently given Marina in wedlock to one of his captains, Juan Jaramillo, of whom little is known beyond the fact that he remarried soon after Marina's death. López de Gómara, however, makes the following somewhat ungallant statement, "I believe that Juan Jaramillo married Marina while he was drunk. They blamed Cortés for allowing it, as he had had children by her."[16] As all other sources indicate that Marina bore Cortés only one son, it would appear that López de Gómara wants the affair to be seen in the worst possible light for all three participants.

Father Bartolomé de las Casas also did his best to undercut any idealizing of Cortés either as commander or romantic hero. Since his purpose was to debunk the glories of the conquistadors in order to heighten his account of the Indians' sufferings, Las Casas was particularly hard on the Spaniards' commander-in-chief. He scoffs at the notion that Cortés showed Machiavellian cunning in his manipulation of one city-state against another. According to Las Casas it would have been obvious to anyone with a modicum of intelligence that the tribes were hostile to one another. Furthermore, with the kind of interpreters available, Las Casas finds it unlikely that any high-level conferences could have taken place, and he gives us the first home-spun version of Marina and Cortés in colloquy. Las Casas specifically refutes López de Gómara's assertions about Cortés' diplomatic perspicacity:

> And Gómara on this point says many foolish things, and even some that are lies, as he always did in order to color the deeds of his master Cortés in that land. For instance, he says that through Marina or Malinche he asked them about the lords of that land, and many other things. This must be false, as it is not credible that such long conversations could be held with so inexpert an interpreter, who could barely use the most common words of that language like "daca pan, daca de comer, toma esto por ello" and everything else by signs. . . .[17]

---

15. Díaz del Castillo, *Historia*, p. 247.

16. López de Gómara, *Crónica general*, pp. 409–10.

17. Fray Bartolomé de las Casas, *Historia de las Indias*, vol. 3, chap. 122. See BAE, vol. 96, 469.

We are a far cry from William Prescott, whose *History of the Conquest of Mexico* tells us three hundred years later that "It was not very long . . . before Marina, who had a lively genius, made herself so far mistress of the Castilian as to supersede the necessity of any other linguist." A feat easily accomplished, it would seem: "She learned it the more readily as it was to her the language of love."[18]

It took the late Romantics to develop fully the image of Marina as ministering angel to the heathen. However, what might be called the "gossip-column" treatment begins only thirty years after Las Casas set to work on his *History of the Indies*, in a work called *Noticias históricas de la Nueva España* (1589) by a Juan Suárez de Peralta, claimed by some to be Cortés' nephew-in-law.[19] Suárez de Peralta was writing relatively soon after the events he described, so he had little excuse for his inaccuracies or salacious asides. Some examples will show how he set an atmosphere of which later writers took full advantage.

First, he calls Marina "not the worst bit of armor" the troops had to their name, and he proceeds to garble horribly the details of her discovery by the Spaniards. According to him, she gave the Spaniards glowing details of all the gold to be found in Moctezuma's capital and promised to lead the army to this tempting treasure trove. Then appears the following passage:

> They were all very pleased with her, and did not leave her alone for a minute, asking her many questions until Hernán Cortés finally said that no one was to talk to her. Malicious people said it was because he was jealous, and we can have no doubt that this was so, as he had six children with her. These were Don Martín Cortés, knight of the order of Santiago, and three daughters, two of them nuns in the order of the Mother of God, in the convent at Sant Lucar de Barrameda, and Doña Leonor Cortés who married Martín de Tolosa. (p. 75)

Not only does Suárez de Peralta mention six children while naming only four, but except for Martín Cortés he had dreamed them all up. Indeed, these five nonexistent offspring are symbolic of the many other fictional accretions which later writers affixed to Marina's shadowy image. (Leonor did in fact exist but was born to Cortés by Isabel, or Tecuichpo, the only legitimate daughter of Moctezuma. Certainly she was not Marina's child.)

18. William Prescott, *History of the Conquest of Mexico* (London and New York: 1909), I, 185.

19. Juan Suárez de Peralta, *Noticias históricas de la Nueva España* (1589; Madrid: Imprenta de M. G. Hernández, 1878).

Suárez de Peralta then turns his attention to Cortés' legitimate son Martín. Both the bastard son of Malinche and the legitimate son of Cortés' second wife, Doña Juana de Zúñiga, were called Martín after their paternal grandfather. The two Martíns were involved in a conspiracy against the Spanish crown, which took place in 1565–1566 and ended in the exile of both from Mexico. At the time of this conspiracy the legitimate Martín was apparently involved with a lady called Marina—the coincidence seems too good to be true—and Suárez de Peralta gives us the following bit of doggerel which he says was running through the vice regal court:

> Para Marina, soy testigo
> ganó esta tierra un buen hombre,
> y por otra deste nombre
> la perderá quien yo diga. (pp. 200–1)
>
> For Marina, I'll bear witness
> a good man won this land,
> and through another of her name
> I'll tell you who will lose it.

And this level of historical discourse is found again in not a few of the so-called biographies of the last hundred years.[20]

During the nineteenth century the issue of Mexican independence and clearly divergent political attitudes to colonialism polarized attitudes toward the conquest and all that pertained to it.[21] Ignacio Ramírez, speaking in 1886 at the commemoration of the proclamation of Mexican independence, described Marina as "Cortés' concubine" and compared her with Eve, adding, "It is one of the mysteries of fate that all nations owe their fall and ignominy to a woman."[22] Yet a

---

20. See, among other such examples, *El amor en la conquista* by Federico Fernández de Castillejo (Buenos Aires: Emecé Editores, 1943); *Doña Marina (la india que amó a Hernán Cortés)* by Felipe González Ruiz (Madrid: Ediciones Morata, 1944); *Malinche: Drama de la conquista* by Ramón Vásquez (Buenos Aires: Distribución exclusiva de Editorial Kraft, 1968); and some accounts in English, a particularly horrendous example of which is *Cortez and Marina* by Edison Marshall (N. Y.: Popular Library, 1963), with Cortés as first-person narrator.

21. Cf. Victor Rico González, *Hacia un concepto de la conquista de México* (Mexico: Instituto de Historia, 1953), which provides a historiographic comparison of the writings of several historians, among them Carlos María Bustamante, William Prescott, Alamán, Orozco y Berra, Alfredo Chavero, and Justo Sierra.

22. Ignacio Ramírez, *Discursos y artículos*, (Mexico: Imprenta Victoria, 1917), p. 5.

North American historian, William Prescott, could say that "the name of Malinche . . . was pronounced with kindness by the conquered races, with whose misfortunes she showed an invariable sympathy."[23] Though Marina/Malinche received considerable attention in histories and so-called biographies during the next half-century, it was not until the writings of Octavio Paz and later Carlos Fuentes that a less simplistic evaluation of her role appeared. Paz's penetration of the national myths is well known; Fuentes' play *Todos los gatos son pardos* moves one step further in political consciousness. The true hero of the play is the Indian people, who, through Malinche, become the Mexican nation. The play is a drama of power and abuse of power, Moctezuma the usurping emperor being replaced by the usurping empire of Spain, with Cortés its unsuspecting emissary. The immediate conflict is between Cortés and Moctezuma, the latter dominated—and paralyzed—by fatalism, the former driven by the power of the will. "Between the opposite shores of power, a bridge: the interpreter Marina who by means of words converts the story of both powers into destiny: knowledge from which there is no escape."[24] Marina does not help Cortés in his conquest in order to betray her Indian people but in order to replace the tyrant Moctezuma with Cortés, who she considers will rule with justice. Her defeat is implicit in that one imperialism is overthrown by another, and she is left with her bastard son, the first Mexican, and her legacy of names:

> Malintzin . . . Marina . . . Malinche . . . You had three names, woman: the one your parents gave you, the one your lover gave you, and the one your people gave you. . . . Malintzin, said your parents: enchantress, goddess of ill fortune and blood feud . . . Marina, said your man, remembering the ocean he crossed to come to this land. . . . Malinche, said your people: traitress, white man's mouthpiece and guide. . . . Goddess, Malintzin; whore, Marina; mother, Malinche. (pp. 13–14)

To her son, *hijo de la chingada*, she leaves the Mexican heritage: death, dreams, rebellion, and love. Of those, death is the easiest to achieve, love the most difficult.

Marina has a counterpart of sorts in the Anglo-Saxon conquest of North America. Lewis and Clark had a Shoshone Indian woman as guide on their journey of exploration up the Missouri River, across the

---

23. Prescott, *History of the Conquest*, I.
24. Fuentes, *Todos los gatos son pardos*, p. 6.

Rocky Mountains, and down the Columbia River to the sea.[25] There are many curious parallels between the life of Sacajawea and that of Malinche, but more significant are the different ways history has dealt with them. Sacajawea's name is virtually unknown in the United States, and to those who do know her, she provides merely a human interest story in the greater epic of Anglo-Saxon expansion.

Marina, however, has been a continually disquieting presence in the Mexican imagination. She disturbs the easy dichotomies into which, without her, the Spanish conquest of Mexico could be resolved. According to the anthropologist Gregory Bateson,[26] there exists in the human mind a tendency to handle differentiations within society by means of bipolar distinctions. The bipolarity of the European settlement of North America is perfectly clear: at the beginning, white man faced Indian. Then among the white men other bipolar divisions became apparent, often shifting within the context of European politics but always clearly delineated by national interests, language, cultural heritage, and so on. The northern hemisphere today retains the clarity of these demarcations in both sociological and political terms, though the lines of division themselves have been shifting with bewildering rapidity in the past decades.

None of this tidy bipolarity exists in Mexico, though for centuries of colonialism an attempt was made to pretend that it did. The Council of the Indies worked hard to clear the field into two camps by appointing administrators directly from Spain. Thus, on an official level the home-born Spaniard stood against all the products of the colony. But the colonials made their own attempt at establishing bipolar order. They could rank themselves as *criollos* (creoles—of pure "white" blood) and *mestizos* (creoles of mixed blood). This dichotomy, however, left out the Indians, who were many, and often troublesome. In the years of upheaval which followed Mexican independence, bipolarity became even more problematic as the lines shifted to and fro across political affiliations, accidents of birth, personal opportunism, and so on. And ultimately all other preoccupations were submerged in the Mexican Revolution of 1910, which released a host of bipolar antagonisms, beneath all of which lay the tremendous division between the haves and the have nots. Since the revolution ended with the aban-

---

25. See the *Journals of the Expedition Under the Command of Captains Lewis and Clark*, ed. Nicholas Biddle (New York: Heritage Press, 1962).

26. Gregory Bateson, "Morale and National Character," *Steps to an Ecology of Mind* (Paladin Books, 1973), pp. 62–79.

donment of radical ideals and a new stratification of society suspiciously reminiscent of that which it had replaced, the issue has continued to present itself, and all the more urgently, as its complexity has defied simple answers.

And so Marina has reappeared constantly in the theoretical and fictional creations of Mexican literature, for at the very moment of its genesis, she made impossible in Mexico the easy dualism of Spaniard versus Indian. Western nations, according to Bateson, are not at ease when a third element disturbs a dichotomy: "They lack the organizational devices for handling triangular systems," he says.[27] It was linguistic necessity which first established the triangle "Spaniard-Malinche-Indian," and this triangle became troublesome when from Malinche herself a very real third component—the mestizo—added itself to the population. During the colonial era the significance of this extra component could be ignored, as the problem of national identity was nonexistent outside the context of Spain herself; it was ignored for as long as possible even after independence. During this time Marina could be dealt with very simply since there existed another convenient bipolar framework into which she could be fitted—that of male and female. She could not escape the dichotomy of sex; hence the proliferation of novels and "biographies," which tried to fit her into stereotypic molds.

The "biographies" also falsified the issue since each author allowed his own proclivities and presented a vision of history compatible with his needs and desires. It has taken the greater enlightenment of recent thinkers and writers to assimilate the facts of their nation's past so that these may illuminate rather than bedevil present and future. In these authors' recreations of Marina there are no easy dichotomies but rather intuitive treatments of complex issues. In fact, Malinche evaporates beneath their hands. For the chroniclers, she was the *lengua*, a word which means the concrete thing, "tongue," as well as the abstract thing, "language." This rhetorical synecdoche has been replaced by a metonymy, in which Marina has disappeared. She has become language and, as such, transparency. In the past, writers looked into her face and saw their own; now they look through her to find themselves.

27. Ibid.

Women Against Wedlock

The Reluctant Brides of Golden Age Drama

Melveena McKendrick

There is no adequate English translation of the Spanish phrase *mujer esquiva*. Disdainful, elusive, distant, shy, cold—*esquiva* contains something of them all. But if the phrase cannot be translated, it can be explained. The *mujer esquiva* of Spanish drama is the woman who, for some reason, is averse to the idea of love and marriage. As a natural outcome of this, she is usually, though not invariably, averse to men as well. The *esquiva* is by far the most popular of the many variations on the theme of the "masculine" woman, so beloved of Spanish dramatists of the Golden Age largely because hers is an abnormality that is not out of place in women who depart in other ways as well from the seventeenth-century female norm. About half the number of female bandits in the drama of this period are *esquivas* when they first appear on the scene. The amazon, of course, is traditionally *esquiva*. *Esquivas* too are many of her seventeenth-century dramatic counterparts, those women who, having been brought up in an atmosphere of freedom which has enabled them to indulge their superior physical strength and skills, resent the threat to their independence that love and marriage represent. However, I do not intend to deal here with those female characters whose *esquivez* is, within context, subordinate to or less interesting than their other "unfeminine" trait or traits but with those heroines whose primary importance to plot and/or theme lies, or seems to lie, in their reluctance to marry.

The *mujer esquiva*, as well as being the most popular manifestation of the masculine woman—making regular appearances from the turn of the seventeenth century until around 1660—is also the most important. She is in fact central to the whole theme of feminism in the Golden Age theater because she, more than any other female type, serves to demonstrate the ideological parameters within which this feminism operated. Her central position is determined by the nature and seriousness of her revolt. Like other female characters who revolt against what they consider to be the unjust laws and conventions of the masculine society in which they live, the *mujer esquiva* is justified in her grievances.

To modern observers, increasingly familiar as they are becoming with human sexuality in all its aspects, the lesbian motif might seem to be implicit in the *esquiva*'s rejection of men. But whether it was intended by the dramatists to be implicit or whether it was seen to be so by contemporary audiences is a different matter. It would be both foolish and arrogant automatically to ascribe our own sexual awareness to other societies, as if such awareness were a universal and static factor. This is particularly true in the case of female homosexuality, which throughout the greater part of European society until the present day has been very much, through ignorance and sublimation, a subterranean phenomenon. That rejection of marriage is often the first psychological manifestation of lesbian tendencies does not mean that it leads inevitably to lesbianism. And in the manufactured world of the Golden Age drama it certainly does not. Those who argue that it does are confusing feminist statements with deviant tastes—an understandable lapse of judgment on the part of the layperson but less forgivable in those in tune with the ethos of the seventeenth-century theater. Careful distinctions must be made if hasty amateur psychology is not to lead to a misunderstanding of the whole nature of the *esquiva*'s revolt. That revolt is prompted not by a desire to reject the essential nature of her sexual being but by the way in which the concept of nature is invoked by men to justify their relegation of woman to an inactive, inferior role in life.

Nonetheless, for the dramatist, nature is involved. Love and marriage are the realms where the essential differences between the sexes are most pointed. In the eyes of the dramatist the *mujer esquiva* is not, ultimately, rebelling against man-made rules, which, given the weakness of human nature, may well be misguided ones. Her defiance, whatever the motive, whatever the incitement, is for them directed against the natural order of things as decreed by God. This natural order may be briefly explained thus: woman was created of man in the Garden of Eden to be his helpmeet; on the temporal level he is therefore her first cause and final end; love and marriage are her birthright;

toward them her entire nature is directed, and in them she finds her fulfillment. To this natural law no woman, unless she has a religious vocation, is an exception, and the foolish, misguided woman who considers herself immune to love, who claims to dislike men or who prefers to avoid matrimony, must therefore be led, or driven, back onto the path of sanity, reason—and true happiness. Such sentiments are repeated time and again throughout the body of plays which have *mujeres esquivas* as their heroines, and the unanimity of opinion among the dramatists on this score can be judged from the fact that not one of the women finally remains voluntarily single. These ideas about the natural role of woman, whether explicitly expressed by the play's dramatis personae or implicitly conveyed by the development of the action, are not, by any means, mere dramatic platitudes; they were seriously held by the men of the age. Lope Félix de Vega Carpio (1562–1635), creator of Spain's national drama, dedicated his play *La vengadora de las mujeres* (The Woman Who Avenged Women)[1] (written between 1613 and 1620) to "la Señora Fenisa Camila" with the words:

> Vanidad es en una mujer despreciar los hombres, pues cuando Aristóteles dijo que la mujer le apetecía como la materia a la forma no pensó que era pequeño el encarecimiento. Mas respondera v.m. que Dios, habiéndole criado, le halló solo, y que le dio la mujer por compañía; de donde querría inferir que él debe apetecerla y que ella puede huirle. El argumento es falso, porque saliendo del mismo, ha de volver a su primera causa,[2] como a la mar los ríos. Él solo, dijo el filósofo que era Dios o bestia; v.m. no puede ser lo primero: mire al peligro en que se pone con lo segundo; y si le ha de suceder lo que a Laura, que con todas sus letras, sus estudios, cuidados y melindres vino a querer sujeto. . . . . . . no intente por vanidad cosas que, no teniendo por fundamento la virtud, se oponen a la naturaleza. No ame v.m., pero no aborrezca; no diga bien de los hombres, pero no los infame; siquiera porque sus padres desearon que lo fuese, y les pesó de que naciese mujer: y aun a la misma naturaleza, que por su falta la hizo hombre imperfecto, título que dieron a la mujer tantos filósofos.[3]

1. The translations of titles and quotations throughout are the author's. Very few of the plays mentioned have been translated into English.

2. Lope uses *primera causa* loosely here in a chronological sense in accordance with the biblical narrative. In strict theological terms, of course, only God can be the first cause (as well as final end) of woman as well as man.

3. In *Obras de Lope Félix de Vega Carpio, Nueva edición* (Madrid: Real Academia Española, 1916–1930), vol. 13, 614 (hereafter cited as *Acad. N.*).

> It is vanity in a woman to spurn man, for when Aristotle stated that woman craved man as matter craves form, he intended the implication to be taken seriously. Your honour will reply that God, having created man, judged him to be lonely and gave him woman for company; from which you would deduce that he must crave her company and she may flee his. The argument is a false one, for issuing as she does from man, she must return to her first cause, like the river to the sea. The philosopher described man alone as being either God or beast; your honour cannot be the former: beware of becoming the latter; and if there befalls you what befell Laura, who for all her learning, her studies, her preoccupations and affectations ended up falling in love with one of her subjects . . . do not through vanity attempt things which, not being founded on virtue, are opposed to Nature. By all means do not love, but do not hate; by all means do not speak well of men, but do not slander them; even though your parents wanted you to be one and were distressed that you were born a girl. Nature made you an imperfect man, a title given to woman by many philosophers.

This age-old conception of woman forms the very basis of the *mujer esquiva* plays. The thesis is almost invariably dramatized after the manner established by Lope: the heroine's aversion to love and marriage; her gradual yielding to love, a process helped along by the pretended disdain of the hero and by the jealousy he succeeds in creating in her; the crisis which precipitates the transformation; and, finally, the willing subjection to the *yugo blando* ("sweet yoke") of matrimony. But obviously the theme of the woman who scorns love in asserting her independence is susceptible of a variety of treatments, and although differences in plot detail are usually unimportant, the differences in the *nature* of the heroine's *esquivez* and in the motives behind it *are* important because they determine the degree of the dramatist's disapproval and hence the whole tone of the play.

The *mujer esquiva* plays can, for the most part, be divided into two groups according to the motive ascribed by the dramatist to the woman concerned. These two motives are vanity and arrogant pride. Their recurrence reveals the dramatists' inability to conceive of any assertion of female independence other than that based on some reprehensible character trait; none of the playwrights of the Golden Age sympathizes with his *esquivas* in the way that Cervantes sympathizes with Marcela in Part 1 of the *Quijote*. When vanity is the underlying cause of the heroine's *esquivez*, the treatment is light-hearted, but when the *mujer esquiva* is guilty of arrogant pride, the theme is sometimes dealt with more seriously, and the play then leaves the plane of light comedy.

I

The woman who glories in being surrounded by despairing suitors appears in the play *Los milagros del desprecio*[4] (The Miracles Worked by Scorn) (written between 1599 and 1603), which if indeed Lope's, as it is assumed to be, must have been one of the earliest plays to deal in depth with the *mujer esquiva*. Doña Juana's is the soon-to-be-familiar story of the girl who is caught on her own hook. Her confessed hatred of men is such that she explodes into hysteria whenever they are mentioned. When she thinks her views are being questioned, she even resorts to physical violence, and any signs of softening in her maid, Leonor, she meets with the threats of punishment typical of her emotionally unstable character. Her denunciation of men has not the authority of personal experience because she has never allowed a man within speaking range, nor even that of vicarious experience, for she proffers none of the usual classical examples of man's worthlessness. Why then the vehement scorn of the displays of violence and bad temper? Lope leaves us in no doubt of the answer—vanity. Juana delights in the fruitless efforts of her suitors; she glories in the power she has over them; she revels in her own haughtiness and untouchability.

> Viendo a un hombre padecer
> me considero gloriosa. (act 2, *Acad. N*, vol. 13, p. 13a)
>
> I glory in seeing a man suffer.

Equally flattering to her vanity is the public respect and esteem her aura of aloofness and unquestionable virtue has earned her, and it is through this regard for her public image that nature will accomplish its revenge. Her hysteria is a response to the growing threat to her public image as Leonor's support gradually weakens. Consistent with her vanity, too, is her self-appointment as an instrument of woman's universal vengeance upon man and her desire to impose her views on all women. Yet, again, it is vanity that makes Juana so unkind to her cousin Beatriz and leads her to betray Beatriz' love affair to her father, Juana's uncle; she wishes to conform to his high opinion of her virtue.

Lope is illustrating the premise that hatred of men is neither natural nor plausible in a woman and that beneath any apparent antagonism

---

4. In *Acad. N.*, vol. 13.

there is some fault of character which makes her behave in this way. Appropriately, therefore, after being subjected to the scorn and neglect with which she has hitherto treated her suitors, Juana is finally punished and made to see the error of her ways through this very fault. Self-deception gives way to self-knowledge. Since vanity is what Juana is accused of, the public pricking of this vanity is her punishment and she is caught on a wet night, disheveled and covered in mud, in actual pursuit of a man. There could scarcely be a more humiliating exposure for the woman who has boasted of her immunity to the follies of love. Scorn and ridicule, after all, are the arch foes of vanity; pride can ride above them, but vanity is helpless in their presence. Juana does make an attempt to justify herself:

> Yo soy. ¿De qué os admiráis?
> Si pensáis que me ha sacado
> de mi casa algún cuidado
> amoroso, os engañáis.
> Las mujeres que nacemos,
> señor don Pedro Girón,
> con sangre y estimación,
> más que las otras sentimos.
> ¡Vive Dios que he de saber
> quién es esta vuestra dama
> por quien mi opinión y fama
> se ha echado tanto a perder!
> que eso solo me ha sacado
> de mi casa. (act 3, p. 26a–b)

> It is I. Why are you surprised? If you think some love affair has brought me from my house you are mistaken. We women of noble blood and high repute, señor don Pedro Girón, feel things more strongly than others. By God, I'll know who this lady of yours is that has cost me my reputation and good name, for that alone has brought me from my house.

To an extent, she is correct, for nature in her wisdom, and aided by the wily Hernando, has used Juana's self-esteem to put her in a position where she has to yield to love. The news that Don Pedro had another lady and had been ridiculing Juana first affected her vanity and only afterwards led to jealousy. The general process of reform is the same in all the *mujeres esquivas*, but in the best plays it is always adapted to the individual character of the particular heroine. The punishment is suggested by the weakness and is therefore the most effective antidote for it.

If Juana personifies an attitude that is alien to woman's true nature, her cousin Beatriz, on the other hand, is all that a woman should be for Lope: warm, appealing, in love, and interested in the love affairs of others. This two-sided portrayal of womanhood is characteristic of many of the *esquiva* plays, the two standing respectively for warning and example. Here Lope prudently strengthens his case by using Beatriz, and not any of the male characters, as a mouthpiece for the claims of love and marriage:

> ¿No somos también mujeres,
> y en las mujeres también
> natural el querer bien? (act 2, p. 14a)

Are we not also women, and is it not natural in women to love well?

and

> Dios obra en el casamiento. (act 2, p. 16a)

Marriage is God's work.

With his *Los milagros del desprecio*, Lope created a genre; some fifty years later the genre culminated in the polished and utterly delightful play by Agustín Moreto y Cabaña (1618–1669), *El desdén con el desdén*[5] (Disdain with Disdain) (probably written between 1652 and 1654). Again the situation is that of the disdainful heroine won over to love by feigned scorn and betrayed by her own vanity. Diana's quarrel, however, is essentially with love, which she considers to be responsible for all the world's tragedies and troubles. Unlike Juana, she bases her views on the knowledge and wisdom she has culled from her books. Her attitude toward the world is one of cold indifference born, so she claims, of disillusionment. The siege that her disdain now undergoes is altogether a much subtler campaign than the barrage of scorn, neglect, and ridicule to which Juana is subjected. To begin with, the efficacy of disdain has already been proved to his chagrin by Carlos, who has fallen in love with Diana in spite of her being a

> hermosura modesta
> con muchas señas de tibia (act 1, BAE, vol. 39, p. 1)

modest beauty with more than a touch of the lukewarm

---

5. In *Comedias escogidas de Moreto*, Biblioteca de Autores Españoles (hereafter cited as BAE), vol. 39 (Madrid: Rivadeneira, 1865).

because for the first time in his life he is unable to take what he wants just for the asking. He is not slow to realize that only the challenge which the unattainable represents for his own egoism will succeed in shaking Diana's, and he therefore poses as an *hombre esquivo* (a man who is for some reason reluctant to marry), daring Diana to try to reduce him to the same state of abject submission as her other suitors. Diana swallows the bait:

> he de hacer empeño
> de rendir su vanidad. (act 1, p. 6c)

> I shall make it my job to overcome his vanity.

She little realizes that with these words she is passing judgment not on Carlos' motives but on her own. Slowly but surely the vanity wounded by Carlos' immunity gives way to a desire not only to impress but to possess, and when Carlos plays his ace card by pretending interest in one of her ladies-in-waiting, Diana is irretrievably lost. As befits the play's subtlety of plot and character, there is no public humiliation of the vain, misguided woman here as there is in *Los milagros del desprecio*. An official declaration of obedience to Diana's wishes on the part of Carlos allows her to grant him her hand with the dignity appropriate to her situation.

Moreto is no less convinced than Lope of the importance of the part which love must inevitably play in woman's makeup, and he likewise stresses that any evasion or denial of love is a revolt against nature itself. Carlos with graphic eloquence states that the result of Diana's studies is

> un común desprecio
> de los hombres, unas iras
> contra el orden natural
> del amor con quien fabrica
> el mundo a su duración
> alcázares en que viva. (act 1, p. 2a)

> a common scorn for men, an anger against the natural order of love with which the world raises to its own continuance castles wherein to flourish.

This conviction that Diana is behaving unnaturally is shared by her friend, Cintia, who exclaims in amazement:

> ¡Que por error su agudeza
> quiera el amor condenar;

> y si lo es, quiera enmendar
> lo que erró naturaleza! (act 1, p. 4a)

To think that her wit should condemn love as an error, and, be it so, that she should strive to reform where Nature erred!

In an extremely interesting article, Bruce Wardropper interprets the theme of the play as being a secularized form of free will, which is radically different from theological free will.[6] Moreto, Wardropper holds, is asking to what extent woman is free to choose whether or not she will marry. This is not the place for an investigation of the full theological implications of this view, but on the evidence provided by the *esquiva* plays, I should like to make several points that necessarily limit the truth of Wardropper's assertions. Although his interpretation of the play and his discussion of the tension in Diana between reason and will correspond to the ideas the play suggests to the reader and are therefore in one respect entirely valid, I should hesitate to state that Moreto is *actively* speculating about this problem of free will. After all, he is writing within a well-worn tradition, with ready-made situations and ideas, and with a ready-made phraseology to draw upon. His play appears to me to be a testimony of faith in an ingrained pattern of belief. In fact, to choose *El desdén con el desdén* to illustrate a secularization of the Spanish theater in Moreto's drama is a mistake. The ideology of self-determination in all the *esquiva* plays is perhaps as far removed from "consciously Christian ethics" as that of the play in question. Each one poses the question (whether consciously or not, it does not matter) of the extent of woman's self-determination, and each one supports the concept of a limited degree of free will, which Wardropper finds only in *El desdén con el desdén*. At the same time, in every case the love force is directed toward the harmony produced by marriage. In other words, the dramatists uphold a secularized free will within the framework of what is essentially, including in Moreto, a Christian social and natural order. Furthermore, the love-reason debate in Moreto's play is even more conventional than the heroine's *esquivez*, and it must not, therefore, be granted too much importance in an assessment of the dramatist's intentions. Finally, Wardropper seems to give the impression that this lack of true freedom was woman's alone. And, of course, it was not. For the Golden Age the natural forces in man were as powerful as those in woman, and he was as sub-

---

6. Bruce W. Wardropper, "Moreto's 'El desdén con el desdén': The *Comedia* Secularized," *Bulletin of Hispanic Studies*, 24 (1957): 1–9.

ject to love as she. The *hombres esquivos* of the theater discover that they are no more free to choose to remain single than the *esquivas* themselves.

The position that Pedro Calderón de la Barca (1600–1681) takes in his play *No hay burlas con el amor*[7] (There's No Playing with Love) (probably written in 1635) is slightly more ambiguous than Moreto's. His heroine, Beatriz, is a vain, conceited, and silly *précieuse* who makes a show of her learning and speaks in an affected manner. The praise she receives from the undiscriminating flatters her conceit and creates in her a self-congratulatory disdain for her suitors.[8] The play also contains one of the several examples in Golden Age theater of the *hombre esquivo*, Don Alonso, a young rake who hates the idea of love and marriage because of the emotional ties involved.[9] Inevitably, he and Beatriz fall in love with each other although both, of course, are loath to admit it. Their attraction is made to seem normal and inevitable, but we can only deduce that it is intended to be seen as the proper outcome for their prejudices by considering the alternatives—promiscuity with lower-class girls for Alonso, conceited spinsterhood for Beatriz. For Calderón does not speak of love and marriage in the reverent tones which Lope tends to adopt. In fact, after having the couple fall in love, he mischievously shifts position and uses them as a warning against love. The bulk of the evidence provided by the play, however, points to the conclusion that Calderón's views were the same as Lope's, and Calderón's other *mujeres esquivas* confirm this. But, unlike Lope, Calderón was capable of speaking of love and marriage tongue in cheek and of expressing the conventional horror of them affected by those out to raise a laugh.

The psychological precept behind the reform of the *mujer esquiva* who suffers from vanity is, of course, the age-old *similia similibus curantur* ("like cures like"). The woman's *esquivez* itself is equally based

---

7. In *Comedias de Calderón*, BAE, vol. 9 (Madrid: Rivadeneira, 1885).

8. In writing this play, Calderón obviously had in mind two plays by Lope: *Los melindres de Belisa* and *Los milagros del desprecio*. From the former, he took the idea of the *melindrosa* heroine; from the latter, he took the delight which Leonor and Inés take in subjecting Beatriz to love and its accompanying emotions, strongly reminiscent of the relish taken by Leonor and Beatriz in Doña Juana's downfall.

9. Carlos in *El desdén con el desdén* only feigns *esquivez*. The other true *esquivos* are the king in Lope's *De los contrarios de amor* (The Obstacles to Love), Don Alonso in Calderón's *No hay burlas con el amor*, Don Juan in Lope's *De cosario a cosario* (Birds of a Feather), Don Félix in Calderón's *Guárdate del agua Mansa* (Still Waters Run Deep), and Don Félix in Juan

on a psychological truism—that we never want what we can get. Thus, the heroine of Moreto's *El poder de la amistad*[10] (The Power of Friendship) (written 1652?), Margarita, although she has no theoretical objections to men or marriage and is neither arrogant nor conceited, will not accept her suitor:

> Por ver que me quiere mucho. (act 1, p. 23b)

Because he loves me so much.

Only when Alejandro makes himself inaccessible does she become conscious of his attractions.

There are two plays which concentrate in particular upon the theme of the counter-suggestibility of human nature in matters of love: *Hacer remedio el dolor*[11] (Heartache Finds a Way) (written 1649?) jointly by Jéronimo Cáncer y Velasco (159?–1655), Moreto, and questionably Juan de Matos Fragoso (1608–1689), and *Lo que son mujeres*[12] (Just like a Woman) (published 1645) by Francisco de Rojas Zorrilla (1607–1648). In both plays, the familiar formula is given its logical conclusion: when the girl is reduced to wanting her suitor, her suitor no longer wants her. Casandra in *Hacer remedio el dolor* is an orphan who, after disdaining her suitors in order to remain faithful to her books, naïvely admits her love for Carlos. At this point, the other plays normally end. But Carlos is a restless, irrational young man, who finds Casandra's capitulation distasteful, and so he betakes himself to Naples to embark upon the conquest of another woman. The story of Casandra and Carlos could well be the sequel to *El desdén con el desdén.* Casandra, however, is quick to realize that the only way to win Carlos back is to create the illusion that he is once more the pursuer and she the pursued. This she does and he is soon brought to heel.

Serafina in Rojas Zorrilla's *Lo que son mujeres* is not so fortunate as Casandra. For her *esquivez* she is humiliated to the point where after each of her four former suitors has rejected her, she is reduced in her desperation to proposing to the servants. She is not even compen-

---

Vélez de Guevara's *Encontráronse dos arroyuelos* (The Meeting of Two Streams). It is illuminating that the men are motivated in their *esquivez* by specific doubts and fears, often related to an incident in their past. They never reject love and marriage on grounds of so-called principles, which have their real roots in vanity or pride.

10. In *Comedias escogidas de Moreto*, BAE, vol. 39.

11. Valencia, 1762 (copy in the University Library, Cambridge).

12. In *Comedias escogidas de Rojas Zorrilla*, BAE, vol. 54 (Madrid: Rivadeneira, 1860).

sated for her loss of dignity by love and a husband. The play, in fact, is a savage one, lacking in the warmth, kindness, and understanding with which Lope, in his plays, treats his *mujeres esquivas*. The disdainful woman is normally humbled by her lover because he loves and wants her, but all that Serafina's suitors want is their revenge. The only sympathetic character in the play is the sister, Matea, and even she is frivolous and unstable. Rojas Zorrilla has, in fact, modified the usual tale of feminine disdain in several ways. First, the *mujer esquiva* is offset by a woman who has an indiscriminate fondness for all men; second, none of the suitors really loves Serafina; third, the change in her is not brought about by jealousy but by pique at seeing the less attractive sister favored; fourth, she does not fall in love with any of the four men; and, fifth, neither of the girls finally marries. These changes are typical of the delight Rojas Zorrilla took in refusing to follow the conventions. His views about women and love, on the other hand, seem to have been entirely conventional, for like Lope he is convinced that woman's place is at man's side,

> Ser inclinada a los hombres
> ni es liviandad ni flaqueza;
> este es un bien natural. (act 1, BAE, vol. 39, p. 194a)

> An inclination toward men is neither frivolity nor weakness but a natural good.

At the same time, the picture he paints of the female character is not a pretty one. Women, he intimates, are fickle, shallow, unreliable, insincere, and motivated by vanity and caprice. Admittedly, his portrayal of the male character is scarcely less unattractive; the suitors are a ridiculous foursome, equally as cruel and capricious as Serafina herself. Obviously, the play is not meant as a serious judgment upon human nature. It is a clever if rather unpleasant satire upon the familiar dramatic situation of the disdainful woman and her admirers.

II

The undercurrent of harshness in *Lo que son mujeres* leads naturally to the second group of *mujer esquiva* plays—those in which the heroine's sin is a less venial one than vanity and in which the treatment of the theme is consequently sometimes more serious. The most important and the subtlest of these plays is Lope's *La moza de cántaro*[13] (The Pitcher Maid) (written before 1627). It is devoted to an examina-

---

13. In *Acad. N.*, vol. 13.

tion of this particular type of woman and might therefore be called the "thesis" play on this subject. The heroine, Doña María, refuses to marry and despises all the suitors who present themselves not only because she considers none of them worthy of her but also because she will not subject herself to the authority of any man:

> Nací con esta arrogancia;
> no me puedo sujetar
> si es sujetar el casar. (act 1, *Acad. N*, vol. 13, p. 648a)

> With this arrogance I was born: if marriage be subjection, subject I will not be.

Her arrogance, to which even her maid dares bear witness, is doubly reprehensible in a woman because it smacks of masculinity, and one of the essential requisites in a woman in the seventeenth century was gentleness and meekness. Doña María's streak of *varonilidad* ("masculinity") is soon displayed in action when she takes upon herself the vengeance for an insult to her father, a task which should fall naturally and properly upon his son. Her arrogance has driven her not only to a defiance of nature (by not marrying) but also to a defiance of society (by usurping her brother's role). For this twofold rebellion she must be punished.

Society's revenge is immediate. Since her vengeance involves murders, she becomes a social outcast. In order to conceal her identity and to earn her living, she is reduced to the life of a servant. Her *esquivez* no longer has the protection and encouragement provided formerly by her elevated station. She is now exposed to the coarse realities of life and is forced to use all her positive masculine qualities to protect herself. At this point nature takes its revenge. María refused marriage on the grounds that she could not submit to any man, even one she loved. Now she is at the beck and call of a foul-mouthed master, who eventually tries to violate her. Hitherto she spurned the most worthy men; now she is forced into contact with the rough, the crude, and the importunate. The lesson is severe, but it is well learned, and once penance has been done, absolution is granted. Lope's attitude is not that of the relentless moralist gleefully witnessing the fall of pride and pronouncing judgment but rather that of the affectionate father who realizes with reluctance that for his child's own good, she must be taught a bitter lesson by experience. Now that nature has punished María, it proceeds to reward her by reestablishing within her its normal claims. With arrogance gone, there is room for love, and María falls in love with a young gallant, Don Juan, her heart touched by the first courtesy and gentleness she has known since she fled fom her home. To ensure that her love is properly motivated and not merely the result of gratitude, she is given a rival to cope with, but finally she achieves royal pardon and marriage to Don Juan.

The thesis of the play is clear—the desire for independence and the impulse to unnecessary (unnecessary because her father has a son to avenge him) self-assertion are improper in a woman. María's punishment is her transformation to a lowly status, which will bring the truth home to her. Once again, the seventeenth-century conviction that there can be no rationale behind a woman's *esquivez*, merely a moral fault, is strongly stated. With marriage, María accepts her female destiny, thereby allowing the order of nature to be restored and ensuring her own happiness.

The same grave view of female arrogance taken by Lope in *La moza de cántaro* is also taken by the unknown author of *De los contrarios de amor*[14] (The Obstacles to Love) and by Tirso de Molina (1580?–1648) in his *El burlador de Sevilla*[15] (The Trickster of Seville) (published 1630). Neither of the women in question here, however, is the protagonist of the play, and their *esquivez* is not the central theme. The queen of Scotland in *De los contrarios de amor* is an arrogant woman who refuses to subject herself to any man. Her hatred of men is matched by that felt by the king of England for women, but whereas his feelings are the result of some personal incident in the past which has embittered him, the queen's are based on arrogance alone. They plunge their countries into war merely to defeat and humble the other, but since the queen's fault is greater, she is the one who must yield. Unconvincing as their ultimate change of heart is, the point is unmistakable. The subplot is, in fact, stating the case for marriage. Marriage, that is the fulfillment of the laws of nature, brings back harmony and prosperity to the two countries. In other words, it is restoring order on a *national* scale and healing the breach created by the queen's wrongful self-assertion.

The marriages at the end of Tirso de Molina's *El burlador de Sevilla* are also a symbol of the restoration of harmony, in this case of the social harmony which has been disrupted by the anarchy of Don Juan. Tisbea, the second of the four women Don Juan deceives and the most interesting of them, is another *mujer esquiva*. This sets her apart from her three co-heroines and makes her the only woman in the play in

14. Published as Lope's in *Acad. N.*, vol. 1.

15. In *Comedias de Tirso de Molina*, Nueva Bibliografía de Autores Españoles, vol. 9 (Madrid: Bailly-Baillière, 1907).

whom any dramatic conflict takes place. The arrogant pride which leads her to reject love and disdain her suitors adds, in fact, a new dimension to the Don Juan theme of pride and self-assertion. Tisbea delights in making men suffer as Don Juan does women. The immunity she claims to the laws of nature is a parallel to his self-assured immunity to divine retribution. She is above love, he, above all social convention. Both are arrogant, both self-assertive, both egoists, and both suffer from a sense of their own superiority.

While Tisbea's contribution to the Don Juan theme is implicit rather than explicit, the playwright's disapproval of her is obvious. She is shown as the victim not of Don Juan but of her own character. Convinced of her superiority to her fellow fishermen, she regards the arrival of Don Juan as a heaven-sent opportunity to rise above her own status. Don Juan's handsome figure and flattering words do not attract her. Before he opens his mouth, her *esquivez* has already disappeared simply because Don Juan's servant, Catalinón, has told her who his master is. In spite of her refrain of misgiving, "plega a Dios que no mintáis" (pray God you do not lie), her dreams of grandeur make her prefer to believe Don Juan's promise of marriage. Her sensitivity about her humble state is apparent before she meets him, and because of her ambition Tisbea refuses love only to succumb to lust. Her pride is humbled; her ambitions shattered. It is absurd to see Tisbea as the hapless victim of Don Juan's charm; Tisbea, no less than the other three women, is an illustration of Tirso de Molina's premise that Don Juan's sexuality relies for its success on circumstances exterior to itself.

The motive of pride is the one most often used by seventeenth-century dramatists in their depiction of the *mujer esquiva* mainly because it is so often the most appropriate. The *esquivez* motif appears frequently in plays whose heroines are superwomen or rulers, and in these situations, the attribution of *esquivez* to an arrogant self-assertion that refuses to subject itself to man is entirely logical. Lucinda in Lope's *La fe rompida*[16] (Broken Faith) (written between 1599 and 1603), Doña María in Lope's *La varona castellana*[17] (The Virago of Castile) (written between 1597 and 1603), Queen Rodiana in Lope's *El soldado amante*[18] (The Soldier Lover) (probably written between 1593 and 1595), and Madama Inés in Calderón's *Mujer, llora y ven-*

16. In *Acad. N.*, vol. 5.
17. In *Obras de Lope de Vega* (Madrid: Real Academia Española, 1890–1913) (hereafter cited as *Acad.*), vol. 8.
18. In *Acad. N.*, vol. 11.

cerás[19] (Woman, Weep and You'll Conquer) (written ca. 1660) are all such women, and all eventually fall in love. The treatment here is more or less conventional and consequently not heavy handed. There is no question of punishment; nature simply takes its course, and the *esquivez* of the heroines evaporates in the face of the stronger compulsion of their newfound love.

Two more complex examples of the *mujer esquiva*, both rulers whose disdain is likewise based on arrogant pride, are Cristerna in Calderón's *Afectos de odio y amor* (Feelings of Love and Hate)[20] (first performed 1657) and Laura in Lope's *La vengadora de las mujeres*[21] (The Woman Who Avenged Women) (written between 1613 and 1620). Their interest lies in the fact that they are not merely *esquivas* but also militant feminists. Cristerna propagates feminism by actually legislating in women's favor, and amongst the laws to be passed are the abolition of the Salic law, the admission of women to public positions, and the stricture that no woman marry beneath herself on pain of death. In support of this last, Cristerna explains:

el amor
no es disculpa para nada.
Porque ¿qué es amor? ¿Es más
que una ciega ilusión vana
que vence, porque yo quiero
que venza? (act 1, BAE, vol. 9, p. 102c)

love excuses nothing. For what is love? Is it more than an illusion, blind and vain, which conquers because I will it to conquer?

This is almost heresy in the seventeenth century, which regarded human beings by their very nature as subject to love, in spite of their reason and their will, and it is immediately obvious that for this arrogant assertion that love is a figment of the conscious imagination, Cristerna will be taught a lesson.

Laura, in *La vengadora de las mujeres*, who, like the female bandit of Golden Age drama, is a self-appointed avenger of women, translates her hatred of men into rather different action. Her proposed vengeance on men for their cruelty and injustice to women takes three courses: she studies hard to equip herself for intellectual battle with men; she gives her ladies-in-waiting lessons in "misandry"; and she refuses to submit to any man by marrying, as society and her royal posi-

19. In *Acad. N.*, vol. 9.
20. In BAE, vol. 9.
21. In *Acad. N.*, vol. 13.

tion demand. She is a much less sympathetic character than Cristerna, who, in spite of her feminist pride, is a brave, wise, and generous queen. Laura is not only extremely arrogant but also presumptuous, rude, and exceedingly vain. Moreover, she neglects her duty by refusing even to consider marriage. She will not entertain the possibility that women do not want to be avenged; her ladies-in-waiting certainly do not.

Both women, of course, gradually and reluctantly have to submit to the normal workings of nature, their pride holding them back, their jealousy urging them forward. Laura, because of her greater arrogance, receives a severe, though temporary, blow to her pride by falling in love with someone who is apparently her social inferior. The plays are both fairly light-hearted, however, and the lesson the heroines are taught is a mild one. The fact that Laura is won in a tournament frees her even from the necessity of admitting that she wants Lisardo. Cristerna's capitulation is more extreme, for she actually bears witness to her new faith, asserting that women are born to be men's vassals:

> Estése
> el mundo como se estaba,
> y sepan que las mujeres,
> vasallas del hombre nacen. (act 3, p. 122c)

Let the world remain as it always was, and know that women the vassals of men are born to be.

Neither of the plays is in any sense a "thesis" play. Calderón is writing in a tradition established years before by Lope. Even though in *La vengadora de las mujeres* the action is contrived largely to make possible a theoretical discussion of a subject—women—which allows of ingenious philosophizing and witty analogies, a verbal battle where the weapons of both attack and defense are quotations from Aristotle and Plato. Nevertheless, both tell the familiar story of the *mujer esquiva*'s reconciliation to love, and both betray the conviction that this reconciliation is right. The capitulation of Calderón's heroine is more extreme than that of any of Lope's. And Lope, of course, would not be Lope if he failed to take this opportunity to express his views on women, love, and marriage. Every character at some time extols the wonders of love and marriage and affirms the inevitable dependence of woman on man. In fact, in both the play and its dedication, Lope describes in detail those views that can be deduced from most of his plays:

Amaldo. . . . al imperio del hombre
se ha de rendir la mujer. (act 1, *Acad. N*, vol. 13, p. 615a)

Amaldo. . . . to man's rule woman must surrender.

III

There remains a group of five plays which fall outside the main body of the *mujer esquiva* plays in that the motives of their heroines cannot be strictly described as either vanity or pride. In three cases out of the five, the heroine's views are much more truly rational and considered than those of the usual *mujer esquiva*, whose attempt to rationalize her motives does not succeed in hiding their true origin. The fourth makes no attempt whatsoever to justify her disdain, for it is purely the result of whimsy. And the fifth, one of the most interesting characters in the whole of the Golden Age theater, is nothing less than a case of psychological narcissism.

The attitude shared by Serafina, duchess of Mantua, in *Galán, valiente y discreto*[22] (Gallant, Courageous and Discerning) by Antonio Mira de Amescua (1574?–1644) (performed in 1632) and Celia in Lope's *De cosario a cosario*[23] (Birds of a Feather) (written between 1617 and 1619), is entirely reasonable. Their wariness is based on the very natural fear of committing themselves to the wrong man. Celia has no desire to give herself and her fortune to any of the worthless gallants about the court, and, similarly, Serafina wants to be loved for herself and not for her wealth and position. Her desire to preserve her independence is born of the dread of surrendering it unwisely. The manner in which love eventually overcomes their fears is different in the two plays, both skillfully handled love intrigues. Serafina proves the love of Don Fadrique by pretending to be her own maid, while Celia is attracted to a man as reluctant to marry as she is and of such uncompromising cynicism that she resolves to humble him.[24] Jealousy, of course, does its work in both plays, and the two women are reconciled to marriage with the "right" man. As usual, Lope cannot resist

22. In *Dramáticos contemporáneos a Lope de Vega*, BAE, vol. 45 (Madrid: Rivadeneira, 1858).

23. In *Acad. N.*, vol. 11.

24. Don Juan has been happily married once but is determined not to fall victim to the golddiggers who he is convinced abound at court. This conflict of like minds is a pleasing variant of the rather overworked "disdain with disdain" theme.

including some of his marriage and love propaganda, but Mira indulges in no theorizing on these topics. He is merely producing an entertaining, graceful play in a popular tradition. When Serafina yields, there is no question of subjugation, just a dignified acceptance of a worthy man. Approval of love and marriage, however, is implicit.

The third more rational *esquiva* is "the warlike Spanishwoman" in the 1616 play *La belígera española*[25] by Ricardo de Turia (pseudonym for Pedro Juan de Rejaule y Toledo), one of the most pleasing of the Spanish theater's unusual women. Her peculiar interest lies in the fact that whereas nearly all the other disdainful women have to learn to accept the fact that love and subjection to man are one and the same thing, Doña Mencía de Nidos has to be convinced that the opposite is true. The very epitome of *varonilidad*, she leads the Spanish settlers against the resurgent Indians in Chile and eventually becomes governor of the city of Concepción.[26] Unlike the usual Spanish virago, however, she is neither haughty nor cruel; she does not mock her suitor Don Pedro nor despise him but explains calmly and rationally that while she likes and respects him she cannot love him. In other words, she behaves like a mature, responsible woman. Nonetheless, hers is a psychologically intricate approach. She has no quarrel with love and marriage for women in general, merely for herself because, she reasons, the courage and endurance demanded of a soldier are incompatible with emotional commitments. Now the interesting point about this objection is that Doña Mencía is so masculine in her character and tastes that she judges love not by its effect on woman but by the effect it has on man. Woman, she is convinced, "para sujeto ha nacido" (was born to be subject), so how can man be at once strong and subject to an already subject being? In her desire to avoid becoming weak and effeminate, her identification with the opposite sex is complete. Even more interesting, however, is the fact that Doña Mencía is not ultimately "reduced" to femininity. Don Pedro's courage proves to her that love is not detrimental and that subjection to it does not imply inferiority; whereupon she yields to her growing love and accepts his hand. But there is no question of her "giving herself" to him; she accepts him as an equal and not as lord and master. Her essential charac-

25. In *Poetas dramáticos valencianos*, ed. Eduardo Julía Martínez, vol. 2 (Madrid: Real Academia Española, 1929).

26. Doña Mencía had a historical existence though much elaborated in Turia's play. She was a doughty city matron who urged the governor to resist the Indian revolt.

ter has not changed, and she will presumably continue as hunter, soldier, and leader. But whereas before she considered herself a man, she can now accept the fact that she is a remarkable woman and that those qualities she recognizes in herself are not alien to femininity. The lesson she learns is that to accept one's womanhood is not to accept inferiority.

Turia's approach to the *mujer esquiva* is obviously a very different one from Lope's. Both believe that woman, like man, is subject to all-powerful love, but Turia is prepared to allow woman her pride and to confine himself to showing her that self-assertion is not incompatible with love and marriage. For Lope, woman's revolt against her sex is heresy; for Turia it is merely unnecessary. Whereas Lope sees the capitulation of the *mujer esquiva* as a humble, grateful submission to man, Turia, like Mira de Amescua in *Galán, valiente y discreto*, can conceive of it as a dignified acceptance. He wrote within the pattern established by Lope but brought to it a personal dimension of liberalism and of imaginative psychological insight.

The severity of Lope's disapproval of the *mujer esquiva* is shown again in his treatment of the fourth heroine in this group. Belisa in *Los melindres de Belisa*[27] (The Affectations of Belisa) (written between 1606 and 1608) is a superb portrayal of the *melindrosa*, the finicky, spoiled child, and a much more complex character than the run-of-the-mill disdainful adult woman. Today she would be labeled maladjusted and emotionally retarded. The indulgence that her parents have shown her since the day of her birth has made her selfish, hysterical, violent, and irresponsible. Her reasons for refusing her various suitors are the purely arbitrary ones of a mentality which delights in contrariness: one has lost an eye, another is too heavy, one is bald, one has large feet and dirty nails, another is merely French, and a sixth she turns down because of the device on the front of his military habit. The touchstone in her conversion is, naturally, love, but the method by which Lope chooses to bring about the transformation from spoiled child to responsible woman is here particularly suitable and impressive, revealing the psychological finesse of which Lope was frequently capable, above all, in his female characters.

Lope's remedy is to subject Belisa's system to a series of shocks which rudely jolt her out of her dream world where everybody seeks to humor her and where everything is designed to please her. First, her infantile temperament is made to cope with an adult emotion, sexual love, and then almost simultaneously, her child's mentality has to grap-

---

27. In *Acad. N.*, vol. 12.

ple with the social problems posed by the fact that she has fallen in love with her slave. The competition provided by Celia and the suspicion that the slave is not all that he appears to be confuse Belisa even further; for the first time in her life, she has lost command of the situation. The final blow is her discovery that her mother, who has formerly gratified her every whim, is also in love with the slave and intends to marry him. This discovery shocks Belisa into a concern for the family honor, a development which in seventeenth-century terms denotes the growth of a sense of responsibility.[28]

Such is the process by which Belisa the child achieves womanhood. The full punishment for her *esquivez*, however, is yet to come, for nature has avenged itself not only by making her conceive a passion for her inferior—this problem is resolved with the revelation of Felisardo's true identity—but also by making that man inaccessible. Felisardo loves Celia, and a chastened and wiser Belisa has to be content with Eliso. She has missed the oportunity of choosing a husband for herself, and as a result she has to accept the man chosen for her. Her reply to her brother's order that she marry Eliso, "Eso es justo" (It is only right), echoes the submission to their female destinies of all Lope's women. Since he was a fervent and consistent champion of woman's right to freedom of choice in love, the significance of this arranged match cannot be mistaken.

The desire to be a man is a common one among the more aggressive types of the masculine woman in the Golden Age theater, a desire born of impatience with the limitations imposed upon these women by the fact of their own sex. It is shared by the heroine of Tirso de Molina's *El vergonzoso en palacio*[29] (The Shy Man at Court) (written before 1611), Serafina. Serafina, however, is salon-bred, and her motives are not nearly as straightforward. In the first act, she is rather an unknown quantity. Much is said about her beauty, but she appears on the scene only rarely. We gather from her father, however, that she is reluctant to marry, a reluctance which he attributes to her carefree youth. A hint that the reason offered by her father might not be the correct one is given at the end of act 1 where although willing to recognize that Mireno is a handsome man, she can summon up no great interest in him. In act 2, it appears that she ardently wishes she had been born a

28. She herself has already decided that her love for the slave is impossible—her order to have him branded is a subconscious attempt to kill love by making the object of it unsightly.

29. In *Comedias de Tirso de Molina*, BAE, vol. 5 (Madrid: Rivadeneira, 1850).

man, and she therefore delights in the opportunity to dress as one, with which the performance of a play presents her. When her duenna, Doña Juana, expresses shocked amazement, she replies:

> no te asombre
> que apetezca el traje de hombre,
> ya que no lo puedo ser. (act 2, BAE, vol. 5, p. 215b)

do not be surprised that I should yearn to dress like a man, seeing that I cannot be one.

Another hint about Serafina's nature is given by Doña Juana's warning to her not to fall in love with herself. Doña Juana is not merely anticipating an event; she unwittingly puts her finger on its cause. Serafina's desire to be a man is soon afterwards amply borne out by the verve with which she enters her part. She identifies herself so completely with the jealous lover she is portraying that she attacks Doña Juana as if she were the rival lover, embraces her as if she were the wife, then attacks the poor woman again as if she were bride, groom, priest and congregation all rolled into one. This absorption in her part is important because it contrasts so strongly with that indifference in her we have already noted. In fact, the final two stages in the development of her character follow from there. First, with extraordinary indifference she ignores Doña Juana's warning that she is secretly being painted; then, as a result of this particular example of apathy, she falls in love with her own portrait. Indifference, the desire to be a man, the ability to identify herself with the jealous lover, and the attraction to her own image, these are the essential building blocks in Serafina's personality. They are related qualities carefully built up by the dramatist to form a coherent whole, a consistent image. Serafina is, in short, a narcissist.

Her indifference is the first pointer to this conclusion. She is incapable of reacting positively to anything outside herself and is utterly self-involved. She enters into her play acting with passion because it allows her to indulge her self-preoccupation. Furthermore, the part she chooses to play is entirely logical, for who is more self-involved than the jealous husband/lover highly conscious of his honor and his dignity? Her masculine role is advisedly chosen since in the drama of the Golden Age, self-preoccupation is normally the prerogative of the male, and her desire for masculinity is based on a subconscious recognition of this fact, presupposing as it does that man's greater self-preoccupation goes hand in hand with an awareness of his greater importance.

It is Serafina's self-preoccupation that makes her reject marriage and that leads her to fall in love with her own image. Her interests are so entirely directed toward herself that there is no room in her psychological makeup for a concern for anybody else. The portrait is a projection of herself; at the same time, it purports to be a man, therefore, she falls in love with it. What is this but a heterosexual manifestation of a narcissus complex? Doña Juana, the play's champion of love, thinks that this is heaven's way of punishing Serafina, and there certainly *is* a nice irony in it. Lope would have regarded it in the same light as Doña Juana, but Tirso depicts it as the logical outcome of Serafina's almost pathological love of self, and the note of condemnation with regard to her *esquivez* is negligible. Nowhere else in the play is her attitude to love criticized. In act 2 she justifies her attitude quite rationally, with what is substantially the same argument as one put forward by Cervantes' shepherdess, Marcela, in Part 1 of *Don Quixote*.

Serafina. ¿Puede ser
el no tener voluntad
a ninguno, crueldad? di
Juana. ¿Pues no?
Serafina. ¿Y será justo cosa
por ser para otros piadosa
ser yo cruel para mí?

Serafina. Tell me, can it be cruelty not to be in love?
Juana. Well, isn't it?
Serafina. And would it be just, in taking pity on others, to be cruel to myself?

The painter who overhears her remark acknowledges the logic of her view,

por dios, que ella dice bien. (act 2, p. 216a)

By the Lord, she is right.

There is no indication that Tirso does not do the same. If he is condemning anything, he is condemning not so much her *esquivez* but the self-preoccupation which gives rise to it, and Serafina is punished for this self-preoccupation with her seduction by Don Antonio and with marriage to him. This punishment aspect, however, is not emphasized. Tirso's interest lies essentially in the psychological curiosity of Serafina's character and not in the morality or propriety of her behavior.

Notwithstanding the variety of treatment given to the *mujer es-*

quiva theme, all the plays in which she appears primarily as *esquiva* (and not, for example, as bandit or amazon) have a very strong family resemblance, and their plots tend to follow the same stereotyped pattern.[30] This pattern was initially created by Lope as a vehicle for his strongly held views on women, love, and marriage. His followers imitated him, and later dramatists then wrote within what was a well-established convention. The *mujer esquiva* is, as a result, one of the most familiar theatrical types in seventeenth-century Spain. Inevitably, her apperance is not always accompanied by interesting variations of treatment and interpretation. Many plays are entirely conventional and unremarkable in this respect.

So predictable did the career of the disdainful woman become, in fact, that Rojas Zorrilla, who loved poking fun at theatrical conventions, wrote a satire of it—*Sin honra no hay amistad*[31] (No Friendship Without Honor) (published 1644). His heroine, Juana, who harbors an entirely unmotivated hatred of men, is converted to love in the usual manner. The difference here is that she does not fall in love with any particular man but with love itself, and she is confronted, therefore, with the dilemma of which man to choose. This is an obvious take-off on the heroine's inevitable subjection to a man through jealousy, and Juana's predicament is clearly intended to be an amusing one. No sooner does she realize that she is loved, not scorned, than she promptly falls out of love again. The satire, however, is not directed wholly toward Juana. The whole ethos of the *comedia* and its traditional preoccupation with love and honor is being gently mocked. Furthermore, there is no hint of a moral, no note of condemnation anywhere in the play. Juana's behavior is always shown as laughable, never as irresponsible or wrong-minded. Bernardo is not criticized for killing Melchor's father, and only Antonio finds his forcible abduction of Antonio's sister at all reprehensible. Melchor is allowed conveniently to forget his vow to avenge his father's death. This lack of moral concern, this absence of any true emotion, this disregard of personal feelings, this humorous treatment of serious matters like murder and rape are all typical of the satirical method. Here the satire is light-hearted both in method and purpose. Rojas Zorrilla is mocking not some aspect of real life but certain theatrical attitudes. His play is a

30. In pointing out the resemblance and in tracing the pattern, one is in danger of reducing the plays to mere schematized units. But of course many of the characters are fascinating individuals in their own right; María in *La moza de cántaro*, for example, is one of Lope's best female portraits, and the development of character throughout is quite masterly.

31. In BAE, vol. 54.

satire on other plays and is therefore twice removed from the plane of reality. There is no place here for the psychological truths contained by many of the plays which belong to the convention he is satirizing. His sole concern is with a type of dramatic plot, and the omission of everything that would make this stereotyped plot meaningful is therefore logical.

The relationship of the woman who shuns love and marriage to the feminist debates of medieval and Renaissance literature has been pointed out by Barbara Matulka.[32] Matulka traces the use made of the debate in several *esquiva* plays and shows how the champions of women in the *comedia* are protagonists in the surviving controversy concerning the specific merits and defects of the sexes. Her thesis is acceptable with certain reservations. Her argument seems to rest on a false premise, for she states that

> this feminist theme usually takes up the age-old controversy of the superiority of men or women by presenting as the leading character a lady who is a *Siglo de Oro* version of the "Belle dame sans merci" who has read of the deceptions of men and the evils which women have suffered through love, and has vowed never to fall a victim to passion but instead sets out to avenge women of their male betrayers (p. 192)

The *mujer esquiva*, in other words, was created to allow the Spanish dramatists to carry the feminist theme onto the stage. But in the majority of the *esquiva* plays the heroine's disdain is not provoked by a desire to wreak vengeance on men, nor is it the result of her literary studies. Furthermore, the feminist debate itself is, in most cases, never mentioned or even echoed, and the woman who demands "equal rights for her sisters" is the odd exception not the rule. Matulka's argument certainly applies to plays like Lope's *La vengadora de las mujeres*, Calderón's *Afectos de odio y amor*, Rojas Zorrilla's *Sin honra no hay amistad* and Juan Vélez de Guevara's *Encontráronse dos arroyuelos* (The Meeting of Two Streams). It does not apply to the female bandits who are *esquivas before* they are dishonored; it does not apply to Lope's *Los milagros del desprecio*, *El valiente Céspedes*, or *La moza de cántaro*; nor does it apply to a host of other plays including Turia's *La belígera española*, Tirso's *El burlador de Sevilla*, nor his *El vergonzoso en palacio*, Lope's *Los melindres de Belisa*, nor even Moreto's *El desdén con el desdén*.

In these plays the origin of the heroine's *esquivez* varies widely

32. Barbara Matulka, "The Feminist Theme in the Drama of the *Siglo de Oro*," *Romanic Review*, 26 (1935): 191–231.

within the spectrum of vanity and pride. Some resent the idea of subjecting themselves to a man; others are so mannish that the very notion of love and marriage is anathema to them. Some think no man worthy of them, and others believe that to fall in love is folly for men and women alike. Occasionally (with Serafina in *El vergonzoso en palacio* and Belisa in *Los melindres de Belisa*, for example), the motive is peculiarly eccentric. I do not wish to deny the importance of the feminist controversy in the formation of the *esquiva* plays. I merely want to suggest that the figure of the *mujer esquiva* is not just a vehicle for the dramatization of a particular literary theme. The crucial question is this: Why, after centuries of discussion about the merits and demerits of women, does the feminist theme suddenly burgeon into a female revolt against love and marriage? Why does it not remain a theoretical discussion as in the early theater? In other words, where did the *esquiva* come from and why did she become a popular dramatic type?

The *esquiva* was not new to Spain with the theater of the late 1590s. The dominant influence on Spanish secular literature of the sixteenth century was the culture of the Italian Renaissance. Petrarchan poetry was built around the image of the cold, hard-hearted, unresponsive mistress; indeed, it depended on her, for the suffering necessary to perfect love rested on the supposition that that love was unrequited. The mistress of the songbooks, of many sentimental romances, of much of the poetry of Garcilaso de la Vega (1503–1536) and Fernando de Herrera (1534–1597) remains immune to her lover's pleas. She is frequently described in terms of snow, ice, rock, and marble, which refuse to be melted by the ardor of her lover's passion. The reason for her *esquivez* is rarely given because it is unimportant; motives, however, the theater could readily supply.

For more specific examples of *esquivez* we have to look no further than the classical literature revived with the Renaissance. Ovid's *Metamorphoses* offers many of them: Diana, Athene/Minerva, Daphne, Proserpina, Atalanta, Pomona, Anaxarete, Arethusa, and, of course, the amazons themselves. The evidence that the dramatists were familiar with these classical myths and had them in mind as they wrote is overwhelming. The amazon plays themselves reveal the attraction this widespread legend held for people at the time, and it would be impossible to count and tedious to relate how many times the disdainful heroines invoke the memory of Pantasilia, Menalipe, and other famous amazon queens, and, above all, the goddess of chastity, Diana.

In the Petrarchan tradition, therefore, and in classical literature, the theater had ready-made *esquiva* figures—figures who did not belong to the traditional medieval controversy of the sexes. The amazons and Diana and her disciples were feminists, of course, but they were not of the feminist theme in its narrow literary sense. Add to these women the most famous contemporary example of the woman who shuns marriage and is equivocal even about love—Elizabeth the virgin queen of England—and there would seem to be inspiration enough for the creation of the type of the *mujer esquiva* as portrayed in the Golden Age drama.

But all this does not solve the problem of why she was created at this particular point and why in Spanish literature. The vogues for Petrarch and for Greco-Roman culture were well established long before the end of the sixteenth century. Both influences were as strongly felt in other countries. The circumstances were admittedly propitious: the continuing hold exerted by medieval and Renaissance love motifs upon the imagination and the enthusiasm for things classical; the medieval feminist debate, which had taken on new life with the Renaissance; the new atmosphere of comparative tolerance toward women which resulted from the teachings of Erasmus; all these contributed.

But something was needed to act as precipitator, and that something was Lope de Vega. The *mujer esquiva* was his creation; she is one of the few manifestations of the *mujer varonil* ("masculine woman") who does not appear in the pre-Lope theater. Lope, as his treatment of the masculine woman in all her forms indicates, was interested to an extraordinary degree in the subject of woman and in her position vis-à-vis love, marriage, and society. Furthermore, he had passionately held views on these matters. He sermonizes about them in a way no other dramatist does. His vehemence and sincerity are so great, in fact, that one cannot but think that something spurred him into action. No one protests as much as he did unless there is something to protest about.

I cannot be persuaded that his indignation was provoked by a handful of literary heroines or by a distant recalcitrant queen. The clue perhaps lies in his dedication of *La vengadora de las mujeres* to Señora Fenisa Camila, who was obviously, from what he says, a real-life *esquiva*, who expressed a dislike of men and refused to marry. Fenisa Camila, however, was not the only woman with such views. Lope's words to Señora Marcia Leonarda (the poetic pseudonym he gave his mistress, Doña Marta de Nevares Santoyo) in the dedication of his play about the amazons, *Las mujeres sin hombres* (Women Without Men)—"no le ofrezco su historia para que con su ejemplo desee serlo, antes bien para que conozca que la fuerza con que fueron vencidas tiene por disculpa la misma naturaleza" (I offer you their story not so that you will follow their example, but rather so that you will realize that the force by which they were vanquished has nature itself for excuse)—apart from being a piece of special pleading on his own behalf, indicate that the message of his play was one that he felt needed to be said. That the arguments of the feminist heroines of the theater were used by women in real life is obvious from the preface María de Zayas Sotomayor (1590–1601?) wrote to her first collection of short stories,[33] and they are, on the whole, arguments which are not used by women's male champions:

> Si esta materia de que nos componemos los hombres y las mujeres . . . no tiene más nobleza en ellos que en nosotras . . . ¿qué razón hay para que ellos sean sabios y presuman que nosotras no podemos serlo? Esto no tiene a mi parecer más respuesta que su impiedad o tiranía en encerrarnos, y no darnos maestros; y así la verdadera causa de no ser las mujeres doctas no es defecto del caudal, sino falta de la aplicación, porque si en nuestra crianza como nos ponen el cambray en las almohadillas y los dibuxos en el bastidor, nos dieran libros y preceptores, fuéramos tan aptas, para los puestos y para las cátedras como los hombres.
>
> If this material of which we men and women are made . . . is no nobler in them than in us, . . . what reason is there for them to be wise and to assume that we may not be? To my mind the only answer to this lies in their cruelty and tyranny in keeping us shut up and not giving us teachers; and thus the true cause of women's not being learned lies not in any defect in ability but in lack of opportunity, for if in the course of our upbringing they gave us books and tutors as readily as they place cambric on our sewing-pillows and patterns on our embroidery frames, we would be as suited as men are for positions and university chairs.

The evidence, therefore, points to the possibility that Fenisa Camila was one of a number of women in Spain at the time who, as a result of their readings, decided that their sex had been hard done by. A very small minority, certainly, but a minority with the intellectual curiosity that led them to think, read, and inquire in the first place, the intelligence which allowed them to assess what they read, the mental stamina which enabled them to cling to their views, and the eloquence which meant they could express them. That their feminism should have taken the form of a revolt against love and marriage is psychologically consistent. Their need to assert themselves would have been

---

33. *Novelas amorosas y ejemplares* (published 1637).

translated quite naturally into a gesture of defiance against the institutions which curtailed their independence most effectively. We know that women sometimes participated in the literary salons, even ran some of them. The position of woman, the feminist theme, in other words, must have been one of the favorite topics of discussion.

The feminst debate, therefore, is behind the *mujer esquiva* plays but not in quite the way Matulka indicated. The *mujer esquiva* of the drama, I would suggest, is not so much the extension of the literary theme of feminism but more the reaction against a contemporary aspect of feminism which was, within a restricted circle, very much alive. Against the background of the traditional debate and of Erasmian influence, Lope reacted to the feminism of his female contemporaries (a feminism born of that debate and that influence) by depicting their *esquivez* on the stage, giving it the motives (vanity and pride) he thought were the true ones, and finally making it submit to the laws of nature. The literary *esquivas* of old were but grist to his mill; he drew on them for plots and situations and for arguments to put into his heroine's mouth. When he wanted his characters themselves to argue his theme, he had the formalized feminist debate to refer to. His heroine became a convention, adopted by other dramatists. Both he and they used her in a variety of ways, employing her *esquivez* now as their main theme, now as an insignificant incident. As a result, the plots in which she appears cover a wide range of subject, treatment and psychological motivation. They are held together as a group not by the controversy of the sexes but by the constantly recurring figure of the *mujer esquiva*. This is why the *esquiva* herself is the real key to the phenomenon of the *mujer esquiva* plays.

As for the theatrical popularity of the *mujer esquiva*, this is not hard to explain, in spite of her lack (more often than not) of the provocative charms of doublet and hose. The challenge offered to masculine pride and the male conquering instinct by the woman who is hard to get is an accepted one, and the popularity of the *esquiva*, a type given as often to verbal as to physical aggressiveness, can be explained only in this way. Watching the inevitable subjection of female to male—the taming of the shrew—was a marvelous opportunity for self-congratulatory male esteem. Each man in the audience could happily identify himself with the hero who, by deceit, by psychological warfare, or by his essential nobility, gradually thawed out and won over the disdainful heroine.

There must have been more than a little of this in the *esquiva*'s attraction for the dramatists themselves. Furthermore, contradictory as it may seem, the *esquiva*'s progress from indifference to warmth and concern probably had a strong hidden appeal for the female members of her audience. What, after all, is the *esquiva* but a more sophisticated version of Sleeping Beauty? Both are waiting to be awakened to love and life. The prince is a stylization of the man who wins the unattainable woman. And the "prince" is probably the most common form of female wish fulfillment. The *esquiva*'s appeal is, in fact, inextricably linked with the dramatists' views on women in general.

Two facts emerge from the *mujer esquiva* plays. First, the Spanish playwrights of the seventeenth century were not prepared to emancipate woman from the demands imposed upon her by nature; and, second, they were not prepared to allow her any worthwhile motives for wishing to assert her independence. Not all of them may have shared Lope's rigid views on this matter or continually had the same axe to grind. Mira de Amescua and Ricardo de Turia may allow their heroines to accept marriage rather than submit to it; Turia may even allow woman her self-assertion. Tirso de Molina may conceive of a more complex and interesting motivation for female *esquivez*. But all of them subscribe to these basic tenets, even Doña Ana Caro, whose *El conde Partinuplés*[34] (Count Partinuplés) (published 1635) is the only play I have found in which a woman writer depicts a *mujer esquiva*. Though popular in its day, it is a poor play and is interesting only in that it reveals to what extent even women of literary pretensions like Caro were conditioned by the general attitude of the age about love and women.

The continual insistence that love is part of the natural order of the universe is, in part, an aspect of the seventeenth century's neo-Platonic inheritance. The interesting question is why much *more* stress is laid upon this theory in imaginative literature in the seventeenth century than in the secular love literature of the sixteenth century. It is certainly not a familiar precept in the pre-Lope drama. The answer seems to be that the Platonic belief in love (in its widest sense) as an integral feature of universal harmony possessed a specific, practical application for the seventeenth century, which still conceived of the world as the reflection of a divine purpose and, therefore, regarded order and balance as essential to well-being and, at the same time, looked for artistic nourishment in the vitals of its own society.

In other words, the Golden Age theater shows Platonic theory at work within a Christian social context. It is in the seventeenth century that the hierarchal order of society with its delegation of authority

34. In *Dramáticos posteriores a Lope de Vega*, BAE, vol. 49 (Madrid: Rivadeneira, 1859).

from God through the king down to the head of each family, receives particular emphasis, and it is in seventeenth-century drama that marriage is used at the end of a play as a symbol of the restoration of the good order of society. The seemingly haphazard batch of marriages with which nearly every plot is brought to an end is not merely an empty convention employed as an easy solution to the action; it reflects a philosophy of life, the belief that continuing security depends on order. Woman has her place in this order as wife and mother. A refusal to accept this place is a threat to the whole pattern of life. In all fairness, however, it must not be forgotten that for the seventeenth-century playwrights, man was as subject to love and marriage as was woman. None of the few *hombres esquivos* escapes them. The greater incidence of *esquivez* among heroines is largely due to their greater entertainment value; in reality, of course, seventeenth-century women had a great deal more to gain from marriage than they had to lose.

The dramatists' inability or unwillingness to conceive of there being any plausible rationale at the bottom of the *mujer esquiva*'s self-assertion is an inevitable one, contingent upon their sex. Being men, they are naturally reluctant to free woman of her traditional dependence upon and dominance by the male. Equally naturally, they cannot imagine that woman is really capable of disliking man, even less of being indifferent to him. That this conviction is not peculiar to the seventeenth-century Spanish theater is clear from the fact that whereas *misogyny* exists to convey the hatred of women, *misogamy* to convey the hatred of marriage, and *misanthropy* to convey the hatred of mankind, no word exists at all to convey the hatred of men; a word like *misandry* would have to be invented for this purpose; a small point, but significant. It would be wrong to expect of the Spanish playwrights of this period an objectivity and a liberality which most men have not achieved even today.

The *mujer esquiva*, in short, represents an invaluable contribution to the theme of seventeenth-century feminism because the treatment accorded her reveals exactly how far the dramatists were prepared to go in their defense of woman and their tolerance of feminist aims. The modern observer will denounce their feminism as very limited indeed. Nevertheless, for men of their day, feminist they were. For all their provisos and qualifications, they were interested in and concerned with the issues that affected woman's life, and they made an honest attempt to reconcile the anomalies they detected with their convictions about the nature of human existence. They would not emancipate woman from man, but neither would they emancipate man from woman. For them, love was the greatest equalizer of all. God-ordained as the workings of nature were, they were immutable, good, and right. The workings of society, although an integral part of God's universe, were dependent on man and therefore susceptible to human weakness. Woman was in many ways a victim of this weakness. The wrongs perpetrated against her by a masculine society—as a victim of sexual aggression, arranged marriages, and an all-pervasive double standard of morality—could and should be put right.[35] But the role appointed her by God for her own happiness and that of mankind was one to be gratefully accepted. The Spanish dramatists accordingly join with Shakespeare's Rosalind in bidding the reluctant bride:

> But, mistress, know yourself: down on your knees,
> And thank heaven, fasting, for a good man's love.

---

35. See Melveena McKendrick, *Woman and Society in the Spanish Drama of the Golden Age: A Study of the "mujer varonil"* (Cambridge: Cambridge University Press, 1974).

The Convent as Catalyst for Autonomy

Two Hispanic Nuns of the Seventeenth Century

Electa Arenal

Until recently, scholars have regarded Saint Teresa of Avila as an isolated instance of a woman of great energy and spirit, the epitome of the unique fusion of the real and the ideal in Spanish life and letters.[1] But the discovery of significant numbers of neglected manuscripts suggests that she was not alone, that around her and in her wake came other dynamic and contemplative women.[2] One of these was Venerable Madre Isabel de Jesús (1586–1648). She was an illiterate Castilian shepherdess and visionary, who struggled

---

I wish to thank Barbara Grant, Marcia Welles, and Helene Farber de Aguilar for reading and criticizing my manuscript, Virginia Youngren and Michele Barefoot for editorial assistance, and Grace Clark for typing.

1. See, for example, E. A. Peers, *Studies of the Spanish Mystics*, 3 vols. (New York: Macmillan, 1927–1930); H. Hatzfeld, *Estudios literarios sobre mística española*, 2nd ed. (Madrid: Gredos, 1965); D. Alonso, *Del siglo de oro a este siglo de siglas* (Madrid: Gredos, 1962).

2. The most important single reference source to works by women is Manuel Serrano y Sanz's *Apuntes para una biblioteca de escritoras españolas desde el año 1401 al 1833* (Madrid: Tipografía de la Revista de Archivos, 1903 and 1905; published in a facsimile edition in Madrid, 1975). I can mention two, Sor María de San José, a favorite of Saint Teresa's, and Juliana Morell, whose work I have traced to the Bibliothèque Calvet in Avignon. See Serrano y Sanz, II, 333–50 and 63–70 (incorrectly indexed). For the most part, how-

for twenty-five years to become a nun. Another, of quite different stamp, was Sor Juana Inés de la Cruz (1648–1695) of New Spain, who previewed the coming age of Enlightenment and defended the right of women to exercise and live by their minds. Without rivals in intellectual scope or artistic projection, the Mexican nun left poetry, plays, and prose, which were not compiled and edited until more than two hundred and fifty years after her death.[3]

Unlike Sor Juana, who was recognized in her own time as being among the greatest intellects and literary talents of the period, Madre Isabel lived in relative obscurity in a self-generated world of religious visions. Sor Juana wrote an autobiographical "letter" not as a literary endeavor but as the defense of an intellectual life in answer to attacks by her superiors; Madre Isabel dictated her life at the request of her superiors, again not as a literary endeavor but as a religious exercise. Sor Juana's autobiography is unique; Madre Isabel's resembles in effect hundreds of lives written in the sixteenth and seventeenth centuries in Spain and its colonies with the aim of inspiring emulation in the faithful.[4]

---

ever, works of this sort have been ignored. I traveled to Spain on a CUNY Faculty Grant in 1973 to do research at the Biblioteca Nacional and the Archivo Histórico Nacional, where documents by women, largely neglected, are plentiful. It was in the manuscript section of the Biblioteca Nacional that I discovered the *Life* of Madre Isabel, catalogued under the author's first name, which is the only way such works are listed in that library. (At the Archivo Histórico Nacional they are listed by religious orders only.) Elsewhere in Spain, the archives of Simancas near Valladolid and of the convent of Las Huelgas in Burgos are also rich sources of manuscripts. Archives, convents, and libraries in many other cities—Seville, Avila, Barcelona—have more of such documents. But in many of these places, getting access to the manuscripts requires a great deal of perseverance.

3. Sor Juana Inés de la Cruz, *Obras completas* (Mexico: Fondo de Cultura Económica 1951–1957), Alfonso Méndez Plancarte, ed., vols. 1–3, Alberto Salceda, ed., vol. 4 (hereafter cited as O.C.). When citing the *Respuesta a Sor Filotea* (hereafter cited as *Respuesta*), I also provide page numbers from Elias L. Rivers' edition, Sor Juana Inés de la Cruz, *Antología* (Madrid: Anaya, 1965); I cite from this edition because it is readily available and reasonably priced.

4. These lives are mentioned, for example, in R. Trevor Davies' *The Golden Century of Spain (1501–1621)* (New York: Harper Torchbooks, 1961), p. 290; and Julio Caro Baroja, *Las formas complejas de la vida religiosa* (Madrid: Akal, 1978), pp. 81, 84, 87. See also Antonio Domíngues Ortíz, *Las clases privilegiadas en la España del Antiguo Régimen* (Madrid: Ediciones Istmo, 1973), p. 202.

For centuries, most of the women who in Virginia Woolf's phrase had "a room of their own" found it in the cloister.[5] As Emily James Putnam stated in *The Lady: Studies of Certain Significant Phases of Her History*, "No institution in Europe has ever won for the lady the freedom of development that she enjoyed in the convent. . . . The impulse toward leadership which kept the men in the world sent the women out of it."[6] The cloister, which common opinion often represents as a refuge (or as a prison), was equally a place in which women could support each other and even cultivate a certain amount of independence. It provided women of greatly divergent personalities with a semiautonomous culture in which they could find sustenance, exert influence, and develop talents they never could have expressed as fully in the outside world. In that sense, the convent was a catalyst for autonomy. It is ironic that the greater inequality of women in Hispanic culture, a result in part of the strength and pervasiveness of the Church, made the very source of restrictions an outlet for freer expression. In effect, nuns found a way of being important in the world by choosing to live outside it.

Despite the rigor of convent life, there was room for variation, even eccentricity, as the lives of these two very different women illustrate. Madre Isabel, a poor shepherdess, worked as a domestic servant both in and out of the convent; Sor Juana, from a moderately wealthy landholding family, was close to the most privileged ranks of society. Madre Isabel was uneducated; Sor Juana was an acknowledged prodigy. Peasant and aristocrat, poor and rich, illiterate and intellectual—the convent, echoing the outer world, held and maintained these contrasts in social status.

One of the aims of this chapter is to add a few threads to the reweaving of the tapestry of women's history and literature. Madre Isabel's recorded experience is part of the background against which Sor Juana's life and thought stands out in sharp relief. The juxtaposition of these two seventeenth-century lives provides us a more complete picture of the times and of the reactions of women within it. Many

---

5. Virginia Woolf, *A Room of One's Own* (1929; rpt. New York: Harcourt, Brace & World, 1957). Although Woolf's book is not directly related to the subject of this essay, it is essential reading for anyone interested in women writers.

6. Emily James Putnam, *The Lady: Studies of Certain Significant Phases of Her History* (1910; rpt. Chicago: University of Chicago Press, 1970), pp. 71, 78.

more women's lives resembled Madre Isabel's than Sor Juana's. In belief, religious ideas, and intellectual set, even the women of the upper classes were closer to the Spanish peasant mystic than to the Mexican preencyclopedist. The Spanish nun conforms to the climate of the times. Her road to exceptionality was a more allowable one; along the route of mysticism and of "holy ignorance," she reached the point of being able to exert influence. Sor Juana was a central figure in the cultural and intellectual life of the court of New Spain. She brilliantly refuted the concept of "holy ignorance" but was refused confession for this defiance—and ultimately capitulated or converted.

Because there is a tendency to regard those women who entered convents simply as nuns—as religious figures—they have been missed as people. Both Sor Juana and Isabel de Jesús felt guilt for taking time out to write (or dictate); both were clever and found ways of getting around obstacles such as the resentments or rulings of confessors and superiors. Although neither attained the political and economic power Putnam discusses (which medieval abbesses held), both struggled for self-realization. And this can be attributed to the fact that they were nuns. Since they were women outside of their sexual function in society—"disembodied" and seen more as spirit than as matter—they were free to deal with philosophical and spiritual issues.

Sor Juana presided as might a philosopher queen over a salon; in her own society, Madre Isabel, a kind of mystical madwoman, was called upon to give advice, make predictions, console those who mourned, and encourage those who wavered. Both held positions of respect within the convent, and both dedicated time to caring for their sisters. For Sor Juana the convent was the least of evils; for Isabel it was the last stop before heaven. For both of them it was essential, allowing them to consider themselves the equals, if not the superiors, of the men around them. Both explicitly claim such equality, Sor Juana by virtue of intellect, Isabel by virtue of spirit.

The two sections of this chapter are necessarily quite different from each other. In the case of Madre Isabel, the discovery of a hitherto unknown document requires an initial description, assessment, and analysis. In the case of Sor Juana, whose work has been discussed by a considerable number of critics and writers,[7] the aim has been to suggest, from a feminist viewpoint, some reassessment of her life and art.

---

7. Pedro Henríquez Ureña, Dorothy Schons, and Ermilo Abreu Gómez compiled the best early twentieth-century bibliographies of Sor Juana's work. Ludwig Pfandl, *Sor Juana Inés de la Cruz: La décima musa de México, su vida, su poesía, su psique*, trans. J. A. Ortega y Medina, introd. Francisco de la

The Life and Work of an Unknown Mystic

Madre Isabel was a seventeeth-century peasant mystic who absorbed the hagiographic language and oral tradition of the convent and then dictated a spiritual autobiography. Born in 1586, four years after the death of Saint Teresa and not far from the saint's home town of Avila, she was in her thirties when Saint Teresa was canonized. She lived during the Counter-Reformation, the Golden Age of Spanish theater (she mentions seeing a play), the age of Cervantes, a time in which Spanish hegemony ended (the Spanish Armada was defeated in 1588). Her autobiography reveals, however, no interest in history but rather a devotion to private and religious life: how she dealt with her poverty, her intelligence, and her madness; how she developed as an individual, her attitudes toward knowledge and revelation. Her largely ahistorical world was determined by her religious culture; it was also a function of her class and her status as a woman.

The title of Madre Isabel's 470-page work is *Vida de la Venerable Madre Isabel de Jesús, recoleta Augustina en el convento de San Juan Bautista de la villa de Arenas. Dictada por ella misma y añadido lo que faltó de su dichosa muerte*[8] (Life of the Venerable Mother Isabel de Jesús, Cloistered Augustinian of the Convent of Saint John the Baptist in the Village of Arenas. Dictated by her, with an Addition Telling of Her Blessed Death). In the artistic sense, a primitive masterpiece, it reveals, practically uncensored, the fantasy life of this obsessively religious woman.

Maza (Mexico: Universidad Nacional Autónoma de México, 1963), provides a chronological bibliography 1873–1935; continued by de la Maza for 1936–1963. For an easily accessible, sizable bibliography, see Anita Arroyo, *Razón y pasión de Sor Juana* (Mexico: Editorial Porrúa, 1971). Both Muna Lee and Samuel Beckett have done fine translations of some of Sor Juana's poems. Sor Juana was introduced by Judith Thurman (in a *Ms.* magazine section called "Lost Women") under the title, "Sister Juana, the Price of Genius," *Ms.*, April 1973, pp. 14–21; in the summer of 1978, a new play about Sor Juana's life by Betty Neustat, also entitled *The Price of Genius*, was produced at the Women's InterArt Center in New York. See the reviews by Richard Eder, "Stage: 'Price of Genius' Vignettes of Sor Juana," *New York Times*, 7 June 1978; and that by Barbara Crossette, "New Face: Susan Stevens, Finding Herself a Mexican Nun," *New York Times*, 28 July 1978.

8. (Madrid: Viuda de Francisco Nieto, 1675). Copy at the Biblioteca Nacional (Madrid); numbers following citations refer to pages in this edition. This translation and all others of both Madre Isabel and Sor Juana Inés de la Cruz that appear in this essay are by the author and by poet and translator Meg Bogin.

The first book has thirty-seven chapters and covers her years of secular life; in many ways this is the most interesting part since she discusses her childhood, marriage, and entry into religious life. The forty chapters of Book 2 span her twenty years as a lay sister. The third book, a seven-chapter appendix written by her confessor, recounts the illness and death of Isabel—a traditional requirement in such biographies—the life and death of her secretary Madre Inés del Sacramento, and the opinions of others regarding the miracles and prophecies responsible for "the saintly fame she left behind her."

Like Saint Teresa, Isabel de Jesús manifested both utter humility and determined self-assertion. Her ambition and her competitiveness emerge clearly. When Isabel's confessor says to her:

> Isabel, yo me holgaría, que tu espíritu sea tan bueno como el de la Santa Madre Teresa. . . . (p. 174)
>
> Isabel, I would be delighted were your spirit to prove as good as that of our Holy Mother Saint Teresa. . . .

she has an immediate inner response:

> Al decirme esto mi Confesor, me dijeron a mi interiormente: no es menos bueno tu espíritu, que el suyo, el suyo era de Dios, y el tuyo también los es. . . . (p. 174)
>
> As my confessor said this to me, voices from within spoke to me thus: Your spirit is in no wise inferior to hers, hers belonged to God as does your own. . . .

Her supreme confidence in her direct line to Christ not only made life bearable; it transformed her into a popular sage and a maverick theologian. After describing her recognition of the principle of three-in-one, the Trinity, she states:

> Dijo me el Señor: ves esto, que te he enseñado aquí, sin costarte ningún trabajo: mira que es mística Teología, y les cuesta a los Teólogos grandisimo trabajo primero que vienen a entenderlo. Sea Dios alabado para siempre, que desde niña me hizo merced de darme esta inclinación como ya tengo dicho. (p. 160)
>
> The Lord said to me, Behold this which I have taught you without any effort on your part; this is Mystical Theology, which theologians must struggle to comprehend. Praise God that it was given to me from childhood to know these things, as I have already said.

Madre Isabel emerges from the autobiography as neither ignorant nor obedient, despite her avowed espousal of these virtues. As the vessel of the Lord's revelations and supreme wisdom, she felt sufficiently confident to criticize those who "gain wisdom by study" and think it is their own work and effort that has made them wise (p. 83). Although she identifies with her sex, nonetheless, she accepts orthodox opinion on the earthly inferiority of women; but her writing reveals that she saw the paradox of Christ's teaching—that the lowliest shall be the highest—working in her favor.

Madre Isabel's life story also illustrates the truism that popular traditional Catholicism fosters a relationship of intimacy between believers and their objects of adoration. Christ becomes family. More than the protagonist herself, He moves as a lively character of her autobiography, speaking in a variety of moods and tones, appearing in various forms, seen at varying distances, and even relating to other, mortal characters of the tale. The dramatic tension thus established unifies the narrative and counterbalances the constant interpretations of visions and the elaborations on their theological meaning. It is a fascinating *desdoblamiento* (in the sense of manifold representations). The impression of flowing, divine love is brought close by the portrayal of Christ in highly affective contexts: a doting, correcting, reassuring, guiding parent; a sensitive and vulnerable lover; an unwavering though moody friend. Colloquial speech often flavors Christ's words to Mother Isabel. When, for instance, she begs that he give "her brothers" some of what he has given her—a Spanish version of a request appearing in the Gospels—he rebukes her emphatically and with almost childish impudence:

> Mira que no doy a todos lo que te doy a ti, sino a quien quiero, y como quiero, y cuando quiero, díjome. (p. 83)
>
> Look, I don't give to everyone what I give to you, but only to whom I wish, and as I wish, and when I wish, he said to me.

This everyday language and the accompanying proverbs and expressions—such as "hay almas que se quieren inclinar a pecar, no solo de paso, sino de asiento" (p. 311) (There are souls that go toward sin not as transients, but as permanent residents)—all drawn from the vernacular of Castile, weave in and out of the narrative as a counterpoint to the biblical tones and the sermonlike cadences that characterize theological interpretations.

> Ea valerosos soldados de la milicia de Cristo bien nuestro, sigamos a nuestro valeroso Capitán, haciendo guerra a nuestro contrario. . . . Ea queridos hermanos en Cristo, sigámosle, pues que es nuestro Hermano mayor, y nos está convidando al eterno descanso. . . . Llegaos os suplico a la piedra imán, que es Cristo: llegaos conociendo que es tan poderoso, que os levantará, atrayéndoos a si. (p. 237)
>
> Hear me, brave soldiers of Christ's militia, let us follow our valiant Captain, making war against our enemy. . . . Hear me! dear brothers in Christ, let us follow him, for he is our eldest Brother, and he invites us to eternal rest. . . . I beg you, approach Christ, the magnet stone; approach, and know that he is so powerful that he will raise you, attracting you to himself.

That Madre Isabel came to the convent from poverty[9] and the life of a Castilian shepherdess, we are not allowed to forget: *rústica pastora* ("rustic shepherdess") and *pobre labradora* ("poor laborer") are the epithets by which she repeatedly and formulistically describes herself. (Her confessor, her secretary, and the churchmen passing judgment on the value of publishing the volume also employ it.) The epithets reminding us of her humble and rustic origins become emblematic. But the reality to which they allude is a center of interest for the modern reader.

Despite the fact that she was one of nine children, loneliness was the dominant theme of her childhood. Isabel, who learned to tend sheep at about the same age Sor Juana learned to read, spent long, solitary hours up in the mountain terrified of being attacked by wolves. Very early, according to her own account, imagination came to her rescue, providing companionship in the form of religious visions. Surely the major influence on the form of this compensation was the indoctrination she received from her mother, who "never misses a mass."

On the insistence of a brother-in-law, she was married to a toothless old man when she was fourteen. By fifteen she was pregnant. She had three children, all of whom died in infancy or early childhood. But the marriage, a torment she overcame by a feat of her imagination, lasted twenty-four years. She conquered her aversion toward her husband by imagining that she was making love to Joseph, the husband of Mary.

---

9. Madre Isabel was a lay nun. Women who did not have enough money to provide a dowry as brides of Christ were admitted to the convent only as lay nuns; there were parts of the convent they could not enter; they worked often as *monjas de coro* ("servants to the dowered").

Mary was the object of her mother's religious predilection, she tells us. But Isabel's own affections led her to Christ and the Trinity. The psychological implications of this affinity are significant: elements of individuation, competition, compensation. Married to an old man, she picked a young and beautiful one to venerate. Left childless by the deaths of her three babies, she chose the child. In the world of her visions she was passionately in love with a protean Christ who appeared to her as a young shepherd, a royal hunter, a beam of light, a fountain, a gold-ringleted infant. She does not make much of the deaths of her children, but the effect of these tragedies surfaces time and time again in the imagery of her religious fantasies.

In one of these fantasies, she sees Christ with engorged breasts nursing dogs.[10] She transforms the metaphor, taken from the reality of her own life, into a symbol of Christ's mercy. The initial image of a Christ with engorged breasts is startling, but Isabel assures us she knows what she's talking about: when her own babies died, she had nursed other women's babies, and even dogs, to relieve the swelling:

> Manifestóme el Señor un día su corazón santísimo, diciéndome que estaba cargado, y que no hallaba quien le descargase los pechos: yo entendí que los pechos de su misericordia . . . me dijo que por haber enfermado sus hijos había dado los pechos a los perros, entendí, que como el pueblo de Dios se rebeló contra Cristo, Hijo de Dios vivo, enfermó, no queriendo recibir su divina palabra le desobligaron los hijos, que él tanto amaba, y que no queriendo sus divinos pechos, los dió a los gentiles, que eran los perros: yo lo entendí muy bien, porque había pasado por mí cuando enfermaban mis niños, y cuando se morían daba mis pechos a los hijos ajenos, y a los mismos perros, porque no cabe la leche en los pechos, y está hirviendo por salir, y como la leche de la misericordia de Dios estaba en el encendido amor, cociendo por comunicarse; para hacernos bien. . . . (pp. 81–82)

> One day the Lord revealed to me his most holy heart, saying that he was engorged and that he could not find anyone to relieve his breasts: I understood the breasts of his mercy . . . he told me that because his children had fallen ill he had nursed dogs. I understood that since God's people rebelled against Christ, the living Son of God, they became ill, refusing his divine word; the

10. A hermaphroditic Christ figures in early gospels (first to third centuries); and God/Christ as nurturing mother appears in the works of medieval religious women such as Bridgit of Sweden, Julian of Norwich, Saint Catherine of Siena, and Margery Kempe.

> children whom he loved so dearly rejected his divine breasts, so he offered them to the gentiles, who were the dogs. I understood it well, because I had experienced the same thing; when my children were ill and when they died, I breast-fed the children of others, and even puppies, because the milk cannot be contained in the breasts, and it presses to issue forth, and since the milk of God's mercy comes from his ardent love straining to be communicated, to do us good. . . .

Making a living was always difficult, and there were constant misfortunes: loss of sheep, of the little land that belonged to the family. Isabel ended up working as a servant in rich people's homes. She had one employer who would not let her out of his sight; another accused her of robbery. Madre Isabel's own life resembles a picaresque novel.

In addition to working outside her home, she had to take care of her infirm husband, one of whose illnesses lasted six years (she describes his incontinence and apologizes for finding the wiping and washing up ghastly). As time went on, she became increasingly observant, hastening to communion and confession with a zeal that aroused the resentment and suspicion of the townspeople. She—and others into whose souls God allows her to peer—was plagued by devils; the hellish characters she describes are as dramatic and grotesque as any to be found in the anonymous murals of Hell at Pisa or in the paintings of Hieronymus Bosch:[11]

> Estaba su corazón tal, cual no esté el de nadie. Tenía dos espantosos demonios en el interior de su alma, teníanle comidas las entrañas, estaba denigrido el hueco del interior, adonde habitaba aquella infernal compañía que tenía. (p. 217) Viendo con los ojos del alma, los terribles tormentos que tiene aparejados aquel señor infernal. . . . le ví echar de su seno, vomitando una pobre alma, echando de si llamas vivas . . . ¡qué penas tan horribles . . . qué rabiosos compañeros tienen! ay que aullidos, y que lamentaciones. . . . (p. 236)

> His heart was as no one's should ever be. He had two horrendous devils within his soul; they had devoured his entrails; the inner hollow was blackened where that infernal company he kept had their abode. . . . Seeing with the eyes of my soul the terrible

11. It has come to my attention by word of mouth and through the *Fourteenth Century English Mystics Newsletter* (4 [September 1978]: 29) that Elvy Setterquist O'Brien of Western Illinois University is studying the iconographic impact of Saint Birgitta's *Revelations* on Bosch and its influence on medieval and Renaissance art. Lina Eckenstein (*Woman Under Monasticism: Chapters*

> torments the infernal lord has prepared. . . . I saw him thrust from his breast, vomiting, a poor soul, alive with flames . . . what horrible punishments . . . what raging companions. Oh! What howls and lamentations. . . .

Indirect dialogue pulls us into the scenes of her visions. Sometimes her visions are self-contained; at other times she brings in references to actual events. Always the phenomena of the outer world are subordinate to those of the interior world of the visions. The transposition is seen in the way natural events are perceived: for example, in her vision of the army of devils, there is first the vision itself and then the assertion of its material presence as a damaging cloudburst.

> Representóseme en una nube gran ejército de demonios: levantóse esta nube repentinamente con grandísimos truenos, y relámpagos, y con tanta piedra que era admiración; daban voces los demonios en las nubes, pidiendo al Señor que nos hundiese que le ofendíamos mucho. . . . Yo suplicaba al Señor . . . que tuviese por bien de guardar los frutos espirituales. Parecíales mal a mis vecinas, que dijese aquello, sino que mirase en qué peligro estaban las viñas, y los panes. El Señor me mandó, que le pidiese para las almas, que muchas había que pedían lo temporal. Hizo grandísimo daño esta nube, y hiciera mucho más, si no la detuviera el Señor con sus Angeles. Yo ví, que entrando en ella, la deshicieron, y parecía que había una lucha dentro de la nube, y los Angeles buenos con los malos. . . . (pp. 101–2)

> There appeared to me in a cloud a great army of devils; the cloud burst suddenly with loud thunder and lightning, and with so many stones it was awesome; the devils in the clouds yelled and screamed, begging the Lord to drown us, for we were sinners. . . . I pleaded with the Lord . . . to see fit to save the fruits

---

on Saint-Lore and Convent Life Between A.D. *500 and* A.D. *1500* [Cambridge: Cambridge University Press, 1896]), speaking of the literary and artistic nuns of the convent of Helfta in the thirteenth century, states:

> For strong natures who rebelled against the conditions of ordinary life, but were shut out from the arena of intellectual competition, found an outlet for their aspirations in intensified emotionalism, and this emotionalism led to the development of a wealth of varying imagery which subsequently became the subject-matter of pictorial art. In course of time the images offered and suggested by Scripture had been supplemented by a thousand floating fancies and a mass of legendary conceits, which were often based on heathen conceptions. . . . (p. 328)

One of the great writers of Helfta, St. Gertrude the Great, is mentioned by Sor Juana; see p. 149, n. 5.

> of the spirit. The neighborhood women were annoyed that I should ask thus, while I paid no attention to the danger to the vineyards and wheatfields. The Lord ordered me to pray for souls because they were many who were praying for temporal goods. That cloud did a lot of damage, and it would have done worse if the Lord had not intervened with His Angels. I saw that as they entered it they destroyed it, and it seemed as if there was a battle going on within it, with the good Angels against the bad. . . .

As always, center stage is taken up by the inner life. Material reality, often seen as backdrop, or as secondary plot, is engulfed. Her husband's death when she was thirty-eight put her in the position to realize her fondest dream: to become a nun. But there remained still one ordeal to undergo; accused by her local church of being a false prophet, she was publicly shamed from the pulpit. The phrase in which she sums up the experience could be taken from the work of any dramatist of the Golden Age:

> Predicó este Padre sus honras, y de camino mis deshonras. (p. 120)

> The priest did his honors, and in passing, caused my dishonor.

Two priests were especially antagonistic toward her. When nuns were imported from Salamanca to found an Augustinian convent, Isabel was recommended as a servant. The two priests spread news of the charges against her and informed the nuns that she had been treated for possession by devils. Predictably, the nuns refused her services, saying that they already had two mad sisters in the convent and that they would not take chances with another. She was finally admitted three years later after first working as a lay aide to Discalced Franciscan monks. She tells how on her first day of work for the Franciscans, she was attacked at the door of the monastery. Her humiliation is a glorious parallel to the sufferings of Christ:

> A pocos días que los acudí, me cocaban los hombres que acertaban a pasar por allí a su trabajo, como me veían a la puerta, que como era forastera reparaban mucho. . . . Luego que me puse el saco de sayal, como me vieron de nuevo salir a un recado (había caido una gran nieve) y ellos dieron en meter piedras, y hacer pelotas con la nieve; tirándome a cual más podía. (pp. 125–26)

> A few days after I had been there, the men who used to pass by on their way to work began to tease me since I was a stranger in

> their town, and stare at me. . . . Then when I had started wearing my burlap robe they saw me going out to do an errand one day. A heavy snow had fallen, and they started to gather stones, and make them into snowballs, which they hurled at me as hard as they were able.

After these and other persecutions, in 1626, at the age of forty, she entered the Augustinian cloistered convent. On the day she took the habit, the roof of the convent caved in; given their susceptibility to superstition, it is a wonder that the nuns did not expel her on the spot. But during her first months in the convent, her joy at finally being a nun was almost destroyed by torments imaginary and real. In the world she had been burdened with an old husband for twenty-four years; in the convent she was to be burdened for the next fifteen years by antagonistic confessors, one of whom thought she was possessed. So violent was the struggle—the trauma of finally reaching her goal? the fear?—that she thought she was losing her mind. She was warring with devils again, and she writes of days and nights spent in constant visionary states.

One source of her torment—her temptations, pain, illness—was the strain imposed by her efforts to obey confessors whose instructions differed so widely from those of her inner voices. The confessors called upon her to meditate on her sins rather than listen to the voices and the accompanying vision. That she saw devils rear up before her, turning her mind to "el espíritu maligno de la fornicación" (p. 167) (the evil spirit of fornication), caused her unbearable mental anguish; interestingly, the trouble ceased when another confessor allowed her to follow her own bent. She accepted and endured the torment since she saw it as suffering for Christ; and it confirmed her in the eyes of many of her fellow nuns and certain of the priests as an authentic mystic.

We should underscore the status Isabel attained within the convent and the sense of power she must finally have found there. In her visions she often played the role of courier and mediator between Christ and her confessors. If she disagreed with a confessor, she would consult with Christ and promptly return to the confessor with a message from the Savior supporting her own point of view. She always managed to have the upper hand. Impressed by her own revelations and concerned because Christ and her confessor were in conflict, Isabel felt an urge to learn to read and write. But the Lord advised against it:

> Él estaba contento con que yo no empiese leer, ni escribir; porque si lo supiera, entendieran cuando yo lo dijera, que lo había yo sacado de algún libro. . . . (p. 170)

> He preferred that I not learn to read or write; for if I had, then people might think that the things I said were taken from books. . . .

The content of Isabel's rich inner life, the variety of visionary, hallucinatory, ecstatic experience is described in detail. In a few instances, she resembles other mystic writers who lament their inability to describe the mystic union:

> Venía diciendo acerca del amor de Dios nuestro Señor, y de los afectos que causan en el alma, y verdad es, que yo no acierto a declararme, sé que lo gozo, y no sé decirlo. . . . (p. 396)
>
> I've been telling of the love of God our Lord, and of the feelings it causes the soul, and the truth is, I can't find the right words, I know that I receive it, and I don't know how to say it. . . .

But in most cases she felt no such verbal impediment and was more than willing to recount the hundreds of visions and miracles that were daily events in her life:

> Yo me arrimé a un mármol. . . . comencé a verter lágrimas . . . a las cuales acude el piadoso Señor, que no tiene corazón para vernos llorar . . . ésta fue la primera vez que le ví, que aunque me abrazaba en su divino amor, no le conocía: y así tomando forma de niño muy pequeñito, me comenzó a hablar. . . . si tu te quieres poner a mi escuela, yo te enseñare. . . . anda acá, vamos a Padre y dirasle, que has tratado acá en el mundo con un mercader engañoso, que te ha prometido y no tiene nada que darte; yo tengo mucho que darte, que he venido muy rico de las Indias de mi Padre. . . . (p. 23) Se me representó la Madre de Dios, con su bendito Hijo en los brazos; ví que no tenía cabeza, y que en el hueco del pecho tenía una gran concavidad negra espantosa, y tenía el alma asomada a aquella concavidad. . . . Causóme grandísimo miedo; quise echar a huir: comenzó a llamar con la cabeza, y a llorar: entendí que me pedía que pidiese a Dios por ella. . . . (p. 68) En medio de estos trabajos estaba una noche, que no sabía de mi, y me habló el Señor en latín, yo lo entendí en romance; y entenderlo, y aliviarse la pesada carga, fue todo a un tiempo. . . . (p. 174)
>
> I leaned against a marble column. . . . I began to gush tears . . . to which the pitying Lord responds, for He doesn't have the heart to see us cry . . . this was the first time I saw Him, because although I burned with the divine love, I had not met Him. . . . And so, appearing in the form of a tiny child, He began to talk to

> me. . . . If you want to join my school, I will teach you. . . . Come here, let's go to Father, and you will tell Him that here in the world you have dealt with a deceptive usurer [her confessor] who has made promises but who has nothing to give you; I have much to give you, for I come with riches from the Indies of my Father. . . . I saw the Mother of God with her blessed Son in her ams; I saw that she was headless, and that from the decapitated hole her soul was peering out. . . . I was frightened to death; I tried to flee; she began to call me with her head [the head of her spirit?] and to weep; I understood that she was asking me to pray to God for her. . . . One night, in the midst of these trials, I was beside myself, and the Lord spoke to me in Latin, and I understood Him in Spanish; and the understanding and the lifting of the grievous burden came to me at once. . . .

As she grew more secure, Madre Isabel also became more dogmatic, and more tedious as a writer. Likewise, she acquired greater theological sophistication. The confidence she gained from knowing she could converse with Christ whenever she pleased gave her strength of character, although at times she was overbearing. The head she had in the heavens was much more real to her than the feet she had on the ground. In her visionary life she transcended the mundane, easily identifying and visiting with the most holy and powerful: Saint Catherine of Siena, Saint Peter, Saint Thomas, Saint Teresa, and Saint Augustine.

Madre Isabel's life bears a striking resemblance to that of Margery Kempe, the medieval English fanatic so magnificently portrayed by Louise Collis.[12] Like Kempe, Madre Isabel was righteous and driven, becoming so extreme in her fervor that many people concluded that she was mad rather than divinely inspired. To win grace, she became grotesque.

Nineteen years after entering the convent and three years before her death, Isabel was assigned a secretary to whom she was asked to dictate her exemplary life for the benefit of nuns to come. She opposed the idea, feeling herself unworthy of such an exalted task. But she changed her mind when God sent word that he wanted her to do it.

> Pero movida por él mismo, como he declarado aquí, y mandada, ya consejada de mis Confesores; no una, sino muchas veces me he venido a rendir a hacer lo que no pensé. . . . en largos años que tengo, he tenido muchos, de los cuales unos han sido en pró, y otros en contra, pero los mas me han mandado que lo haga

12. Louise Collis, *Memoirs of a Medieval Woman: The Life and Times of Margery Kempe* (New York: Thomas Y. Crowell, 1967).

para gloria, y honra de Dios nuestro Señor, que no se puede perder nada en hacerlo, a mi me parece que estoy perdiendo aquí tiempo por cuanto tengo ocupada una hermana, que está haciendo lo que yo había de hacer, y por no saber leer, ni escribir, mi Confesor se lo ha mandado a ella, dáme escrúpulo, por cuanto tiene buenas manos de labor, y está el Convento pobrísimo. . . . (p. 9)

But moved by God himself, as I have declared, and ordered and advised by my Confessors, not once, but many times, I have finally agreed to do what I didn't think I would. . . . In my long years I have had many [confessors] some of whom have been in favor and some against, but most have ordered me to do it for the glory and honor of the Lord our God, since nothing can be lost in doing it. But I feel I am wasting time because I am occupying a sister in doing what of rights I should be doing. Because I don't know how to read or write my Confessor has assigned her the task. It worries me, especially because she has good hands for sewing and this Convent is very poor. . . .

While dictating, she became conscious of form, making references to the manner in which she was speaking and recording, commenting about reiterations—"como ya tengo dicho" (p. 160) (as I have already said)—about breaks in time sequence, admitting feelings of insufficiency, revealing plans of the telling. Many formal elements of the narrative place it in the Teresaian modality: they are direct and immediate, popular and oral in nature. Repetitions become formulas for the framework of the telling:

"Estando un día" (pp. 63, 181) (One time)
"Díjome el Señor" (pp. 83, 90, 103) (The Lord says/said to me)
"Otra vez" (pp. 74, 84) (On another occasion)
"Volviendo a" (pp. 58, 87, 189) (Going back to [a story, a time])
"Dejando esto aquí" (p. 61) (Leaving this aside).

For openings of episodes:

"También me sucedía ver" (p. 102) (I also used to see)
"Estando un día" (pp. 9, 131, 157) (One day when I was)

For praises to the Lord:

"Sea Dios alabado" (pp. 48, 73) (May God be praised)
"Cristo bien nuestro" (pp. 49, 63) (Christ our good)

> "Hízome su Divina Magistad otra grandísima merced" (pp. 76, 78) (God did me the great favor)

and so on. Characteristic of the style is the frequent use of contrast and comparison, of explication and apostrophe, of indirect dialogue, of repetitive underscoring, and of augmentatives and diminutives.[13]

Echoing the tradition of the epics and ballads, tenses are combined fluidly; imperfect, preterite, and present appear in the same or adjoining phrases, adding freshness and immediacy as well as a timeless, poetic quality, as can be noticed in the passages cited in these pages. Madre Isabel knows how many sheets have been filled, the space of time allotted, the deadlines:

> Hasta aquí he podido llegar, porque se me ha acabado ya la obediencia, y a mi Prelada Isabel de Santa Mónica el oficio, y no puedo pasar a mas; ha llegado a número de ciento y tres pliegos. . . . (p. 397)

> This is as far as I've been able to come, it is the end of my assigned time and of my Superior Isabel de Santa Monica's time in office, and I cannot go beyond; it comes to one hundred and three sheets. . . .

Her relationship with her secretary who, being dowered, was of higher rank, was a complex one. Inés del Santísimo Sacramento, a reader of lives of saints, had early developed admiration for Madre Isabel and welcomed the opportunity to serve her. The sessions took place in secret so as not to disturb the convent routines or cause a stir and, therefore, were held late at night. When Madre Inés was finished with her daily chores, she would send a mental message to which Madre Isabel would respond, appearing at her cell. Deep bonds of affection developed between them. On occasion Madre Isabel even speaks in the first person plural:

> Ya he dicho que veo de ordinario una hermosa luz, cuando estamos escribiendo. . . . que no sé yo que haya escrito pliego ninguno, en que no se haya recibido esta merced del Señor. . . . (p. 397)

> I have already mentioned that ordinarily when we are writing I see a beautiful light. . . . Hardly a sheet has been written without this gift from the Lord. . . .

---

13. Intensification is achieved through reiteration of some of the same common words employed by Saint Teresa ("tornar," "tan," "gran," "tanto," "gran-

From the beginning Madre Isabel had taken on the assignment as a wifely duty. She reasons: if the king goes after a shepherdess and asks her hand in marriage, is it just for her to refuse? And it is the wife's duty to give in to the husband's desires. She also hears the Lord saying to her:

> Conmigo eres, pregonera de mis grandezas
>
> You are with me, a town crier of my magnificence.

And she adds:

> También me llamó trompeta, y campana. (p. 9)
>
> He also called me his trumpet and his carillon.

Madre Isabel was almost sixty-five when she began dictating to Inés del Santísimo Sacramento the book that was not to be published until almost thirty years after her death in 1675. Although committed to paper, it remains essentially an oral history. With her proverbs and popular wisdom, her faith in the reality of her imaginings, and her portrayal of the various points of view of her family, her neighbors, and of ecclesiastics in disagreement with each other, Mother Isabel suggests a Cervantine perspectivism[14] that is astonishing in view of the limits of her own experience.

The Life and Work of a Well-Known Poet

Sor Juana Inés de la Cruz, the great Mexican poet, playwright, and intellectual, last of the great seventeenth-century Hispanic Baroque writers, was born Juana Inés Ramírez y Asbaje, in the colony then called New Spain. She was known as a *gongorista*, after the Spanish mannerist poet, Góngora. Quevedo, Gracián, and Calderón were her contemporaries.

Juana Ramírez lived at the hub of New Spain's vice regal society, the most splendid and complex of the Spanish colonial empire. Five vice regal regimes succeeded each other during her lifetime. By education, she belongs to medieval scholasticism and Renaissance humanism; in her poetic and dramatic output to the Baroque or mannerist period; in her intellectual orientation to the dawning of the Age of

---

dísimo/a"). See Randolph Pope, *La autobiografía española hasta Torres Villarroel* (Bern: Herbert Land, 1974), pp. 62, 68–71.

14. The concept is José Ortega y Gasset's; see his *Meditaciones del Quijote* (Madrid: Revista de Occidente, 1957); English translation by Evelyn Rugg and Diego Marín, *Meditations on Quixote* (New York: W. W. Norton, 1961).

Reason. But Sor Juana cannot be categorized because her genius and her womanhood prevented her from becoming part of a particular school or university tradition; the educational isolation which she at times lamented kept her in touch with herself.

Sor Juana, like most geniuses, was ahead of her time. Exceptionality, however, is treated differently in men than in women. What I want to suggest is not that we forget that Sor Juana was a woman but that we must reverse the manner in which we respond to that fact. Because Sor Juana Inés is one of the only two women who figure consistently and universally in the annals of Hispanic literary history before the nineteenth century, her position has an importance for women that it does not have for men.

The lives of Sor Juana and Saint Teresa are exceptions that prove the oppressive rule. Besides extraordinary talent and production, it took unusual circumstances and potent sources of support for both St. Teresa and Sor Juana to prevail. Could they have been the only women of such talent? Were they not perhaps the only ones with the cluster of requirements needed to break through the barriers against the success of women in the public world? Saint Teresa had the support of her mystical union with God, and of some prestigious earthly beings as well. Sor Juana was called by her contemporaries "the Tenth Muse,"[15] an epithet perpetuated by later scholars who have kept her ensconced on a literary pedestal.

Nancy Miller, in an essay on women's autobiography in France, advances one hypothesis in this regard. Observing that maleness and humanity are conflated by both male authors and most critic-consumers of autobiography, she introduces the notion of a gender-bound reading: "I would propose . . . a practice of the text that would recognize the status of the reader as differentiated subject; a reading subject named by gender and committed in a dialectics of identification to deciphering the inscription of a female subject."[16] Miller's proposed method will be kept in mind in this section.

15. Such epithets were common in the seventeenth century. Applied to Sor Juana, it became part of the title of the first edition of her poems in Spain: *Inundación castálida de la única poetisa, musa dézima: Sor Juana Inés de la Cruz* (Madrid: Juan García Infanzón, 1689). The sexist nature of the carryover into modern times of such epithets is what concerns us here.

16. Nancy K. Miller, "Women's Autobiography in France: For a Dialectics of Identification," in *Women and Language in Literature and Society*, ed. S. Connell-Ginet, R. Borker, and N. Furman (New York: Praeger, 1980), p. 267.

Women—necessarily influenced by patriarchal culture and scholarship, but nevertheless, as women, reading differently—have contributed significantly to studies of Sor Juana. In bibliographies one of course finds many fewer works by women, and in the most widely distributed and popular anthologies even fewer.[17] Well-trained and first-rate or first-rated women critics are rare; the paternalistic and condescending underpinnings of university and publishing systems do little to encourage a change.

And yet women played an essential role in publicizing Sor Juana's work both during and after her lifetime. The marquise of Mancera, who doted on her, was a major affective support—if indeed a distraction—first in the court and later in the convent. She rescued Sor Juana from her first overly rigorous convent and visited her regularly in the second. A few years after the marquise's death, the countess of Paredes, wife of the new vice regent, occupied her place in Sor Juana's affections. A woman of culture who wrote poetry herself, she took Sor Juana's poems and plays to Spain to have them published. She shares responsibility for the solid grounding of Sor Juana's reputation in Spain and the colonies. Along with other figures of seventeenth-century literature, Sor Juana's fame waned in the eighteenth and nineteenth centuries.

Serrano y Sanz doesn't even mention the *Respuesta a Sor Filotea de la Cruz* (Reply to Sister Filotea de la Cruz) (1691) in summarizing Sor Juana's life and work in his bio-bibliography of women writers.[18] Pedro Henríquez Ureña and Manuel Toussaint began this century's rediscovery. And a North American scholar, Dorothy Schons (1925), pioneered in finding documents, amplifying bibliography, investigating dates, and placing Sor Juana in her period. Her slim volumes and articles remain difficult to locate. Two other North American women

---

17. Of the relatively widely distributed popular paperback anthologies and presentations for students, Rivers lists 5 women among 45 entries; Xirau, 6 of 34; Veiravé, 1 of 24; Flynn, 3 of 23; and Monterde, 4 of 31. In Dorothy Schons's 1925 bibliography there are among "Articles and Studies" two that are anonymous, which must always be suspected, one with initials only, and 4 women's names out of 55. Pfandl (for 1873–1935) lists 3 women out of 35, and de la Maza (for 1936–1963) lists 31 of 213 (plus 3 that are doubtful). Anita Arroyo's bibliography of 179 entries contains 36 by women, 7 or so doubtful, and 2 anonymous. Of the authors participating in homages to Sor Juana, the one published in Mexico in 1951 presented no women critics among eleven authors; the one published in Colombia represented none among four.

18. Serrano y Sanz, *Apuntes*, I, 289–97.

scholars, Lota Spell (1947) and E. J. Gates (1939), also contributed to the research. Several Spanish and Spanish-American women scholars brought attention to Sor Juana.[19]

If one accepts the concept of gender-linked reading, there follows an understanding of the special sense of identification, sympathy, and consequently, the recognition evident in the work of women who have approached the work of Sor Juana. For example, Anita Arroyo responds, with a conviction based on her own female experience, to the sources of Sor Juana's torment and passion. Respecting Sor Juana's reticence, she argues that the absence of total confession does not detract from the essential meanings of Sor Juana's work. Arroyo also reviews briefly the contributions of women in a chapter on Sor Juana and the literary critics. Mirta Aguirre's short but excellent book, *Del encausto a la sangre: Sor Juana Inés de la Cruz* (From Imperial Red Ink to Blood), and Rachel Phillips's short essay "Sor Juana: Dream and Silence"[20] cut through mystifications and convolutions in tracing the probable chain of events—and Sor Juana's reaction to them—which led to her silence and finally her death. As women, they respond more to the seriousness and less to the "charm" of her work.

Like Saint Teresa and Madre Isabel, Sor Juana displayed self-effacement and humility, on the one hand, and, on the other, competitiveness, ambition, and a quality that some would call arrogance, others self-assertion and confidence. In speaking of her trials and tribulations, she compares herself to Saint Peter, Saint Jerome, and to Christ himself. She emphasizes her dedication to her chosen vocation of study and learning; natural ability was complemented by constant hard work and frequently by contention with the material being studied or created as well as with surrounding circumstances.

---

19. Dorothy Schons's results are published as *Some Bibliographical Notes on Sor Juana Inés de la Cruz* (Austin: University of Texas Bulletin no. 2526, 1925); and "Some Obscure Points in the Life of Sor Juana Inés de la Cruz," *Modern Philology*, 24(2) (November 1926): 141–62. The work of Lota Spell and E. J. Gates is cited in Rivers, *Antología* (Madrid: Anaya, 1965), pp. 12, 15. From the review and citations given by Arroyo (*Razón y pasión*, pp. 163–66), I gather that a significant interpretation of Sor Juana and the Baroque—that Arroyo does not entirely agree with—was made by Jesusa Alfau de Solalinde, "El barroco en la vida de Sor Juana," *Humanidades* (Faculty of Philosophy and Letters of the University of Mexico) 1 (1943); I have not been able to locate this periodical.

20. Mirta Aguirre, *Del encausto a la sangre: Sor Juana Inés de la Cruz* (Havana: Casa de las Américas, 1975); Rachel Phillips, "Sor Juana: Dream and Silence," *Aphra*, 3(1) (Winter 1971–1972): 30–40.

Sor Juana transcended the demands of gender and the limitations of what are to this day called in Hispanic countries "the tasks proper to her sex" because of an unusual combination of factors, among them her having been a child prodigy. Already too strong in intellectual development at the age when precocity in women is directly or subtly stifled, her life did not take the course usual for a woman of her class. It was her own idea in 1655, at the age of seven, to ask her mother to dress her in men's clothing and send her to the university in Mexico:

> Teniendo yo después como seis o siete años, y sabiendo ya leer y escribir, con todas las otras habilidades de labores y costuras que deprenden las mujeres, oí decir que había Universidad y Escuelas en que se estudiaban las ciencias, en Méjico; y apenas lo oí cuando empecé a matar a mi madre con instantes e importunos ruegos sobre que, mudándome el traje, me enviase a Méjico, en casa de unos deudos que tenía, para estudiar y cursar la Universidad. (IV, 445–46; p. 78)

> When I was about six or seven, having already learned to read and write, along with other skills such as embroidery and dressmaking which were considered appropriate for women, I heard that in Mexico City there was a university and schools where one could learn science. As soon as I heard that, I began to torture my mother with insistent and annoying pleas that she change my clothes and send me to live with relatives of hers in Mexico City so I could study at the university.

She had devoured the books in her maternal grandfather's library near the provincial town of Amecameca; they had provided her with an unsystematic but thorough education. All the autobiographical anecdotes and episodes offered by Sor Juana in the *Respuesta* refer to her precocity, her self-discipline, and her drive: in sum, to her education. She laments the lack of teachers and of the stimulation of student peers, and she underscores the sense of loneliness that hindered her intellectual development. When, in 1665, at the age of seventeen, she became a lady-in-waiting at the court of the Marquises of Mancera, despite the fact that she was nurtured by a close and loving relationship with them, the court treated her as a freak. One event organized by the viceroys recalls the tests found in old fairy tales: there gathered at the palace a group of the most learned men to examine Juana in their respective disciplines. She astonished them all. She was paraded, shown off, and expected to produce original poems and plays for all occasions. This episode was not recorded in the *Respuesta* but in the short essay of her first biographer, Diego Calleja, whom later commentators followed.[21] Sor Juana's own reactions passed into her drama and verse.

Sor Juana's switch from court to convent, which occurred when she was nineteen, was abrupt and remains partially unexplained. Nevertheless, in the *Respuesta* she says clearly:

> Para la total negación que tenía al matrimonio, era lo menos desproporcionado y lo más decente que podía elegir. (IV, 446; p. 78)
>
> Given my complete opposition to the idea of marriage, it was the least shocking and most decent thing I could have chosen.

Her choice to stay in the world or to enter the convent she saw as fraught with difficulties for her main purpose in life, "de querer vivir sola; de no querer tener ocupación obligatoria que embarazase la libertad de mi estudio . . . el sosegado silencio de mis libros" (IV, 446; p. 79) (to live alone, to avoid any obligation which might disturb my freedom to study, the tranquil silence of my books). She chose religious life not because it was her true vocation but because it seemed the only way of attaining that purpose.

But Sor Juana's abode in the cloister was no ascetic cell; on the contrary, it came to be more like a salon. She was visited by people at the upper levels of the Church, the vice regal family, scholars, writers, and travelers from abroad. According to Padre Calleja, her private library held four thousand volumes.[22] She collected musical and scientific instruments. She became poet laureate, continuing to produce occasional poetry for lovers of the court, for birthdays, anniversaries, and deaths, and sacred poetry and plays for the celebrations of religious holidays at the great cathedrals of Mexico.

Writing played a major role in Sor Juana's life from her teens until her early forties when, shortly after composing the *Respuesta a Sor Filotea*, she signed away in blood—literally—her earthly pursuits and, in effect, her life. At this time, tremendous external economic and political crisis coincided with her own experience of censorship, persecution, isolation, and disillusionment. For more than twenty years she had flourished under difficult circumstances, in which, nevertheless, the balance had been weighted toward recognition and support of her work.

---

21. Diego Calleja, "Aprobación del Reverendíssimo Padre Diego Calleja, de la Compañía de Jesús" in Sor Juana Inés de la Cruz, *Fama y obras posthumas del Fénix de México* (Madrid: Antonio G. de Reyes, 1714), unpaginated.

22. Dorothy Schons suggests four hundred volumes; see O.C. , I, lxi.

Sor Juana's tremendous drive helped her to cope with practical impediments and with her own emotional sensitivities. Convent routines and duties were demanding. And when there were moments for leisure, her sisters and the servants would often enlist her aid or attention, wishing mediation of quarrels, advice, conversation. Her description of her response to such demands is often quoted. She would give herself a period of ten days or so of solitude. Then her conscience would begin to prod her for neglecting her sisters, and she would put aside her own work and take up her social duties. A tone of muffled resentment characterizes her references to incursions on her time. One must recognize, on the other hand, the advantages that her privileged position offered her. Although it is perhaps true, as Sor Juana humorously claims, that Aristotle would have been a greater philosopher had he cooked, it is also certain that had *she* had to do more cooking—or sewing, or cleaning, or washing or ironing—she would not have produced the body of writing that she did.

In the *Respuesta*, Sor Juana describes her facility for writing as a double-edged gift. It encroached upon time she would have preferred to spend studying, and it provoked envy and resentment on the part of people of lesser talent. Reprimanded for her profane verse and rebuked for the theological trespass, as we shall see, she had good reason to describe herself as a writer only under duress.[23] Although she may have considered some of the assignments as encumbrances, she accomplished most of what she did with intensity and polish. She felt sensitive pride in being one of the two (with Carlos de Sigüenza y Góngora) official writers of the court.

Several studies have noted Sor Juana's hypersensitivity—how she became enraged by the attacks of enemies, upset by the criticism of friends, vain, exhibitionistic, and grudge-bearing, and sensitive to a fault.[24] But could it have been otherwise when she had been treated as an oddity from the beginning of her solitary childhood? In a sense her status as a "rare bird" gave her a perch for many years, though this same status was later to make her vulnerable to the attacks of those who resented her independence, her fame, and her exercise in scholastic discourse.

23. Dario Puccini, in his heavily footnoted study of Sor Juana, discusses this question and comes to a similar conclusion. See his *Sor Juana Inés de la Cruz: Studio d'una personalità del Barocco messicano* (Roma: Edizioni dell'Ateneo, 1967), pp. 91–96.

24. See Francisco de la Maza, "Sor Juana y Don Carlos: Explicación de dos sonetos hasta ahora confusos," *Cuadernos Americanos* 145 (2) (March–April 1966): 190–204.

The ethical, philosophical, literary, and feminist implications of Sor Juana's autobiographical essay and of her entire legacy have yet to be fully explored or disseminated. Why they have not been is in part a feminist question since it is related to the fact that it was not until three hundred years after her birth that her *Obras completas*—plays, poetry, and prose—were gathered together and published.[25] Her secular theater includes two comedies, two one-act intermezzos (*sainetes*), fourteen dramatic poems (*loas*), and one soiree (*sarao*). The longest speech in *Los empeños de una casa* (The Trials of a [Noble] House) is the female protagonist's narrative of her life, in which Sor Juana put much of herself—experience, feelings, reactions—telling of the zeal with which she studied and learned, the spread of her fame, and of a disappointment in love (IV, 36–43). For the Church she wrote three sacramental plays (*autos sacramentales*), three dramatic preludes (*loas*) to these plays, and another *loa* in praise of the Immaculate Conception (III, 3–278). *El Divino Narciso* (The Divine Narcissus), one of the sacramental plays, and the *loa* written to precede it are considered her dramatic masterpieces. For Church celebrations she also wrote *villancicos*, sets of poems to be combined with prayers and masses, employing all the metric forms popular at the time. In the *villancicos* to Santa Catarina, Sor Juana identifies with this saint renowned for her wisdom:

> De una Mujer se convencen
> todos los Sabios de Egipto,
> para prueba de que el sexo
> no es esencia en lo entendido. (II, 171)
>
> By a Woman all the Sages
> of Egypt are convinced,
> as proof that one's sex
> is not the essence of the mind.

Among these *villancicos* are poems in Nahuatl and Nahuatl and Spanish and several imitating the Spanish of the blacks, in which she expressed their resentment, resistance, and the urge for freedom.[26] The

---

25. For existing translations of Sor Juana, see: Margery Resnick and Isabelle de Cortivron, eds., *Women Writers in Translation: An Annotated Bibliography* (New York: Garland Press, 1981).

26. Mirta Aguirre (*Del encausto a la sangre*), mentioning the fact that Sor Juana had a slave among her servants, places the poems in a nonromanticized focus: "They are not insurrectional poems. . . . Sor Juana is not to be taken as an abolitionist. But slavery hurts her; one feels her sympathy . . ." (p. 84).

fifty love poems have been debated and dissected for their confessional meanings. The discussions sometimes seem to obscure the fact that Sor Juana wrote some of the most beautiful love poems in the Spanish language, poems characterized by uncanny insight into human psychology.

Sor Juana's most famous poem is the "Sátira filosófica" (Philosophical Satire), which begins, "Hombres necios, que acusáis" (I, 228–29) (Foolish men, who accuse). School children memorize it, but in the colleges it is not often enough seen in perspective as the culmination and refinement of a theme used and abused for several centuries, a masterful formal achievement, that sums up one of the debates between misogynists and philogynists so popular in that period. Sor Juana's protest against sexual abuse and her humor in showing that women are damned if they do and damned if they don't added a vibrancy to the poetic theme.[27] In Sor Juana's longest and perhaps her own favorite poem, "Primero sueño" (I, 335–59) (The First Dream), she casts herself as Phaëthon, who dared to steer his carriage toward the sun. Moving through the philosophical knowledge of her day, as she seeks to unravel the nature of the universe and of thought, she describes the stages of her own intellectual development, its difficulties, and her final sense of failure.[28] Courtly poems and philosophical, historical, and mythological sonnets complete Sor Juana's production in verse.

As is the case with most writers, there is autobiographical material throughout Sor Juana's work. In addition to Leonor's speech in *Los empeños de una casa*, the *villancicos* to Santa Catarina cited above, and the abstract yet significant "Primero sueño" there is the *romance*,

---

27. In Pilar de Oñate, *El feminismo en la literatura española* (Madrid: Espasa-Calpe, 1935), I found the texts of earlier rather mediocre poems on the same subject. Méndez Plancarte (*O.C.*, I, 488–92) also documented some poetic precursors and subsequent refutations in the notes to the poem.

28. Vicente Gaos, the Mexican philosopher, considers this poem in a class by itself, unequaled in the poetry of intellectual disillusionment; see his "El sueño de un sueño," *Historia de México*, 10(37) (July–August 1960): 70–71. Rachel Phillips ("Dream and Silence"), following Octavio Paz and agreeing with his estimation of it as one of the most complex poems in the Spanish language, gives a fine summation and claims that it "bears witness to human dignity" (p. 40). Alfonso Reyes called it, with the *Respuesta*, the front and back of the same fabric; see his *Letras de la Nueva España* in his *Obras completas*, vol. 12 (Mexico: Fondo de Cultura Económica, 1960), p. 371; English translation by Harriet de Onís in Alfonso Reyes, *The Position of America* (New York: Knopf, 1950), p. 126.

"Señor: para responderos" (Sir, in response to you), in which Sor Juana answers "un caballero del Perú" (I, 136–39) (a gentleman from Peru) who had sent her verses suggesting that she turn into a man. Her rebuke seems relevant to modern ears accustomed to discussions of issues of masculinity and femininity and the search for androgyny:

> porque acá Sálmacis falta,
> en cuyos cristales dicen
> que hay no sé qué virtud de
> dar alientos varoniles.
> Yo no entiendo de esas cosas;
> sólo sé que aquí me vine
> porque, si es que soy mujer,
> ninguno lo verifique.
> Y también sé que, en latín,
> sólo a las casadas dicen
> *uxor*, o mujer, y que
> es común de dos lo Virgen.
> Con que a mí no es bien mirado
> que como a mujer me miren,
> pues no soy mujer que a alguno
> de mujer pueda servirle;
> y sólo sé que mi cuerpo,
> sin que a uno u otro se incline,
> es nuestro, o abstracto, cuanto
> sólo el Alma deposite. (I, 138)

> For Salmacis is not to be found here
> in whose crystal ball they say
> there is I know not what power to
> endow one with manly spirit.
>
> I am not acquainted with such things:
> I know only that I came here
> so that, if indeed I am a woman
> no one might be led to prove it.
>
> And I also know that in Latin
> only married women are called
> *uxor*, or woman, and that
> virginity is expected of both.
>
> So that it is not considered correct
> that I be seen as a woman
> for I am not a woman
> who serves as anyone's woman;

and I know only that my body
without favoring one or another,
is neutral, or abstract, since
it houses only the Soul. . . .

Woman and wife are used synonymously in Spanish, which allows for the word play in the fourth stanza above. The most exaggerated analysis of these verses is to be found in Pfandl, who sees in them the declaration of her defective nature and her "psychic tragedy."[29]

Sor Juana's *Respuesta a Sor Filotea* is the major and most direct source of her autobiographical writing, and it is an essential document of seventeenth-century feminism.[30] As I indicated earlier, there exists an abundance of still unstudied autobiographical documents by women of this period; some may eventually prove exceptional, though it is doubtful that any will be comparable with Sor Juana's, which runs counter to the Counter-Reformation. No "holy ignorance" for her. The implication of all her writing is that she saw life as a loving labor in pursuit of knowledge. In the introduction to the second volume of her poems and plays, and again in the *Respuesta*, she uses a quotation from Saint Jerome that could stand as the epigraph to her work and as the epitaph on her tomb:

> Quid ibi laboris insumpserim, quid sustinuerim difficultatis, quoties desperaverim, quotiesque cessaverim et contentione discendi rursus inceperim; testis est conscientia. (IV, 451; p. 84)

> Of the effort I made, of the difficulties I suffered through, of how many times I despaired, and how many others I gave up and started again in my determination to learn, my conscience is the witness.

It is unlikely that Sor Juana would have written this autobiographical essay had she not been stunned by the reprimand and threat of damnation contained in the letter to which it was the reply. The year before, impressed by her theological reasoning in conversation, Don

---

29. Pfandl, *La décima musa de México*, pp. 188–89.

30. Puccini (*Studio d'una personalità*) calls Sor Juana's feminism premature (p. 148). Salceda calls it "the Magna Carta of intellectual freedom of the women of America" (*O.C.*, IV, xliii). Arroyo (*Razón y pasión*) calls it the "first manifesto of women's spiritual liberation" (p. 126). Octavio Paz claims it is "one of the most important documents in the history of Spanish culture and in that of the intellectual emancipation of women," in *Anthology of Mexican Poetry*, trans. Samuel Beckett, compiled by O. Paz, preface C. M. Bowra (London: Thames & Hudson, 1958), p. 204.

Manuel Fernández de Santa Cruz, bishop of Puebla, asked her to record for him her disagreement with a sermon written in 1650 by a famous but controversial Portuguese Jesuit, Antonio Vieyra. Without consulting her, the bishop had the essay printed as the *Carta Atenagórica* (Athenagoric Letter) (1690).[31] Don Manuel had long been one of Sor Juana's powerful friends, but he was involved in the internecine ecclesiastical warfare going on at the time. It is not clear whether or not he was innocent and acting alone in having Sor Juana's essay published. If her profane work had caused a stir (1689), the publication of her religious text caused her ultimate silence.[32]

Through an ironic twist of fate, her theological refutation came to be used as an "attack" on the liberal wing of the Jesuits and led to the marshaling of forces against Sor Juana that should have been in her favor. At the time of this crisis in her life, Sor Juana's relationship with members of the vice regal and Church establishment had changed. The vice regents who had befriended and supported her had died or returned to Spain. Further, the reaction set off by the publication of her poems in Spain and of her theological disputation in New Spain estranged her from her nearly life-long confessor, Antonio Nuñez de Miranda.

With the *Carta Atenagórica*, the bishop also published a preliminary letter to Sor Juana, criticizing her dedication to profane subjects, some of the arguments against Vieyra, and expressing worry about her salvation. He signed it with the pseudonym Sor Filotea.

If anything was typical of the seventeenth century it was that almost nothing was taken—or expressed—at face value. Neither life nor let-

---

31. The *Athenagoric Letter* (or *Letter Worthy of Athena*), then, was her refutation of Vieyra's "Maundy Thursday Sermon." (It was subsequently printed as *Crisis sobre un sermón*; see O.C., IV, 631–32). One of his main theses is that God does human beings the great favor of putting the need to love one another above the need to love Him. In her refutation, Sor Juana's primary claim is that the greatest proof of God's favor is to go against His own nature, to refrain from doing us good, in order that we may learn. Although there is not the space here to discuss the subject further, it may interest readers in comparative literature and women's studies to know that the concept of God as a cause of pain (as well as of pleasure) and of the usefulness for learning of passing through pain and suffering was affirmed in a letter of 1693, written by the first English feminist, Mary Astell (1666–1731). It will be reprinted in a forthcoming book by the woman who has rediscovered her, Ruth Perry, of M.I.T. Letters between John Norris and Mary Astell were published in London in 1695.

32. See Puccini, *Studio d'una personalità*, pp. 34–49; Arroyo, *Razón y pasión*, Part 1, Chap. 3; Aguirre, *Del encausto a la sangre*, pp. 42–50.

ters were approached simply and directly in that Baroque time. It is surprising that so many critics have understood both the letter from Sor Filotea and the answer to it as generous and almost ingenuous. But in view of attitudes about women, it is not surprising.[33] Smart women were seen as precocious children (*monjita, damita*). Women who wrote autobiographies were supposed to be making total confessions. Scholars such as Salceda, Cossio, Castro Leal, and Rivers claim that the ostensible reprimand for not applying her intelligence more to sacred and less to profane subject matter was really a friendly way of presenting Sor Juana with the opportunity of defending herself and of discoursing at length on her favorite subjects. In essence, it seems to have presented her with the need to make what she knew was a vain attempt at self-defense: it spurred her to write her intellectual and spiritual testament. The weight of Counter-Reformation ideology and of the personally devastating criticism she was trying to contest proved an overwhelming condemnation and turned Sor Juana ultimately to seek death and salvation in the manner eternally asked of women—self-sacrifice for the sick and dying. Within three months of receiving Sor Filotea's letter, she had replied with what she called a simple "narración de mi inclinación" (IV, 445; p. 78) (narrative regarding my inclination to letters), which is a not-so-simple *apologia pro vita sua*.

A demonstration of her mental virtuosity, a portrait of the origins and development of her intellectual passion and of the suffering it caused her, a defense of the education and intellectual life of women, the *Respuesta* is also a protest against ecclesiastic—and all kinds of—stupidity and repression.

At one point she was prohibited from reading, a prohibition which she treats with light and condescending humor:

> Una prelada muy santa y muy cándida que creyó que el estudio era cosa de Inquisición . . . me mandó que no estudiase. Yo la obedecí (unos tres meses que duró el poder ella mandar) en cuanto a no tomar libro, que en cuanto a no estudiar absolutamente, como no cae debajo de mi potestad, no lo pude hacer, porque aunque no estudiaba en los libros, estudiaba en todas las cosas que Dios crió, sirviéndome ellas de letras, y de libro toda esta máquina universal. (IV, 458; p. 90)

33. See Margaret Adams, "The Compassion Trip," and other essays in *Woman in Sexist Society: Studies in Power and Powerlessness*, ed. Vivian Gornick and Barbara K. Moran (New York: Basic Books, 1971); Elise Boulding, *The Underside of History: A View of Women Through Time* (Boulder, Colo.: Westview Press, 1976); *Becoming Visible: Women in European History*, ed. Renate Bridenthal and Claudia Koonz (New York: Houghton Mifflin, 1977).

> A religious but simple-minded mother superior who thought that study was a matter for the Inquisition . . . ordered me not to study. I obeyed her (for the three months that she lasted in office) as far as not taking a book in hand. But as far as absolutely not studying, it wasn't in my power, I couldn't do it. For even though I wasn't studying in books, I studied in God's works, taking *them* as letters and the whole Creation as my book.

More is here than meets the eye. By ridiculing the "simple-minded" from a lofty position, Sor Juana is urging her reader to abjure the common attitudes and practices of the times. Would even a mother superior make such a prohibition without consulting her confessor? Was she the only one who thought that study was a matter for the Inquisition? Behind the prohibition stood surely confessor and other Church authorities who were gradually restricting her freedom.

The *Respuesta*'s full beauty and meaning become apparent only after more than one reading. It is full of Latin quotations (in most editions they are translated in footnotes). There is tight scholastic logic, classical aphorism, Renaissance harmonic play, and in a few instances familiar and popular expressions. Anger, defiance, challenge, humility, tenderness, and despair alternate as Sor Juana describes her childhood struggles to educate herself. As she affirms her love of study above all else, she defends the right of women to learn and to exercise the freedom to think and reflect and opine. She defends her right to refute the theological arguments of the famous Jesuit and to put forth her own. And she even speaks belligerently:

> ¿Llevar una opinión contraria de Vieyra fue en mi atrevimiento? . . . Mi entendimiento tal cual ¿no es tan libre como el suyo, pues viene de un solar? (IV, 468; p. 101)
>
> It was bold of me to oppose Vieyra? . . . My mind is not as free as his, though it derives from the same Source?

Time and again she refers to the inalienable freedom of the mind.

The most important source of support for her defense was one she herself had marshaled to her side in the course of a lifetime of reading: a long line of "tantas y tan insignes mujeres" (IV, 460–61; p. 93) (learned and powerful women of the past). For she buttresses her self-defense with more than forty-two examples of her female predecessors—names drawn from classical, mythological, biblical, and contemporary sources.[34] This company assured her that, despite the odds, she

34. Some of the learned and powerful women she mentions are the mother of John the Baptist, Saint Paula, Saint Teresa, Deborah, the Queen of Sheba,

had a right to move in the world as she did, to follow her own bent.

The *Respuesta* itself is too rich and complex to be discussed in full here. But the essence of Sor Juana's convictions is present in the Latin quotations she employed in the essay. I have abstracted and examined seventy-eight such citations. Some must have occurred to her as she wrote; others she must have searched for in her effort to build her defense, which is also a challenge and a veiled announcement of her ultimate resolution. Seen thus, isolated, the quotations offer a sharp-focused and intensified version of the essay as a whole. They are not, as some critics have claimed, superfluous. The first quotation refers to the effect of *beneficio* ("favor"), "*Minorem spei* [*sic*], *maiorem benefacti* [*sic*] *gloriam pereunt* [*sic*]" (IV, 646; p. 73)[35] (Hopes produce less, favors produce more glory). The sentence immediately following is "In such a way that they silence the favored." By the last citation of the essay, she has come full circle back to the same concept. The implication is clear: she has been betrayed. The "favor" was the publication—with the flattering title (Athenagoric)—of ideas that she had expressed orally and in private and then upon request had written down, for private consumption only. Of those quotations she selects, both the first, from Quintilian, and the last, from Seneca, match the reference to the classically titled publication.

As is common in the work of the other great Baroque masters, there are frequently double edges and multiple meanings in the allusions, citations, and metaphors she employs. The first citation shows Sor Juana's understanding of her own and women's (let that stand for human) psychology. Real support does often give better results than promises. But in this case, of course, the support was a cruelty and an outrage. Lest the intent of the quotation be obscured by the most obvious meaning, she repeats it in the final statement—a bitter, regretful state-

---

Abigail, Esther, Rahab, Anna, the Sibyls, Minerva, Argentaria, Tiresias, Zenobia, Arete, Nicostrata, Aspasia Milesia, Hispasia, Leoncia, Jucia, Corina, Cornelia, Catherine, Gertrude, Paula Blesila, Eustoquio, Fabiola, Falconia, Queen Isabel, Christine Alexandra, the Duchess of Aveyro, the Countess of Villaumbrosa, Marcela, Pacatula, Leta, Bridgette, Salome, Mary the mother of Jacob, Sister Mary of Antigua, and Mary of Agreda. O.C., IV, 460 et passim; Rivers ed., p. 93.

35. Medievalist Barbara Grant and Latin scholar Ellen Quackenbos have pointed out to me three errors in the citation: (1) *spei* should read *spes*; (2) *benefacti* should read *benefacta*; and (3) *pereunt* should read *pariunt*. I have checked the 1700, 1714, and 1725 editions. The errors appear in all three and were, therefore, probably either errors of Sor Juana's or misreadings by the Spanish printers of the original ms. They passed uncorrected into the O.C.

ment of her fate: "*Turpe est beneficiis vinci*" (IV, 663; p. 107) (What a humiliation [shame] to be vanquished by favors).

Other citations refer to justice, judgment, trials, accusations, and secrecy. They build her case and reveal her awareness that not only is Sor Filotea a disguise for her friend the bishop of Puebla but that behind him stand her confessor and other less friendly and more powerful forces. Both friends and enemies are defeating her, the first more painfully than the second.

It is notable that the quotation "*mulieres in Ecclesia taceant*" (Women are to be silent in church) is repeated three times. "*Mulier in silentio discat*" (Women are to learn in silence) and the universalizing "*Audi, Israel, et tace*" (Listen, Israel, and be silent) appear after the first two repetitions and before the third, adding impact to the theme (IV, 656, 660; pp. 94, 98, 100). It also associates the silencing of women—and of herself—with that of the wise, the innocent, the dominated.

The subtlety of Sor Juana's reasoning is evidenced throughout. For instance, in the citation of Martial on the very subject of understanding (closely related, through Gracián, whose writing she knew well, to ingenuity): "Rare is the one who will recognize the superior understanding of another." She has been discussing envy as a motivation for enmity and destruction, and the citation has a triple meaning in the context in which it is placed. On the first plane, it is a dismayed protest at the envy aroused by her intellectual superiority. On a second plane, it relates to her vying against her own human limitations—like Icarus and Phaëthon in whom she projected herself in her great poem, "Primero sueño"—for cosmic understanding. On a third and less apparent plane I detect an association with her own less glorious personal struggles with the emotion of envy.

The misogynistic, anti-intellectual,[36] "turgid atmosphere of uneasy orthodoxy,"[37] of New Spain is exemplified both affectively and symbolically through the citations. Misunderstanding of the Scriptures and of the interpretations of the Scriptures are highlighted. Not lack of faith but envy and stupidity are most to blame. It is Sor Juana's conviction that the road to God is paved by the process of learning and that women of rights must also travel that road. Beauty, understanding, and tireless effort to gain knowledge are what is truly holy; the holy is persecuted. Throughout the citations, a vivid sense of resentment, ex-

---

36. See Manuel Durán, "El drama intelectual de Sor Juana y el anti-intelectualismo hispánico," *Cuadernos Americanos*, 21(4) (July–August 1963): 238–53.

37. Phillips, "Dream and Silence," p. 30.

pressed with irony and bitterness, culminates in the final, disconsolate submission. In the Latin references she explains, defends, and clarifies: her disagreement with Vieyra was not an attack on him, nor on the Jesuits. She cites both according to what she might think her judges want to hear and to what she wants and needs to say.

Four of the citations refer to versifying, and they are presented with a tone of overt impatience with those who consider verse making sinful. From Cassiodorus she takes the statement that verse had its origin in the Holy Scriptures. From Ovid she draws a statement to support her tendency to say everything in verse, and, going further, she reminds the reader that Saint Paul associated verse with being itself.

Five Latin quotations are given in addition to the three already mentioned to substantiate women's right to learn and teach. From Quintilian, a citation that seems to espouse the cornerstone of modern philosophies of education—intellectual freedom and education through knowledge of the self: "*Noscat quisque, et non tantum ex alienis praeceptis sed ex natura sua capiat consilium*" (IV, 661; p. 101) (Let all learn and not from the precepts of others but rather from the teachings of their own nature). Having followed this advice, she claims herself formally unprepared to do even what is allowed to women in Church tradition—to teach by writing. By publishing what she wrote, the bishop had transformed it into what she had not intended it to be.

The need for guidance and independence but also the fear and sorrow attendant upon the acquisition of knowledge/understanding are the themes of citations that build toward a parallel with the greatest sufferer—Christ. The citations convey her sense of martyrdom to the cause. From Saint Jerome comes the description of the road toward knowledge as a Calvary (see p. 174). Another citation, from Saint Cyprian, hints at the dangers of writing, while ostensibly continuing the explanation of the dearth of religious subject matter in her works: "*Gravi consideratione indigent quae scribimus*" (IV, 660; p. 101) (That which we write requires careful [serious] consideration). Great consideration is being given to this *Respuesta*.

Sor Juana fulfilled her purposes magnificently in this essay-letter: she excuses and explains her dedication to secular rather than religious letters. But she did much more. A superficially most ladylike defense exposes its author as a superb ironist. Claiming lack of adequate preparation, she displays her theological erudition; insisting on how little she knows, she shows how much less those who consider themselves sages know; apologizing for digressions, she creates cadenzas of wit; overly courteous, she unleashes her anger. The *Respuesta* can be and has been read also as a treatise on interdisciplinary study, a discussion of educational theory, a dissection of a society in which the excellent and the extraordinary were not only discouraged but not even tolerated. And yet in three hundred years we have not come so far. That no other Sor Juana has surfaced in the Hispanic literary world is surely in great part a result of the social circumstances that have kept women in "their place."

In spite of the fact that she was famous and her work well known, until quite recently the study of Sor Juana has been with few exceptions both limited and distorted.[38] Attitudes about morality, religion, and sexuality have charged Sor Juana criticism with bias and tendentiousness and have led to curious literary battles. Some critics have wanted to see her as a mystic, others as an atheist; some as a jilted or fallen woman, others as a tortured lesbian. For example, Ermilo Abreu Gómez calls Sor Juana's a viriloid nature;[39] Ezequiel Chávez describes her as a bird of paradise;[40] to Elias Rivers she is a "damita intelectual" (an intellectual little lady), a "monjita" (little nun), and "una ave tan rara" (such a strange bird).[41] Castro Leal calls her "un milagro" (a mir-

---

38. I do not wish to suggest that Sor Juana scholarship is lacking in value. I do, however, wish to point up and underline the limiting and distorting effects of sexist attitudes—which are both conscious and unconscious—inherent in the scholarship to which we are accustomed. See *Feminist Literary Criticism: Explorations in Theory*, ed. Josephine Donovan (Lexington: University of Kentucky Press, 1975). Octavio Paz, for instance, in a recently published article entitled "Juana Ramírez," *Vuelta* (Mexico), 2 (April 1978): 17–23, quotes, as lamentably still true, Dorothy Schons's comment, made in 1926: "Sor Juana's biography has yet to be written." He sets the record straight for a large reading public on the date of her birth, 1648, as established by Guillermo Ramírez España and Alberto G. Salceda, rather than 1651 as claimed by Calleja at the beginning of the eighteenth century and repeated in most subsequent studies. He reviews the history of her family and discusses the "illegitimacy" of Juana Ramírez, of her siblings, and of other relatives. But in summarizing and noting the virtues and failures of Pfandl's Freudian study of the poet, he seems to accept Freudian tenets himself without question. He points out that J. R. *had* to have become "masculinized" in order to accede to knowledge in a "masculine culture." A feminist examination of the question of intellect in a patriarchal culture would have a different focus. For example, why the label "masculine" for all outstanding intellectual products by women?

39. Ermilo Abreu Gómez, *Semblanza de Sor Juana* (Mexico: Ediciones Letras de México, 1938), p. 41.

40. Ezequiel Chávez, *Sor Juana Inés de la Cruz: Ensayo de psicología y de estimación del sentido de su obra* (Mexico: Editorial Porrúa, 1970), p. 36.

41. Sor Juana Inés de la Cruz, *Antología*, ed. Elias L. Rivers (Madrid: Anaya, 1965), p. 6.

acle) and "un ornamento de su siglo" (an ornament to her century)[42] and claims that her desire for knowledge did not detract from her femininity and charm. Pedro Salinas, affirming how advanced Sor Juana was for her time, envisions her as an American college girl riding a bike, wearing glasses, her hair blowing in the wind.[43] Américo Castro, pointing out her intellectual martyrdom, on the one hand, calls her "pobre monjita" (poor little nun), on the other.[44] (No one ever called Fray Luis de León or San Juan de la Cruz "poor little monk.") Sexist criteria continually obtrude in books and articles that otherwise contain much of value on Sor Juana's times, her life, and her work. Irving Leonard calls her "an ambivalent personality of feminine emotion and masculine intellectuality."[45] Pfandl, basing his Freudian analysis of her as a "classic psychoneurotic" on her urge to enjoy masculine intellectual pleasure, goes even further: "Her tragedy was this: that although she was born a woman, she should not have been."[46] These and similar labels and opinions, passed on from one critic to another and from critic to student or reader, have too long gone unquestioned.

Modification of sexist criteria can come only after the explosion of erroneous assumptions through intelligent and unrelenting insistence. Women in the field are going back to reckon with a giant who has so often been presented to us through the lens of diminution or condescension or deification. Those in other literatures, it is to be hoped, will soon include Sor Juana's work in seventeenth-century studies. The *Respuesta a Sor Filotea* deserves to take its place in the canon of basic feminist writings alongside the works of Christine de Pisan,[47] Flora

---

42. Sor Juana Inés de la Cruz, *Poesía, Teatro y Prosa*, ed. Antonio Castro Leal (Mexico: Editorial Porrúa, 1968), p. vii.

43. "En busca de Juana de Asbaje," in Pedro Salinas, *Ensayos de literatura hispánica* (Madrid: Aguilar, 1958), p. 124.

44. Américo Castro, *De la edad conflictiva*, 2nd ed. (Madrid: Taurus, 1961), pp. 155, 157.

45. Irving Leonard, "The *encontradas correspondencias* of Sor Juana Inés: An Interpretation," *Hispanic Review*, 23 (January 1955): 33; this phrase is quoted in Gerard Flynn, *Sor Juana Inés de la Cruz* (New York: Twayne, 1971), p. 119.

46. Pfandl, *La décima musa de México*, p. 311; this is the passage selected for quotation in Sor Juana Inés de la Cruz, *Selección poética*, ed. Alfredo Veravé (Buenos Aires: Kapelusz, 1972), p. 162.

47. Christine de Pisan was a fifteenth-century French poet who wrote a treatise on women's education, protested against Ovid's *Ars Amatoria*, and participated in a controversy regarding *Le Roman de la Rose*. She was celebrated and attacked as a champion of her sex. See Eileen Power, *Medieval Women*, ed. M. M. Postan (Cambridge: Cambridge University Press, 1975), pp. 12–13, 31–34, et passim; for bibliographic references, see note 2, p. 100.

Tristan,[48] Mary Wollstonecraft,[49] John Stuart Mill,[50] Virginia Woolf,[51] and Simone de Beauvoir.[52]

I have described some of the contrasts between Madre Isabel and Sor Juana Inés de la Cruz. Both women can be tied to earlier periods—the one to medieval mysticism, the other to the medieval abbesses of the Double Abbeys (those in the system of unified monasteries and convents), renowned for development and conservation of learning and the arts. If we can project them backward and place them in an earlier historical period, we can also project them forward and see them in relation to trends of more modern times. Madre Isabel might then remind us of the continuing relegation of women to beatitude and nonschooled culture, still the lot of millions of Hispanic women; Sor Juana is closer to the developments we associate with the age of Enlightenment (rational thinking, scientific inquiry, and experimentation), to the continuing increase in the numbers of women who participate in fields long the domain of men, and to the spreading movement of women's liberation.

---

48. Flora Tristan, a utopian socialist, best known as the grandmother of Gauguin, and a precursor of Marx, wrote in defense of the English and French working class, especially of the women of that class, in the third and fourth decades of the nineteenth century. See Dominique Desanti, ed., *Oeuvres et vie mêlées [par] Flora Tristan* (Paris: Union Générale d'Editions, 1973).

49. See Mary Wollstonecraft, "A Vindication of the Rights of Women," in *Feminism: The Essential Historical Writings*, ed. Miriam Schneir (1798; rpt. New York: Vintage, 1972).

50. See John Stuart Mill, *The Subjection of Women* (1869; rpt. Cambridge, Mass.: M.I.T. Press, 1970).

51. See Virginia Woolf, *A Room of One's Own* (1929; rpt. New York: Harcourt, Brace & World, 1957).

52. See Simone de Beauvoir, *The Second Sex* (French 1949; English 1955; rpt. New York: Bantam, 1970).

A School for Wives

Women in Eighteenth-Century Spanish Theater

Kathleen Kish

Logic, the handmaid of that eighteenth-century goddess Reason, leads one to expect that at least a few semiliberated females graced the stage during the Enlightenment. Was there not a general campaign for human dignity? Were not tyranny and servitude roundly condemned? Did not reformers strive to eradicate ignorance and to improve the human condition? And where better than in the theater—whose resonance can be equated to that of today's mass media—can one look for traces of woman's autonomy as a function of social evolution at the dawn of the modern age?

A preliminary survey of well-known dramatic works of the period seems to indicate that women (or at least their theatrical doubles) were indeed "coming of age." The century's most famous tragedy, Vicente García de la Huerta's *Raquel* (Madrid premiere 1778), features as title figure and sole female character an ambitious beauty whose persuasive powers induce her royal lover to surrender his throne to her. Just as triumphant, though less illustrious, as befits the social world in which she moves, is the heroine of the most popular of the comedies to come from the pen of the century's outstanding dramatist, Leandro Fernández de Moratín. Paquita, the lead in his *El sí de las niñas* (The Maiden's Consent) (premiere 1806), can look forward to a happy union with the young officer whom she loves instead of to an arranged marriage with a much older man. Other manifestations of female autonomy can be found in a third variety of theater, the *sainete* ("interlude"), whose recognized master is Ramón de la Cruz. Besides depicting a series of self-supporting women of the working class, Cruz on occasion shows women standing up for themselves. The amazon creatures in his *La república de las mujeres* (The Republic of Women) (premiere 1772), for example, have the upper hand in a struggle with men, and his *Las mujeres defendidas* (Women Defended) (premiere 1764) demonstrates that men are responsible for women's defects.[1]

It would be easy—and misleading—to multiply these examples of apparently independent females so as to paint a picture of eighteenth-century playwrights as champions of women's rights. That such a view is far from accurate can be shown with only a slightly less superficial examination of the works just mentioned. Raquel's moment of glory, for instance, is brief. Labeled as a *ramera vil* (l. 62) (vile prostitute) by the tragedy's one truly noble protagonist, she proves to be unworthy of the throne. A mere puppet of her evil male adviser, she dies by his hand as just recompense for her guilty ambition. If her deep love for the king ennobles her (or at least endears her to the audience), its self-effacing nature accentuates her essential lack of identity:

> Yo amo a Alfonso, y primero que le olvide,
> primero que en mi pecho descaezca
> aquel intenso ardor con que le quise,
> no digo yo una vida, mil quisiera
> tener para poder sacrificarlas
> a mi amor. (ll. 2182–87)

> I love Alfonso, and rather than forget him, rather than have that intense ardor with which I have loved him decline, I would wish to have not one life, but a thousand, in order to be able to sacrifice them to my love.

---

1. Vicente García de la Huerta, *Raquel*, ed. Joseph G. Fucilla, Biblioteca Anaya, no. 70 (Salamanca: Anaya, 1965); Leandro Fernández de Moratín, *La comedia nueva. El sí de las niñas*, ed. John Dowling and René Andioc (Madrid: Clásicos Castalia, 1968); Ramón de la Cruz, *Sainetes*, ed. Emilio Cotarelo y Mori, Nueva Biblioteca de Autores Españoles, vols. 23 and 26, 2 vols. (Madrid: Bailly-Bailliere, 1915–1928); *La república de las mujeres* appears as no. 131 in this collection, II, 263–70; *Las mujeres defendidas*, as no. 31, I, 162–68. Subsequent references to these works (as well as to others, following their first full bibliographical citation) will be inserted in the text. Spelling and accentuation will be modernized in quotations. All translations are my own. There are, however, two English versions of Moratín's most famous play: *The Maiden's Consent*, trans. Harriet de Onís (Great Neck, N.Y.: Barron's Educational Series, Inc., 1962), and *When a Girl Says Yes*, trans. William M. Davis, in Ángel Flores, ed., *Spanish Drama* (New York: Bantam Books, 1962).

Moratín's Paquita is also denied autonomous action. The product of a repressive convent education, she is treated by her mother Doña Irene as an economic asset, which can be invested to advantage now that the girl is marriageable material. Paquita's happy prospects at the end of the play are not of her own doing; they result from the prudent kindness of the elderly suitor approved by her mother, who cedes his claim to Paquita's hand in favor of his young nephew.

Unlike these two heroines, some of the women protagonists of Cruz's *sainetes* can act independently—to a degree. The superior beings in *La república de las mujeres* live in an upside-down fairy tale world where male slaves do woman's customary work, but after the comic effect of this extraordinary situation is fully exploited, these "liberated" women (whose pettiness and incompetence receive some humorous knocks along the way) agree to return to normal society, provided that men agree to several conditions, the first being

> que la que novio no tenga
> por sí misma a los quince años,
> se le ha de buscar por cuenta
> del Estado. (II, 270)

> that the state seek out a bridegroom for any girl who has not by the age of fifteen secured one for herself.

This idea of female dependency is underlined in *Las mujeres defendidas*, where it is established that undesirable feminine behavior (neglect of domestic and maternal duties, obsession with stylish appearances, ignorance) has developed in response to men's desires and expectations.

Dramatists other than Ramón de la Cruz afford the best possibility for drawing a composite of woman as both a reflection of eighteenth-century reality and as an idealized vision. I believe this to be due to the tendency to distortion by the humor with which Cruz treats his vast array of characters. Authors of serious drama (whether comedy or tragedy), on the other hand, were intent on the clarity of their message. Their obeisance to the period's literary first commandment, *utile dulci* ("to teach while entertaining"), in contrast with Cruz's attitude, favored its didactic component. In addition to rescuing Spanish literature from the depths of degradation into which they believed it had sunk (symptomatic of which were the outlandish dramatic spectacles which enjoyed great popularity), these writers strove to achieve a salubrious effect on the society of their day. Theater, as a highly visible art form accessible even to the illiterate masses, provided them with an ideal mechanism for confronting the defects (both literary and human) which they saw around them.

Judging from their dramatic production, these reform-minded authors deemed woman's correction a top priority concern. Her image is on balance negative, which is not surprising, given the didactic bent of the medium in which she appears. Her almost universal depiction as wife (actual, potential, or former) is equally easy to comprehend since such was her "natural" role at the time—even nuns, as brides of Christ, could be fitted into this slot. What is perhaps unexpected is the kind of lesson the so-called progressive spirits of the Enlightenment wished to teach wives and those responsible for them. The school for wives embodied in eighteenth-century Spanish theater did little to encourage feminine advancement. The small gains which do emerge resulted not from any desire on the part of the reformers to champion women's rights as a goal in itself but rather as a side effect of the advocacy of their real purpose: social stability.[2]

The Negative Image of Woman

The great majority of female characters in eighteenth-century comedy and tragedy display unattractive personality traits, ranging from laughable foibles to outright vices. None of these escapes chastisement although the degree of punishment is graduated in accordance with the seriousness of the defect. Thus, the querulous chatter of Paquita's mother Doña Irene in *El sí de las niñas* is merely held up for ridicule whereas the corrupt Doña Mónica in Tomás de Iriarte's *El señorito mimado* (The Pampered Youth) (premiere 1788), who poses as an aris-

2. For a thorough treatment of the interdependence of drama and society, see René Andioc, *Teatro y sociedad en el Madrid del siglo XVIII* (Theater and Society in Eighteenth-Century Madrid) ([Madrid]: Fundación Juan March/ Editorial Castalia, 1976). Andioc's ideas, as well as his acute analyses of many of the plays discussed in the present study, had been formulated earlier in his *Sur la querelle du théâtre au temps de Leandro Fernández de Moratín* (On Theatrical Debate at the Time of Leandro Fernández de Moratín) (Tarbes-Bordeaux: Imprimerie Saint Joseph, 1970). They have been of immeasurable aid. Of related interest are Jorge Campos, *Teatro y sociedad en España 1780–1820* (Theater and Society in Spain 1780–1820) (Madrid: Editorial Moneda y Crédito, 1969); and a fascinating interpretation of mores during the period: Carmen Martín Gaite, *Usos amorosos del dieciocho en España* (Amorous Practices in Eighteenth-Century Spain) (Madrid: Siglo veintiuno de España, 1972). For a balanced picture one should consult also John A. Cook, *Neo-Classic Drama in Spain: Theory and Practice* (Dallas, Texas: Southern Methodist University Press, 1959); and I. L. McClelland, *Spanish Drama of Pathos, 1750–1808*, 2 vols. (Liverpool: Liverpool University Press, 1970).

tocrat and runs a secret gambling operation, sees her plot to secure a rich husband foiled and is arrested to boot.[3] Many of the negative attributes ascribed to women characters derive from a single source: feminine pride. Its theological implications aside (religious considerations are always secondary in the profane milieu of the dramas in question), pride in women is shown as pernicious because it can cause them to ignore time-honored restraints in their quest for personal fulfillment.

Egocentric behavior on the part of women is presented as intolerable. Only negative results await any wife (present, past, or future) who is misguided enough to attempt to satisfy her own wishes instead of bowing to custom. Female rebels in the drama flout the established class system and/or some element of generally recognized authority. Their presumption causes at least a momentary disruption of the normal social order, which is the underlying reason for the punishment they receive. "Pride comes before a fall" could well be the maxim which these characters are intended to illustrate.

That the rigid system of social stratification characteristic of the *ancien régime* was beginning to crumble in the eighteenth century is well known. As a reflection of the transition to a more homogenized social structure, the drama shows how some individuals who would have hitherto been resigned to their birthright as have-nots struggle for economic self-improvement and the aura of grandeur which could accompany a step up the social ladder. That such social mobility was frowned upon by dramatists is easy to demonstrate: characters who imitate the behavior of their social betters as well as those who attempt to use marriage as a means for social climbing are made to suffer.

One female protagonist who combines these two elements is the title figure of Nicolás Fernández de Moratín's *La petimetra*[4] (The Female Fop) (published 1762). The financially embarrassed Doña Jerónima, in hopes of attracting a rich husband, adopts the ostentatious styles of the comfortable classes and advertises a dowry that she does not possess. She is ultimately punished with a worthless partner and a

---

3. In *Colección de obras en verso y prosa de Don Tomás de Yriarte* (Madrid: Benito Cano, 1787), IV, 123–326. The reader may now consult this play and its companion piece *La señorita malcriada* (The Ill-Bred Miss) in a new edition. See Tomás de Iriarte, *El señorito mimado; La señorita malcriada*, ed. Russell P. Sebold (Madrid: Castalia, 1978).

4. In *Obras de Don Nicolás y Don Leandro Fernández de Moratín*, ed. Buenaventura Carlos Aribau, 2nd ed., Biblioteca de Autores Españoles, vol. 2 (Madrid: Rivadeneyra, 1848), pp. 66–84 (hereafter cited as BAE, II). The author of *La petimetra* is the father of Leandro Fernández de Moratín.

symbolic stripping. The removal of her inappropriate finery, in addition to humiliating her, reveals her for what she really is: a woman who has tried and failed to barter a disguise into a Cinderella fate for herself.

The specter of unequal marriages rises again in the work of the younger Moratín, haunting all of his plays. The one closest in spirit to his father's comedy is *El barón*[5] (The Baron) (premiere 1803). In it the socially ambitious Tía Mónica, a poor peasant, is prepared to sacrifice her daughter to a repugnant suitor who claims to be a nobleman. Harboring the additional hope of an advantageous second marriage for herself (one of the castles in the air conjured up by the bogus baron), Tía Mónica suffers a painful awakening with the unmasking of the baron—and of her own foolish vanity.

An indication of the degree of disapproval accorded to female pretensions of grandeur is its censure even in tragedy. In the monologue in which she attempts to justify her acquired role as queen, the beautiful Jewess Raquel, who has lived as the king's mistress for seven years, concludes that, "No hay calidad sino el merecimiento: / la virtud solamente es la Nobleza" (ll. 1849–50) (There is no rank but merit: Virtue is the only nobility). Her denigration from the play's outset makes this notion suspect, however, and the closing lines of the work specify Raquel's flaw and the cause of her downfall, *soberbia* (l. 2313) ("excessive pride").

Pride, then, is the motivational factor which dramatists see as the root of woman's assault on the social hierarchy. Judging from the profile of the fictional characters with whom they endow this vice and from its consequences, it is an evil which must be stamped out. Not only is it shown as unbecoming but also as capable of producing confusion (for example, difficulty in distinguishing true nobility from its counterfeit) and even social upheaval. Still a greater threat is inherent in feminine pride, however, and one with even more noxious results: the challenge to established (that is, male) authority.

Calming the Stirrings of Autonomy: The Education of Wives

The female in the eighteenth-century drama is represented as an essentially dependent being. Until coming of age (that is, taking the bridal or religious veil), she is subject to her father or his representative (her male guardian or her widowed mother). As an adult she is subject to her husband (earthly or divine). If her husband dies, she relies on the inheritance he leaves (as does the mother of Iriarte's pam-

5. In BAE, II, 373–91.

pered youth) or is forced to seek the assistance of some new male protector through her own remarriage or through orchestrating a match for her daughter (as L. Moratín's Tía Mónica and Doña Irene—who has already made the trip down the aisle three times—try to do). Tragic heroines, in addition to loyalty to the head of the family, owe allegiance to the fatherland.

What is assured by the smooth working of this system of female subservience is the stability of the institution of the family and, by extension, of the entire society built upon this basic unit. Conversely, when women overstep their traditional bounds, they begin to unravel the whole carefully woven fabric of social order. This is the danger which dramatists must have sensed as inherent in any challenge to male authority and which they must have hoped to forestall by creating female characters whose every move toward independence, motivated, as these authors show it, by egotism, is somehow frustrated.

Failing to demonstrate the respect due to a father is such a serious error that it is punished even when the authority figure seems distinctly unworthy. The pious charade practiced on her father by Doña Clara in L. Moratín's *La mojigata*[6] (The Female Hypocrite) (premiere 1804) is clearly presented as a reaction to her father's ignorance and greed (he has destined her for a convent life so that he can spend the inheritance which she would otherwise receive as a dowry), but it is not shown as justified. Instead, Doña Clara must face her father's righteous fury when he discovers her duplicity, and she is doomed to marriage with an undesirable partner. Another kind of defiance of paternal authority is displayed by the doting mother in Iriarte's *El señorito mimado*. Ignoring the instructions of her son's guardian (her deceased husband's brother), she indulges the boy's every whim and is blamed for his degenerate habits not only by her brother-in-law but also, ultimately, by her repentant offspring. Such is the bitter reward for an incompetent female father-substitute.

No greater is the success that awaits the rebellious wife who attempts to stand up to a husband. The heroine of L. Moratín's *El viejo y la niña*[7] (The Old Man and the Young Girl) (premiere 1790), manipulated by her dishonest guardian into a marriage not to her liking, seizes the only opportunity she has to escape her elderly spouse's cruel jealousy after her true love departs for a life on the high seas: she decides to bury herself in a convent. N. Moratín also depicts a desperate wife—this time driven by maternal love to oppose her husband.

---

6. In BAE, II, 392–417.

7. In BAE, II, 335–55.

Doña María, wife of the title figure in *Guzmán el Bueno*[8] (Guzmán the Good) (published 1777), tries every means she can devise to persuade the hero to forego his patriotic duty in order to secure their son's release by the Moorish enemy. Her disrespect for her husband reaches its climax when she hints that his failure to act may be motivated by cowardice. Later, however, she sees the error of her ways and then is proclaimed *esposa digna de Guzmán el Bueno* (p. 139) (a wife worthy of Guzmán the Good). Her incipient autonomy thus nipped in the bud, she is reduced to crying out for vengeance (to be carried out by men, of course) after her son has been put to death.

An especially well-developed exposition of the challenge to male supremacy in the marriage partnership is found in Iriarte's *La señorita malcriada*[9] (The Ill-Bred Miss) (premiere 1791). In this play the spirited Pepita, aged twenty, whose outrageous behavior has gone uncorrected by her carefree father Don Gonzalo since his wife's death ten years earlier, is subject to the disruptive influence of Doña Ambrosia, a very merry widow with designs on Pepita's father. The two women discuss at length how to subvert the marriage institution by feigning indifference, depression, affection, or illness, as the case might require. They agree that these dishonest tactics are justified and that women deserve to be profligate spenders since they must put up with children and housekeepers. Doña Ambrosia is even bold enough, in her proposal of marriage to Pepita's father, to suggest that they share an open relationship so that both partners can continue to enjoy their individual freedom. Her punishment, however, and that of her disciple are not long in arriving: neither of them lands a husband in the end. Doña Ambrosia learns that she has been collaborating with the scoundrel who had swindled her deceased husband, and the now wiser Don Gonzalo retracts the promise of marriage she had extracted from him. Pepita's intended (Doña Ambrosia's discredited ally) turns out to be a false marquis, who has abandoned a wife in Paris, and the respectable candidate for her hand withdraws because of her scandalous behavior. With the aim of rendering the girl marriageable, Don Gonzalo decides to send her to a convent school for correction, much to her chagrin.

8. In BAE, II, 118–40.

9. I have worked with a published version bound in the Borras Collection for the Study of Spanish Drama, vol. 23, no. 12, in the Library of the University of North Carolina at Chapel Hill. The colophon indicates the place of publication as Barcelona (Librería de la Viuda Piferrer) but mentions no date. It is known that the play was first published in 1788. See now the modern edition by Russell P. Sebold, cited in note 3, above.

The implication of woman's seeking to satisfy her internal dictates instead of the externally determined goals which she should be taught is clear: the rupture of normal social relations. In the case of female opposition to the authority of fathers or husbands, the danger is neatly summed up by one of Iriarte's mouthpieces, Pepita's aunt Doña Clara:

> Por unas locas como éstas,
> Por sus caprichos, sus gastos,
> Y mala crianza, pierden
> Su fortuna más de cuatro
> Dignas de una ventajosa
> Colocación. Recelando
> Los hombres la general
> Censura; los malos ratos,
> Las deudas, y otros perjuicios,
> Huyen de tomar estado. (p. 44)

> On account of a few women like these, because of their whims, their expenditures, and bad upbringing, quite a few women who are worthy of an advantageous match forfeit their good fortune. Men, fearing general censure, debts, and other harmful effects, flee from matrimony.

Perhaps even more disturbing than the female revolt against the power structure within the family were the potential inroads by women into other bastions of male supremacy, notably the realms of the intellect and of politics. That women should eschew any advanced exercise of their mental faculties is vividly pointed out in L. Moratín's *La comedia nueva o El café*[10] (The New Play or The Café) (premiere 1792). Here, not only is ridicule heaped on the former servant girl Doña Agustina for her literary pretensions, but also the censure of "educated" women is generalized when they are praised by a thoroughly discredited pedant. Equally vicious are the attacks on women who dare to challenge the authority of the state. Besides Huerta's Raquel and N. Moratín's Doña María, two other tragic heroines yield to their personal desires to the detriment of the fatherland and to their own ultimate destruction: Olvia in Ignacio López de Ayala's *Numancia destruida* (Numancia Destroyed) (premiere 1778) and Hormesinda in Manuel José Quintana's *Pelayo* (premiere 1805).[11]

Olvia displays an apparent impetus to self-sacrifice: she agrees to

---

10. In *La comedia nueva*, pp. 59–134.

11. Ignacio López de Ayala, *Numancia destruida*, ed. Russell P. Sebold, Biblioteca Anaya, no. 94 (Salamanca: Anaya, 1971); Manuel José Quintana, *Pe-*

forfeit her childhood sweetheart in favor of a suitor from the enemy camp who has promised to aid her besieged city, and she even decides not to take vengeance on him for having killed one of her brothers. Although she seems altruistic, she is, nevertheless, punished in the end: through an error she is mortally wounded by her true love, and her surviving brother, who is also leader of the city, proclaims her to be the cause of its holocaust. In terms of the plot she is responsible because she has unknowingly contravened the command of an oracle. On a deeper level, though, it can be seen that Olvia's real error was having attempted to act *on her own*. In this regard her admission to the town's high priest that she has kept her plan for enlisting the enemy's aid from her brother (both father figure and embodiment of the fatherland) takes on special significance. Clearly, there is no room at the top for feminine intervention, even when it is well intentioned.

A similar message is brought out by Quintana's rendition of the popular story of Pelayo.[12] His heroine, torn between patriotic duty and love, succumbs to the dictates of her heart and marries the infidel leader Munuza, thus incurring the wrath of her brother and head of the resistance against the Moors, Pelayo. He will not be appeased by Hormesinda's explanation that her marriage was motivated in part by the desire to help her people. Her attempt to serve two masters fails: she is despised by both. Having been stabbed by her husband, she admits with her dying breath that hers has been a guilty love and expresses the hope that her brother will come to remember her with affection.

Quintana's Hormesinda represents a kind of distilled essence, a compendium of the negative traits of women and the dangers inherent in leaving them to their own devices. Frail by nature, prone to emotional excesses, which they are incapable of subduing because of their imperfect rational faculties, it is most important that they be carefully educated (that is, managed). Otherwise, the consequences are disastrous, as Hormesinda's case shows. She betrays her responsibility to paternal authority, to her husband, to the fatherland, and even (through

---

layo, in *Tesoro del teatro español desde su origen (año de 1356) hasta nuestros días*, ed. Eugenio de Ochoa (Paris: Librería europea de Baudry, 1838), V, 537–56.

12. The same incident was dramatized by both N. Moratín and Gaspar Melchor de Jovellanos. The former entitled his tragedy *Hormesinda* (BAE, II, 85–101). For the latter's version, see *Pelayo*, in vol. 1 of *Obras publicadas e inéditas de Don Gaspar Melchor de Jovellanos*, ed. Cándido Nocedal, Biblioteca de Autores Españoles, vol. 46 (Madrid: Librería de los sucesores de Hernando, 1924), pp. 50–76.

her non-Christian marriage) to God the Father. Furthermore, her having chosen a mate without her male guardian's permission is a direct affront to masculine superiority in general and to Pelayo in particular. It is in spite of this stain on his honor, and because it is considered temporary, that he is elected king. The symbolic cleansing of this stain which is accomplished by Hormesinda's death conveys the final message of this statement on the ravages of feminine independence. Standing over his dying sister's body and issuing a call to arms to his troops, Pelayo announces that *his* blood is pouring out to save Spain. Hormesinda is thus reduced to a kind of Adam's rib, a sacrificial lamb with no separate identity. This is the brand of woman needed to ensure the preservation of society.

In Praise of Woman: The Feminine Ideal

With the ideal female character, eighteenth-century dramatists could counterbalance the basically negative image of woman and round out the lesson they sought to teach by creating positive role models and demonstrating that "good" women can expect rewards commensurate with their virtue. Few differences separate the admirable comic and tragic heroines. The outstanding characteristic of both is an unquestioning acceptance of woman's role as obedient daughter turned obedient wife.

Typically, the positive female figure in a comedy has received a careful upbringing free from or impervious to disruptive influences. She is sexually innocent, modest, skilled in housekeeping and not averse to it, minimally schooled, and always ready to bow to authority. Sometimes she appears as a foil to a rebellious woman. Such is the role of N. Moratín's Doña María, cousin of the *petimetra* ("female fop"), Doña Jerónima, whose virtue—dowry—win her a partner far worthier than the one her cousin must settle for. Similarly, the ignorant but industrious Doña Mariquita in L. Moratín's *La comedia nueva* shows up the folly of her lettered aunt Doña Agustina. The sixteen-year-old Mariquita's obsession and her only goal in life is marriage, and the author's spokesman Don Pedro holds out hope that she will indeed find a husband if only she will stop trying quite so hard. Once again women are cautioned against independent action, even when their purpose is entirely honorable.

Passivity, on the other hand, is rewarded. Doña Flora, the young lady who is at first attracted to Iriarte's pampered youth, is undeceived, thanks to the guidance of her other, better suitor, whom she accepts once she is assured of her father's *benigno asenso* (p. 323) ("benign assent"). Likewise, Doña Isabel in L. Moratín's *El barón*, her future jeopardized by her mother's insane ambition but unwilling to default on her respect for parental authority, is rescued by her uncle's intervention and guaranteed a marital union to her liking. A similar structure operates in this author's *El sí de las niñas*.

Selfless behavior is the single common denominator among positive tragic heroines. In the two renditions of the Pelayo story which complement Quintana's version, the hero's sister (called Hormesinda by N. Moratín and Dosinda by Jovellanos) steadfastly resigns herself to any amount of private suffering in order to serve the common good. Both women cite honor as their primary motivation and never falter in their role as dependent (not to say possession) of Pelayo. They are rewarded by being snatched from the arms of death. In addition, Dosinda is restored to her betrothed whereas Hormesinda is reconciled with the brother who had erroneously counted her as treacherous.

The single case in which a tragic heroine dies apparently an innocent victim provides the final contours necessary for outlining the image of the positive female. Lucrecia (in N. Moratín's play by the same name) (published 1763),[13] a Roman matron renowned for her extraordinary marital fidelity, is faced with an exquisite dilemma. Should she submit to the amorous advances of the crown prince Tarquino or die unblemished but unable to defend herself against the false scandal which Tarquino promises to spread about her if she chooses the latter course? Lucrecia decides to yield to her aggressor, considering infamy the greater of the two evils. Her unwilling adultery is forgiven by all three of the symbolic representatives of male authority—her father, her husband, and Bruto, who is both spokesman for the fatherland and champion of virility). Lucrecia, nevertheless, takes her own life, calling to mind those medieval Spanish adulteresses who asked for death as payment for their offense.[14] Her dying wish, that

---

13. In BAE, II, 102–17.

14. See, for example, the ballad which begins, "Blanca sois, señora mía, / más que el rayo del sol," (My lady, you are whiter than the sun's ray) in C. Colin Smith, ed., *Spanish Ballads* (Oxford: Pergamon Press, 1964), pp. 197–98. Although the girl in this poem differs from Lucrecia in that she is a willing, even eager, adulteress who is caught in the act, she, too, acknowledges death as the ultimate fate of the unfaithful wife. After responding dishonestly to a series of incriminating questions from her husband, she gives the following answer to his query about a lance he has seen in the room:

> ¡Tomadla, conde, tomadla,
> matadme con ella vos,
> que aquesta muerte, buen conde,
> bien os la merezco yo! (p. 198)

her name go down in history with honor, is the only recompense she asks for her self-sacrifice.

With her dramatic suicide, Lucrecia joins the ranks of those positive heroines who illustrate that female virtue (that is, submissiveness) is always rewarded. Whether the prize be earthly (rescue from danger, reunion with a loved one) or sublime (eternal fame), its intention is the same: to show that happiness and/or glory await a woman who foregoes self-indulgence and opts instead for passivity in the service of masculine authority. This is the typical message of eighteenth-century theater vis-à-vis woman's role, but a final assessment will be possible only after a look at some exceptions to the rule.

One Step Forward, Two Steps Back: Signs of Woman's Advancement

Eighteenth-century dramatists show little evidence of having envisioned, much less espoused, any significant changes in woman's lot. Not even the title figure in Nicasio Álvarez de Cienfuegos' *Zoraida*[15] (generally recognized as the best of his tragedies) (premiere ca. 1798), who bears a distinct resemblance to numerous operatic prima donnas, is a truly revolutionary heroine. Zoraida wrestles throughout the play with the conflict between her duty to the repulsive man she has married and the affection she continues to feel for her true love. In the end, she accepts her lover's invitation to prove the depth of her feeling for him by killing herself with the same bloody weapon he has just used on himself. Thereafter, Zoraida's confidante, who has been the voice of reason throughout, tells the guards: "Llorad conmigo; / Que estas lágrimas solas recompensan / A las virtudes en el mundo ingrato" (p. 506) (Cry with me, for these tears are the only reward for virtues in the ungrateful world). If these words signal a new era, in which the cause-and-effect relationship between behavior and its consequences no longer reflects at least poetic justice, they do not substantially alter the nature of the positive female image. Zoraida is just another example of the virtuous, dependent woman. If anything, her undeserved

---

> Take it, Count, take it, kill me with it, for this death, good Count, I well deserve from you!

The death wish of this woman and that of Lucrecia arise in dissimilar circumstances, but each enjoys a final moment of dignity while submitting to what she perceives as her inevitable penalty. As Smith points out (p. 199), the "high seriousness" of the treatment of the theme of the punishment of the adulteress "in Castile—country of Calderón and the *drama de honor*" contrasts sharply with the coarse or even humorous treatment elsewhere in Europe.

15. In *Tesoro del teatro español*, V, 489–506.

death is even more appalling than Lucrecia's since it serves a more private, and hence less sublime, ideal. A victim of her lover's unjustified scorn, she dies to satisfy *his* doubts: hardly a case of feminine self-realization.

The few instances in which women are allowed to overstep their normal bounds with impunity or to rehearse new social roles can usually be seen as quirks. The occasional outburst of a maid is one such case. In L. Moratín's *El viejo y la niña*, for example, the servant declares that a virgin death is preferable to life with a grotesque mate and complains about one of the limitations imposed on women:

Y nosotras encerradas
En esta cárcel estrecha,
Si no es a misa, jamás
Damos por ahí una vuelta. (p. 351)

And we women, locked up in this narrow jail, can never go out anywhere, except to Mass.

The exemplary value of these unusual sentiments is doubtful. Indeed, they seem to respond primarily to a desire for dramatic variety. They are, moreover, suspect because their source is of the humblest social station.

When "advanced" notions issue from credible characters though, they deserve more careful scrutiny. That Doña Inés, the cousin of L. Moratín's female hypocrite and her virtuous foil, is rewarded in the end with an inheritance, which she herself can administer but with *no* husband in sight, is surprising and significant since it hints at the possibility of a limited self-reliance for women. Another "progressive" outlook is presented in Iriarte's *La señorita malcriada*. Here the title figure is advised by her worthy suitor Don Eugenio to cultivate her mind by studying history, morality, geography, languages, and fine arts so as to develop an aversion to the tyrannical system:

De los que, según estilo
Musulmán, no consideran
A las mujeres nacidas
Sino para esclavas necias
Del hombre, y las privan casi
Del uso de las potencias. (p. 22)

of those who, à la Mussulman, consider women born only to be man's foolish slaves, and who nearly deprive them of the use of their faculties.

An educated woman would be capable of pleasant conversation, he says, and the combination of "natural viveza [y] . . . útil conocimiento" (p. 22) (natural perspicacity and useful knowledge) would render her that much more desirable. One cannot escape the conclusion that Don Eugenio's advice to Pepita is intended less to enlighten her than to subject her to his will.

The incorrigible Pepita refuses to take the bait, leaving Iriarte's proposal of female "higher education" in a state of limbo, but he manages in this same play to strike a somewhat more effective blow for woman's progress. Not only does he give Pepita's prudent aunt Doña Clara a weighty role as the epitome of common sense (in opposition to her brother), he also endows her with a *male* friend, in the person of Don Eugenio. This platonic relationship has the blessings of Doña Clara's husband—the only fly in the ointment since the clear implication is that this ideal female would never maintain the friendship if her husband disapproved.

L. Moratín's plays contain no such spectacular reversals of normal expectations about woman's image, but they do plant two important seeds for the development of female autonomy, albeit in a very tentative way. In Doña Beatriz, the sister of Don Roque (the cruel husband in *El viejo y la niña*), he creates a unique character: the effective female ally of another woman (confidantes tend to be either negative or of minor significance). Doña Beatriz is no out-and-out rebel (she advises her young sister-in-law to resign herself to the loss of her true love), but she does side with the girl in her decision to abandon her husband and enter a convent. The importance of this female alliance, even though temporary in nature and well within the bounds of decorum, should not be underrated since it indicates that woman may not be destined forever to face the world of men helpless and alone.

The second advanced idea conveyed by L. Moratín's theater (and echoed in Iriarte's) is more fundamental—and perhaps more intentional. It is, stated simply, that girls should not be forced to marry against their will. As his most complete exposition of the question shows, however, much more than a woman's decision is at issue—and at stake. The kindly Don Diego (the author's spokesman in *El sí de las niñas*) outlines the problem:

> Ve aquí los frutos de la educación. Esto es lo que se llama criar bien a una niña: enseñarla a que desmienta y oculte las pasiones más inocentes con una pérfida disimulación. Las juzgan honestas luego que las ven instruidas en el arte de callar y mentir. Se obstinan en que el temperamento, la edad ni el genio no han de tener influencia alguna en sus inclinaciones, o en que su voluntad

> ha de torcerse al capricho de quien las gobierna. Todo se las permite, menos la sinceridad. Con tal que no digan lo que sienten, con tal que finjan aborrecer lo que más desean, con tal que se presten a pronunciar, cuando se lo manden, un sí perjuro, sacrílego, origen de tantos escándalos, ya están bien criadas, y se llama excelente educación la que inspira en ellas el temor, la astucia y el silencio de un esclavo. (p. 263)
>
> Behold the fruits of education. This is what is called raising a girl well: teaching her to lie and to hide the most innocent passions with perfidious dissimulation. Girls are judged decent once they have been instructed in the art of keeping silent and lying. People obstinately maintain that neither temperament, nor age, nor character will have any influence on their inclinations, or else that their will should be twisted in accordance with the caprice of the one who governs them. They are allowed everything except sincerity. So long as they do not say what they feel, so long as they pretend to hate what they most desire, so long as they agree to pronounce on command a perjured, sacrilegious yes, the origin of so many scandals, they are indeed well reared, and an upbringing which inspires in them the fear, the silence, and the astuteness of a slave is called excellent.

Through this passage, L. Moratín clearly condemns the abuse of parental authority as well as the kind of education that can produce only a hypocritical woman. But is the dramatist advocating that women be allowed to act with natural spontaneity, unfettered by outside pressures? The answer is an unequivocal no. In the first place, Moratín never arranges things so that the power structure which operates within society is open to attack. Even unworthy or inept authority figures (Don Roque, for example, or Doña Irene) are spared—or rehabilitated. Second, to judge from Don Diego's remarks, the underlying reason for proposing a reform in woman's education and her freedom of choice in matrimony is quite distinct from any sympathy for her plight as the victim of her elders' oppression. It is to preclude her developing "the astuteness of a slave" which could enable her to cause "scandals," that is, to defy the normal rules of society.

What Moratín holds up as the ideal for emulation by the "modern" family is a rational compromise: the selection of a girl's husband should satisfy both the bride-to-be and her father or his substitute. This is, of course, a storybook solution, which in everyday life would doubtless run up against all manner of difficulties, but not for that reason should it be taken lightly. Indicative of just how far the master of eighteenth-century Spanish theater was prepared to advance the cause of woman's autonomy, it points the way for a final appreciation of the message about (and to) women implicit in their dramatic image.

And They Lived Happily Ever After, So Why Change Things?

The world picture presented in eighteenth-century drama is conservative, if not reactionary. Apparently desirous of preventing the breakdown of the social order, the playwrights of the epoch used the theater to preach a sermon on the benefits of the reigning ideology. Of central importance for the success of their cause was the control of women, who were viewed as the cornerstone of society's integrity since they were the nucleus of its basic structural element, the family. In the climate of intellectual ferment, economic progress, and social evolution that characterized the period, there was a constant threat that the sporadic outbursts of the masses against established authority might find an echo in a revolt by women against their ordained role in life—a sure portent of fundamental damage to the social fabric.

Dramatists had recourse to the "carrot and stick" method in hopes of preventing this (in their eyes) disastrous development. On the one hand, they peopled the stage with negative female types whose rebellious instincts were consistently frustrated. On the other, they created a series of positive heroines whose practice of self-effacing virtue always paid off. Through both punishment and reward, then, woman is taught her rightful role: subservience. If she will but follow the rules, that is, if she will be a "good wife" and resist the temptation to develop any potential for independence, she can look forward to living happily ever after, whether on this earth or in eternity.

The feminine image in eighteenth-century theater is designed to demonstrate that woman has good reason to be satisfied with her traditional role so that any attempt to alter it substantially will appear superfluous. The minor triumphs she is granted (such as her having some say in the determination of her marriage partner), while indicating that dramatists were not oblivious to the winds of change, only incidentally improve her lot. They are pragmatically, not philosophically, motivated. Their goal, like that of the positive and negative object lessons embodied in the entire cast of female dramatic characters, is to convince the audience that all is basically right with the world. The obvious implication is that only cosmetic reforms are needed to perpetuate the existing social structure, a structure in which power is entrenched in male-dominated institutions. Clearly, there is little room for women's liberation in a literary world whose byword is, "Long live the status quo!"

Gertrude the Great

Avellaneda, Nineteenth-Century Feminist

Beth Miller

When I first began working on Gertrudis Gómez de Avellaneda in 1972, I imagined that she must have been a visible and controversial "personality" in her time, somewhat like Gabriela Mistral or Norman Mailer in theirs. Actually, Avellaneda seems to have been less self-conscious a performer than these twentieth-century counterparts although she was no less aware of antagonistic audiences and was often very sensitive to unfair criticism. Now that I am more familiar with her work and with Avellaneda scholarship, I find the woman and her writings far more fascinating even than the public persona. She reminds me in some ways of Erica Jong (a victim of the notoriety of *Fear of Flying*), Lina Wertmüller (in the creation of character and in a contradictory combination of conservative and anticonservative thought), or Anne Sexton (for the expression of private suffering and sense of shared history).

In any case, Avellaneda was indeed a public figure; Fernán Caballero's sarcastic epithet, "Gertrudis la Magna" (Gertrude the Great), implies no less. We tend to forget, however, that the instantly famous remark uttered by another of Avellaneda's contemporaries—"es

---

This article is a much revised and expanded version of a paper read at the International Avellaneda Symposium, Lake Mohonk, N.Y., and the State University College of New York, New Paltz, 27 and 28 October 1973; in its original form it appeared in *Revista/Review Interamericana*, 4 (1974): 177–83; and, in a slightly revised Spanish translation, in Beth Miller, *Mujeres en la literatura* (Mexico: Fleischer, 1978), pp. 20–25.

mucho hombre esta mujer" (this woman is quite a man)—was a comment on her work, one destined to become a (male supremacist) critical cliché.[1] Such mixing up of her art and life by the public as well as by critics is best explained by their common sociohistorical context. Avellaneda (1814–1873) was a dashing character, an exotic Cuban expatriate in Europe. She was also a genuine nineteenth-century Romantic poet and a great woman. It is hard to keep in mind that she was a woman who wrote in a sexist culture and period. Had she lived and worked in New York, London, or Paris, she might have faced fewer obstacles than she had to contend with in the narrow and repressive cultural climate of Seville, Corunna, Havana, and—capital city that it was—Madrid.

The fact that she was a female writer largely biased Avellaneda scholarship from the beginning. A recent literary historian of the 1840s in Spain writes that Avellaneda received numerous enthusiastic reviews in the Madrid press but emphasizes that these tended to mingle literary comment with praise for her beauty and her performance as an "eternally young, female prodigy."[2] In many ways Avella-

---

1. Fernán Caballero (1796–1877) was the pen name of Cecilia Böhl de Faber, who was born in Switzerland and died in Seville. Among her chief works were: (novels) *La Gaviota*, 1849; *Clemencia*, 1852; *La familia de Alvareda*, 1856; *Un servilón y un liberalito*, 1857; *Un verano en Bornos*, 1858; (folklore and tales) *Cuentos y poesías andaluces*, 1859; *Cuadros de costumbres populares andaluzas*, 1852; *Relaciones*, 1857. The remark is variously attributed to the dramatist Manuel Bretón de los Herreros, to the poet Juan Nicasio Gallego, and to an unnamed spectator at the first night of Avellaneda's play *Alfonso Munio* (Madrid, 13 June 1844). Edwin B. Williams, in *The Life and Dramatic Works of Gertrudis Gómez de Avellaneda* (Philadelphia: Publications of the University of Pennsylvania, Series in Romanic Languages and Literatures 11, 1924), p. 24, says it was at the first performance of *Alfonso Munio*, at the Teatro de la Cruz, "that someone made the famous remark: 'Es mucho hombre esta mujer,' which later gave rise to much discussion of the relative importance of the masculine and feminine elements in Avellaneda's art, and which it has been said, the authoress often repeated herself with great satisfaction." On the other hand, José María Chacón y Calvo, in *Gertrudis Gómez de Avellaneda: Las influencias castellanas, examen negativo* (Habana: Imprenta "El siglo XX," 1914), p. 8, says that the phrase was "atribuído al gran poeta civil del Dos de Mayo" (attributed to the great civic poet of the Second of May).

2. Salvador García, *Las ideas literarias en España entre 1840 y 1850* (Berkeley: University of California Press, Publications in Modern Philology 98, 1971), p. 67. All translations of the Spanish texts in this essay are my own. I have sometimes omitted the original Spanish and occasional page references in the interests of readability.

neda seems to have seen herself much as the critics did. That is, she was conscious of being a woman writer and, ever mindful of adverse circumstances, often viewed her life and later her works as exemplary, especially for other women.

I am concerned here, however, not with Avellaneda's "feminine art" but rather with her feminism. Her literary production is feminist for its time in some of its themes, plots, characters, and statements. In her letters, her autobiographical writings, and her other nonfiction prose works, as well as in her poetry, plays, and novels, Avellaneda reveals much about herself as a woman and identifies with female characters and authors. According to Carmen Bravo-Villasante, "Everything in her work is autobiographical, from her poems and letters to the characters in her plays and fiction."[3] Whether or not this interpretation is correct, my approach and concern here are not precisely biographical. Avellaneda's writings reflect not only her life experience but also her artistry and thought.

From a historical and feminist perspective, probably the single most important thing Avellaneda achieved was endurance. She is one of a meager number of female Romantic poets to appear in anthologies a hundred years after first publication. Among her close contemporaries in Spain and Cuba, the only other survivors are Carolina Coronado and Luisa Pérez de Zambrana. In her own period, Avellaneda succeeded, as the others could not, in penetrating the male-dominated Spanish literary scene. She knew—or was at some time in communication with—prominent literary figures of the day, including Gallego, Lista, Mesonero Romanos, Quintana, García Tassara, Valera, and Zorrilla. She also maintained, or tried to maintain, professional and/or friendly relationships with women, most of them very different from herself and, of course, less famous. She greatly admired and often mentioned Mme. de Staël and George Sand. Like these French writers, Avellaneda became a celebrity, a successful and envied literary artist, a woman of letters. For her public, understandably, what she was and what she did were as interesting as what she wrote, and her life was inevitably read into her works.

The persona which has survived through her writings and which still emerges, miraculously, despite a great heap of bad and biased scholarship that obscures her corpus, is not enigmatic or shy or vague. An ambitious and energetic woman, Avellaneda smoked tobacco,

---

3. Carmen Bravo-Villasante, *Una vida romántica: La Avellaneda* (Barcelona: Editora y Distribuidora Hispano Americana, Col. El Puente, 1967), p. 219.

wore dresses which exposed fashionably her large breasts, and had numerous marriages and love affairs, and an illegitimate child. She seems to have willed herself to be strong-minded since she admits, for example, in the *Autobiografía*, first published in *La Ilustración* in 1850, that in her youth she was impetuous, violent, and intent on having her own way.[4] Although she mellowed as she matured, she continued to hold some advanced and liberal opinions. She was inevitably embroiled in literary politics, controversies, and scandals, the biggest event being her candidacy for and rejection by the Royal Spanish Academy in 1853. She became, as far as I know, the first woman to edit a Spanish-language journal, the short-lived *La Gaceta de las Mujeres* published in 1845 (later entitled *La Ilustración de las Damas*), and, what is more, did so in her early thirties.[5]

She wrote and rewrote a great deal, sometimes obsessively. Her rewriting of poems and other works is of particular interest since it reflects not only the emotional vicissitudes of her loves and life but her ideological development. The many variants found in her work attest to her literary ambition and professionalism. An example of the first kind of revision is the poem "A él," written in November 1840 to her lover Ignacio de Cepeda y Alcalde and published in the first edition of her *Poesías* (1841). By 1850 their romance had ended, and Avellaneda had had a brief and ultimately disastrous love affair with Gabriel García Tassara, after which she married a man who died within a few months; subsequently, there was a brief renewal of her affair with Cepeda. The consequence of these events was an extensive revision of the love poem "A él" in the second edition of her *Poesías* (1850). The nineteen additional years that elapsed before the publication of the first volume of her collected works gave Avellaneda the detachment necessary for a final artistic ordering of emotional experience, and the third version of "A él," in the 1869 *Obras*, is so thoroughly rewritten that it is in effect a new poem.[6]

---

4. In a love letter she writes of two powerful natures in herself: "la de una mujer y la de un poeta" (that of a woman and that of a poet) (in Gertrudis Gómez de Avellaneda, *Cartas inéditas existentes en el Museo del Ejército*, ed. José Priego Fernández del Campo [Madrid: Fundación Universitaria Española, 1975], pp. 42–44).

5. García, *Las ideas literarias*, pp. 192–93.

6. The first edition of Avellaneda's collected poems is *Poesías de la Señorita D^a^. Gertrudis Gómez de Avellaneda* (Madrid: Establecimiento Tipográfico, 1841); the second edition is *Poesías de la Excelentísima Señora D^a^. Gertrudis Gómez de Avellaneda de Sabater* (Madrid: Imprenta de Delgrás Hermanos, 1850); the third edition is *Obras literarias de la Señora Doña Gertrudis*

There are a number of writings that show important ideological revision. In 1843 Avellaneda addressed to the adolescent Queen Isabel II an enthusiastically loyal poem, of which the last stanza emphasizes the devotion of Cuba, "pearl of the Mexican seas," to queen and motherland. In the 1869 *Obras* (Isabel had been deposed in the previous year, and Cuba had for two decades been struggling intermittently for independence), the last stanza warns that the distant and forgotten island longs for liberty.[7] There is a much more drastic revision of Avellaneda's sonnet to George Washington, first published in 1841. In the 1869 *Obras*, only the title and the first two lines of the original sonnet are retained, the ornate style and classical allusions are replaced by a plainer and more functional style, and there is a radical change in the poet's world view and political attitude. The 1869 sonnet is pacifist and democratic and has a markedly American emphasis. These changes may be traced to the historical events of the years between 1841 and 1869 and to the changing political and intellectual climate in both Europe and America.[8]

In many other cases, poems are reworked, as far as one can see, less for any compelling emotional or ideological reason than for aesthetic ones that suggest the seriousness with which Avellaneda viewed her work. The changes are sometimes small, as in the sonnet she wrote on leaving Cuba in 1836, which was published in the 1841 *Poesías* and which reappeared in the 1850 *Poesías* with a changed twelfth line.

Gómez de Avellaneda. Colección completa, 5 vols. (Madrid: M. Rivadeneyra, 1869). The standard compilation of all Avellaneda's work is the Centenary Edition, *Obras de la Avellaneda. Edición Nacional del Centenario*, 6 vols. (Habana: Imprenta de Aurelio Miranda, 1914). The Centenary Edition is generally the basis for other editions and selections, including *Obras de Gertrudis Gómez de Avellaneda*, ed. José María Castro y Calvo, Biblioteca de Autores Españoles, vol. 272 (Madrid: Atlas, 1974). Mexican printings of Avellaneda's work are discussed in Edith L. Kelly, "Observaciones sobre algunas obras de la Avellaneda publicadas en México," *Revista Iberoamericana* 3 (1941), 123–32.

7. This change is discussed by Emilio Cotarelo y Mori, *La Avellaneda y sus obras: Ensayo biográfico y crítico* (Madrid: Tipografía de Archivos, 1930), pp. 84–85. Cotarelo accuses Avellaneda of "a great and notorious falsehood" in pretending that the lines which reflect her views of 1869 were present in the original poem of 1843. Obviously, Cotarelo does not take sufficiently into account Avellaneda's intentional reworking of her writings to reflect her changing attitudes and ideas. Also see Antonio Lazcano, "Gertrudis Gómez de Avellaneda: Ideas About Cuban Society of Her Times in Her Prose," dissertation, University of Minnesota, 1977.

8. See Beth Miller and Alan Deyermond, "The Metamorphosis of Avellaneda's Sonnet to Washington," *Symposium*, 33 (1979): 153–70.

Often, however, they are extensive: the twenty-nine-stanza "A la poesía" (*Poesías*, 1841) becomes in the 1850 *Poesías* a new seventeen-stanza poem, which uses a few lines from the original (the first four lines of the opening stanza are preserved, and four other stanzas survive in a greatly changed form). The 1869 *Obras* includes a modified version of the 1850 poem, changing eighteen lines and leaving eighty-four unaltered. "Al mar," which has twenty-three stanzas in 1841, is reduced to twenty in 1850 (four stanzas are suppressed, a new one is added, three have variants in every line, and four have lesser changes). In the 1869 *Obras*, another stanza is suppressed, and there are new changes in thirteen of the surviving nineteen stanzas. Rewriting on this scale shows an abiding concern with poetic craft and literary reputation.[9]

In her plays and narratives Avellaneda created many strong female characters, and although these were literary creations generally not meant to represent the author, most of them led lives as exciting and, often, as unconventional as her own. Ermesinda in the play *Egilona* (1845) has two husbands, one a Christian and the other a Muslim, and she loves them both. The heroine of *El cacique de Tumerqué* (1860) has only one husband but two lovers. On the other hand, female victims of many sorts abound. In *La montaña maldita* (1851) a son throws his innocent mother out into a storm. In *Alfonso Munio* (1844) a daughter is killed by her father for a slight offense to his honor. In *Dolores* (1851) a young woman is locked in a tower to prevent her from marrying the man she loves; she eventually retires into monastic solitude, rejecting the society that victimized her. Avellaneda allows the victims in her works dignity and even grandeur. The virtuous Elda in *Baltasar* (1858), although a slave, delivers some magnificent lines, as when she proudly declares to the king of Babylon, "My life is yours, but my soul is mine!" Matilde in *Tres amores* (1858), abandoned by her lover, a poet who has gone off to find his destiny, exclaims, "He is donning the crown of glory. Very well! But I want that crown too! I want to rise to those heights, live in that marvelous world of intellect

---

9. See Aurora J. Roselló, "La poesía lírica de Gertrudis Gómez de Avellaneda," dissertation, University of Southern California, 1973, Chap. 5; and Alan Deyermond and Beth Miller, "On Editing the Poetry of Avellaneda," *Studia Hispanica* (1: Homage to Rodolfo Cardona) (Austin and Madrid: Ediciones Cátedra, 1981), pp. 41–55. Avellaneda also made substantial changes in works of other genres; see, for example, Joseph V. Judicini, "The Stylistic Revision of La Avellaneda's *Alfonso Munio*," *Revista de Estudios Hispánicos* (Alabama), 11 (1977): 451–66.

and fame!" (One is tempted to see in this an allusion to Avellaneda's love affair with the poet Gabriel García Tassara, who abandoned her. The parallel should, however, not be pushed too far; Avellaneda's literary career was well established before her relationship with Tassara began.) Of all Avellaneda's heroines, the wronged and rebellious Natalia, in *La aventurera* (1853), achieves the greatest and most feminist vindication, overcoming all obstacles and enlightening her seducer in the act of humiliating him.

In some of these works, as in her nonfiction prose writings, Avellaneda criticizes the cultural concepts of masculine and feminine (or violent/passive), even making haughtily tongue-in-cheek remarks about "the weak sex." She criticizes the double standard and defends women who are seduced by men and women who choose lives of celibacy. She criticizes patriarchy and advocates voluntary marriage. These issues, which were significant in the mid-nineteenth century, should not be dismissed as stock literary topics in her works, nor should they be considered as purely autobiographical allusions. The attitudes implicit in her novels and plays reflect the positions she enunciates clearly in her correspondence and essays. For instance, in a letter to her lover Cepeda, she expresses her view on the institution of marriage (a similar view is set forth in an 1846 letter to the novelist Juan Valera, in which she compares marriage to monarchy):

> El matrimonio es un mal necesario del cual pueden sacarse muchos bienes. Yo lo considero a mi modo, y a mi modo lo abrazaría . . . con la bendición del cura o sin ella: poco me importaría; para mí el matrimonio garantizado por los hombres o garantizado por la recíproca fe de los contrayentes únicamente, no tiene más diferencia, sino que el uno es más público y el otro más solemne . . . el uno es más *social* y el otro más *individual*.[10]
>
> Marriage is a necessary evil from which much good can be derived. I judge it in my fashion and would adopt it in my own way . . . with or without the priest's blessing: it doesn't matter to me. For me, there is no difference between matrimony guaranteed in the customary way and matrimony guaranteed solely by the reciprocal faith of the betrothed, except that one is more public, the other more solemn . . . one is more *social*, the other more *individual*.

---

10. Quoted from Raimundo Lazo, *Gertrudis Gómez de Avellaneda: La mujer y la poetisa lírica* (Mexico: Porrúa, Col. "Sepan Cuántos" 226, 1972), p. 90; the emphasis in this and all other quotations in this chapter are Avellaneda's. For her letter to Valera, see Cotarelo, *La Avellaneda*, pp. 434–35.

Her novel *Dos mujeres* (1842) implies the same view—at least, until she appears to lose her nerve toward the end. This novel, in which critics have detected a strong influence of George Sand, is the story of a young husband who, while having to live away from home for a time, falls in love with an attractive widow. The wife arrives just as the lovers are preparing to leave the country, and recognizing that this is a more passionate and deeper love than she had experienced in her marriage, she is willing to resign her claims on her husband. This is the position at the end of the third volume of the novel, but the fourth, and much shorter, volume produces a surprising reversal: the widow, rather than destroy her lover's marriage, commits suicide. Cotarelo argues that this hurried ending to the novel, like Avellaneda's statement that in it she had "limited herself to sketching realistic characters and natural passions" without any moral or social aim, reflects her nervousness about public reaction and that the view implied at the end of the third volume—the primacy of love over marriage—is the one she really held.[11] The letters to Valera and Cepeda substantiate Cotarelo's interpretation.

Similarly, Avellaneda's dramatic solution of *deus in convento* may be viewed as a feminist statement as well as a convenient literary device and a reflection of her religious fervor. Margaret Fuller, one of the most widely read feminist writers of the time and editor of *The Dial*, recommended that women seek strength and solace in interiority and solitude.[12] Although not a transcendentalist like Fuller, Avellaneda sought that dramatic solution in her own life, as when she spent several months in a convent at Bordeaux after the death of her first husband in 1846. His illness and death seem to have intensified her piety.[13] On her return to Spain from the convent, she wrote a devotional work, which was ready for publication in 1847. It did not appear because the

---

11. Cotarelo, *La Avellaneda*, pp. 80–84, 434–35.

12. *Memoirs of Margaret Fuller Ossoli*, ed. Ralph Waldo Emerson, William Henry Channing, and James Freeman Clarke, 2 vols. (Boston, 1874). The *Memoirs*, first published in 1852, contain some of Fuller's letters and extracts from her journals. Although these volumes are valuable as primary source material, some of the contents have been bowdlerized by the editors; also, in some cases information is missing or unclear. See also *Margaret Fuller, American Romantic: A Selection from Her Writings and Correspondence*, ed. Perry Miller (Garden City, N.Y.: Doubleday, 1963). In 1855, Margaret's brother, Arthur B. Fuller, published a new edition of *Woman in the Nineteenth Century*, reprinted by W. W. Norton, 1971.

13. For a different interpretation, see Florinda Álzaga, *Las ansias de infinito en la Avellaneda* (Miami: Ediciones Universal, col. Polymita, 1979), pp. 35–68.

publisher went bankrupt, but the manuscript has recently been rediscovered.[14] The author's religious fervor lasted for the rest of her life; she published a new and longer *Devocionario* twenty years later, and she chose to end the poetry volume of her 1869 *Obras* with six religious poems. Thus, for Avellaneda, as for many of the nineteenth-century American feminists, the struggle for political, social, and professional rights was accompanied by a profound sense of religious commitment.

Another point of similarity between Avellaneda and some of her contemporaries in the United States is that she was first an abolitionist and subsequently a feminist: in her, as in them, there is a natural intellectual progression from the idea of racial to that of sexual equality. Her abolitionist novel *Sab*, set in Cuba, was written in the late 1830s and published in 1841, eleven years before *Uncle Tom's Cabin*. At that time, few Cubans shared Avellaneda's abolitionist beliefs, and it was not until thirty years later that the planters of the island were willing to countenance even gradual emancipation. Some critics have tried to minimize the abolitionist nature of *Sab*, alleging that the novel is primarily a love story and secondarily a picturesque portrayal of the Cuban background and that it makes little or no protest against the institution of slavery.[15] It is, however, significant that the Cuban journal *El Museo*, publishing *Sab* in serial form in 1883, prefaces the text with this comment:

> Se publicó en Madrid, en 1841; pero la corta edición que se hizo fue, en su mayor parte, secuestrada y retirada de la circulación por los mismos parientes de la autora, a causa de las ideas abolicionistas que encierra. Por la misma causa fue excluida de la edición completa de las obras de la Avellaneda, ya que de seguro se le habría negado la entrada en esta Isla si hubiera figurado *Sab* en ella.[16]

---

14. *Manual del cristiano: Nuevo y completo devocionario por la excelentísima señora doña Gertrudis Gómez de Avellaneda de Sabater*, ed. Carmen Bravo-Villasante (Madrid: Fundación Universitaria Española, 1975).

15. Cotarelo, *La Avellaneda*, p. 75; Bravo-Villasante, *Una vida romántica*, p. 85. Bravo-Villasante soon changed her view, stressing Avellaneda's egalitarian and abolitionist concern, in "Las corrientes sociales del romanticismo en la obra de la Avellaneda," *Cuadernos Hispanoamericanos*, 76 (1968): 771–75.

16. Domingo Figarola-Caneda and Emilia Boxhorn, *Gertrudis Gómez de Avellaneda: Biografía, bibliografía e iconografía, incluyendo muchas cartas, inéditas o publicadas, escritas por la gran poetisa o dirigidas a ella, y sus memorias* (Madrid: Sociedad General Española de Librería, 1929), p. 77. The evidence is reviewed by Helena Percas Ponseti, "Sobre la Avellaneda y su no-

> It was published in Madrid in 1841, but most of the small edition which was printed was bought up and taken out of circulation by the author's relatives because of the abolitionist ideas which it contains. For the same reason it was excluded from the author's complete works [the 1869 *Obras*] since that edition would surely have been prohibited in Cuba if *Sab* had formed part of it.

Novels such as *Dos mujeres* and *Sab* created a stir because of their daring political implications and, occasionally, their accusations against men. Not a man-hater, Avellaneda nevertheless directs her barbs with amazonian superiority in many of her letters to male correspondents.[17] She wrote works not only about women but for women readers and often dedicated pieces to women she liked and respected. In a letter of 1852 in which she defends her *Dolores*, urging its publication in the *Semanario Pintoresco Español* of Madrid, she writes that she hopes its reading will provide "complete solace and entertainment for loyal subscribers, but especially for female readers."[18] She was as aware of the image of woman in literature as George Sand herself. In 1859, she answers a male author who had sought her opinion on his book with the assurance that his women are superior to Hugo's four-legged beasts and that, in fact, they "are not as monstrous as some allege."[19]

As I have already indicated, some of Avellaneda's letters and autobiograpical writings may be read as feminist documents. In January of 1853, during her unsuccessful campaign for entry into the Real Academia, she writes that, as a "poor female poet," she cannot help wishing for some kind of honor even though she is disqualified, on account of her sex, from aspiring to the government grants received by male

---

vela *Sab*," *Revista Iberoamericana*, 28 (1962): 347–57, who sets *Sab* in the context of other Cuban abolitionist writings and rejects Cotarelo's opinion. Also see Ivan A. Schulman, "The Portrait of the Slave: Ideology and Aesthetics in the Cuban Antislavery Novel," *Annals of the New York Academy of Sciences*, 292 (1977): 356–67.

17. Some of her letters are contained in Cotarelo, *La Avellaneda*, others in Figarola-Caneda and Boxhorn, *Gertrudis Gómez de Avellaneda*. See also Gertrudis Gómez de Avellaneda y Arteaga, *Antología. Poesías y cartas amorosas*, ed. Ramón Gómez de la Serna (Buenos Aires: Espasa-Calpe, Austral 498, 1948); Avellaneda, *Diario de Amor*, ed. Alberto Ghiraldo (Madrid: M. Aguilar, 1928); and Avellaneda, *Autobiografía y cartas (hasta ahora inéditas)*, ed. Lorenzo Cruz de Fuentes (Madrid: Imprenta Helénica, 1914). The 1975 collection, *Cartas inéditas existentes en el Museo del Ejército*, contains much valuable, previously unpublished material.

18. Quoted in Figarola-Caneda and Boxhorn, *Gertrudis Gómez de Avellaneda*, p. 210.

19. Ibid., p. 220.

colleagues who do not surpass her either in laboriousness or in love of letters. She says she hopes that the academy will find some way to demonstrate that "no es en España un anatema el ser mujer de alguna instrucción; que el sexo no priva del justo galardón al legítimo merecimiento" (it is not anathema for a woman in Spain to have some education; that one's sex does not deprive one of proper reward for legitimate merit). However, in another letter, she correctly predicts:

> Los que tienen interés en eliminarme, ventilarán antes de la cuestión de merecimiento la de *posibilidad*, porque, no obstante los ejemplos anteriores de mujeres académicas, ejemplos que parecían decisivos y capaces de borrar los menores escrúpulos, todavía se vuelve a la objeción del sexo, a falta de otra.
>
> Those who have an interest in eliminating me will air the question of *possibility* before that of merit because, despite the prior examples of academic women, examples which seemed decisive and capable of erasing every trace of doubt, still they go back to the objection of sex, since there is no other possible objection.

She jokes:

> Creo que si el ejército de damas que recelan algunos académicos acude a invadir sus asientos desde el momento en que se me dispense uno . . . la Academia y la España deben felicitarse de un suceso tan sin ejemplo en el mundo.
>
> I think that if it really happens, as some academicians fear, that an army of ladies come to invade their chairs as soon as I am granted one . . . then the academy and Spain ought to be congratulated for an event so without parallel or precedent in the world.

In a letter of 1856, three years after her exclusion by the academy, she is more bitter. For a writer in Spain, being a woman is an "eterno obstáculo" (eternal obstacle):

> Soy acaso el único escritor de España que jamás ha alcanzado de ningún Gobierno distinción ni recompensa grande o chica. Mi sexo ha sido un eterno obstáculo a la buena voluntad que algunos Ministros me han manifestado, y mi amor propio herido ha tenido, sin embargo, que aceptar como buenas las razones que, fundándose en mi falta de barbas, se han servido alegar.[20]

---

20. The letters which she wrote to the academy after her rejection are printed in ibid., pp. 212–17.

> I am perhaps the only writer in Spain who has never obtained from any government some compensation, some award, large or small. My sex has been an eternal obstacle to the good will shown me by some ministers. With wounded vanity I have had to accept their reasons as valid, although they are based merely on my lack of a beard.

She maintained this attitude and indictment until her death. In her last will and testament she begs the academy's pardon for any "ligerezas e injusticias" (lack of respect or justice) on her part, explaining that she was of course resentful when the academy decided "no admitir en su seno a cualquier individuo de mi sexo" (not to admit into its bosom any individuals of my sex).[21] Another aspect of this prejudice was manifested when it was alleged that her poems were really the work of Juan Nicasio Gallego, who had written a preface to her *Poesías* (1841). Such accusations of plagiarism have been made against women writers throughout the centuries.

I think Avellaneda wanted not only to survive, but to survive as a feminist. There is some evidence of her feminist leanings and intentions even in some very early writings. The point which has seldom been made about Avellaneda is that she understood clearly that her personal as well as professional problems were reflections of broad cultural and social problems shared by many. In a letter of 1845 she speaks plainly about her situation and feelings, which are empathic but ambivalent. A woman doubly victimized, she laments that she has been continually wounded by the envious multitude of women seeking vengeance for their degradation by social slavery.

In the following two decades Avellaneda's feminism becomes more constructive and activist. In 1860, one year after her return to Cuba, she undertook the direction of a journal for women, the *Album Cubano*.[22] In its twelve issues she included her polemical series "La mujer" and her biographies of famous women. These articles were contemporaneous with writings, speeches, and political activities of pioneer North American feminists, as well as with milestone women's rights conventions and legislation in the United States. Avellaneda, born in 1814, belonged to the same generation as Susan B. Anthony (b. 1820), Ernestine Potowski Rose (b. 1810), Elizabeth Cady Stanton (b. 1815), and Lucy Stone (b. 1818). Avellaneda's "La mujer" series

---

21. Quoted in Bravo-Villasante, *Una vida romántica*, pp. 187–88.

22. The complete title of the magazine was *Album cubano de lo bueno y lo bello. Revista quincenal de moral, literatura, bellas artes y modas. Dedicada al bello sexo y dirigida por doña Gertrudis G. de Avellaneda.*

was identical in many of its concerns and purposes with Margaret Fuller's popular book, *Woman in the Nineteenth Century*, published in 1845. I have already indicated some coincidences of attitude and intellectual development between Avellaneda and her North American contemporaries.

Kate Millett writes that "the sexual revolution was born in the thirties and forties of the nineteenth century" although "it enjoyed . . . a very generous period of gestation in the womb of time." Millett adds, "these years saw the emergence of actual political organization on the issues of a sexual revolution, and in literature, an obsessive concern with the emotions and experiences of such a revolution."[23] In the 1850s Avellaneda published in the prestigious Madrid biweekly the first of the "La mujer" articles and a biographical piece entitled "Luisa Molina." Later she wrote for the *Album* a number of such articles on notable women: Sappho, Vittoria Colonna, Saint Teresa, and others. Her celebrated poem to Cuban women ("A las cubanas") dates from 1860, as does the publication of "A Magdalena" (a woman, after all), and her *Dolores* in the *Diario de la Marina*. It was in the same year, 1860, that—in a reciprocity perhaps based on rare female bonding—Carolina Coronado's article on Avellaneda appeared in Spain (in the "Galería de poetisas contemporáneas" in *La América*), and, in Cuba, Avellaneda published her prologue to Luisa Pérez de Zambrana's *Poesías*. In the larger context of women's history, 1860 was an important year, for it was in that year that the Married Women's Property Act finally became law in New York state.

The Women's Rights Convention of 1848 at Seneca Falls, New York, was the beginning of what was to become the international women's movement. According to the Seneca Falls "Declaration of Sentiments and Resolutions": "The history of mankind is a history of repeated injuries and usurpations on the part of man toward woman, having in direct object the establishment of an absolute tyranny over her." The major premise of the "Declaration" is simply and succinctly stated: "We hold these truths to be self-evident: that all men and women are created equal. . . ."[24] Avellaneda, in the same spirit, goes even further; her intention in the "Mujer" series, she says, is to demonstrate the intellectual equality of men and women and further: "no ya la igualdad de los dos sexos, sino *la superioridad del nuestro*" (not

23. Kate Millett, *Sexual Politics* (Garden City, N.Y.: Doubleday, 1970), p. 65.

24. *Feminism: The Essential Historical Writings*, ed. Miriam Schneir (New York: Random House, 1972), pp. 77–78.

only the equality of the sexes, but *the superiority of ours*). Another article in her series (as announced in its title) treats woman "considerada particularmente en su capacidad científica, artística y literaria" (considering particularly her scientific, artistic, and literary capabilities) and angrily criticizes the "sexo dominador" (the domineering sex).[25]

In the future it would be useful and interesting to study further Avellaneda's *Album* and to investigate the possibility of direct connections with North American feminists and the international women's movement. We know that by the time of our Second National Women's Rights Convention in 1851, the movement had already excited interest in England and France. Although Avellaneda did not visit the United States or England until 1864, she was, in Gertrude Stein's sense, "contemporary." Through the years the majority of her male critics have continued to view her as a Romantic heroine.[26] However, the noblest of real-life heroines in Avellaneda's time—and she was one of them—were working for women's rights, whether in politics, in literature, or in education. In one of her letters Avellaneda reports that the critics label her art *varonil* ("manly") and say she is less a "poetess" than a "poet." Criticizing these critics, she comments dryly, "I do not believe that is precisely true." While corresponding and competing with men, Avellaneda sympathized and identified with other women. All in all, "fue mucha mujer."

---

25. Cotarelo, *La Avellaneda*, p. 350.

26. The tradition persists, even in authoritative reference works: Geoffrey Ribbans, writing in *Spain: A Companion to Spanish Studies*, ed. P. E. Russell (London: Methuen, 1973), p. 395, dismisses her as "the sentimental and discursive Cuban poetess."

Notes Toward a Definition of Gabriela Mistral's Ideology

Fernando Alegría

It is possible that with the passing of time the oral poetry of Gabriela Mistral (Chile, 1889–1957) will be considered the most profound and valuable expression of her creative genius. By "oral poetry" I mean the improvised talks she gave at university halls or at private gatherings, the conversations she carried on all night, sipping her scotch whiskey and smoking cigarettes, as well as her famous *Recados*, articles written on the spur of the moment covering a wide variety of subjects, in which, more than a style of writing, a tone of voice is recognized.[1]

Her written poetry is, of course, something else. *Desolación* (1923), heavy as it is with ritual images and archaic ornamentation, is basically a testimony of love and religious crisis. The book's popularity was due mainly to its dramatic eloquence and anecdotal content. *Tala* (1946), on the other hand, is an intricately woven structure of symbols conveying a state of alienation in a Hispanic-American world of ancient mountains, forests, and oceans; it is also an austere verbal discourse composed of both modern and neoclassical rhetoric.

---

1. Two fine examples of these improvised talks were at the University of Chile, 11 September 1954 and at the Chilean Government Palace (La Moneda) 9 September 1954. On the latter occasion Mistral addressed a crowd of more than a hundred thousand people at the invitation of President Carlos Ibáñez del Campo. Oblivious of what was really going on in Chile at the time, she thanked the president for an agrarian reform he never dreamed of implementing and for the distribution of land to the Indians and peasants, something Ibáñez had never done.

These books still form the basis of her reputation as a poet, yet they alone do not account for her fame. Gabriela Mistral was a living legend in her own time, a personality of such charismatic force that people accepted her as a great artist solely on the basis of what she said and did, and without knowing much about her art. Her voice, full of cadence and gentle rhythms, never failed to come through in all its complex density. It was a rare mixture of unrefined, ambiguous, and, at the same time, aggressive naïveté, the voice of a people, Mistral's rugged, simple, country folk of Chile's northern province.

It is difficult to say what Mistral's place will be in the history of Latin American poetry. She once said that Chile's greatest poet was Pablo Neruda. She could have gone down the list recognizing the superiority of other poets, but if we consider the impact of her ideas on the social development of Chile during the early twentieth century, Mistral becomes a unique factor in a vast movement toward a second liberation for the whole of Latin America. Social history, then, and the history of ideas seem to be the main realms in which to judge her merit.

Around 1910, a year when most of the Latin American nations celebrated the centennial of their political independence from Spain, a generation of great prose writers and poets was emerging in Chile. A few of them gained international recognition: Pedro Prado, Eduardo Barrios, Vicente Huidobro, and Pablo de Rokha. Their time was one of evolution from regionalism to neosymbolism, from narrow nationalism to awareness of an expanding new world. Politically, Chile had seen the last days of a flamboyant plutocracy, once power-drunk after Chile's victorious war against Peru and Bolivia, now rapidly losing strength as a consequence of a disastrous economic policy.[2]

Arturo Alessandri Palma, the Lion of Tarapacá (president of Chile, 1920–1924; 1932–1938), was the voice of an ambitious and enterprising middle class, and Luis E. Recabarren emerged as the champion of syndicalism and the founder of the Chilean Communist party.[3] Military leaders were already rattling their sabers waiting for an opportunity to place themselves at the service of a resuscitated oligarchy. A young and handsome colonel, Carlos Ibáñez del Campo, would be the first to succeed.[4]

---

2. See Francisco A. Encina, *Nuestra inferioridad económica* (Santiago: n.p., 1912).

3. See F. Alegría, *Recabarren* (Santiago: Antares, 1938).

4. Campo ruled briefly as a military dictator and was the legally elected president of Chile when Mistral visited Santiago in 1954.

However tumultuous this period of unrest, strikes, and political skirmishes may have been, a curious sort of artistic life continued to flourish, centralized, like everything else, in Santiago. Young writers and musicians, painters and sculptors, a gentle company of dropouts, isolated themselves in rural colonies fashioned after the Tolstoyan dream of social equality and collective work. Such was the unwritten program of Los Diez, a group of mildly anarchic worshippers of beauty, battling against the bureaucracy of the Chilean bourgeoisie. They had already settled on a farm near Santiago when Mistral first heard about them. There, they strove to work the land and failed, inexperienced farmers, dreamers in peasant clothes, losers in their own world of make-believe and Tolstoyan utopia. Mistral, of course, never joined Los Diez. Women were expected to adhere to a cause but never to participate militantly in it. She grew and matured with them at a distance, sent her poems to them, and fell in love with one of them, the poet M. Magallanes Moure.[5] She clearly understood their style and Fabian socialism. Let us remember that she never cared much for Spanish peninsular liberalism, which she found pompous and empty. The generation of 1898 had two points of attraction for her, namely, the somnambulist poetics of Juan Ramón Jiménez and Miguel de Unamuno's violent, passionate interpretation of Christianity.

As we have stated, it was not so much her written poetry that elicited the admiration of her elders as her physical appearance and spoken words. Testimonies by Pedro Prado, Eduardo Barrios, Hernán Díaz Arrieta ("Alone"), and J. S. González Vera offer ample proof to this fact.[6] Mistral brought with her a kind of truth, or better yet, the search for a truth that could not fit into the sophisticated frame of modernism's philosophy. For one thing, she blithely and knowingly confused literature with sociology and education. Her purpose was not to write for any type of elite or to be accepted by *Pacific Magazine*, the glossy haven of Chilean modernists. From the very beginning she had set her mind on rocking the boat of a bourgeois society smothered in carefully protected self-satisfaction. Being a young teacher, she fought bigotry, social prejudice, hypocrisy, and dogmatism in the schools. Sensing the changing times for women in Europe and America, Mistral was a feminist from the start, supporting political reforms

5. See *Gabriela Mistral: Cartas de amor*, ed. Sergio Fernández Larraín (Santiago: Editorial Andrés Bello, 1978).

6. See Hernán Díaz Arrieta, *Gabriela Mistral* (Santiago: Nascimento, 1946), and *Los cuatro grandes de la literatura chilena* (Santiago: ZigZag, 1963); and J. S. González Vera, *Algunos* (Santiago: Nascimento, 1959).

considered too radical by her superiors in the school system. Winning the poetry prize of the Chilean Writers Society in 1916 gave her sudden fame. Literary groups began inviting her to read or talk about her poetry. Instead, she discussed John Dewey's and Mme. Montessori's theories on education and Gandhi's doctrine of passive resistance against the English. She pointed at social conditions in Chile and suggested the need for agrarian reform, for laws intended to protect women's rights, for more and better schools in the countryside. Her reputation as a social leader grew, and by the time the Mexican government invited her to work with Vasconcelos in the organization of an advanced system of rural schools, Mistral's ideas (rather than her poetry) were internationally known and respected.

Yet, about the same time, 1922, the first edition of her poetry in book form was published in the United States at the initiative of the American Association of Teachers of Spanish and Portuguese and under the personal guidance of Columbia University professor Federico de Onís. Mistral sailed away to Mexico, then to Europe, and would never come back to live in Chile. With the exception of *Rondas*, which Chilean school children memorize and chant, and "Sonnets of Death," which has steadily remained the *pièce de résistance* of every major Latin American *diseuse*, Mistral's poetry never has been justly appreciated by the common reader in her native country. As a matter of fact, it has not been poetry that people have associated with her voluminous and ceremonial presence. They have enjoyed making a legend of her unconventional ways of dressing and speaking, underlining the bold nature of some of her pronouncements and the strong individualistic quality of her behavior.

Paul Valéry, placed in the uncomfortable position of having to write a prologue for a poet he never quite accepted, said of Mistral's poetry that it should be *felt* as an organic response to the hidden forces of a continent;[7] he did not say "read." Other men of equal intellectual weight have uttered similar opinions. One begins to suspect that the most profound and moving evaluations of Mistral's art are not to be found in critical, scholarly studies but in informal testimonies of persons who were exposed to the magnetism of her physical presence.[8]

I suppose compiling all the talks, lectures, interviews, and im-

7. Paul Valéry, "Gabriela Mistral," *Atenea* (Concepción-Santiago), nos. 269–70, November–December 1947, pp. 313–22; this essay appeared originally in *Revue de Paris*, February 1946.

8. See, as an example, Pablo Neruda, *Confieso que he vivido: Memorias* (Buenos Aires: Losada, 1974).

provisations, to say nothing of the correspondence, which Mistral poured out all over the world, is an unsurmountable task. There must be thousands of letters scattered throughout the world waiting to be collected and published. We know that not even her articles have been listed completely. The very commendable anthology edited by Alfonso Escudero, as he himself concedes, is flawed by many and important omissions.[9] The only compilation that has been made so far of her *Recados* cannot be considered an anthology. Since it obviously represents only an attempt to publicize the most harmless of Mistral's editorial comments.

How does one go about trying to define Mistral's ideology if we cannot count on a sufficient number of texts to provide a solid foundation? Something can be accomplished if, instead of dealing with the bulk of her prose output, we follow only certain currents of her thought in one particular field—political in this case—ideas that are easily recognizable and, perhaps, universally acceptable. As a contribution to this study, I would like to propose five categories which may be judged essential to the definition of her social ideas:

1. Human rights: specifically, the problems of political and racial minorities.
2. Social Christianity: the social responsibility of the church in reference to economic and political injustice and its duty to defend and protect civil rights within the structure of a liberal democracy.
3. Antitotalitarianism: opposition to all forms of political extremism and to militaristic aggression.
4. Pacifism: support of the nonviolent movement as represented by Mahatma Gandhi; condemnation of imperialist wars and of the proliferation of nuclear weapons.
5. Americanism: conceived as an exaltation of indigenous communal organization and promotion of agrarian reforms.

These five currents of critical thought, abundantly supported by examples taken from books and articles and from speeches, suggest an ideology with a Christian basis rooted in the theories of Henri Bergson, Teilhard de Chardin, and Jacques Maritain. I will refer here only to three examples of Mistral's political ideology. The three examples are "La palabra maldita" (The Cursed Word), "Palabras para la Universidad de Puerto Rico" (Words for the University of Puerto Rico),

9. *Recados contando a Chile*, ed. Alfonso M. Escudero, O.S.A. (Santiago: Editorial del Pacífico, 1957).

and a text divided into two parts, "Sandino" and "La cacería de Sandino" (The Hunt for Sandino). I shall discuss these texts in reverse chronological order, leaving for the last the earliest one, which, in my opinion, reveals her political position most clearly and poignantly.

"La palabra maldita" (*The Cursed Word*) (1951)

This pacifist manifesto is a defense of writer-friends, who, for having signed the famous Peace Declaration of Stockholm, were subjected to ruthless persecution by reactionary governments and by anti-Communist circles in Europe and America. "'No se trabaja y crea sino en la paz' . . . 'es una verdad de Perogrullo, pero que se desvanece apenas la tierra pardea de uniformes y hiede a químicas infernales.'"[10] ('One cannot work or create except in peace,' says Mistral. 'This is a commonly accepted truth but one that goes unheeded as soon as the earth turns brown with uniforms or begins to stink under war chemicals').

From this passionate diatribe, three conclusions may be drawn. First, Mistral defends peace in order to counterattack an international conspiracy orchestrated by the strategists of the Cold War. There is nothing abstract about this manifesto, nor is it presented in romantic or sentimental terms. Mistral speaks specifically of persons who are being victimized and abused as a result of their antiwar stance and whom she urges not to weaken in their resistance. Second, Mistral's position here is not strictly political but also ethical and religious, as borne out by her insistent references to the Bible and the word of Jesus. Third, this militant pacifism involves an indirect opposition to the Soviet Union's intervention in Finland and Hungary.[11]

"Palabras para la Universidad de Puerto Rico" (Words for the University of Puerto Rico) (1948)

Addressing the students and faculty of the University of Puerto Rico, Mistral attempted to reconcile controversial viewpoints. On the one hand, she defends a conservative policy that would limit the political rights of the student body. She calls for more discipline and obedience, for more time devoted to study, and for less participation

---

10. "La palabra maldita" is reprinted in Matilde Ladrón de Guevara, *Gabriela Mistral, rebelde magnífica* (Santiago: n.p., 3rd ed., 1957), pp. 107–110. This and all other translations in this article are my own.

11. See Gabriela Mistral, "Campeón finlandés," in her *Lagar* (Santiago: Editorial del Pacífico, 1954), p. 21; and Gabriela Mistral, "En defensa de Hungría," *Cuadernos* (Paris), 23 (March–April 1957), pp. 8–11.

in the struggle of the Puerto Rican people for national liberation. On the other hand, she voices a libertarian creed based on the vacuous liberalism of Ortega y Gasset's *Misión de la universidad*. However, she manages, at least, to underline the idealism involved in the political activities of the university students. Remembering Ruskin, she says: "Lograron ustedes lo que quiso el viejo fabiano: que no manden sobre la visión cotidiana ni el casino de juego ni bancos prósperos . . . ni aún las moradas de los ricos" (You have achieved what the old Fabian desired: that neither gambling casinos nor prosperous banks . . . nor even the homes of the wealthy should dominate the life of a city). She adds: "Busca la juventud de hoy más o menos estas cosas: un orden social en el cual las diferencias de clase no sigan correspondiendo a nombres y a dineros, sino a la capacidad comprobada por el oficio o la profesión. . . . [E]lla va buscando a tanteos penosos una espiritualidad nueva"[12] (Today's youth is searching more or less for a social order in which class differences no longer are attached to family name and wealth, but rather to proven ability in one's job or profession . . . [young people] are painfully searching and groping for a new spirituality.

It is interesting to note that in the course of this speech, Mistral makes some timely observations about the state of colonialism prevalent in most of Latin America today: "En dos tercios de la América seguimos siendo los países de las materias primas . . . los parientes del Africa primaria"[13] (In two-thirds of America, we continue to be producers of raw materials . . . the relatives of primitive Africa). Yet Latin Americans must pay a high price in their native currencies to purchase imported manufactured products. Mistral asks rhetorically why Latin Americans must buy foreign carpets to cover the floors of their houses if they have fine native weavers? She comments that the rich travel the length of Europe acquiring expensive china and pottery, without stopping to consider the precious craft of native artisans. She comments ironically that countries with forests and jungles where trees reach the sky import their matches and paper from Scandinavia.[14] This is Mistral at her best, criticizing the elitism of the upper bourgeoisie in Latin America. But then she proceeds to condemn the leftist militancy of university students and to place a negative stamp upon everything tainted by what she understands as "socialism."

Mistral fears that unjust social conditions, political coercion, per-

12. Mistral, *Palabras para la Universidad de Puerto Rico*, pp. 7–8 and 16–17.

13. Ibid., p. 26.

14. Ibid., pp. 11–12.

secution, and economic abuses will bring forth anarchy, not revolution, and that the nations of the Third World will fall prey to manipulators of disorder. She longs for a kind of humanism related to the ideas of liberalism as understood by the leaders of the nineteenth century wars of independence in Latin America. Failing to recognize the true nature of colonialism and neocolonialism, Mistral prefers to forget the economic factor whle holding fast to a sort of benevolent utopia that her young listeners could not accept.

She preaches in ambiguous terms: "Cuida tu bien: es pequeño y se confunda con tu alma"[15] (Take care of your property: it is small and can be easily mistaken for your soul). Property? What kind of property? She seems to allude to a wealth of wisdom passed down the generations by the likes of Andrés Bello and Eugenio María de Hostos, a lofty heritage to be preserved against the materialism of social revolution. It could be that in this case Mistral's words might reflect a pragmatic purpose: she was speaking in support of the rector of the university at a time of crisis, in which he had been forced to confront the bitter opposition of a revolutionary student body. Mistral cast her lot with that of her friend and host.

"Sandino" (1928) and "La cacería de Sandino" (1931)[16] *(The Hunt for Sandino)*

In 1928, responding to a questionnaire in Paris, Mistral expressed in courageous and vigorous terms her unconditional support of Sandino's struggle for freedom in Nicaragua. At the same time she took the occasion to denounce the imperialist maneuvers of President Herbert Hoover. She says to a newspaperman:

> Me pregunta usted . . . lo que pienso sobre la resistencia del general Sandino a las fuerzas norteamericanas. Me pone usted en apuros: yo oigo hablar de política la mitad del año—el tiempo que paso en Paris—, pero yo no querría saber nada de todo eso. Sin embargo, voy convenciéndome de que caminan sobre la América vertiginosamente tiempos en que ya no digo las mujeres, sino los niños también, han de tener que hablar de política, porque política vendrá a ser (perversa política) la entrega de la riqueza de nuestros pueblos; el latifundio de puños cerrados que impide una decorosa y salvadora división del suelo; la escuela vieja que no

15. Ibid.

16. Both of these articles were published in newspapers in Santiago, Chile: "Sandino," *El Mercurio*, 4 March 1928, p. 5; and "La cacería de Sandino," *El Mercurio*, 7 June 1931, p. 7.

> da oficios al niño pobre y da al profesional a medias su especialidad; el jacobinismo avinagrado, de puro añejo, que niega la libertad de cultos . . . las influencias extranjeras . . . .[17]
>
> You ask me what I think about General Sandino's resistance against the North American forces. You place me in an embarrassing situation. Politics is all I hear when I am in Paris. But I would rather spend my time at other things. Nevertheless, I am becoming convinced that the time is fast approaching when I must say that not only women, but children as well, will have to speak of politics because politics will eventually mean better distribution of the wealth of our nations, the destruction of the landed estate which today prevents a dignified and equitable division of land, the death of the old educational system which does not teach skills to the poor child and only halfway prepares the professional for his specialty, the end of Jacobinism, stale and sour with age, that denies the freedom of religion, and the rejection of evil foreign interests.

Mistral is stating here a political program that echoes some basic proposals of the Mexican Revolution of 1910. Dividing the land means agrarian reform, combating "foreign interests" means antiimperialism, doing away with traditional education is tantamount to challenging the predominance of private schools in most of Latin America.

This first article is made up of two parts. In one, Mistral explains the international significance of Sandino's epic struggle, the true character of his armed revolt. Sandino is described as the model of a leader seeking the liberation of his country from foreign economic domination in order to establish social and political justice. In the second part, she offers a warning to the United States, much in the same manner as Rubén Darío had already done,[18] against embarking on a geopolitical adventure which might prove to be a double-edged weapon. In essence, such a policy will only achieve the polarization of uncontrollable forces and will bring about a Latin-American unity that will transcend its partisan factions.

She readily grants that it is difficult for her to have a complete picture of what is going on in Nicaragua. Yet, she says, even if one does not have all the pertinent details, the main point of Sandino's fighting

17. "Sandino," *El Mercurio*, 4 March 1928, p. 5.

18. See, for example, Darío's widely anthologized "A Roosevelt" (1905), in *Poesía política nicaragüense*, ed. Francisco de Asís Fernández (Mexico: Universidad Nacional Autónoma de México, Textos de Humanidades 12, 1979), pp. 21–23.

is sufficiently clear. This is a duel between two well-defined forces: one is pursuing a policy of world domination according to an unwritten "manifest destiny;" the other, deeply divided since the native oligarchy sides with the invaders, resists through the concerted action of a people's army, workers, students, and peasants. When the North American seven-league boots stride toward the South, says Mistral, "se acordarán de 'los dos mil de Sandino' para hacer lo mismo"[19] (people will remember the example set by 'Sandino's two thousand' and will resist). She foretells an age of guerrilla warfare, a gaining of ground inch by inch, and a sort of rewriting of the wars of independence—a time in which history will recognize the meaning of popular resistance. Some of Mistral's suggestions for helping the Nicaraguan cause must have been startling even for the staunchest supporters of Sandino. She wanted immediate action and made rousing pleas for support: "Nunca los dólares, los sucres y los bolívares suramericanos, que se gastan tan fluvialmente en sensualidades capitalinas, estarían mejor donados"[20] (The dollars, *sucres*, and *bolívares*, which are spent so ostentatiously on sensual pleasure, could not be better spent [than in aiding Sandino's struggle]).

In 1931 Gabriela Mistral published in the *ABC* of Madrid a second article about Nicaragua entitled "La cacería de Sandino" (The Hunt for Sandino), which was reproduced in *El Mercurio* of Santiago the same year. More than just an account of the military campaign, it is a passionate and vibrant call to the defense of Sandino. It is also a premonition of defeat, a sad, almost desperate, final message. But she manages, once again, to sound the alarm for the dangers involved in President Hoover's policy toward Latin America:

> Mister Hoover ha declarado a Sandino "fuera de la ley." Ignorando eso que llaman derecho internacional, se entiende, sin embargo, que los Estados Unidos hablan del territorio nicaragüense como del propio porque no se comprende la declaración sino como lanzada sobre uno de sus cuidadanos.[21]
>
> Mr. Hoover has declared Sandino an "outlaw," oblivious to what is called international law. The United States government speaks of Nicaraguan territory as if it were its own, since declaring someone an "outlaw" cannot be understood except as it applies to one of its own citizens.

19. "Sandino," *El Mercurio*, 4 March 1928, p. 5.
20. Ibid., p. 5.
21. "La cacería de Sandino," *El Mercurio*, 7 June 1931, p. 7.

Sandino, then would be "outside of North American law." With true political instinct, she blames the local politicians for asking the North Americans to intervene against Sandino. They cannot imagine, she states, that "la cadena de derechos que han creado al extraño y [el] . . . despeñadero de concesiones por el cual echaron a rodar su país" (in doing so they have started a chain reaction. Privileges and concessions are being piled into the hands of the invaders and will topple over the heads of these traitors for years to come).

Sandino's image stands out in epic proportions in Mistral's articles. He appears as a mythological leader whose struggle is rooted in the great tradition of American liberators. Mistral comments that not since 1810 has Latin America witnessed a crusade for freedom like the one waged by Sandino. She says sarcastically: "Mister Hoover, mal informado a pesar de sus veintiún embajadas, no sabe que el hombrecito Sandino, moruno, plebeyo e infeliz, ha tomado como un garfio la admiración de su raza"[22] (Mr. Hoover, who has been badly advised despite his twenty-one embassies, does not know that this insignificant Sandino, dark-skinned, plebeian, and ingenuous, has taken up the admiration of his people as a weapon).

Like Pablo Neruda in his poem "Que despierte el leñador" (May the Woodcutter Awake), Mistral goes beyond mere complaint and denunciation. She delivers a bellicose warning:

> Los marinos de Mr. Hoover van a recoger en sus manos un trofeo en el que casi todos los del Sur veremos nuestra sangre . . . y un voto diremos bajito o fuerte que no hemos dicho nunca hasta ahora, a pesar de Santo Domingo y del Haití.[23]
>
> Mr. Hoover's marines are going to hold in their hands a trophy in which nearly all of us from the South will see our own blood . . . We are cursing them, quietly or loudly, in words we have never used before, despite Santo Domingo and Haiti.

Mistral's conclusion is clearly stated: in the tragedy and apparent defeat of a Latin-American nation we must find the reason for renewed resistance because the will to fight is the result of unity won through sacrifice. She believes guerrilla warfare has scarcely begun, predicting:

> . . . a la muerte de Sandino se hará de un golpe . . . . El guerrillero es, en un solo cuerpo, nuestro Páez, nuestro Morelos, nuestro Carrera y nuestro Artigas. La faena es igual, el trance es el mismo.

---

22. Ibid., p. 7. 23. Ibid., p. 7.

> Nos hará vivir Mr. Hoover, eso sí, una sensación de unidad continental no probada ni en 1810 por la guerra de la independencia, porque este héroe no es local, aunque se mueva en un kilómetro de suelo rural, sino rigurosamente racial. Mister Hoover va a conseguir, sin buscarlo, algo que nosotros mismos no habíamos logrado: sentirnos uno de punta a cabo del Continente en la muerte de Augusto Sandino.[24]

> . . . after Sandino's execution [a sense of identification] will occur suddenly. . . . In Sandino we see our Páez, our Morelos, our Carrera, and our Artigas. The task is the same, as is the predicament.
>
> Mr. Hoover will cause us to experience a feeling of continental unity never achieved before, not even in 1810, because the hero is not just a local figure, even though he operates within a radius of one kilometer of rural territory. Mr. Hoover is going to attain, without intending to do so, something which we ourselves have not been able to accomplish: to see ourselves, from first to last, from the beginning to the end, as one person in Augusto Sandino's death.

The currents of thought that we have attempted to identify in these three articles by Mistral cannot, of course, be taken as anything but a brief introduction to the study of her social and political ideas. A complete collection of her *Recados*, lectures, improvised addresses, and articles, as well as a good sample of her letters, will have to be put together before someone undertakes a thorough examination with a view toward defining what might be called Mistral's ideology. Once studied and critically analyzed, Mistral's prose works will come to be considered the expression of a decisive period in the social history of Latin America, a candid image of half a century of violence and upheaval, of popular heroism and individual sacrifice.

Mistral saw American men and women as instruments of a creative passion. She identified herself with the working classes so that her message—deeply Christian as it was—had a sort of socialist projection, insistent on the brotherhood of men, solidarity through knowledge and beauty, and the search for justice far beyond sectarian prejudices and hatreds. Obviously, this element of socialism was never recognized by her. It is essential, then, to see through her prose and poetry and find meaning between the lines. But, above all, it is necessary to study her life and spoken word to capture her creative power, which in itself is a lesson in moral courage and an example of unwavering ideological consistency.

---

24. Ibid., p. 7.

Female Archetypes in Mexican Literature

Luis Leal

The characterization of women throughout Mexican literature has been profoundly influenced by two archetypes present in the Mexican psyche: that of the woman who has kept her virginity and that of the one who has lost it. The violated woman emerged in literature during the conquest. Doña Marina, interpreter and lover of Cortés, became the prototype of this character, having been abandoned by the Spanish conqueror after he had made her the mother of his son Martín (see pp. 97–114). At the same time, Marina became the epitome of the person who betrays the homeland by aiding the enemy.

Doña Marina is one of the characters in Mexican literture who can be traced back to the earliest writers such as Bernal Díaz del Castillo, the sixteenth-century chronicler of the conquest of Mexico. That Marina's mysterious life became a legend early in the history of Mexico is suggested by a well-known dictionary: "Las novelas forjadas a la sombra de esta leyenda son casi todas vacías de contenido histórico"[1] (The novels that have arisen from the shade of this legend [Marina's] are always empty of historical content).

One of the first novels, perhaps the very first, in which Doña Marina appears as a fictitious character is the anonymous *Jicotencal*,

---

1. *Diccionario Porrúa de historia, biografía y geografía de México* (Mexico: Editorial Porrúa, 1964), s.v. "Malinche." My translation, as are all which follow, except those from Octavio Paz.

published in Philadelphia in 1826.[2] In this historical novel Doña Marina represents the forces of evil and is characterized as wily, perfidious, deceitful, and treacherous. Her mythical nature is strengthened by the association that the author makes between Marina and the serpent, which placed her under the light of two feminine archetypes, one European and the other Mexican; that is, Eve and Coatlicue. Of the Aztec goddess, Father Ángel María Garibay says, "un sentido de maternidad mana de este monstruo monolito,[3] pero hay un dejo de guerra y de muerte, a través de aquellos corazones y de aquellas serpientes"[4] (although a maternal sentiment flows from this monster, there is a taste in her of war and death, both of which manifest themselves in the necklaces of hearts and serpents). And Fray Juan de Torquemada, the early-seventeenth-century historian, dramatically, in his *Monarquia indiana*, has Coatlicue speak in these terms:

> Si vosotros me conocéis por Quilaztli, yo tengo otros cuatro nombres, con que me conozco. El uno es Cuacihuatl, que quiere decir 'mujer culebra'; el otro Cuahuicihuatl, que quiere decir 'mujer águila'; el otro Yaocihuatl, 'mujer guerrera'; el cuarto Tzitzimicihuatl, que quiere decir 'mujer infernal'.[5]
>
> You know me as Quilaztli, but I have four other names by which I am known. One of them is Cuacihuatl, which means "woman-serpent"; another is Cuahuicihuatl, which means "woman-eagle"; another is Yaocihuatl, "warrior-woman"; and the fourth is Tzitzimicihuatl, which means "infernal-woman." And according to the characteristics inherent in these four names, you shall see who I am and the powers that I have and the evil that I can do to you.

Octavio Paz has identified la Malinche, a term derived from the name Marina, with the mythical *la Chingada*,[6] and José Clemente Orozco, in another medium, painting, with Eve. In 1885 Manuel Martínez de Castro published the novel *Eva*, in which the protagonist is

---

2. *Jicotencal*, 2 vols. (Philadelphia, Pa.: Imprenta de Guillermo Stavely, 1826), I, 133, 134, 168.

3. The historian and critic Garibay is here describing the monumental statue of Coatlicue at the National Museum of Anthropology in Mexico City.

4. Ángel María Garibay, *Historia de la literatura náhuatl*, 2 vols. (Mexico: Editorial Porrúa, 1953), I, 115.

5. Fray Juan de Torquemada, *Monarquía indiana*, ed. Miguel León Portilla, 3 vols. (Mexico: Editorial Porrúa, 1969), I, 81a.

6. Octavio Paz, *The Labyrinth of Solitude*, trans. Lysander Kemp (New York: Grove Press, 1961), p. 86.

a woman raped by a group of soldiers. To avenge herself, she turns her hatred against all men. She, therefore, antecedes Doña Bárbara, Rómulo Gallegos' heroine, and La Negra Angustias, the leading character in the novel of the same name by the Mexican Francisco Rojas González. The violated figure reappears a few years later in another Mexican novel, *Toña Machetes* (1956), where Toña (Antonia), the offspring of the patron's weak daughter, has been seduced by a common but strong horse trainer. Toña wishes to vindicate her mother's honor and to avenge herself for the humiliation she has suffered.

Rosario Castellanos, in *Mujer que sabe latín* (1973), observes that "la concubina india fue tratada como un animal doméstico y como él desechada al llegar al punto de la inutilidad"[8] (the Indian mistress was treated like a domestic animal, and, like it, discarded when she was no longer useful). Before publishing that collection of essays, Castellanos dramatized the problem of the Indian woman in her novel *Balún-Canán* (1957), in which we find a character, Don César, who is a direct descendant of the conquistadors; he honors the Indian women by favoring them. The Indian males always saw in them the virtue that had attracted the *patrón*.[9]

The violated woman has her opposite, the pure woman, whose symbol in Mexican literature is the image of the Virgen de Guadalupe. She is associated with Tonantzin, the Aztec goddess-mother, thus uniting two myths, one European, the other native.[10] The Virgin of Guadalupe is an Indian symbol, represented as dark-complexioned and as having manifested herself to the Indian Juan Diego. She is identified with what is truly Mexican as opposed to what is foreign. If la Malinche sided with the foreign invader and helped him conquer her own people, the Virgin of Guadalupe protects the Indian, the Mestizo, and the Creole, that is, the representatives of the new Mexican nation. She

7. Manuel Martínez de Castro, *Eva: Memorias de dos huérfanos* (Mexico: Tip. Lit. de Filomeno Mata, 1885); Rómulo Gallegos, *Doña Bárbara* (Barcelona: Araluce, 1929); Francisco Rojas González, *La Negra Angustias* (Mexico: Edición y Distribución Ibero Americana de Publicaciones, S.A., 1944; 2nd ed., 1948); Margarita López Portillo, *Toña Machetes* (Mexico: Ediciones Botas, 1956).

8. Rosario Castellanos, *Mujer que sabe latín* (Mexico: SepSetentas, 1973), p. 26; this title is the first part of the popular Spanish saying "Mujer que sabe latín, ni encuentra marido ni tiene buen fin" (A woman who knows Latin [who is educated] cannot find a husband, and comes to no good end).

9. Rosario Castellanos, *Balún-Canán*, 2nd ed. (Mexico: Fondo de Cultura Económica, 1961), p. 80.

10. See Jacques Lafaye, *Quetzalcóatl and Guadalupe* (Chicago: University of Chicago Press, 1976).

is also the shield behind which the poor, the humble, and the helpless take refuge.

In a more restricted manner she represents women confronted by the opposite sex. When the woman in Rojas González' *La Negra Angustias* (1944) (The Black Angustias) dons the uniform of one of her lieutenants as a symbol of her superiority over men, she discovers the image of the Lord of Chalma attached to the hat. "Con la punta de los dedos desprendió la estampa del Señor de Chalma y dijo al Güitlacoche:—Este se lo pones a tu sombrero; yo no necesito machos que me cuiden . . . . Búscame una estampita de la Virgen de Guadalupe"[11] (With the tip of her fingers she dislodged the image of the Lord of Chalma and said to Güitlacoche: 'This you can wear on your hat. I do not need machos to defend me. . . . Find me an image of the Virgin of Guadalupe').

The Virgin appears in Mexican literature during the colonial period as well. In the pastoral novel, *Los sirgueros de la Virgen* (Songs to the Virgin), published in Mexico City in 1620 by Fray Francisco Bramón, the feminine characters (Marcilda, Florinarda, Arminda, etc.) are idealized shepherdesses who are as pure and chaste as the Virgin they worship and to whom they sing. The Virgin Mary appears in a dream to Palmerio, one of the male characters, in the guise of a huntress, like Diana, and she wounds him with an arrow in a scene reminiscent of the myth of the death of Orion by the Greek Diana (Artemis), who slew him with her arrow because he made an attempt upon her chastity. A parallel is also drawn between some of the feminine characters and Diana's maids. On their way to celebrate a feast in honor of the Virgin, Menandro and Anfriso (the two principal male characters) meet "cuatro hermosísimas zagalas . . . como . . . las doncellas que a la casta Diana acompañaban"[12] (four beautiful shepherdesses, worthy of accompanying the chaste Diana). The novel ends with an allegorical play, "Auto del triunfo de la Virgen y gozo mexicano" (Play of the Triumph of the Virgin and Mexican Praise), in which we already find the association of the myth of the founding of the Aztec empire to the cult of the Virgin. Among the allegorical characters in this short play, the most original is the Mexican kingdom, who appears "riquísimamente vestido con una tilma de plumería y oro, costosamente guarnecida"

---

11. Rojas González, *La Negra Angustias*, 2nd ed., p. 108. It must be pointed out that the name Guadalupe is used by both men and women. It is often shortened to Lupe for both sexes.

12. Francisco Bramón, *Los sirgueros de la Virgen* (Mexico: UNAM, 1944), p. 37; my free translation.

(p. 108) (opulently dressed, with a cloak fastened by a knot made of feathers and gold, richly embroidered). On his left arm he carries a shield decorated with the emblem of the Mexican empire, an eagle over a nopal. The association between that symbol, which represents the founding of the Aztec nation, and the cult of the Virgin is to be found in the inscription under the emblem on the shield, which reads:

> Pues tal luz le da María,
> renovaréla en su día. (p. 109)
>
> For Mary gives it such light,
> I shall renew it on her day.

Bramón's Virgin is still the Virgen de los Remedios, the Virgin brought to Mexico by Hernán Cortés. Soon, however, its cult is substituted by that of the Virgen de Guadalupe.[13] In the work of another seventeenth-century writer, Carlos de Sigüenza y Góngora, we already find the Virgen de Guadalupe as the protectress of the inhabitants of New Spain. In his novel, *Infortunios de Alonso Ramírez* (Misfortunes of Alonso Ramírez), published in Mexico City in 1690, whenever the narrator is in danger he appeals to the Virgin of Guadalupe.[14] During the period of independence the Virgin of Guadalupe becomes associated with the national spirit. Father Hidalgo uses her image as a banner during the struggle for independence from Spain. The cult of the Virgin flows from its divine and religious aspects into the worship of human beings such as the mother, the sweetheart, and, in general, all pure and good women.

Thus, we arrive at two contrasting types, the good woman and the bad woman, which have their origins in antiquity. In Mexican literature, recalling again the novel *Jicotencal*, we find Teutila, an angelical Indian woman who is virtuous, honest, and faithful as a wife, as opposed to la Malinche. The former is called "ángel bajado del cielo" (II, 174) (an angel descended from heaven), is characterized as the innocent victim of the tyrant Cortés, and is contrasted to Marina, "una astuta serpiente" (I, 190) (the astute serpent). Dedicated to help the unfortunate, she becomes, like the Virgin of Guadalupe, the refuge of the helpless.

---

13. During the year 1666 the first attempt was made to document the apparition. Several books were published, the most famous being that of Luis Becerra Tanco, *Origen milagroso del Santuario de Nuestra Señora de Guadalupe* (Mexico: Viuda de Bernardo Calderón, 1666).

14. See Carlos de Sigüenza y Góngora, *Infortunios de Alonso Ramírez*, in *Obras históricas* (Mexico: Editorial Porrúa, 1944), pp. 47, 64, 65.

The Virgin, in her role as mother, also symbolizes the earth. Here, again, we detect the survival of pre-Hispanic myths. For the Aztecs one of the symbols of the goddess Coatlicue, the obsidian butterfly, according to Father Garibay, "es la tierra en su personificada maternidad, que en su regazo abarca a vivos y a muertos"[15] (is the earth in its maternal personification, who in her bosom embraces the dead and the living). In the poems collected by Fray Bernardino de Sahagún in Tepepulco during the middle of the sixteenth century, we find the following verses:

> Amarillas flores abrieron la corola.
> ¡Es Nuestra Madre, la del rostro con máscara!
> . . .
> Blancas flores abrieron la corola.
> ¡Es Nuestra Madre, la del rostro con máscara!
> . . .
> ¡La deidad sobre los cactus redondos;
> Nuestra Madre, Mariposa de obsidiana![16]
>
> The yellow flowers opened their corolla.
> It is Our Mother, the one with the masked face!
> . . .
> The white flowers opened their corolla.
> It is Our Mother, the one with the masked face!
> . . .
> The deity over the round cacti:
> Our Mother, the obsidian butterfly!

The transition from the adoration of the Virgin to the adoration of the mother is an easy one. In Mexico, the mother is always characterized as suffering, humble, and passive. In literature no better example can be found than *La Luciérnaga* (*The Firefly*), the protagonist in Azuela's novel of the same name. Conchita, as she is called, symbolizes the exemplary mother and dedicated wife by refusing to leave her husband, Dionisio, despite his profligacy.[17] The narrator describes her as "la esposa cristiana que sigue a su compañero, así esté lacrado por las enfermedades, por la miseria, por el vicio, o por el crimen mismo. Si la misión de la luciérnaga es hacer más negra la noche con su lucecilla, la luciérnaga, cintilando, cumple con su misión"[18] (the Christian wife

---

15. Garibay, *Historia*, I, 117.

16. Garibay, *Historia*, I, 117, 118.

17. The names are symbolical, Conchita being the diminutive of Concha, and this the abbreviated form of Concepción, or Sagrada Concepción.

18. Mariano Azuela, *La Luciérnaga*, in his *Obras completas*, ed. Francisco Monterde, 3 vols. (Mexico: Fondo de Cultura Económica, 1958–1960), I,

who follows her companion, even if he has been lacerated by illnesses, or by poverty, or by vices, or even crime. If the mission of the firefly is to make the night darker with her little light, by glowing she fulfills her mission). Conchita is humble, obedient, unpretentious, quiet, faithful, and submissive. Torres-Ríoseco calls her "alma humilde y grande, épica en su sencillez y en su silencio"[19] (a humble and great soul, epic in her simplicity and her silence).

In the novel *El desierto mágico* (The Magic Desert) published in 1961 by Concha de Villarreal we find, as in *Jicotencal*, the two opposed types, the good and the evil woman. The pure, humble, dedicated, and shy Engracia, as well as the provocative, aggressive, and bold Paula are both in love with Ventura, the local schoolteacher. Engracia wins when Ventura realizes that his illicit relations with Paula are unworthy since they degrade his character. The good woman, however, does not always triumph. In *Fruto de sangre* (Blood Harvest), a novel published in 1958 by Rosa de Castaño, the husband, Martín, abandons his suffering, humble wife to live with a woman whose husband is away. And in *Yo como pobre* (1944) (*Someday the Dream*), a novel by Magdalena Mondragón, Julia, the good, passive wife, dedicates herself to helping the poor people of the slum where she lives after losing her husband and son.[20]

Variants of the virginal female are the innocent and pure sweetheart, the untouchable nun, and the dedicated schoolteacher whereas the violated woman emerges as the accessible girlfriend and the prostitute. The first group is made up of women who are respected, the second by those who can be reviled. An intermediate group between these two extremes includes the spinster and the flirt.

The relationship of mother-sweetheart is obvious in the romantic poem "Nocturno a Rosario" (Nocturne to Rosario) by the nineteenth-century poet Manuel Acuña, where the following verses appear:

---

663. This novel has recently been translated by Frances Kellam and Bernice Berler, *Three Novels by Mariano Azuela: The Trials of a Respectable Family; The Underdogs; The Firefly* (San Antonio, Tex.: Trinity University Press, 1979).

19. Arturo Torres-Ríoseco, *Grandes novelistas de la América hispana*, vol. 1, "Los novelistas de la tierra" (Berkeley: University of California Press, 1941), p. 26.

20. Concha de Villarreal, *El desierto mágico* (Mexico: Ediciones Botas, 1961); Rosa de Castaño, *Fruto de sangre* (Mexico: Populibros "La Prensa," 1958); Magdalena Mondragón, *Yo como pobre* (Mexico: Ediciones "Ariel," 1944), trans. Samuel Putnam, *Someday the Dream* (New York: Dial, 1947).

Camino mucho, mucho, y al fin de la jornada
la forma de mi madre se pierde en la nada
y tú de nuevo vuelves en mi alma a aparecer.

¡Qué hermoso hubiera sido vivir bajo aquel techo,

los dos una sola alma, los dos un solo pecho,
y en medio de nosotros, mi madre como un dios![21]

I walk, walk, and at the end of the journey
My mother's silhouette vanishes into nothingness
And you again and again, in my soul appear.

How beautiful it would have been
To live under that roof.

The two of us as a single soul
The two of us a single self
And between us
My mother like a god!

In other poets, the pure sweetheart, whose prototype is the mythical sleeping beauty, is untouchable. Ramón López Velarde is inspired by a pure, detached woman. The association of Virgin-mother-sweetheart appears in his poem "Elogio a Fuensanta" (In Praise of Fuensanta):

Humilde te he rezado mi tristeza
como en los pobres templos parroquiales
el campanario ante la Virgen reza.

Antífona es tu voz, y en los corales
de tu mística boca he descubierto
el sabor de los besos maternales.[22]

Humbly I have prayed my sadness to you
as in the poor country churches
the farmer to the Virgin prays.

Antiphony is your voice, and in the c(h)orals
of your mystical mouth I have discovered
the taste of maternal kisses.

Upon marriage, the sweetheart who is pure becomes a faithful wife and unassuming mother. If she remains single, she becomes a *solte-*

---

21. Manuel Acuña, "Nocturno a Rosario," in José Emilio Pacheco, ed., *La poesía mexicana del siglo XIX: Antología* (Mexico: Empresas Editoriales, 1965), pp. 263–64.

22. Ramón López Velarde, *Poesías completas y el minutero*, 3rd ed. (Mexico: Editorial Porrúa, 1963), p. 13.

rona ("old maid"), a nun, a *beata* ("overly religious woman"), or a schoolteacher. The *solterona* is a common character in Mexican literature. She appears in *Polvos de arroz* (Face Powder) (1958), a novelette by Sergio Galindo, and in several short stories by Raquel Banda Farfán, Elena Garro, and Carlos Fuentes. Galindo's character combines the problem of the *solterona* with that of the virgin and the violated woman. Camerina becomes a *solterona* as a result of her fiancé's seduction of her sister Augusta, but the emotional problems of Camerina, as a *solterona*, are what Galindo is interested in exploring.[23]

The *solterona* usually appears as a simple stereotype of homeliness. Galindo presents Camerina as an extremely fat woman. Raquel Banda Farfán, in her numerous short stories, often attributes to her *solteronas* the single physical characteristic of ugliness. Jova, in the story "Una extraña enfermedad" (A Rare Disease), is representative of this stereotype:

> Jova era la solterona del rancho, esa solterona que hay en todas partes, sin amigas con quienes comentar su desgracia, porque una doncella que ha llegado a cierta edad, ni puede hacer ronda con las jóvenes ni tampoco con las mujeres casadas. . . . Se recordaba bien que Jova nunca fue bonita, ni siquiera a los quince, cuando se dice que no hay muchacha fea. Era una güera pizque que no podía mirar la luz del día sin hacer gestos, y para colmo, tenía la dentadura de fuera y le era imposible juntar los labios.[24]

> Jova was the ranch's *solterona*, that *solterona* found everywhere, without friends with whom to share her misfortune because a maid that has reached a certain age can neither join the young nor the married women. . . . They remembered that Jova was never pretty, not even when she was fifteen, when, they say, there is no ugly girl. She was a squinty-eyed ash blonde who could not look at the light of day, and to make it worse she had protruding teeth and could not close her lips.

Another of Banda Farfán's characters is the twenty-three-year-old heroine of her story "Por un piropo" (For a Compliment). Dionisia is a *solterona* so ugly that "los hombres la veían con la indiferencia con

23. Sergio Galindo, *Polvos de arroz* (Xalapa: Universidad Veracruzana, 1958); Raquel Banda Farfán, *El secreto* (Mexico: Editorial Diana, 1960), and *Un pedazo de vida* (Naucalpan: Editorial Comaval, 1959); Elena Garro, *La semana de colores* (Xalapa: Universidad Veracruzana, 1964); Carlos Fuentes, *Cantar de ciegos* (Mexico: Joaquín Mortiz, 1964).

24. Raquel Banda Farfán, "Una extraña enfermedad," in her *El secreto*, p. 121.

que puede verse a una vaca"[25] (men looked at her with the indifference with which they looked at a cow). However, Herculano is attracted to her. Why? Because "nunca antes hombre alguno la tentó ni con los ojos" (p. 9) (she had not been touched by any man, not even with the eyes). He makes love to her, though he says, "Es fea la indina, fea como un zopilote, por eso de día ni siquiera la miro" (p. 9) (The Indian girl is ugly, ugly as a buzzard, which is why in the daylight I won't even look at her). Banda Farfán's *solteronas* are ugly, but they finally get married, even if they have to marry a dying man, as does Chona in another of her stories, "La cita" (The Date).[26]

This is not so with the stories of Carlos Fuentes, as we can see in "A la víbora de la mar"[27] (Sea Serpent), in which a *solterona* is deceived and robbed of her savings during a boat trip from Acapulco to Miami. Isabel, from Mexico City, is in her forties and rather good-looking. "Cuál sería la palabra [para describirla]? Dowdy, I guess." (p. 138) (How would you describe her? Dowdy, I guess). In spite of her shyness, she falls in love with the North American Harrison Beatle, who marries her in a mock ceremony and then steals her money. Three days before reaching Miami, where Harrison and his male lover plan to leave the boat, Harrison says, "De todas maneras, pobrecita. Empezaba a quererla, como a una tía vieja. Pensar que tenemos que hacer la comedia tres días más, ¡ooooooh!" (p. 208) (Poor thing. I was beginning to like her, like you like an old aunt. And to think that we have to act out this comedy for three more days, ooooooh!). If Galindo and Banda Farfán see their *solteronas* with sympathy, Fuentes sees them with sarcasm, without pity.

The *beata* or overly religious woman is very close to the nun, a familiar character in Hispanic literature since its origins. Both appear frequently in Mexican literature, the nun especially in romantic fiction, in such extravagant novels as *Monja y casada, virgen y mártir* (1868)[28] (Nun and Married, Virgin and Martyr) by Vicente Riva Palacio. His heroine, Sor Blanca, is placed by her brother in a convent, from which she escapes, marries, is tortured by the Inquisition, escapes again, is captured by a bandit, and, finally, falls to her death from a precipice, still a virgin.

---

25. Raquel Banda Farfán, "Por un piropo," in her *Un pedazo de vida*, p. 6.
26. Raquel Banda Farfán, *La cita* (Mexico: Ediciones de Andrea, 1957).
27. Carlos Fuentes, "A la víbora de la mar," in his *Cantar de ciegos*. The title of this story is the name of a popular children's game; quotations from the 4th ed., 1969.
28. Vicente Riva Palacio, *Monja y casada, virgen y mártir* (Mexico: Imprenta de "La Constitución Social," 1868).

In modern fiction, the *beata* is characterized by Agustín Yáñez. In his novel *Al filo del agua* (1947) (*The Edge of the Storm*) the *beatas* appear as a group, as members of the religious association "Hijas de María" (Mary's Daughters). All women joining this association must forego marriage. In the novel, Maclovia Ledesma disobeys this rule, marries, and leaves the association, producing difficulties for her and her husband. He loses money in every business he undertakes; she has two miscarriages; and finally she loses her mind. "Maclovia; desde recién casada fue víctima de una tristeza mortal, que nada ni nadie podía disiparle; tras la primera frustración dio en sentirse perseguida, ya por sus parientes políticos, luego por su marido, finalmente por el diablo en persona"[29] (Maclovia, from the day she married, was a victim of a mortal sadness which no one could dispel. After the first frustration she believed she was persecuted, first by her relatives, then by her husband, and finally by the devil in person). But the daily life of the other members of the association (Teófila, Elvira, Maximina) is just as unbalanced. Yáñez sympathizes with the *beata*, connecting her sufferings to those of other people rather than ridiculing her celibacy.

Not so Juan Rulfo, who, in his short story "Anacleto Morones," presents a biting characterization of the *beata*. The story opens with the description by the male narrator Lucas, of a group of ten *beatas*:

> ¡Viejas, hijas del demonio! Las vi venir a todas juntas, en procesión. Vestidas de negro, sudando como mulas, bajo el mero rayo del sol. La vi desde lejos como si fuera una recua levantando polvo. Negras todas ellas. Venían por el camino de Amula, cantando entre rezos, entre el calor, con sus negros escapularios grandotes y renegridos sobre los que caían en goterones el sudor de su cara.[30]
>
> Old hags, daughters of the devil! I saw them coming all together, like a procession. Dressed in black, sweating like mules under the rays of the sun. I saw them from afar, like a pack of mules throwing up dust. Black all over. They came from the direction of Amula, singing and praying, in the heat of the day, with their large, fat, blacker-than-black scapularies, over which the perspiration from their faces was falling in large, thick drops.

---

29. Agustín Yáñez, *Al filo del agua* (Mexico: Editorial Porrúa, 1955), pp. 223–24; trans. Ethel Brinton, *The Edge of the Storm* (Austin: University of Texas Press, 1963).

30. Juan Rulfo, "Anacleto Morones," in his *El llano en llamas* (Mexico: Fondo de Cultura Económica, 1953; 2nd ed., 1970), p. 119.

Lucas is cynical, as he had been deceived by his wife, daughter of the holy man Anacleto, whom the *beatas* seek to canonize. The ten women who have come to persuade Lucas to testify as to the holiness of Anacleto Morones are misguided *beatas* who worship the memory of a fake, a fact known to Lucas. In Rulfo's story some of the *beatas* are even willing to make love, and one of them stays with Lucas all night. She ends the story with this remark, which proves that Lucas is not lying: "—Eres una calamidad, Lucas Lucatero. No eres nada cariñoso. ¿Sabes quién sí era amoroso con una? —¿Quién? —El Niño Anacleto. Él sí que sabía hacer el amor" (p. 135) ('You are a calamity, Lucas Lucatero. You are not at all affectionate. You know who was really loving with one?' 'Who?' 'El Niño Anacleto. He really knew how to make love').

The *beata*, however, is traditionally averse toward sex, as Mariana, a *solterona beata* who appears in the novel *La vida y yo* (1954) (Life and I) by Blanca B. Mauries, succinctly tells us. She has a profound horror for the sins of love.[31] As a rule, the nun, the *solterona*, and the *beata* are not pursued by men. On the other hand, the man considers it a normal activity to try to seduce a flirt, who is characterized as loose and fickle, easily becoming a mistress or a prostitute. In the 1948 novel, *Senderos de pasión* (Paths of Passion) by Dina Rico, one of the leading characters, Conchita, finally succumbs to Armando's demands, an act condemned by the closed society in which she lives. This leads to her tragic suicide. Another feminine character, Leonor, makes this observation:

> Yo no podía comprender por qué, cuando delinquía una mujer, en lugar de ofrecerle una mano amiga, un hogar honesto—aun contra su propia voluntad—donde pudiera olvidar su pecado y redimirse, se la lanzaba al arroyo, obligándola, las más de las veces, a seguir rodando por la pendiente iniciada por amor.[32]
>
> I could not understand why, when a woman breaks the rigid sexual rules, instead of being offered a helping hand, providing her with a decent home—even against her own will—where she could forget her sin and redeem herself, she is cast into the gutter, forcing her, most of the time, to keep on falling down the road initiated by love.

A variant of the flirt is the girl who risks her virginity, often with the intention of losing it. The best examples of this type are the girls

31. Blanca B. Mauries, *La vida y yo* (Mexico: Ediciones Botas, 1954).
32. Dina Rico, *Senderos de pasión* (Mexico: B. Costa-Amic, 1948), p. 40.

found in "Las rorras Gómez" (The Gómez Dolls) by Francisco Rojas González. The action of the story takes place during the years of the revolution, and has to do with the behavior of two beautiful young sisters who are hidden by their mother to save them from the hands of the soldiers. After searching the house in vain, the soldiers see a brick move on the wall, discover the hidden girls, and rape them. The discovery was not, of course, by chance. One of the sisters says,

> mi novio era muy tímido, ¿sabes? y yo, yo tenía ganas de desmayarme entre los brazos de un hombre fuerte, fuerte . . . ! Y entre los [revolucionarios] chavistas había tantos hombres fuertes . . . Por eso movía la puerta del postigo.[33]
>
> My sweetheart was very timid, you know, and I yearned to pass out in the arms of a strong man. . . . And among the revolutionaries there were so many of them. That's why I moved the brick.

Later on one of the sisters marries but the other becomes a prostitute.

Not all fallen flirts become prostitutes. Often they wish to redeem themselves and take up a profession such as nurse, social worker, or schoolteacher. An example of this transformation is Leonor, who has been violated by the painter Juan José, in the novel *Senderos de pasión*. When her son is stillborn, she dedicates herself to teaching the sons and daughters of others. It is not unusual for a schoolteacher to participate in social causes on behalf of the poor, as did Dolores Martínez, the protagonist of the novel *La maestrita* (1949) (The Schoolteacher) by María Luisa Ocampo.[34] This humble, idealistic, and openhearted woman dedicates her life to teaching the townspeople. She joins the Zapatista movement and fights to provide a better life for the *campesino* ("peasant"). Nevertheless, when she is made a prisoner, she is executed without pity and without anyone's coming to her defense. Some teachers are more fortunate. Their dedication to improve the standard of living of the people often elicits the admiration of men. In the novel *El enganchador* (1951) (The Contract Agent) by Carmelinda Pacheco de Haedo, the peon Felipe says, "¡Bendita sea la maestra! ¡no hay persona más buena, en toda la ribera! Ella nos enseña, nos anima . . . parece el sol que nos da luz, nos da calor y llena de esperanza nuestra alma"[35] (Blessed be the teacher! There is no better person in all

33. Francisco Rojas González, "Las rorras Gómez," in his *Cuentos completos* (Mexico: Fondo de Cultura Económica, 1971), p. 22.

34. María Luisa Ocampo, *La maestrita* (Mexico: n.p., 1949).

35. Carmelinda Pacheco de Haedo, *El enganchador* (Villahermosa, Tabasco: Cía. Editora Tabasqueña, 1951), p. 46.

the community! She teaches us, she encourages us . . . she is like the sun who gives us light and heat, and fills our soul with hope).

The shift from the available girlfriend to the prostitute is one of the most common literary devices in world fiction. In Mexican literature we have Santa, the protagonist in the novel of the same name by Federico Gamboa. Santa falls to the charms of Ensign Márquez, and her mother and brothers throw her out of the house into prostitution. Agustina, her benign and unquestioning mother,

> no la maldecía, porque impura y todo, continuaba idolatrándola y continuaba encomendándola a la infinita misericorida de Dios . . . pero sí la repudiaba, porque cuando una virgen se aparta de lo honesto y consiente que la desgarren su vestidura de inocencia; cuando una hija mancilla las canas de su madre, de una madre que se asoma a las negruras del sepulcro; cuando una doncella enloda a los hermanos que por sostenerla trabajan, entonces la que ha cesado de ser virgen, la mala hija y la doncella olvidadiza, apesta cuanto la rodea y hay que rechazarla, que soponerla muerta y que rezar por ella.[36]

> did not curse her because, impure and all, she continued to idolize her and continued to entrust her to the infinite mercy of God. . . . But she repudiated her because when a virgin withdraws from what is honest and consents to have her dress of innocence torn apart; when a daughter stains her mother's white hair, a mother who has one foot in the grave; when a maiden bemires her brothers that have to work for her upkeep; then the one who has stopped being a virgin, the bad daughter and forgetful maid, infects everything that surrounds her and it is necessary to reject her, to assume that she is dead and pray for her.

Why this submission of women to men in Mexican literature, which we assume to be a reflection of real life? Octavio Paz, who has reflected upon this question explains:

> Like almost all other people, Mexicans consider women to be an instrument, either of the desires of man, or of the ends assigned to her by law, society, or moral codes. Ends, it must be said, about which she has never been consulted and in whose execution she only participates passively as depository of certain values. Whether as a prostitute, goddess, *grande dame*, or mistress,

36. Federico Gamboa, *Santa* (Madrid: Casa Editorial Bailly-Bailliere, 1910), p. 67.

> women transmit or preserve, but do not [create],[37] the values and energies entrusted to them by nature or society. In a world made in man's image, women are only a reflection of masculine will and desire.[38]

In *Mujer que sabe latín* Rosario Castellanos blames not only men, as Sor Juana had done in the seventeenth century, but also society. She says:

> Por eso desde que nace una mujer la educación trabaja sobre el material dado para adaptarlo a su destino y cultivarlo en un ente moralmente aceptable, es decir, socialmente útil. Así se le despoja de la espontaneidad para actuar; se le prohibe la iniciativa de decidir; se le enseña a obedecer los mandamientos de una ética que le es absolutamente ajena y que no tiene más justificación ni fundamentación que la de servir a los intereses, a los propósitos y a los fines de los demás. (p. 14)

> From the very moment that a woman is born, the educational system works on the material at hand to make it adapt to its destiny and turn out a being morally acceptable, that is to say, socially useful. Thus she is dispossessed of her spontaneity to act; she is denied the initiative to decide; she is taught to obey the commandments of an ethic that is absolutely strange to her, that has no justification or foundation other than that of serving the interests, purposes, and ends of others.

There is no doubt that Mexican literature, like all other literatures, reflects the prejudices of the ages and creates types that are remolded within the limits of these prejudices, most of them derived from the past. Feminine archetypes, therefore, reflect the characteristics, good or bad, that have been attributed to women throughout the years. Because of this long literary tradition, it is a monumental task to rid literature of these archetypes. Considering the fact that society changes, it is to be supposed that literary types will also change. The Mexican sociologist, Francisco González Pineda, has said that

> [En la sociedad mexicana] la reclusión de la mujer va desapareciendo, y con ello la posibilidad de preservar a las hijas con el medio externo de barrotes y chaperones; las jóvenes van tendiendo, cada vez con mayor frecuencia, a experimentar lo sexual

37. I have changed "believe in" to "create" since it seems to be an obvious error of translation; see p. 32 of the 1959 Spanish edition.
38. Paz, *Labyrinth of Solitude*, p. 35.

> con mayor o menor libertad. . . . Las clases medias se están quedando cada vez con menos vírgenes para los casamientos idealizados de las novias de estas clases, y el hombre mexicano, a tanto agredir mujeres, está comprobando que ya no hay mucho que agredir y se está quedando sin oportunidades para probar su masculinidad.[39]
>
> In Mexican society the seclusion of women is disappearing, and with it the possibility of keeping young women confined by means of bars or chaperons. Young women, more and more, tend to experiment with a greater sexual liberty. . . . The middle class is being left with fewer and fewer virgins for the idealized marriages, and the Mexican man, as a result of his many sexual aggressions, is realizing that there is not much left to violate, and has fewer opportunities to prove his manhood.

The social changes referred to by González Pineda can be verified in the new Mexican literature by young writers such as José Agustín, Gustavo Sainz, José Emilio Pacheco, Juan García Ponce, Juan Tovar, René Avilés Fabila, Margarita Daltón, Esther Seligson, Carmen Rubín de Celís, and others in whose works we can discover the image of a new Mexican woman, a woman that is finally breaking away from the stereotyped characterization based on traditional archetypes.

---

39. Francisco González Pineda, *El mexicano: Psicología de su destructividad* (Mexico: Editorial Pax-México, 1961), p. 163.

Sara de Etcheverts

The Contradictions of Literary Feminism

Francine Masiello

In the decade of the 1920s, Argentine intellectuals formed a professional consciousness about the nature of their writerly task. The creative endeavor was perceived as a special function of a highly trained, vanguard elite; literary criticism was promoted as an autonomous discipline, and the little magazine became the arena for debate about the possibilities of artistic invention.[1] Liberal writers in Argentina devoted seemingly endless energies to the preparation of literary manifestoes, magazines, and public presentations, which positioned the artist as a harbinger of what was new. But the frivolous self-confidence of the *belle époque* was called to a sudden halt by the military coup of Uriburu in September 1930. Dethroned from their once privileged positions, intellectuals began to take careful stock of their social responsibilities, tailoring a cosmopolitan outlook to the demands of a bleak national reality.[2] Historical events assumed a pro-

---

1. For an insightful evaluation of the writer as professional in this period, see Adolfo Prieto, *Literatura y subdesarrollo* (Rosario: Editorial Biblioteca, 1968).

2. The following books are typical expressions of the writer's concern for his national realities and for the failure of Argentine liberalism in the 1930s: Raúl Scalabrini Ortiz, *El hombre que está solo y espera* (Buenos Aires: Gleizer, 1931); Ezequiel Martínez Estrada, *Radiografía de la pampa* (Buenos Aires: Babel, 1933); Eduardo Mallea, *Historia de una pasión argentina* (Buenos Aires: Anaconda, 1938); and Manuel Gálvez, *La Argentina en nuestros libros* (Santiago: Ercilla, 1935). These essays represent efforts to jus-

tagonic role in Argentine texts of the 1930s, superseding the whimsical experiments with metaphor and language play that attracted writers during the previous decade.

The feminist response during this period is particularly intriguing for its oftentimes contradictory analysis of women's problematic role within an intellectual elite.[3] Norah Lange, Victoria Ocampo, and Alfonsina Storni, the best-known women writers of this time, deal unevenly with their literary self-representations, each resorting to escapist fantasies in order to handle the unwelcoming historical situation. Storni, who best understands the oppression of her sex, transforms her poetic expression from a lyric of innocent romance (in the 1920s) to an anguished, subjective voice designed to challenge openly the social injustices as she perceived them.[4] Her despair before unanswered questions leads her to suicide in 1938. Norah Lange first published her lyric poetry under the banner of the aggressive avant-garde movement that was known as ultraism; she later retreats to fantasies of childhood and adolescence as literary compensations for the hostile realities of the 1930s.[5] Victoria Ocampo, in her essays, turns away from Argentina's national crisis and looks, instead, to the metropolitan centers of Europe and the United States to find suitable models for imitation.

---

tify the role of the man of culture within the national context. Among other reasons, their inability to resolve the contradictions that emerged in the so-called "infamous decade" of Argentine history led many writers to suicide, among them Quiroga, Storni, Lugones, and Guillot. Dario Puccini gives a general overview of the Latin American writer in this decade in his article "America Latina: Il prezzo dell'autocoscienza," *Quaderni Storici*, 12, Fasc. 1 (January–April 1977): 79–98. See also David Rock, *Politics in Argentina, 1890–1930: The Rise and Fall of Radicalism* (Cambridge: Cambridge University Press, 1975), for an excellent historical study of the years before the Uriburu coup.

3. For a good historical synopsis of the social position of Argentine women during the first half of this century, see Nancy Caro Hollander, "Women: The Forgotten Half of Argentine History," in *Female and Male in Latin America*, ed. Ann Pescatello (Pittsburgh, Pa.: University of Pittsburgh Press, 1973), pp. 141–58.

4. Compare, for example, the different sensibilities that separate Storni's early romantic volumes such as *La inquietud del rosal* (1916) and *Languidez* (1920) from her last volume, *Mascarilla y trébol* (1938), where she takes up the question of woman's role in society.

5. One may contrast Lange's early poetic texts, *La calle de la tarde* (1925) and *Los días y las noches* (1926), where the *ultraísta* metaphor predominates, with her later prose fictions such as *Cuarenta y cinco días y treinta marineros* (1933) or *Cuadernos de infancia* (1937), in which the writer emphasizes a melancholic lament and escapist fantasy.

The pages of *Sur* reflect Ocampo's preference for male-inspired literary modes and consistently betray her affirmations for women's self-realization through writing.[6] Ocampo's intuitive way of comprehending the cultural task, seen in her numerous biographical notes and *Testimonios*, reproduces the vision of a solidly entrenched elite that mystifies contemporary realities and stalls historical process.

Feminist journals of the period also circumvent national concerns of Argentine women by drifting toward issues of transnational importance. *Mujeres de América* (1933–1936), for example, sought the integration of a broad-based Pan-American feminist movement designed to reach all women of the Americas, inspiring them to take action in political struggle. Its director, Nelly Merino de Carvallo, centralized the journal's focus on the oppression of Latin-American women.[7] *Mujeres de América* called upon women to struggle for agrarian reform or to mediate the peace settlements of the Chaco War. Carvallo urged her readership to action:

> Compañeras: las fronteras desaparecen frente a las desgracias que nos legó el pasado. Frente al hambre de América . . . está igualmente el hambre de todos los pueblos y la tragedia de la mujer sin derecho a la vida limpia y libre, expuesta al primer manotón viscoso de deseo detrás de cada pedazo de pan.[8]
>
> Comrades: the boundaries that separate us disappear before our common legacy of affliction. Before the hunger of America . . . there is the hunger of all people and the tragedy of woman, whose right to a decent and free life has been threatened by her desperate need for each crumb of bread.

---

6. For a criticism of *Sur*'s orientation toward foreign models, see Bertha Aceves et al., "Revista *Sur*: Una forma de colonialismo," *Crítica militante*, 1(1) (March–April 1978): 15–19; or Nicolás Rosa, "*Sur* o el espíritu y la letra," *Los libros*, 2(15–16) (January–February 1971): 4–6. Doris Meyer, by contrast, gives an impassioned defense of Ocampo's literary politics in *Victoria Ocampo: Against the Wind and the Tide* (New York: Braziller, 1979). Ocampo established separate domains for the work of men and women and repeatedly made clear her disinterest in competing with men for positions of privilege. See, for example, Ocampo's essay, "La mujer, sus derechos y sus responsabilidades," in her *La mujer y su expresión* (Buenos Aires: Sur, 1936).

7. In one editorial, Carvallo claimed the need for "woman's active participation in the struggle for life and the need to situate her in the world in conditions advantageous to her sex." Cited in *Mujeres de América*, 2(6) (February 1934): 19.

8. "Proa," *Mujeres de América*, 2(6) (February 1934): 20. All English translations are mine.

Despite the journal's seemingly progressive internationalist position, it still defined women as "helpers," advocates for the important issues that were to be resolved by knowledgeable men. At the same time, the foreign orientation of *Mujeres de América* avoided the Argentine problematic and women's role in the historical juncture of military dictatorship. Although the ideological premises of this magazine differed substantially from those of *Sur*, *Mujeres de América* also managed to avoid the national context by diluting Argentina's political issues in an internationalist solution.

La literatura argentina (1928–1936), in a similar way, obfuscated the preoccupations of Argentine women in the decade of the 1930s. This journal initiated a monthly page of feminine literary criticism under the direction of Raquel Adler, who took to task the diffusion of women's literature in Argentina.[9] In her columns, she exposed the sexist exclusion of women writers from Argentine literary history and from the literary contests and competitions of her day. In one essay, Adler asserted:

> Al clasificar su obra, literariamente hablando, no es entonces el caso de separarla de los hombres escritores, sino de unir su valor intelectual de la producción literaria. Sabemos asimismo que se ha premiado hasta ahora a un reducido número de escritoras. Y premiar una obra femenina no consiste tan solo en lo que aporta de vanidad literaria o de consagración inmediata. Convencerse de que en nuestro país hay un número algo crecido de mujeres de talento es contraer la costumbre y la consideración a la obra femenina.[10]

> We evaluate the literature of women not for the purpose of separating the writer from her male colleagues, but in order to emphasize the intellectual value behind the literary product. We also know that few women writers have received prizes in recognition of their work. Not that the prize is a simple issue of public

9. Adler actively publicized books written by women, feminist literary clubs, and book expositions. In fact, she was among the first to write a lengthy article on the works of Sara de Etcheverts: "Exposición femenina del libro latinoamericano," *La literatura argentina*, 3(36) (August 1931): 366–72.

10. Raquel Adler, "Consideraciones sobre los premios femeninos," *La literatura argentina*, 4(37) (September 1931): 10. On literary prizes, Teresa González commented in a different article: "The collective action of men drives me to rebellion when I see how they join together with more force and less responsibility to favor or deny the merits and virtues of women." "Las escritoras versus el Jurado Municipal," *La literatura argentina*, 4(42) (February 1932); 185.

> prestige or immediate consecration for the writer. It demands that we defy habit and our usual evaluation of women's work by recognizing an ever-increasing number of talented women writers in our country.

Adler disclaimed a separatist position; instead, her plans to enrich feminist literary culture relied upon a sturdy integration of women writers within the male-dominated artistic mainstream. In this way, the Club del Progreso and the Jockey Club were held as models for imitation.[11] Feminists like Adler and her colleagues, who formed part of the oligarchic sector of Argentine society, saw themselves tied more than ever to the male-controlled cultural domain: an independent creativity for women would have to wait.

Sara de Etcheverts, whose fictions have received little attention either in her native Argentina or abroad, provides a valuable summary of these ambivalent feminist perspectives in Argentine literature. Her five novels, published between the late 1920s and 1944, offer lessons in literary history as they mark phases of transition in a changing esthetic sensibility. While Argentine writers of the twenties were divided into disputatious camps of social realists and avant-garde esthetes, identified respectively as the Boedo and Florida movements, Etcheverts follows an independent course that at once absorbs the experimental tendencies of the cosmopolitan mode and projects a social awareness of the inequities of modern Argentine life.[12] The first stage of her writing reflects the disengaged esthetic principles of *belle époque* art, which was formed by audacious formal games and language play. Etcheverts' attraction to futurism is unmistakable: a strident resurrection of Marinetti's cult of the machine, velocity, and violence gives radical energy to her narratives. Etcheverts follows not only the principal tenets of futurism as conceived by Marinetti but also leans upon those writers who actively shared the European modernist fever: references and parodies of Lawrence, Montherlant, and D'Annunzio punctuate the

---

11. This conciliatory position of Adler and her colleagues (Margarita Arsamasseva, Margarita Abella Caprile, and Rosa Bazán de Cámera) was sharply rebuked by Enrique de la Gatín in his article, "Las literatas y el movimiento revolucionario," *Claridad*, no. 215 (September 1930).

12. Alberto Pineta, in *Verde Memoria* (Buenos Aires: Zamora, 1962), describes Etcheverts as an associate of Gómez de la Serna, Norah Lange, Girondo, Vignale, and the González Tuñón brothers, a fact which would suggest Etcheverts' preference for the aestheticizing group known as the "Florida Street" coterie. Nestor Ibarra, in his book *La nueva poesía argentina* (Buenos Aires: Molinari, 1930), indicates that Etcheverts attempted to develop an avant-garde, ultraist prose style.

pages of her fictions. Etcheverts' texts reveal an uncritical absorption of European modernism; in fact, she even uses—not ironically—the misogynist declarations of those writers to describe her supposedly independent female characters. This pattern is especially evident in Etcheverts' first novels, *El animador de la llama* (The Flame Bearer) and *El constructor del silencio* (The Sculptor of Silence) in which she exalts the artist as iconoclast and innovator.[13] Etcheverts' heroes—artists, actors, and alienated wanderers who roam the streets of Buenos Aires—generate a series of discussions on aesthetic sensibility and posit to the reader modes of interpretation of contemporary reality. Characters meet in literary salons and thus construct a textual situation that invites debate on modes of representation in art and the possibility of self-discovery through fiction. Through structured inquiries of this kind, Etcheverts presents the contradictions of the modern intellectual who at once is seriously attracted to the contrivances of the avant-garde and genuinely believes in her own originality. Revealing the writer's indebtedness to a foreign discourse, Etcheverts' characters invariably act out the prescriptive declarations of European literary manifestoes, as if to announce a clear dependence upon distant models. In her later books, *El hijo de la ciudad* (Child of the City), *Una mujer porteña* (Buenos Aires Woman), and *Convivencia* (Convivial Life), she turns to a deliberately essayistic prose that forcefully questions the failures of Argentine liberalism and revaluates the productive conditions of the artist and her obligations to society.[14] In her search for literary solutions for the problems of everyday life, Etcheverts fills her narratives with contradictory assertions about culture and feminism: a forced amalgam of borrowed ideas again mediates her understanding of national political alternatives. National identity, the essence of Argentine character, and the future of national democracy are resolved by the artist amidst the clatter of the automobile and the

---

13. *El constructor del silencio* (Buenos Aires: Tor, 1929) won the first prize in the Buenos Aires Municipal Contest (1929). *El animador de la llama* (Buenos Aires: Tor, n.d.) contains two novels, *El animador de la llama* and *El imperialismo de la vida interior*. We can speculate that *El animador* was written between 1926 and 1928 because of Etcheverts' references to Güiraldes' *Don Segundo Sombra* (published in 1926), to Honegger's musical oratorio *Le Roi David* (which made its Buenos Aires debut in August 1925), and to President Marcelo de Alvear, whose term in office expired in 1928. Etcheverts' insistence on contemporary events allows one to speculate that the novel was written while Alvear was still in office.

14. *El hijo de la ciudad* (Buenos Aires: L. J. Rosso, 1931); *Una mujer porteña* (Buenos Aires: Tor, 1934); *Convivencia* (Buenos Aires: Claridad, 1944).

wonders of modern aviation. Although immigration, colonization, and the dissonant perspectives on life that separate the metropolis from the provinces occupy much of the narrative discussion of her later fictions, Etcheverts makes it clear that the solution for Argentina's problems will not come from the popular sectors but from the artist qua innovator who promises democratic restoration through literary invention and machinery. Technology (of the futurist brand) provides adventure for her narrative heroes while it paradoxically denies them their claims to uniqueness.[15] Etcheverts examines problems of individual alienation and provides questionable solutions through the strategies of imported literary lessons. Her five novels project the common themes of the Argentine writer of the 1930s while they offer the reader a mode of reconsidering modern literary history.

In her earliest novels, *El animador de la llama* and *El constructor del silencio*, the *ultraísta* mode dominates the discourse as the writer experiments with games of literary form.[16] These novels present aesthetic solutions for contemporary political realities. Etcheverts' characters wander through the streets of Buenos Aires in the hope of discovering a relevant alternative for an otherwise senseless life. In each novel, a scanty plot generates a series of discussions on the function of art and literature and the possibility of a revived national culture. In *El animador de la llama*, one of two novels contained in Etcheverts' first volume of the same title, young artists and actresses comment on contemporary aesthetic modes. Mariano Goyena, who serves as *chef d'école* for the bohemian denizens of the novel, establishes guidelines for the perception and evaluation of art, while he inspires his colleagues to engage in the adventure of modernist aesthetics. All relationships among characters are mediated by the exigencies of art, so that even his lover, Delfina Hurtado, an aspiring stage actress in the capital city, serves as a narrative vehicle to promote a discussion about the function of modern theater.

---

15. Walter Benjamin's now classical essay, "The Work of Art in the Age of Mechanical Reproduction," synthesizes some of the literary problems that Etcheverts raises, particularly with respect to the artist's role in a technological age. See Benjamin's *Illuminations*, trans. Harry Zohn (New York: Schocken, 1978), pp. 217–51. His comments are particularly interesting if we consider the contemporaneous visions shared by him and Etcheverts.

16. Alfonsina Storni, in the prologue of *El animador de la llama*, praises Etcheverts' management of *ultraísta* imagery in prose (pp. 5–6). Alfonso Sola González has studied *El constructor del silencio* as an example of *ultraísmo* in his book *Capítulos de la novela argentina* (Mendoza: Biblioteca San Martín, 1959).

In addition, characters discuss the relative merits of European writers and the problem of their influence in Argentine art. Although they urge an independent creative spirit freed from the bonds of tradition, the bohemians of this novel ultimately turn to D'Annunzio and Marinetti for poetic inspiration. Like those Italian writers, who suggest models for literary behavior, the protagonists consider the artistic act as a spontaneous adventure in form, a fleeting gesture that denies prolonged engagement with anecdote. In this way, the characters of Etcheverts' fiction hail technical virtuosity as the necessary skill of the modern writer. Art should emphasize its own form and call attention to the moment of creation. At the same time, it should inspire the viewer, eliciting a mystical sensuality that transcends one's adherence to anecdote (p. 31). The passion of religion is contrasted to the mystical experience of art, and, naturally, the characters decide in favor of the sustenance provided by the aesthetic endeavor.

The narrative actions of this thinly elaborated novel call attention to those prescriptions. Characters urge movement over silence and action over contemplation in an attempt to surpass the constraints of rational discourse. Honegger's *Roi David* appropriately accompanies these discussions as characters prepare to escape from their responsibilities by taking flight, disappearing in automobiles and airplanes.[17] Goyena flees to Paris, the revered center of metropolitan culture, but first he initiates his rites of passage on a plane called the Victory of Samothrace. As if to announce an undisguised debt to Marinetti, the image of classical sculpture is appended to the aviator's dream and provides, in the final analysis, a futurist emblem for escape. Yet the play between technology and art leads finally to the artist's defeat, demystifying his demagogical role and causing a crisis of Self.

Even Etcheverts' treatment of women characters approaches and then retreats from the propositions of the Italian vanguard. Delfina Hurtado, for example, duplicates the models of D'Annunzio's *femme fatale* (although her arrogant sensuality and her participation in the theatrical world also remind us to some degree of the heroine of Eugenio Cambaceres' novel *Sin Rumbo*).[18] Invincible, sensual, and some-

17. The actions of Etcheverts' characters bear a startling resemblance to those of D'Annunzio's characters in his *Forse che sí forse che no*. In that work, D'Annunzio's heroes are also taken by the wonders of modern aviation and the autmobile. It is no surprise that Etcheverts cites the Italian writer so frequently in her novels.

18. Mario Praz offers a valuable analysis of D'Annunzio's *femme fatale* in *The Romantic Agony*, trans. Angus Davidson (New York: Meridian, 1963).

what sadistic, Delfina Hurtado struggles to free herself from the men who attempt to control her. She seeks emancipation from traditional roles in order to realize her career as a stage actress. Ironically, she portrays, in her culminating role, the character of Clytemnestra, suggestive of the wanton cruelty that defines Delfina in the eyes of men. As an interpolated tale in the novel, dramatic action on stage distills the real and projected problems of the actress. Unable to comply with the expectations placed on her, Delfina takes her life and leaves the other characters to continue their dispassionate contemplation of art, removed from the realities of human interaction. Far from projecting a positive image of her female characters, Etcheverts locks her heroine into a static role with no fruitful alternatives for action.

Through a lengthy discussion of art and theater, the novelist reveals a true allegiance to the patrician sectors of society. Even the real-life figures who populate the narrative announce Etcheverts' directions for artistic reform. In one scene, politicians and writers prepare to enter the Casa de la Llama theater. A procession of luminaries comes to pay homage to Delfina: Lugones, Melián Lafinur, Larreta, Güiraldes, Rojas, and Echagüe corroborate the privileged perspective of the narrator as they exchange critiques of the spectacle observed (pp. 57–66). Leading this coterie of intellectuals are President Marcelo de Alvear and his wife Regina Pacini. The Argentine First Lady's theatrical background is particularly interesting in this novel since it strongly suggests that the marriage of art and politics is not simply the story stuff of fiction. More importantly, the dominant figures of cultural and political life in Argentina bear witness to Etcheverts' evaluation of the artist in society; clearly, they agree that the modification of history comes from a special circle of initiates.

El imperialismo de la vida interior, the second novel that comprises *El animador de la llama*, reiterates this ideological position. Renato Mistral seeks self-definition through the cult of the machine. Invigorated by the unrestrained force of velocity, Mistral turns to the potential of speed and movement to compensate for an otherwise meaningless life. Movement fills the emptiness of existence and allows the hero to make sense of his role in society. Action shifts from the fashionable districts of central Buenos Aires to the ranches of the southern pampas, where Mistral contemplates the irreconcilable disparities of his heritage and of his national culture. Much like the Nietzschean hero of *Thus Spoke Zarathustra* (who inspires Renato Mistral), the protagonist, at thirty years of age, leaves for the country to reconsider possibilities for a future life. The D'Annunzian superman aesthetics that informed *El animador de la llama* are replaced in this novel by the

Nietzschean cult of the *Übermensch*: "el hombre tiene que ser superado" (p. 227) (man must be surpassed), declares Mistral as he seeks a son who will inherit his calling as a social redeemer. It is no mistake that the resolution of national problems is found, in *El imperialismo de la vida interior*, by a member of society's privileged class. The poor have no voice in the novel except as a picturesque leitmotif; the valiant ones among them are later discovered to share family bonds with the elite.[19] Women are relegated to maternal roles and serve as Mistral's assistants in his social project. Like the novel that preceded it, *El imperialismo de la vida interior* calls upon exceptional figures of society to redirect the course of history. Mistral renounces his oligarchic past in exchange for a more promising future as a civilizing force in the pampas. He changes his name to Pedro Flama, and, invoking the emblem of the Victory of Samothrace, he flees from the constraints of the metropolis.[20] Etcheverts' open-ended narrative leaves the fate of her hero unknown and, at the same time, invites speculation on the prospects for success of Mistral's liberal project.

In Etcheverts' second volume, *El constructor del silencio*, vanguard models control the action of a tightly woven plot about urban alienation and loneliness. The hero, Andrés Marza, examines the failures of his spiritual life and contemplates creative alternatives. Spatial inversions, temporal reversals, and masked appearances contribute to a narrative in which the writer emphasizes the distances that alternately confuse and then separate subjective and objective worlds. Etcheverts manipulates a mirrorlike game of reflections that fragments the perspectives on old and new and signals a focus on surface realities as a compensation for a hollow interior life. Appearances, then, displace the inner contradictions of the hero as silence is transformed into movement to form a panache of cinematic images:

---

19. Etcheverts reveals a clear debt to Güiraldes' *Don Segundo Sombra* when she sends her hero, Mistral, to the country. In the provinces, Mistral meets his relatives of the Cáceres family; the name, of course, reminds one of the young hero of Güiraldes' novel. It is notable also that Mistral's entrance in the country home parallels Don Segundo's appearance in the Güiraldes narrative.

20. When Mistral renounces his past and changes his name to Pedro Flama in order to start life anew, one is reminded of *Thus Spoke Zarathustra*, the admitted model for Etcheverts' narrative: "You must wish to consume yourself in your own flame: how could you wish to become new unless you first become ashes?" asks Zarathustra, thus foreshadowing Mistral's designs for change; cited from *Thus Spoke Zarathustra*, Book 1, in *The Portable Nietzsche*, ed. and trans. Walter Kaufmann (New York: Viking Press, 1963), p. 176.

> Andrés Marza sintió con desesperación la impresión de otras veces: que él vivía continuamente en una sala de cine y que todo llegaba a su receptividad a través de ese cosmos de sombras sin palabras, de esa humanidad de apariencias que es la película. (p. 44)

> Andres Marza experienced the desperate sensation of earlier times, that he was living continually in a movie theater and that all impressions reached him through that cosmos of silent shadows, through a humanity based on appearances that governs the film image.

It comes as no surprise that film images should direct the dominant metaphors of motion in this novel. Like the hero Goyena before him, Marza wants to convert his interior silence into action and to project his aspirations onto the cult of the modern in order to forge an epic of movement:

> Quería dar a los hombres el poema de la epopeya moderna, el poema que llevaba dentro con una succión de llaga, donde narraría en cien episodios dislocados el origen del avión y del piloto como de una humanidad no creada, sino construída por el hombre mismo y con los mismo errores garrafales de la humanidad creada por los dioses. Pero con una ventaja: la construcción de la ultra audacia, no la audacia guerrera y sí la audacia desnuda de la hazaña. (p. 26)

> He wanted to give men the modern epic poem, the sorely tormenting poem that he carried within him, a poem in which he would narrate in one hundred fragmented episodes the birth of aviation and of the pilot of man, comparing it to a creation story. But one in which man himself created life and with the same fatal errors that belong to the humanity created by the gods. But with one advantage: he would construct the ultimate audacity, not the martial boldness, but the naked temerity that is found in the heroic feat.

Paul Morand with his "Pullman de imágenes" (p. 18) (Pullman of Images) inspires Marza and his inventor to forge an achronological text that focuses on movement, velocity, and color. The narrative becomes a vivid topography of Buenos Aires and its environs, recalling the lyric experiments of the *ultraísta* poets:

> Retiro. Eructos de gente por las bocas de las plataformas. Andrés Marza entró por una de ellas, se sentó en un banco, miró hacia

> arriba: el inmenso techo de cristal limitando el cielo, transformándolo en una usina de nubes. (pp. 28–29)
>
> Palermo con sus canchas rojas como las encías infladas de las sandías. El Hipodromo encerrado en el propio movimiento de punta a punta, enredándose con sus mismos talones. Los sauces autoacariciadores, masturbados. El Plata, carta estrujada y tachada de distancias. (p. 31)
>
> Villa Urquiza desgañitándose, como un crupié, desde un alto parlante, placero del aire. (p. 32)
>
> El eucalipto frente a la casa, orquesta típica de gorriones. El jardín regado de soledad. Un molino viejo, en el fondo, charlando con el viento en la trastienda de una nube. (p. 35)

> Retiro. The cavity of the train station belched hordes of people. Andres Marza entered, sat down on a bench, and looked up; the immense glass roof enclosed the sky, transforming it into a factory of clouds.
>
> Palermo with its red track, like swollen gums of watermelon. The Hippodrome encircled in its own movement from tip to toe, caught up in its own heels. Self-caressing willows, excited. The River Plate, a rumpled card, erased by distances.
>
> Villa Urquiza shrieking like a croupier, from a loudspeaker, marketer of air.
>
> The eucalyptus tree in front of the house, an orchestra of sparrows. The garden watered with solitude. An old mill, in the distance, chatting with the wind in the garret of a cloud.

Through personification, inversion, and metonymic reductions, Etcheverts deconstructs a visual panorama of the city. She distorts common geography in a metaphoric displacement of spatio-temporal markers, reminiscent of the early poetry of Girondo, Borges, or Lange. Urban and rural scenes collapse in a cinematic collage that defies symbolic decoding; at the same time, the viewer's sense of order is necessarily distorted. This visual way of making sense of the world confirms Marza's hypothesis: "Todo era la sensación . . . nunca el sentimiento" (p. 122) (everything was sensation, never passion).

As Etcheverts converts the city into a diagram of colorful objects and intersecting planes, she simultaneously denies the potential of human labor. This becomes particularly evident in her descriptions of the work site. The hero, Andrés Marza, takes a job in an automobile factory, but the physical effort of workers is transcribed by Etcheverts as a spectacle of automation, sound, and movement. Labor is explained as an exhilarating celebration of the machine, and the writer effectively ignores the human dynamic. Etcheverts anesthetizes the personal dimension of work and converts social labor into a technological, artistic act. Reminding us of the futurist games in her earlier narratives, the writer blithely dismisses worker exploitation by textualizing the wonders of automation as an imagistic design. The *guarango* and the *cocoliche*—popular urban types who designate Argentina's lower classes—are still-life figures within this novel; as signs, they bear no real meaning within the Argentine social hierarchy portrayed or within the internal dynamics of the text. Instead, Etcheverts uses these social labels as a way to distance us from the human interests described in the factory. As matchstick figures, they stand on the margins of narrative progress. Marza, meanwhile, fails to make sense of his life; creative labor through writing or assembly-line tasks fails to bring him his desired liberation. Unable to reconcile his ignominious position in life with his aspirations for success, he escapes in an automobile, surrendering his power of self-determination to the force of the machine. Clearly, the novel's ending suggests that artistic alienation knows no resolution in a technological age.

The characters of these early novels willingly turn to art as a possible panacea for the ills of modernity, but, invariably, they find themselves caught in the contradictions of this disputable solution. In Etcheverts' later novels, *El hijo de la ciudad*, *Una mujer porteña*, and *Convivencia*, the historical juncture that inspires character alienation is examined in greater detail. Etcheverts gives thematic preference to popular concerns about fascism, imperialism, and the erosion of national confidence. *El hijo de la ciudad*, for example, presents an epic drama of early twentieth-century Argentine history. The novel reviews significant events that anticipate the "infamous decade" of the 1930s; the rise and fall of Yrigoyen, the effect of the Russian revolution, anarcho-syndical uprisings in the Patagonia, and the "tragic week" of 1919 form the story stuff of this narrative. In *Convivencia*, characters debate the effects of English and North American imperialism on a dependent national culture. They study the phenomena of immigration and the tyranny of political bosses while they review the implications of capitalism on the productive labor of the artist. The ills of the modern world must be corrected, they declare, in order to free the individual and to enhance one's creativity. The political issues raised in *Convivencia* and *El hijo de la ciudad* are countered by a series of facile literary solutions. In *El hijo de la ciudad*, characters turn to technology to redeem the artist from his anonymity; in *Convivencia*, the heroes invoke the spirit of Krishna and D. H. Lawrence to compensate for an otherwise unfulfilling existence. Torn between the attractions of the sensual and the spiritual, the characters ultimately renounce their understanding of history in order to indulge the pleasures of the moment. In both novels, the individual is exalted for his potential creativity, which develops in a social vacuum. Etcheverts' heroes operate unquestioningly on the principle that the artist can redeem society without direct participation in daily life. In this way, history is reduced to a rhetorical filler designed to punctuate the self-serving activities of cosmopolitan writers. Fascism and capitalism become pretexts for aesthetic meditations. At the same time, the heroes of these two novels take stock of their own limitations when they try to understand history. Yet poets fail miserably when they try to describe their reality; rather than forge a social vision of their world, they retreat into a private and solipsistic universe. "Compartir es dejar de ser y yo quiero ser" (p. 61) (To share with others is to lose one's sense of self), affirms a heroine of *Convivencia* in a feeble attempt to withdraw from her social environment. Etcheverts projects the contradictions of liberal writers of her generation who abuse contemporary history in the interests of the literary experience. Political events are withdrawn from their context to serve as leitmotifs of otherwise ordinary narrative tales about individual success or failure. Even the characters' attempts to integrate all forms of artisic expression in one narrative situation reflect this eclectic and conciliatory illusion. Thus, strophes from immigrant theater merge with the precious lyric of vanguard experimentalism, the voice of the popular sectors joins the chorus of society's elite. This facile erasure of class differences in literature coincides with the writer's perceived mission as a savior of the modern age. But the narrator betrays her expressed beliefs in the possibility of a fruitful change; ultimately, the characters fail, each in his own way. Following much discussion, escape, and travel, the hero of *El hijo de la ciudad* concludes with a perplexing question: "Retornar es partir de nuevo . . . . Pero ¿quién redime al hombre de vivir todos los días?" (p. 221) (To return is to start anew . . . . But who can save man from the trials of everyday life?).

The integration of history and fiction is central to the narrative strategy of *Una mujer porteña*. Etcheverts describes the aspirations of woman in modern society and elaborates, through a series of flashbacks, the historical constraints that inhibit her character's freedom. Luciana, an artist, struggles against historical determinism in order to justify her vocational choice. The youth is a misfit among her peers; in order to escape the routine expectations demanded of her (love, marriage, and the promise of children), she evaluates her family history and tries to envisage a course for the future. Situated in a handsome suburb of Buenos Aires, *Una mujer porteña* issues a fierce condemnation of the wasteful follies of privileged youth and criticizes the ideals of more tempered conservative adults who cling to the last vestiges of an oligarchy in decline. Friendships, family, and marriage among the characters of this novel reflect outmoded forms of behavior that inhibit the progress of history and deny the possibility of change. Recollections of family traditions—the unitarian party heritage and the glitter of the 1880s—are juxtaposed to the present moment to control the dialectical tension of the heroine's struggle for identity. Luciana pays special attention to her mother's role and to the restrictions placed on her through marriage and family responsibilities. Hiding in the shadow of her spouse, Luciana's mother represents the cowardly aspect of the Argentine woman, who is afraid to take an independent course of action. Recalling her mother's experience, Luciana asserts the necessity of a work ethic as the only hope for woman's survival. But Luciana faces a classical dilemma: she can accept recognized forms of behavior that bring with them the protection of an easy future, or she can move forward into the uncertainty of loneliness.[21]

Accompanying this interweaving of past and present realities is a creative exploration of the function of art. Luciana finds inspiration in Henry de Montherlant's novel *Aux fontaines du désir* (1927) and decides to parody the explicit course elaborated by that writer.[22] Following Montherlant's propositions, Luciana indulges the protean fount of artistic creativity and seeks in every experience a sense of adventure that serves to conquer her limitations. This outlook, in turn, encourages a plan for escape: "Partir no es morir, sino verificarse, revelar sugerencias que estaban dentro" (p. 192) (Leaving is not death, but a mode of self-verification; a way to reveal those secrets hidden in one's soul). Luciana's flight, in the shadow of Montherlant's misogynist propositions, only points to the paradoxical nature of one's presumed liberation: derivative ideas allow the heroine to cradle an illusion of freedom.

Una mujer porteña works from a series of flashbacks that recall national traditions and offset the present realities. In both historical mo-

21. As Luciana contemplates her options, she also reads Colette's *La vagabonde*; the heroine of Colette's novel suffers a crisis similar to Luciana's.

22. Here, Luciana turns to a clearly misogynist writer for inspiration. Etcheverts has positioned each of her heroines before an unwelcoming male writer, anticipating, in a way, a self-destructive course for each of her narrative women.

ments, the writer suggests that women are bound to the rule of patriarchy. Fascism, the military, and the alienation of city life offer little hope for the creative endeavors of women. Like the other characters of Etcheverts' novels, Luciana challenges these historical restrictions by escaping into the future. She abandons her project of integrating past and present; renouncing her family tradition, she sets sail for Paris in the fantasy of self-realization abroad. The European metropolis again provides a remedy for any *criollo* disorder.

Sara de Etcheverts' novels serve as an apprenticeship for the larger aesthetic and political problems of the modern Argentine writer. Protecting the interests of the intellectual in a hostile and commercialized society, Etcheverts allows her heroes to elaborate plans for self-redemption. She locks her protagonists in the comfortable structure of the intellectual coterie wherein all dialogue and actions are generated. This bohemian group creates a private world for Etcheverts' characters, insulating them from contemporary Argentine realities. At the same time, it permits them a comfortable space in which to nurture an esoteric spiritualism or the illusions of utilitarian reform. Argentine history, then, becomes a pretext for literary discussion. Characters never engage directly in the major events of their day but, instead, take advantage of historical data to serve the interests of debate and meditation. Etcheverts introduces foreign literary models in order to legitimize the role of the artist in society, but the presence of writers such as Marinetti and Montherlant only serves to reinforce the intellectual dependency that characterizes Etcheverts' heroes and especially dominates the female protagonists. The borrowed European project fails in each of the novels because of the dissonant cultural perspectives that separate Argentina from the cultural centers abroad and serves as a metaphor for the dependent ideological formulations that emerged from Argentina in the decades of the 1920s and 1930s. In no case do Etcheverts' heroes—male or female—compensate for their inadequacies as fallen gods in a technological age. Instead, their specious analyses only point to the false consciousness that informs the artist in a world of questionable values. Etcheverts offers no solutions for her characters; like her contemporaries, she projects in fiction the writer's despair before the crisis of modernity.

The Greatest Punishment

Female and Male in Lorca's Tragedies

Julianne Burton

In 1898, the year Federico García Lorca was born, Spain lost the last of her New World colonies to the expanding empire of the United States. The event precipitated a profound economic and spiritual crisis in a country which had for centuries based its identity on past imperial glories. The young Lorca arrived in Madrid from his native Andalusia shortly after the end of World War I. Europe was still shaken by that conflict and by the menacing reverberations of the Russian revolution. In his twenty-fifth year, Lorca witnessed the installation of Primo de Rivera's military dictatorship. The young poet was living at Columbia University when the Great Crash of 1929 rocked Wall Street and all of America. In 1930 he returned home and the following year witnessed the demise of the Spanish monarchy and the advent of the first Spanish Republic.

Reform and revolution were in the air. Lorca saw the social advances made by the Republicans—labor and land reforms, the secularization of the schools, decentralization of governmental power, the institution of divorce—gradually pushed back after 1933 by an increasingly conservative wave of reaction. Then, in February of 1936 came the electoral victory of the Popular Front with the united forces of the Left against the monarchists, clerics, and Falangists. Lorca visited Barcelona under the "Generalitat" and again just a few months before the rise and fall of the tumultuous and tragic Catalonian republic. He returned to Andalusia just days before Franco's Nationalist forces took over his native Granada. It was then that historical timing betrayed him. His death at the hands of the fascist troops coincided with the outbreak of the Spanish Civil War and the destruction of the principles which Lorca had embraced.

It hardly seems tenable to assume that an artist who lived in such times of turbulence and change, especially a poet whose art was so firmly grounded in popular soil, could remain impervious to the social and political upheaval surrounding him or that his works would not bear the traces of those experiences. Yet forty years after the poet's tragic death and even in this new, post-Franco era, Hispanists still insist on viewing Lorca as "ahistorical," "atemporal," and "apolitical."[1] These critics consistently fail to recognize the ideological bias inherent in their attempt to liberate Lorca from ideology.

In the face of those who would interpret Lorca as above and beyond his social and historical context, I would like to propose an alternative view. His experiences abroad and the circumstances at home sensitized him to the social realities of the Spain of his day: an archaic, hypocritical, and crippling morality; a hierarchical, even tyrannical family structure; extreme social stratification and exploitation of the humbler sectors; and a social-sexual code which privileged men at the expense of women's autonomy, participation, and self-realization. His perception of these social ills, combined with other personal factors, such as his mother's repeated protests against the senseless waste of Spanish womanhood and his own perception of women as the transmitters of culture, led him to present female experience as the core of the three tragedies he wrote toward the end of his life. These plays present a vision of what some anthropologists now call the sex-gender system of southern Spanish society. The depth and scope of Lorca's social dimension suggest a concerted attempt to expose and denounce the social system which gives rise to such irreconcilable conflicts and untenable contradictions.

The seriousness of Lorca's commitment to exploring the complexities of sexual politics is apparent in the opening scenes of the first play, *Bodas de sangre* (*Blood Wedding*) (1933). All possibilities of marital status are present in act 1: a widow and her unmarried son in the first scene, a married couple in the second, an unmarried woman and her widowed father in the third. By using generic rather than proper names throughout the first play (Father, Wife, Mother-in-Law), Lorca suggests that the individuality of his characters is subordinated to their function as representatives of certain social roles or

1. For a recent and sophisticated statement of this view, see Sumner N. Greenfield, "Lorca's Theater: A Synthetic Reexamination," *Journal of Spanish Studies: Twentieth Century*, 5(1) (Spring 1977): 34–37.

institutions. Lorca's female characters absorb more and more of his attention in succeeding plays: from his special focus on the mother and the bride (*novia*) in *Blood Wedding*, through his detailed exploration of the plight of a barren woman in *Yerma* (1934), to the sixteen female characters of *La casa de Bernarda Alba* (*The House of Bernarda Alba*) (1936), who, though they often feel the force of masculine presence, never once share the stage with a man. The main themes of the three plays make Lorca's interest in society as experienced by women even more explicit: *Blood Wedding* explores marriage, bereavement, and widowhood; *Yerma* is a study of married life and sterility; *The House of Bernarda Alba* offers an austere picture of matriarchy and spinsterhood.

The struggle between social prescription and individual impulse is at the core of Lorca's trilogy and of all of Lorca's work. The tragedies revolve around those characters who are unable or unwilling to resign themselves to their *sino* ("fate"). A grasp of the alternative interpretations of the *sino* is crucial to understanding the social dimension of Lorca's tragic vision. Whereas his characters most often perceive themselves as the hapless victims of mysterious forces beyond their control, Lorca weaves a counterview into the fabric of the plays, which suggests that definable social and material causes are responsible for the fate of individual characters. More specifically, four concrete factors account in the playwright's eyes for what the characters view as arbitrary destiny: environment, economic status, heredity, and the influence of *el qué dirán* ("community expectations") on the lives of individuals. His heroines' determination to transcend the social and moral confines of their sex in order to lay claim to the possibilities for self-determination traditionally reserved for men gives impetus both to their heroism and their tragedy.

"Hilo y aguja para las hembras. Látigo y mula para el varón"[2] (For women, needle and thread. Mules and whiplashes for the men), decrees Bernarda Alba (*BA*, p. 24) imposing society's rigid differentiation upon her five aging, yet still unmarried, daughters. Indeed, this distribution of tools is indicative of the sexual segregation of the whole society. The association of man with the whip, symbol of dominance over the brute beast, also suggests the man–weapon association, an especially prevalent theme throughout the poems of Lorca's famous

2. Translations are my own. Page numbers refer to the editions of Buenos Aires: Losada, 1969, except for references to *Blood Wedding*, which use the Aguilar edition (Madrid: 1969) of the *Obras Completas*. Codes: *BW*: *OC* = *Blood Wedding*, *Y* for *Yerma*, *BA* for *The House of Bernarda Alba*.

Romancero gitano (*Gypsy Ballads*) and in *Blood Wedding*, where the mother laments, "Los varones . . . tienen por fuerza que manejar armas" (Men . . . are compelled to wield weapons) (*BW*: *OC*, p. 1228). These associations are consistent with man's role as arbiter, avenger, and ruler. In the society which Lorca depicts, a needle is the nearest approximation to a tool or weapon accessible to women.[3] When she is finally driven to violence, a woman has only her bare hands and the strength of her pent-up rage and long-repressed potential. The mother in *Blood Wedding* fears that one of the enemy family might be buried in the same plot as her slain husband and son. Infuriated at this idea, she threatens, "¡Y eso sí que no! ¡Ca! ¡Eso sí que no! Porque con las uñas los desentierro y yo sola los machaco contra la tapia" (And that will never happen! No! That will never happen! Because I'll dig them up with my fingernails and, all by myself, I'll crush them to pieces against the wall" (*BW*: *OC*, p. 1176). And when Yerma's repressed fury is turned against her husband, Juan, she strangles him to death.

With their needle and thread women painstakingly labor over trousseaus, fill hope chests, make baby clothes, and, in their leisure, fashion frilly, nonessential things. The lullaby Leonardo's wife and mother-in-law sing boasts of the child's steel cradle with its pillow and coverlet of fine linen (*BW*: *OC*, p. 1185). These—and her children—make up a woman's only wealth,[4] a wealth, which, unlike the man's, has no exchange value and thus offers no economic independence. Many references are made in the plays to other female occupations—cooking, cleaning, washing clothes, marketing, child rearing—all do-

---

3. Bernarda, the most authoritarian of Lorca's characters, actually does use a rifle against Pepe, but she excuses her own inaccuracy: "No fue culpa mía. Una mujer no sabe apuntar" (*BA*, p. 123) (It wasn't my fault. A woman doesn't know how to take aim).

4. Mourning the death of her last son, the bridegroom's mother laments, "Vendrán las vecinas y no quiero que me vean tan pobre. . . . Una mujer que no tiene un hijo siquiera que poderse llevar a los labios" (*BW*: *OC*, p. 1268) (The neighborwomen will come, and I don't want them to see me so poor. . . . A woman without a single son to take to her lips). María avoids visiting Yerma since Yerma always cries at the sight of María's son. "Me da tristeza que tengas envidia," María tells her. "No es envidia lo que tengo; es pobreza," Yerma replies (*Y*, p. 62) ('It saddens me that you are envious.' 'What I feel is not envy, but poverty'). Children are the fulfillment and the legitimization of women, which is why Yerma so desperately seeks a child. They are also insurance for the legitimate wife. The social rights of Leonardo's wife are assured because she has borne him one child and awaits another. She can spurn him and dedicate herself to her children, preserving her own honor intact despite her husband's infidelity and disgrace.

mestic and without market value.[5] The mule and the whip are tools in the creation of male wealth, for man tills the fields and harvests the crops, shears the sheep, presses the oil and the wine, then exchanges his products for currency or for other goods necessary for his family's well-being.

In Lorca's plays, man's world radiates outward from the home; woman's activities confine her within it except for her occasional trips to the well for water, to the store for goods, or to bring lunch to her husband in the fields. She may leave the house to perform only the most essential duties, for most husbands share Juan's sentiments: "No me gusta que salgas . . . . La calle es para la gente desocupada" (*Y*, p. 15) (I don't like you to go out. . . . The street is for people with nothing to do).[6] If she tarries along the way, she risks incurring the anger of her husband, as Yerma does when Juan comes upon her talking to his friend Victor: "¡Qué haces todavía aquí! . . . Debías estar en casa. . . . No comprendo en qué te has entretenido. . . . Así darás que hablar a los gentes" (*Y*, p. 38–39) (What are you doing here still? . . . You should be at home. . . . I don't understand what has kept you. . . . Now you'll give people something to talk about). Man, however, can roam at will and even has horses to take him "al límite de los llanos" (*BW*: *OC*, p. 1187) (to the edge of the plains), equivalent for Leonardo's wife and mother-in-law, confined as they are to their *mala choza*, to "el fin del mundo" (*BW*: *OC*, p. 1189) (the end of the world).

Lorca underlines the fact that man is woman's master, and as father or brother or husband, governs her activities. He exercises this prerogative by virtue of his role as provider, as the case of Juan's two spinster sisters illustrates. Juan imports them to watch over Yerma, and they are obliged to accept their role as her wardens, for they have no other man to support them and no possibility of independent livelihood. On one occasion Juan scolds them for letting Yerma go out alone: "Una de vosotras debía salir con ella, porque para eso estáis aquí comiendo en mi mantel y bebiendo mi vino" (*Y*, p. 55) (One of you should go out with her. After all, that's why you're here drinking

5. The only exception is the reference made by Leonardo's wife to the women who gather capers, an occupation so humble and painstaking that it is relegated to women.

6. This injunction is particularly unjust and ironic in Yerma's case, for there is no one more unoccupied than she, or more reluctant to be so. When Juan tells her that a woman's place is in the home, she protests, "Cuando las casas no son tumbas. Cuando las sillas se rompen y las sábanas de hilo se gastan con el uso" (*Y*, p. 57) (When the home is not a tomb. When chairs get broken and the linen sheets wear out from use).

my wine and dining at my table). Women's status is no more than that of a slave to the man; as Martirio, one of Bernarda's daughters, bitterly puts it, "una perra sumisa que les dé de comer" (*BA*, p. 34) (a submissive she-dog to give them their food). As long as she is dependent upon a man, she must serve him, preserve his honor, and be subject to his will.

At certain points Lorca suggests that women in this society are viewed as mere extensions of the kinds of property controlled by men. For example, it is not until after a young man has acquired land that he can take a wife. With the children she then bears him his estate will be complete. The neighbor woman points out the almost causal relation between the two processes in the first scene of *Blood Wedding*: "¡[Tu hijo] al fin compró la viña! . . . ¡Ahora se casará!" (*BW*: *OC*, p. 1174) ([Your son] has bought the vineyard at last! . . . Now he'll get married!). Because she is his personal property, Juan has the socially sanctioned right to chide Yerma for her wanderings, confine her to the house, and summon his sisters to keep watch over her. As he tells her during an argument, "No debía decirte: perdóname, sino obligarte, encerrarte, porque para eso soy el marido" (*Y*, p. 60) (I shouldn't say 'forgive me,' but rather force you, lock you up because that's what I'm the husband for).

Woman's only autonomy comes when the dominant male figure in her life disappears. The bridegroom's widowed mother arranges his wedding, and since she tells him how many gifts he can buy, it is clear that the family finances are in her hands. In the absence of her husband it falls to her to maintain tradition and prepare her son for his new role. She is herself a victim of the desolation and incompleteness of a woman alone in that society. Yet when her widowhood gives her the opportunity to take a stand against male domination, even she works to perpetuate the most oppressive aspects of the patriarchy. This is dramatically illustrated in the advice she gives the bridegroom on his wedding day:

> Con tu mujer procura estar cariñosa, y si la notas infatuada o arisca, hazle una caricia que le produzca un poco de daño, un abrazo fuerte, un mordisco y luego un beso suave. Que ella no pueda disgustarse, pero que sienta que tú eres el macho, el amo, el que mandas. Así aprendí de tu padre. Y como no lo tienes, tengo que ser yo la que te enseñe estas fortalezas. (*BW*: *OC*, p. 1240)

Try to be affectionate with your wife, and if you notice her acting conceited or stubborn, caress her in a way that will cause

> her a bit of pain: a strong embrace, a bite followed by a soft kiss. Not enough to anger her, but enough to let her know that you are the *macho*, the one who gives the orders. This is what I learned from your father. Since you no longer have him, I have to be the one to teach you these manly defenses.

When the engagement is finalized, each parent presents his or her child to the other:

> *Madre.* Mi hijo tiene y puede.
> *Padre.* Mi hija también.
> *Madre.* Mi hijo es hermoso. No ha conocido mujer. La honra más limpia que una sábana puesta al sol.
> *Padre.* Qué te digo de la mía. Hace las migas a las tres, cuando el lucero. No habla nunca; suave como la lana, borda toda clase de bordados y puede cortar una maroma con los dientes.
>
> (*BW*: *OC*, p. 1198)

> *Mother.* My son has what it takes and knows what to do with it.
> *Father.* So does my daughter.
> *Mother.* My son is handsome. He has never known a woman. His honor shines brighter than a clean sheet in the sun.
> *Father.* No need to tell you about my daughter. She prepares the bread at three, when the morning star shines. She never speaks. She is soft as wool, embroiders all kinds of fancy work and can cut a strong cord with her teeth.

In the man, strength, capability, beauty, honor, and purity are praised whereas the woman's praises center around her docility, industriousness, and practical skills. The discrepancy between Lorca's representation of society's standards and his personal ones is clear, for his heroines are women of moral and spiritual (not merely physical) strength and resilience, women who do not eschew the traits their society cultivates but exceed them.

The social environment discourages the full expression of the qualities and potential of Lorca's heroines. Barring open rebellion, they are left with only two responses to their restricted sphere of activity, and both serve only to exacerbate the problem. Women can turn their attention outward by casting themselves in the role of custodians of their neighbor's honor; and this is an alternative chosen by many. Gossip is a rewarding occupation, for it is one of the few paths to power open to women. Their guardianship of local morality through public commentary occasions an intense and hypocritical preoccupation with *el qué dirán* on the part of their fellow townspeople. This occupation also confers on the womenfolk the important role of oral "historians," shaping popular opinion and perpetuating local tradition. The injustice and the irony is that women, the most active repositories of such information, are also the main victims of the collective effort to maintain a rigid moral standard by means of verbal inference and censure. In this way, women become custodians of the evidence to be used in the domination and prosecution of their own sex.

Lorca's heroines, on the other hand, often remain aloof from this collective scandal mongering, choosing the second alternative. They turn their energies inward, developing an insight and sensitivity that the male views as foreign and often threatening. Yerma and Víctor agree that for a man, "Es todo lo mismo. . . . Vais a lo vuestro sin reparar en las delicadezas" (*Y.*, pp. 67–68) (It's all the same . . . you go for what's yours without bothering about subtleties). Yerma typifies the woman who is more discriminating, more sensitive to the quality of life. In Yerma and Juan one sees the split between the man as realist, dealer in the concrete and immediate sensual perceptions; and the woman as dreamer, idealist, dweller in the abstract and potential. Juan says:

> Ha llegado el último minuto de resistir este continuo lamento por cosas oscuras, fuera de la vida, por cosas que están en el aire. . . . Por cosas que no han pasado y ni tú ni yo dirigimos. . . . Por cosas que a mí no me importan. . . . A mí me importa lo que tengo entre las manos. Lo que veo por mis ojos. (*Y*, pp. 98–99)
>
> This is the last time I'll stand for this continued lament for things which are outside of life, for things that are in the air. . . . For things that have not happened and are not under your control or mine. . . . For things that don't matter to me. What matters to me is what I can hold in my hands. What I can see with my own eyes.

The sensitivity of Lorca's heroines enables them to perceive painful ironies and injustices, but it only increases their sense of hopeless impotence. For women are constantly urged by men and women alike to endure patiently, suffer in silence, and resign themselves to their fate. As La Poncia, Bernarda's housekeeper, warns, "la que no se conforma se pudre llorando en un rincón" (*BA*, p. 55) (the one who doesn't resign herself to her lot will rot crying in a corner).

Men are prone to spontaneous and violent action, but most often it is women who are forced to sustain the pain of the aftermath. The impassioned monologues of the mother in *Blood Wedding* are eloquent testimony to the pain of past loss, the frustration of woman's inability to avenge her dead, and the impotent fear of renewed bereavement:

> Pero no es así. Se tarda mucho. Por eso es tan terrible ver la sangre de una derramada por el suelo. Una fuente que corre un minuto y a nosotros nos ha costado años. Cuando yo llegué a ver mi hijo, estaba tumbado en la mitad de la calle. Me mojé las manos de sangre y me las lamí con la lengua. Porque era mía. Tú no sabes lo que es eso. En una custodia de cristal y topacios pondría yo la tierra empapada por ella. (*BW*: *OC*, pp. 1228–29)
>
> [Children do not happen in a day.] It takes a long time. That's why it's so terrible for a woman to see her blood spilled upon the ground. A fountain that flows for just a moment, but has cost us women years. When I got to see my son, he lay fallen in the middle of the street. I wet my hands in his blood and licked them with my tongue. Because it was my blood. You [men] don't know what that is like. In a glass and topaz shrine I'd put the earth moistened by his blood.
>
> Me duele hasta la punta de las venas. En la frente de todos ellos yo no veo más que la mano con que mataron a lo que era mío. ¿Tú me ves a mí? ¿No te parezco loca? Pues es loca de no haber gritado todo lo que mi pecho necesita. Tengo en mi pecho un grito siempre puesto de pie a quien tengo que castigar y meter entre los mantos. Pero me llevan a los muertos y hay que callar. (*BW*: *OC*, p. 1227)
>
> It hurts me to the very tips of my veins. On the foreheads of all the members of the Felix family, I see only the hands with which they killed what was mine. . . . Don't you think I'm crazy? Well, I'm crazy from not having screamed everything my breast requires. In my breast there's always a shriek ready for the one I must punish and put under the sheets. But the dead are carried away and one has to keep still.
>
> La navaja, la navaja. . . . Malditas sean todas y el bribón que las inventó. . . . Y las escopetas, y las pistolas, y el cuchillo más pequeño, y hasta las azadas y los bieldos de la era. . . . Todo lo que puede cortar el cuerpo de un hombre. . . . No sé cómo te atreves a llevar una navaja en tu cuerpo, ni cómo yo dejo a la serpiente dentro del arcón. . . . ¿Cómo no voy a hablar viéndote salir por esa puerta? Es que no me gusta que lleves navaja. Es que . . . que no quisiera que salieras al campo, . . . Que me gustaría que fueras una mujer. (*BW*: *OC*, pp. 1172–74)

> Knives, knives. . . . Let them all be damned, along with the scoundrel who invented them. . . . And guns and pistols and the smallest table knife, and even hoes and pitchforks. . . . Everything that can cut a man's body. . . . I don't know how you dare to carry a knife nor how I allow this serpent to dwell in the chest. . . . How can I refrain from speaking when I see you go out that door? It's just that I don't like you to carry a knife. It's just that . . . I wish you wouldn't go out to the fields . . . that I wish you were a woman.

For Yerma the pain is more potential than actual. Barren since her marriage to Juan several years ago, she longs to endure the suffering of childbirth: "tronchada y rota soy para tí. ¡Cómo me duele esta cintura donde tendrás primera cuna!" (*Y*, p. 24) (How broken-stemmed and torn I am for you. How it aches, this waist where your first cradle will be!). She tells her neighbor María, "Yo he visto a mi hermana dar de mamar a su niño con el pecho lleno de grietas y le producía un gran dolor, pero es un dolor fresco, bueno, necesario para la salud" (*Y*, p. 21) (I have seen my sister nursing her baby with her breast full of cuts, . . . but it was a healthy, refreshing pain). Recognizing that as a woman she is destined to endure pain and suffering in one form or another, Yerma chooses the pain of loss rather than the pain of never having possessed:

> Aunque yo supiera que mi hijo me iba a martirizar después y me iba a odiar y me iba a llevar de los cabellos por las calles, recebiría con gozo su nacimiento, porque es mucho mejor llorar por un hombre vivo que nos apuñala, que llorar por esta fantasma sentado año tras año encima de mi corazón. (*Y*, p. 78)

> Even though I knew that my son was going to inflict great suffering on me later, that he would hate me and drag me through the streets by the hair, I would greet his birth with joy since it's much better to cry over a live man who stabs us with a dagger than to cry over this ghost who sits year after year upon my heart.

The male-dominated society which Lorca explores in these plays manifests the following paradox: by keeping women confined, ignorant, and passive, male-dominated society cultivates female weakness and leaves women virtually defenseless prey to stronger (that is, other male) forces. La Poncia realizes that Bernarda, headstrong and overconfident of her own power, "no sabe la fuerza que tiene un hombre entre mujeres solas" (*BA*, p. 110) (doesn't know the power one man wields over solitary women). And the bride reproaches Leonardo: "Un hombre con su caballo sabe mucho y puede mucho para poder estrujar a una muchacha metida en un desierto" (*BW*: *OC*, p. 1214) (A man with a horse has the knowledge and the power to put a lot of pressure on a girl stuck in a desert). As the bodies of her fiance and her lover are being brought back to the village, the bride presents herself before the mother, challenging the elder woman to avenge her son's honor by killing her, but not before the mother has seen for herself that the young woman—a virgin twice "widowed"—still retains her virtue intact. In one of the most powerful and moving speeches of the entire trilogy—one which transcends differences of age, position, and moral status—the bride appeals to the common condition of all women:

> ¡Porque yo me fui con el otro, me fui! Tú también te hubieras ido. Yo era una mujer quemada, llena de llagas por dentro y por fuera, y tu hijo era un poquito de agua de la que yo esperaba hijos, tierra, salud; pero el otro era un río oscuro, lleno de ramas, . . . Y yo corría con tu hijo que era como un niñito de agua fría, y el otro me mandaba cientos de pájaros que me impedían el andar y que dejaban escarcha sobre mis heridas de pobre mujer marchita, de muchacha acarciada por el fuego. Yo no quería, ¡óyelo bien!: yo no quería. Tu hijo era mi fin y yo no lo he engañado, pero el brazo del otro me arrastró como un golpe de mar, . . . y me hubiera arrastrado siempre, siempre, siempre, aunque hubiera sido vieja y todos los hijos de tu hijo me hubiesen agarrado de los cabellos! (*BW*: *OC*, p. 1269)

> Because I ran off with the other one; I ran off! *You would have gone, too.* I was a woman burning with desire, full of wounds inside and out, and your son was a little bit of water from whom I hoped for children, land, health; but the other was a dark river, full of branches. . . . And I ran along with your son, who was like a little boy made of cold water while the other one sent hundreds of birds which blocked my way and left frost on my wounds—the wounds of a poor withered woman, of a girl caressed by fire. I didn't want to. Listen carefully to what I say! I didn't want to. Your son was my destiny and I have not deceived him, but the other's arm dragged me along like the pull of the sea . . . and would have kept me forever, forever, forever, even if I were an old woman and all your son's children were holding me by the hair! (my emphasis)

The passionately reckless response of Bernarda's youngest and most attractive daughter, Adela, to her oldest sister's fiancé is a similar consuming passion fired by her rebellion against a similar confinement. In the bloom of her youth she is sentenced to eight years of mourning and forced to remain with her sisters within Bernarda's conventlike walls.

She says to her sister Martirio, "Ya no aguanto el horror de estos techos después de haber probado el sabor de su boca" (*BA*, p. 119) (I can no longer stand the horror of these walls after having savored the taste of his lips). She uses the same imagery as the bride in *Blood Wedding*—"El me lleva a los juncos de la orilla" (*BA*, p. 119)[7] (He carries me off to the rushes along the shore)—to describe the sexual attraction Pepe holds for her. So great is her desperation that she is prepared to sacrifice honor, social position, family ties—everything—to assume the most despised place in society's eyes:

> Seré lo que él quiera que sea. Todo el pueblo contra mí, quemándome con sus dedos de lumbre, perseguida por los que dicen que son decentes, y me pondré la corona de espinas que tienen las que son queridas de algún hombre casado. (*BA*, p. 119)
>
> I will be whatever he wants me to be. Let the whole town turn against me, burning me with their flaming fingers,[8] let me be pursued by those who claim to be decent folk, and I will put on the crown of thorns worn by women who are the mistresses of some married man.

Both young women view their illicit lovers as saviors who will, by the warmth of their bodies and the strength of their passion, transform an unendurable existence. Throughout the trilogy, the overwhelming energy and determination of the female response loom disproportionately over the meager male stimulus. The growth of such desperate passion out of alienation, fear and stifling powerlessness renders its tremendous grip understandable. The ambivalence which other elements of the society feel toward this surrender to passion and the con-

---

7. Adela's phrase echoes the opening lines of Lorca's gypsy ballad "La casada infiel" (The Unfaithful Wife): "Y que yo me la llevé al río . . ." (And so I took her off to the river . . .). Adela's allusion to the reeds along the shore is clearly figurative since many references have been made to her town's lack of a free-flowing water source. Variations on this image, symbolizing a complete and satisfying sexual encounter, are frequent in Lorca's poetry and plays. The most graphic instance occurs in the tragical farce *Amor de don Perlimpín con Belisa en su jardín*, when Belisa, standing half-naked on her balcony, sings: "Amor, amor / Entre mis muslos cerrados, / nada como un pez el sol. / Agua tibia entre los juncos, / amor" (Love, love / between my closed thighs / the sun swims like a fish. / Warm water among the rushes / love). *Obras completas*, (Madrid: Aguilar, 1969), pp. 982, 987.

8. This is clearly a reference to the mob attack on La Librada's daughter, reputed to have given birth to and destroyed an illegitimate child. Bernarda incites the angry townspeople, crying, "¡Carbón ardiendo en el sitio de su pecado!" (*BA*, p. 90) (Burning coals on the site of her sin!).

sequent rejection of public morality is relayed through the choruslike exchange between the woodcutters, who agree that Leonardo and the bride have done right to flee: one woodcutter says that a man must follow where his blood leads, but his companion reminds him that "blood which sees the light of day gets drunk up by the earth." They conclude that "Vale más ser muerto desangrado que vivo con ella podrida" (*BW*: *OC*, p. 1246) (It's better to bleed to death than to live with your blood rotting inside you).[9]

It is clear that women are not the only victims of a confining moral and social code. Leonardo's fate is to a large extent also collectively determined; he has been discriminated against because of his family history and modest means.[10] But the cumulative impact of the three tragedies indicates that, for Lorca, the structure of Andalusian society causes women to fall prey to its contradictions and impossible demands far more often than men do. As we have noted earlier, one of the ironies of this social system is that women, its most frequent victims, are the most uncompromising in their condemnation of one another and the most unrelenting in their demand for punishment and retribution. The chorus of washerwomen, for instance, soon overrules the only woman among them who shows sympathy for Yerma. The ruthlessness with which women pass judgment upon other members of their sex is necessary for the maintenance of a "shame culture." The possibilities for harsh judgments are multiplied by the fact that no proof is necessary since violation of the code does not require any *actual* transgression but merely the *possibility* of it. So generalized is the social distrust—particularly of women since they are clearly the vic-

9. It is quite possible that these sympathetic judgments are not a factor of a relaxed moral standard employed by men but rather depend upon the woodcutters' inferior social status. Throughout the plays, servants, day laborers, and others of lowly social rank seem to enjoy a moral freedom, which society does not allow its more prominent groups. This point is of course difficult to decide conclusively because of the scarcity of evidence in the plays themselves as well as the lack of a detailed and independent description of Andalusian social hierarchy. At any rate, the relative moral tolerance demonstrated by the woodcutters is somewhat undercut by their fatalism: their conviction that the mortal price will inevitably be extracted for the surrender to passion precludes in their own minds the risk of ever having to act in accordance with their relatively liberal attitudes.

10. Leonardo reveals that his humble economic condition prevented him from marrying the bride: "But two oxen and a poor cottage are hardly worth a thing. That is the thorn." The public commentary on his family's propensity for violence and the popular belief that he will come to no good help create the very conditions to realize those predictions. *Obras completas*, p. 1123.

tims of the social system's double bind—that whoever has the opportunity to violate existing codes of behavior is assumed to have done so.

Yerma (as well as Bernarda's daughters Amelia and Magdalena) directs mild criticism against *el qué dirán*. But only Adela, because she has herself transgressed the moral code and has therefore been compelled to look at the system as one outside it, protests its brutality. As her sisters run out to witness the mob's slaying of a young girl whose illegitimate child has been discovered by the townspeople, Adela screams, "¡Que le dejen escapar! ¡No salgáis vosotras!" (*BA*, p. 90) (Let her escape! Don't go out!).

Of all the tragic heroines, Yerma sustains the longest battle with her fate. Over a period of some five years she hopes and struggles to conceive, desperately seeking her fulfillment as a woman through the only means society allows her. Aware of her unutilized physical and spiritual strength and frustrated by a society which blocks her every impulse, she rebels in isolated actions, such as spending the night at the threshold of her house and participating in the magic rites of Dolores the Sorceress; but she never once questions the justice or appropriateness of the role society has decreed for her. Her struggle is always to fulfill that role, never to escape, undermine, or destroy it although that is, of course, the indirect result of her final action. Given the ambivalence of Lorca's ending, we cannot predict what Yerma's future will be. Although the uncompromising nature of the society she lives in makes it look bleak, we know that after having murdered Juan and thus having eliminated all hope of a child—"¡Yo misma he matado a mi hijo!" (*Y*, p. 101) (I myself have killed my son!)—she feels free and confident at last: "Marchita. Marchita, pero segura. Ahora sí que lo sé de cierto. Y sola. Voy a descansar sin despertarme sobresaltada, para ver si la sangre me anuncia otra sangre nueva. Con el cuerpo seco para siempre" (*Y*, p. 101) (Withering. Withering, but steady. Now I know it for sure. And all alone. I'm going to rest without waking with a start, trying to detect whether my blood is proclaiming another's new blood. My body barren forever more). The relief she feels when at last she is totally alone echoes that of the bridegroom's mother: "Aquí quiero estar. Y tranquila. Ya todos están muertos. A medianoche dormiré, dormiré sin que ya me aterren la escopeta o el cuchillo" (*BW*: *OC*, p. 1267) (This is where I want to be. And at peace. Now they are all dead. At midnight I'll be sleeping—sound asleep and no longer terrified by shotguns or knives). Still, the destiny of a woman alone is a grim and lonely one, as Lorca stresses throughout the course of his plays. We remember the fate of Leonardo's widow: "Tú, a tu casa. / Valiente y sola en tu casa. / A envejecer y a llorar. / Pero la puerta cerrada. / . . . Claveremos las ventanas. / Y vengan lluvias y noches / sobre las hierbas amargas" (*BW*: *OC*, p. 1264) (Confined to your house, brave and alone. To age and to weep. But with the door shut. . . . We will nail down the windows. And let the rains and the nights pass over the bitter grasses).

Upon hearing the news that his daughter has run away with Leonardo, the bride's father is incredulous. He seems to wish for her another fate: "No será ella. Quizá se haya tirado al aljibe" (*BW*: *OC*, p. 1244) (It must not be her. Perhaps she has thrown herself into the cistern). The bridegroom's mother counters him: "Al agua se tiran las honradas, las limpias; ¡ésa, no!" (*BW*: *OC*, p. 1244) (Only pure, honorable women throw themselves into the water; not that one!). This is but one illustration of the fatal dilemma into which a ruthless social code forces nonconforming women. The mortal paradox is that only through dying can a woman prove her honor. Those women who endure their tragedy are soiled and shamed in society's eyes, although death would often appear an easy solution when contrasted to a life of ostracism, isolation, frustration, and remorse. We know this is what awaits the bride; the last exchange between her and the mother makes it quite clear: "Déjame llorar contigo." "Llora. Pero en la puerta." (*BW*: *OC*, p. 1270) ('Let me weep with you,' the bride pleads. 'Go ahead and weep,' comes the sullen reply. 'But in the doorway'). Earlier, the bride had sought her own death repeatedly: she asked Leonardo to kill her "como víbora pequeña" (*BW*: *OC*, p. 1256) (like a little viper), or to put the barrel of the gun into her "manos de novia" (bridal hands). Later she swears she will die with him because "Es justo que yo aquí muera / . . . mujer perdida y doncella" (*BW*: *OC*, p. 1260) (It is just for me to die here, dishonored and still a virgin), but she returns alive to her mother-in-law's house, where for the third and last time she asks to be put to death. Adela, in contrast, disposed of herself as society demands, enabling Bernarda to preserve her precious façade by giving her daughter a virgin's funeral. Adela hanged herself in despair, believing her lover and savior had been slain by Bernarda. But her suicide was also an act of self-defense. She knew too well the revenge which an overly self-righteous society sees fit to take upon those women who have transgressed its codes and who no longer have a man to protect them.

Lorca sharply contrasts this savage severity, which castigates even minor infractions committed by women, to the liberal tolerance shown to men. The bride is admonished by her future mother-in-law: "¿Tú sabes lo que es casarse, criatura? . . . Un hombre, unos hijos y una pared de dos varas de ancho para todo lo demás" (*BW*, *OC*, p. 1200)

(Do you know what it means to get married, child? A man, some children, and a wall two rods wide for everything else). Men are allowed a freedom and self-indulgence women could never dream of. La Poncia informs Bernarda's daughters of the male's marital "obligations": "A vosotras que sois solteras os conviene saber de todos modos que el hombre a los quinces días de boda deja la cama por la mesa y luego la mesa por la tabernilla" (*BA*, p. 55) (As unmarried women it behooves you to know anyway that two weeks after the wedding the man deserts the bed for the table and later the table for the tavern). Lorca incorporates Adelaida's bizarre family history in *The House of Bernarda Alba* to illustrate the society's unremitting tolerance of male infractions:

> *Martirio.* Su padre mató en Cuba al marido de su primera mujer para casarse con ella. Luego aquí la abandonó y se fue con otra que tenía una hija y luego tuvo relaciones con esta muchacha, la madre de Adelaida, y se casó con ella después de haber muerto loca la segunda mujer.
> *Amelia.* Y ese infame, ¿por qué no está en la cárcel?
> *Martirio.* Porque los hombres se tapan unos a otros las cosas de esta índole y nadie es capaz de delatar. (*BA*, pp. 32–33)

> *Martirio.* While in Cuba her father killed his first wife's husband in order to marry her. Then he deserted her here and ran off with another who had a daughter, then later had relations with that girl, who is Adelaida's mother. He married her after his second wife went mad and died.
> *Amelia.* And why isn't that despicable character in jail?
> *Martirio.* Because men cover each other's tracks in these matters, and no one has the nerve to denounce them.

The same double standard is apparent in the first scene of *Blood Wedding*. "Una mujer con un hombre, y ya está" (*BW*: *OC*, p. 1176) (A woman has one man, and that's all there is to it), the mother decrees. A wife must never look at anyone else, and should she one day lose her husband, she must lock herself in her house and stare at the bare wall. Yet in the same scene she espouses a very indulgent standard for male behavior: "Tu padre sí que me llevaba. Eso es de buena casta. Sangre. Tu abuelo dejó a un hijo en cada esquina. Eso me gusta. Los hombres, hombres; el trigo, trigo." (*BW*: *OC*, p. 1174) (Your father was the one who used to carry me away. That's what good stock is. Good blood. Your grandfather left a son on every corner. That's what I like—for men to be men, for wheat to be wheat). That she so openly condones flagrant promiscuity on the part of the male sex stands in ironic juxtaposition to her enraged denunciation of one woman's unconsummated infidelity, which causes her to incite her only surviving son to revenge and death.

This contrast points up the central contradiction in Andalusian society, both as portrayed by Lorca and as analyzed by anthropologists such as Julian Pitt-Rivers[11]: a man's virility—upon which, in part, his honor depends—requires numerous sexual conquests whereas a woman's honor demands that she be above suspicion, that is, free even of the possibility of sexual contact with a man who is not her husband or a member of her immediate family. The female sex bears the brunt of pressure and punishment in this sytem of incompatible codes of behavior.

The most radical social criticism in the trilogy comes from a very minor character, a young girl whom Yerma meets one afternoon on the way back from the fields. Their conversation begins as she tells Yerma, "De todos modos, tú y yo con no tenerlos vivimos más tranquilas" (*Y*, p. 32) (No matter what, you and I live more peaceful lives without children). Yerma wonders why she got married. The girl replies:

> Porque me han casado. Se casan todas. Si seguimos así no va a haber solteras más que las niñas. Bueno, y además, . . . una se casa en realidad mucho antes de ir a la iglesia. Pero las viejas se empeñan en todas estas cosas. Yo tengo diecinueve años y no me gusta guisar, ni lavar. Bueno, pues todo el día he de estar haciendo lo que no me gusta. ¿Y para qué? ¿Qué necesidad tiene mi marido de ser mi marido? Porque lo mismo hacíamos de novios que ahora. Tonterías de los viejos. . . . También tú me dirás loca, ¡la loca, la loca! Yo te puedo decir lo único que he aprendido en la vida: toda la gente está metida dentro de sus casas haciendo lo que no les gusta. Cuánto mejor se está en medio de la calle. (*Y*, p. 33)
>
> Because they married me off. All the women get married. If things go on like this, the only unmarried women will be the schoolgirls. And besides, . . . the truth is that a girl gets married long before she goes to the altar. But the old women insist on all these things. I'm nineteen years old and I don't like to cook or to

11. Julian Pitt-Rivers, *The People of the Sierra*, rev. ed. (Chicago: University of Chicago Press, 1971).

> do laundry. So, I'm supposed to spend my days doing what I don't like to do. And for what? What need is there for my husband to be my husband? Because as sweethearts we did the same thing we do now. Old folks' foolishness. . . . You'll call me crazy, too. The crazy girl! The crazy girl! Well, I can tell you the one thing I've learned in my life: everybody is stuck inside their houses doing what they don't like. How much better you feel in the middle of the street.

This speech is perhaps the most problematic of any in the three tragedies. It sets in sharp relief the hypocrisy and coercive moral power of the old folks (particularly *las viejas*) and the unnaturalness of what the society considers to be the natural state of women. It advocates a refusal to conform to conventional social and moral obligations and the abandonment of house-bound confinement for the freedom of the street. One might argue against the relevance of this speech, for Lorca puts these words into the mouth of a secondary character who appears only twice in the play, a young girl who Yerma thinks is naïve and who the townspeople apparently think is crazy. She turns out to be the daughter of Dolores the Sorceress and thus a somewhat disreputable and marginal member of society. Yet for these very same reasons Lorca can have her lay claim to an objectivity and originality inaccessible to his other characters, confined as they are within the rigidly structured society which he expends so much effort to portray. In such a closed society, only with the marginal, the heretical, or the insane can opposing ideas or new perceptions originate. In her lunacy, María Josefa, Bernarda's mother, demonstrates a similar clairvoyance.

The distinguishing characteristic of Lorca's tragic heroines is their refusal to resign themselves to the fate society has decreed for them. Their rebellion takes various forms. One of the most significant is the attempt to bridge the separation between male and female roles. Adela wishes she could go out to the open fields and work like the men. The bride, only child of an aging father, is proud of her ability to do a man's work: "¡Ojalá lo fuera!" (*BW*: *OC*, p. 1203) (I wish I were one!) she exclaims. And Yerma tells María, "Muchas veces bajo yo a echar la comida a los bueyes, que antes no lo hacía, porque ninguna mujer lo hace y cuando paso por lo oscuro del cobertizo mis pasos me suenan a pasos de hombre" (*Y*, pp. 63–64) (Many times I'm the one to go down and give the oxen their food—something I didn't do before because no woman does—and when I go through the dark part of the shed my footsteps sound to me like those of a man). Bernarda, the most authoritarian of all the characters, is known for her ability to "bregar como un hombre" (contend with difficulties like a man). La

Poncia says that she is of the same school as Bernarda, and her accounts of how she used to keep her husband in line delight the daughters and cause them to exclaim, "¡Así deben ser todas las mujeres!" (*BA*, p. 56) (That's the way all women should be!). All the heroines flout convention in minor ways long before they are actually compelled to break with it. Adela sheds her mourning clothes to parade in a party dress before the barnyard animals; the bride refuses to open her engagement presents, ominously throws her orange-blossom wreath to the ground and indecorously receives Leonardo in her petticoat; Yerma wanders seeking the texture of the earth on her bare feet and spends a night alone under the stars at the threshold of her house—all symbolic acts which foreshadow the coming crises.

In a society which prefers to silence truths it cannot accommodate, Lorca's heroines persist in verbalizing their frustrations. Yerma and the bridegroom's mother are unrivaled in their articulateness. The old neighborwoman has said to the mother, "A nosotras nos toca callar" (*BW*: *OC*, p. 1182) (It's our turn to keep still), but that is the one thing the widow cannot do; her tongue is her only weapon. Yerma, initially open and frank, grows increasingly closed as her desperation mounts. She summarizes her frustrations in one symbolic passage: "Quiero beber agua y no hay vaso ni agua, quiero subir al monte y no tengo pies, quiero bordar mis enaguas y no encuentro los hilos" (*Y*, p. 59) (I want to drink water but find neither the water nor the glass, I want to climb the mountain but have no feet, I want to embroider my petticoats but I can't find the threads). She thirsts after water, a symbol of male virility; she longs to climb the hill and make contact with the earth, a symbol of female fecundity;[12] and the elusive embroidery thread symbolizes her incapacity to realize the female role she so ardently desires to fulfill.

The fabric of Andalusian society, as Lorca depicts it, is rent in two along sexual lines. In no case do we witness the sustained fruition of a relationship between a man and a woman.[13] Lorca's heroines, trapped

---

12. A thorough study of the imagery in the three tragedies reveals that womanhood is associated with the earth, either barren or fertile, but always permanent and long-suffering. The male element is associated with more transitory and mutable symbols: wind and water, the latter especially associated with virility. See Julianne Burton, "Earth, Air, Fire, and Water: Imagery and Symbol in the Tragedies of Federico García Lorca," *García Lorca Review*, 3(2) (September 1975): 99–120.

13. It might be argued that both the mother in *Blood Wedding* and Yerma's friend María enjoyed fulfilling relationships with their respective husbands. It must be remembered, however, that neither relationship was sustained. The

and beaten down by society's constraints, never reject the society itself but rebel only against certain isolated manifestations of its injustice. Yerma, for example, struggles desperately to uphold the most sacred precepts of her society: female marital fidelity, motherhood, and honor. The defiant Adela breaks Bernarda's hold upon her when she breaks her mother's cane, symbol of superior authority. Ironically, she sheds one tyrannical yoke for another, declaring, "En mí no manda nadie más que Pepe" (*BA*, p. 121) (Pepe is the only one who can tell me what to do).

In the kind of sex-gender system which Lorca portrays, the female sector is noncohesive. The focus of female attention is always on the male realm, and women take any opportunity to defect by claiming one of the other side for their own, never realizing that real integration is impossible. Simone de Beauvoir's characterization of women as comrades in captivity applies perfectly here, for Lorca's tragic heroines also "help one another endure their prison, even help one another prepare for escape; but [they expect] their liberation will come from the world of men."[14] When there is competition for the same escape route, all ties among the women concerned are severed. Even those bonds which are viewed as inherent to the whole society no longer hold. As La Poncia says of Bernarda's repressed and frustrated daughters, "Son mujeres sin hombre, nada más. En estas cuestiones se olvida hasta la sangre" (*BA*, p. 111) (They are simply women without a man, nothing more. In such matters even the blood tie is forgotten). The final encounter between Adela and Martirio proves her observation correct. Martirio calls Adela out from her secret tryst with Pepe, for Martirio, too, is in love with him and, jealous of Adela, tries to convince her to abandon him:

Adela. Martirio, Martirio, yo no tengo la culpa.
Martirio. ¡No me abraces! No quiero ablandar mis ojos. Mi sangre ya no es la tuya. Aunque quisiera verte como hermana no te miro ya más que como mujer.
Adela. Aquí no hay ningún remedio. La que tenga que ahogarse que se ahogue. (*BA*, p. 119)

Adela. Martirio, Martirio, I'm not to blame.
Martirio. Don't put your arms around me! I don't want my fury to abate. My blood and your blood are no longer the

---

bridegroom's mother is widowed after just three years of marriage, and María, a very secondary figure, is a newlywed.

14. Simone de Beauvoir, *The Second Sex* (New York: Knopf, 1950), p. 515.

same. Even if I wanted to regard you as my sister, I can't see you now as anything but another woman.

Adela. There is no way out here. Let the one who has to drown herself get on with it.

According to Lorca's vision in *The House of Bernarda Alba*, neither compassion nor honor nor blood ties—nor any social precept which women are expected to uphold without genuine participation in the society which requires their conformity—can bind two women together once a man has come between them.

In these three tragedies, Lorca explores the alternatives open to a woman who rejects enforced resignation to her lot: either she commits suicide like Adela (and symbolically Yerma); or she destroys her husband, as Yerma does with her own two hands, and as the bride does more indirectly. Widowhood, the most common fate of Lorca's women, serves as a metaphor for female destiny. Isolation, frustration, bereavement, and remorse constitute a bitter fate, yet they are preferable to the anguished coexistence with the male. This end is consistent with the thematic ascendancy and endurance of the female, a virtue which, like the other feminine virtues that Lorca portrays, goes unrewarded. Whether she plays the game or breaks the rules, woman is bound to lose, for, in Amelia's words, "Nacer mujer es el mayor castigo" (*BA*, p. 66) (The greatest punishment is to be born a woman).

Is such categorical despair a reflection of Lorca's own views? These plays are in no sense programmatic. They do not posit solutions to the problems they raise. But the thoroughness and intricacy of their social vision is both an expression and a product of Lorca's commitment to a more egalitarian, humane, and personally fulfilling society. It is no accident that the fullest understanding of a particular social system should come at a time when conditions are ripe for its transformation.

The Changing Face of Woman in Latin American Fiction

Marcia L. Welles

The portrayal of woman in twentieth-century Latin American literature by male novelists is a different matter from her portrayal by female authors. The portrayal of women by male authors tends to facile stereotypes, drawn more from the dimension of myth than from that of actuality. Studying the part played by women in Mexican literature, the critic Carlos Monsiváis concludes that they play the role of "landscape"; they are the backdrop for the performance of the male.[1] The characterization of women by female authors is more convincing because the outlines are less distinct, less articulate. These women can no longer be readily identified as types. They fit into no specific classifications—as wife, mother, virgin, or prostitute. The all-good or all-evil feminine archetype does not exist. Despite the complexity and subtlety of these female images, certain structural and thematic elements are recurrent and indicate a shared perspective, especially discernible in the works of four distinguished women novelists, the Chileans María Luisa Bombal and Elisa Serrana and the Argentinians Silvina Bullrich and Marta Lynch. The novels I will discuss here are María Luisa Bombal's *La última niebla* (The Last Mist) (1935); Silvina Bullrich's *Bodas de cristal* (Crystal Wedding) (1951); Elisa Serrana's *Chilena, casada, sin profesión* (A Chilean Married

1. Carlos Monsiváis, "Sexismo en la literatura mexicana," in *Imagen y realidad de la mujer*, ed. Elena Urrutia (Mexico: SepSetentas, 1975), p. 107.

Woman Without a Profession) (1963); Marta Lynch's *La señora Ordóñez* (Mrs. Ordóñez) (1967); and *Mañana digo basta* (Tomorrow I Say Enough) (1968) also by Silvina Bullrich.[2] The specific components of their individual cultural and social milieus are by no means identical, yet their literary and human concerns show a decidedly common core. In all five works, the alienation of woman from her traditional role as wife and mother constitutes a central theme. At the same time, and in some ways predictably, the solitary and somewhat estranging first-person technique common to these authors becomes indispensable.

This structural feature is of greatest importance in these works: the author and character are merged in the persona of a female protagonist in a first-person narrative structure. This fusion prevents the static presentation of an objectified female character. The intensely personal point of view releases the female "I" from imprisonment in voiceless stereotyped characterizations of her being and allows her to reveal herself as a dynamic "becoming," creating a fictional world through her perceptions. The choice of such a narrative structure by all four authors is not coincidental; it is part of the intent of these novels, all of which offer a portrayal of woman's identity as distorted by societal expectations and rendered unnatural even to herself. This in itself is a transgression of a cultural assumption. For although Freud discusses men's eternal concern about the enigma of woman, he adds that "to those of you who are women this will not apply—you are yourselves the problem."[3] In these novels the object of concern has now become the concerned subject.

The thematic connection in the works in question is clear in the similarity of their plot sequence. In each case, the character's world is the urban middle to upper class, which defines and limits the possibilities of the protagonists. As these are married women, status is conveyed through the professional affiliation of the husband. Although Blanca Ordóñez in Lynch's novel is an artist and Alejandra in *Mañana digo basta* is both artist and critic, their work is limited to the feminine

---

2. The following editions have been used: María Luisa Bombal, *La última niebla*, 5th ed. (Buenos Aires: Ed. Andina, 1970); Silvina Bullrich, *Bodas de cristal*, 3rd ed. (Buenos Aires: Ed. Sudamericana, 1959); Elisa Serrana, *Chilena, casada, sin profesión*, 4th ed. (Santiago de Chile: Ed. ZigZag, 1964); Marta Lynch, *La señora Ordóñez* (Buenos Aires: Ed. Jorge Álvarez, 1967); and Silvina Bullrich, *Mañana digo basta* (Buenos Aires: Ed. Sudamericana, 1968). All translations are my own.

3. Sigmund Freud, "Femininity," in *New Introductory Lectures on Psychoanalysis*, trans. and ed. James Strachey (New York: W. W. Norton, 1965), p. 113.

sphere because it falls within the irrational and creative realm of the imagination as opposed to the rational, logical, and scientific order of the male. Besides, that work does not provide economic independence.

The outward events revolve around romance and marriage, more accurately, romance *or* marriage since the pattern is one of disappointed expectations. Paralleling this plot sequence in the outer world is a more significant internal plot consisting of the complex reactions of each narrator to external events as they impinge upon her sense of self. There then arises in each of these women a new awareness of the incongruity between the inner and the outer worlds. The protagonist, now in a state of *dis*-ease, views her formerly comfortable social world as a place of inauthentic values, rejects as hypocritical her previously satisfying diversions and as meaningless her habitual patterns of social interaction. In the process, her inner world is reduced to a state of constant dissatisfaction, reaching the level of anguish at its most intense moments. Each protagonist's project, that is, marriage, fails either through lack of communication or through monotony. As the subjective experiences described by the characters are not distinctive in each case, their malaise must be considered situational not individual.

Alienation—defined as powerlessness, meaninglessness, isolation, normlessness, and self-estrangement[4]—is fundamental in these novels. The transference of these sociopsychological categories from the domain of industry to that of marriage is warranted by the asymmetrical power structure between the male and the female in marriage, which gave rise to Engels' still apt observation, "Within the family he is the bourgeois, and the wife represents the proletariat."[5]

Frustrated expectations perpetuate female powerlessness. This is especially obvious in the case of the nameless protagonist of *La última niebla* and of Teresa in *Chilena, casada, sin profesión*, women whose husbands keep themselves aloof. At the psychological level neither woman can exert any influence whatsoever to change this situation, and at the material level there is no possibility of self-determination. Teresa realizes that

> No contempló otra abertura, otra posibilidad que el amor, la maternidad, la casa. Camino y vocación viniendo del hombre; es-

---

4. M. Seeman, "On the Meaning of Alienation," *American Sociological Review*, 26 (1961): 753–58, as discussed by Joachim Israel in *Alienation: From Marx to Modern Sociology* (Boston: Allyn & Bacon, 1971), pp. 208–15.

5. Frederick Engels, *The Origin of the Family, Private Property, and the State*, trans. Alex West (1942; rpt. with introduction and notes by Eleanor Burke Leacock, New York: International Publishers, 1972), p. 137.

> tabilidad emocional también. . . . ¿Otros intereses? Eran fáciles de oír y de dar los consejos, pero ya nada le interesaba bastante. . . . Amor fracasado, maternidad frustrada, obras sin amarra, ninguna fuente de vida. Deseaba coger algo, lo deseaba tan desesperadamente que alcanzó angustia. (p. 79)
>
> She did not foresee another opening, another possibility, beyond love, maternity, a home. Direction and vocation coming from men; emotional stability also. . . . Other interests? It was easy to listen to and to give advice, but nothing any longer interested her enough. . . . Unsuccessful love, frustrated motherhood, works without substance, no fountain of life. She wished to seize upon something, she desired it so desperately that she experienced anguish.

In *La última niebla* the only alternative to marriage for the narrator would have been to remain a "solterona arrugada" (p. 40) (a wrinkled old maid), and Blanca Ordóñez recalls that "Pensar que Teresa y yo no soñábamos más que con casarnos. ¿Qué otra cosa se hubiera podido hacer?" (p. 62) (To think that Teresa and I didn't dream of anything other than getting married. What else could one have done?). The narrator's sense of powerlessness is so overwhelming in *La última niebla* that she no longer functions as an autonomous entity, for her loss of will and self-direction reduce her to the behavior of a robot as she follows her husband:

> Lo sigo para llevar a cabo una infinidad de pequeños menesteres; para cumplir con una infinidad de frivolidades amenas; para llorar por costumbre y sonreír por deber. Lo sigo para vivir correctamente, para morir correctamente, algún día. (p. 103)
>
> I follow him to complete an infinite number of trivial chores; to carry out an infinite number of pleasant frivolities; to cry through habit and smile through duty. I follow him to live correctly, to die correctly some day.

Meaninglessness is expressed in continued references to emptiness. Teresa feels that "El vacío fue total, profunda la soledad, como la noche, como la nada a su alrededor" (p. 84) (The emptiness was total, the solitude profound, like the night, like the nothingness around her), and as her husband departs in the morning, the unnamed wife of *Bodas de cristal* thinks "Y ahora hasta la noche, mi soledad, mi vacío" (p. 29) (And now until evening, my solitude, my emptiness). The experiences of normlessness and isolation are closely connected as they appear in the novels and are related to the characters' inability or refusal to define themselves within the traditional role expectations. In Serrana's novel, Teresa, unable to bear children, cannot decide what to do with herself, and both Blanca of *La señora Ordóñez* and Alejandra of *Mañana digo basta* rebel against their children's demands. The women's condition of *anomie* is summarized by the husband in *Bodas de cristal* in his observation that

> las mujeres se le aparecían de pronto como seres divagantes, caídos de otro planeta. Se las arreglaban mal sobre la tierra, a veces hasta parecía que el aire les resultaba irrespirable, se inventaban mundos fantásticos, amores desmedidos, recorrían la vida como alucinadas. (pp. 100–01)

> suddenly women seemed to him like wandering beings, fallen from another planet. They managed badly on earth, it even seemed at times that they could not breathe the air, they invented fantastic worlds, exaggerated love affairs, they went through life as though in a state of hallucination.

The rupture between the individual and her role expectations gives rise to a sense of isolation, formulated in similar metaphors. Detached from a solid familial identity, Blanca Ordóñez finds herself "tan sola y alejada como si fuera un velero fantasma, sacudiéndose en su rada" (p. 64) (as alone and distant as though she were a phantom sailboat, flapping its sails in its bay), and Teresa admits that "a veces sueño con que me dejan sola en un desierto o en un mar, no sé, y despierto sin haberlo sabido; en la pesadilla todos se van sin mí" (p. 75) (sometimes I dream that they leave me alone in a desert or in a sea, I don't know, and I awaken without having known it; in the nightmare they all leave without me). Although such symptoms of alienation—powerlessness, meaninglessness, normlessness, isolation—are not necessarily sex-linked, self-estrangement *is* directly related in these novels to the protagonists' being-in-the-world as females. It is connected, therefore, with the usage of the term "alienation" in existentialist philosophy.

Jean-Paul Sartre treats as natural and inevitable the alienation occasioned by a subject's awareness of his own objectivity in the presence of another.[6] The polemical implications of this phenomenon are discussed by Simone de Beauvoir in her definition of woman as the "second sex." Woman is a being who exists as "Other" in a world in which

---

6. Jean-Paul Sartre, *Being and Nothingness*, trans. Hazel E. Barnes (1953; rpt. New York: Washington Square Press, 1968), pp. 340–400.

man is the "Subject." She becomes an object, even to herself.[7] Thus, in the novels under analysis, the characters experience a strange detachment of consciousness. Blanca Ordóñez does not recognize her *self* in the mirror, where she sees "Casi el rostro de una mujer que no era ella" (p. 114) (Almost the face of a woman who was not herself). The dissociation between the consciousness and the body is acute in moments of sexual intimacy. In *Mañana digo basta* Alejandra remembers her body reacting to caresses, "mientras yo, la *verdadera* yo, librada de mi estructura terrestre, miraba irónicamente a esa pareja cincuentona que fingía tener ganas de hacer el amor" (p. 106) (while I, the *real* I, freed from my terrestrial structure, looked ironically at that pair of fiftyish-year-olds that was pretending to feel like making love). Blanca Ordóñez so removes herself from her body during copulation, described as the "acto mecánico y ritual" (p. 46) (a mechanical, ritualistic act), that she wonders if she is not slightly schizophrenic.

The clearest indication of the insecurity of these characters is their obsessive concern with the mirror. They subject themselves to an interminable self-scrutiny, resulting not from narcissism but from the endless assessment of their desirability to a man. The body, meaningful only as a synthesis, is fragmented into separate parts of erotogenic significance as these women observe themselves as outsiders, adopting the male point of view. For instance, in *La última niebla* the narrator notices that "Mi seno está perdiendo su redondez y consistencia de fruto verde" (p. 63) (My breasts are losing their roundness and their consistency of a just-ripening [green] fruit), and the thirty-five-year-old protagonist of *Bodas de cristal* notes that "ya mis pechos, menos rígidos, no levantaban con tanta insolencia la seda del camisón" (p. 15) (my breasts, less taut, no longer raised the silk of my nightgown with such insolence). The judgment is sometimes favorable, as when Blanca Ordóñez says of herself "Buena cintura, buenos pechos, hasta las pantorrillas que mamá calificaba de fornidas resultaron ser un buen par de piernas" (pp. 101–02) (Good waist, good breasts, even the calves that mother regarded as robust turned out to be a good pair of legs). Usually, however, the reaction to the alien body is negative, as occurs to Teresa: "Mientras se desvestía, sintió también repugnancia de sí misma, de su cuerpo, de su ser. . . . Por primera vez se odió" (p. 34) (As she undressed, she also felt repugnance toward herself, toward her body, toward her being. . . . For the first time, she

7. Simone de Beauvoir, *The Second Sex*, trans. H. M. Parshley (1952; rpt. New York: Vintage Books, 1974); see "Introduction," pp. xv–xxxiv.

hated herself). The most extreme example of the loss of self-esteem occurs in *La última niebla* , whose narrator ceases to exist except as an object of desire, with the result that the discovery of her supposed lover's blindness annihilates her.

The body is thus a sign, an indicator of a woman's being-in-the-world as an object valued for its erotic attraction and fertility. For all these women one pathological consequence of the objectification of the body is its metonymic reduction. In Lynch's novel, for example, a woman is appreciated for "un buen útero para concebir" (p. 199) (a good uterus for conceiving); to the father "los hímenes de sus hijas eran sagrados" (p. 156) (his daughters' hymens were sacred); Blanca's sister is admired for "su visible facultad de procrear, tal como si tuviera la matriz entre las cejas" (p. 65) (her visible ability to procreate, as though her womb were between her eyebrows).

This continual conversion of real identity into terms of potential "use-value" for the outside world is a major force in psychic degeneration. The emotional experiences described by the protagonists are reactions to the general social process of reification, defined as "the transformation of all activities and products into commodities,"[8] including the conversion of human beings into objects. In the exchange process of marriage the male assumes the position of the "buyer" who selects the "commodity," his wife, who has a direct "use-value," her ability to procreate, as well as an "indirect use-value," her ability to provide aesthetic pleasure or status to the buyer primarily because of her beauty.[9] As stated by Gloria in *Bodas de cristal*:

> No debemos engañarnos: el amor es ante todo un pacto físico. . . . Una mujer fea puede ser querida con tanta fuerza como una mujer bonita, y sin embargo, ¿por qué solemos verlas solas y solteras? (p. 48)
>
> We should not deceive ourselves: love is above all a physical pact. . . . An ugly woman can be loved as strongly as a pretty one, yet nevertheless, why do we usually see them alone and single?

Because the value of a woman is not intrinsic but extrinsic, dependent upon the evaluation of others, the characters are painfully aware that their commodity value decreases with age. After all, the rate of exchange for an old woman is quite different from that of a young

8. Israel, *Alienation*, p. 287.
9. Terms used by Israel in his discussion of exchange-values, ibid., p. 315.

woman. The mirror is once again the prime witness to this process of evaluation, and the appearance of facial lines produces reactions of anguish. The relationships outside of the monogamic structure which appear in the novels cannot be viewed as liberating experiences, as positive rebellion against what Marcuse terms the "surplus-repression" of a society that delimits the sex instinct into a carefully circumscribed terrain.[10] These narrators seek lovers not to affirm their right to erotic fulfillment but to assuage their fear of aging. The motivation being negative, the relationships serve only to increase anxiety, especially if the lover chosen is a younger man, as occurs in *La señora Ordóñez*. This form of escape is but another facet of woman's status as object.

Simone de Beauvoir has noted that "along with the authentic demand of the subject who wants sovereign freedom, there is in the existent an inauthentic longing for resignation and escape."[11] The dialectical tension in the inner plot of the novels is precisely this conflict within each protagonist between the longing for the transcendence of the self as subject and the equal, or stronger, longing for the emotional neutrality of an object. Such escape takes various forms. In *La última niebla* the narrator withdraws into her phantasmagoric world; in *Chilena, casada, sin profesión*, Teresa, in India, resolves her anguish by means of the dissolution of self into the cosmic unity of Oriental religion. The wife of *Bodas de cristal* glorifies feminine passivity in contrast to male activity in such statements as the following:

> Las mujeres argentinas . . . tienen algo de esa gran resignación del campo o del mar, pero los hombres tienen esa furia ciega de la lluvia que los azota o de las olas que cuando abrazan golpean, revuelcan, nos arrojan jadeantes sobre la arena. (p. 158)

> Argentine women . . . have something akin to that mighty resignation of the land or the sea, but the men possess that blind fury of the rain that beats them or the waves that when they embrace, bruise, overturn, toss us breathless onto the sand.

In *La señora Ordóñez*, Blanca's rebellion proves totally impotent. The opening and closing passages of the novel are practically identical, and Blanca, exhausted by this futile struggle, can say only that "hice todo lo que pude" (p. 375) (I did all that I could). The diarist of *Mañana digo basta* in fact *never* says "Enough!"

---

10. Herbert Marcuse, *Eros and Civilization* (Boston: Beacon Press, 1966), pp. 35–38.

11. De Beauvoir, *The Second Sex*, p. 335.

As we read these novels, we experience the shock of "defamiliarization."[12] The female protagonist is not the fixed, unidimensional one to which we are accustomed. The extreme self-consciousness of these characters, however unhappy or inconclusive, marks a radical departure from Spanish-American literature and suggests a new approach to the portrayal of "woman's love and life" in modern literature. The sex-linked alienation described in the novels has a fundamental critical intention. Although the alienation or reification of the narrator of *La última niebla* is latent in the text and must be deduced from the empirical data presented, in the more contemporary novels such estrangement is a conscious experience to which the protagonists react with anger and bitterness. The pervasive first-person, the voice of self-awareness, makes possible novels in which women can remember, relate, and re-form experience. As in psychoanalysis, memory becomes the vehicle for the attainment of truth as these female characters grope toward an understanding of their being-in-the-world.

The works considered in this essay offer the reader rare glimpses of previously unnoticed lives. Virginia Woolf once remarked that male values predominate in literature as in life, prejudicing our critical evaluation: "This is an important book, the critic assumes, because it deals with war. This is an insignificant book because it deals with the feelings of women in a drawing room."[13] These novels by Bombal, Serrana, Bullrich, and Lynch are important precisely because they do not deal with war but rather with the feelings of women in drawing rooms or bedrooms or dining rooms.

---

12. Concept of Victor Shlovsky as discussed in his *Russian Formalist Criticism: Four Essays*, trans. and introduction by Lee T. Lemon and Marion J. Reis (Lincoln: University of Nebraska Press, 1965), pp. 3–24; and in Fredric Jameson, *The Prison-House of Language* (Princeton, N.J.: Princeton University Press, 1972), pp. 50–54.

13. Virginia Woolf, *A Room of One's Own* (New York: Harcourt, Brace, 1929), p. 128.

The Censored Sex

Woman as Author and Character in Franco's Spain

Linda Gould Levine

To write about post-Franco Spain is necessarily to write about the barrage of "isms" that have recently bombarded Spanish politics: Santiago Carrillos' Eurocommunism, Felipe González' socialism, and Adolfo Suárez' conservatism. Too little, unfortunately, has been said about another "ism" which has become an increasingly strong force in Spain: feminism and the Spanish women's movement. There are more than fifty different feminist groups in Spain today, with ideologies that run the gamut of the women's movement in the United States and abroad—from those which view feminism as a revolutionary struggle independent of men and political parties and which actively seek the destruction of the family unit and of women's oppression as a separate class to those which work in conjunction with the male-dominated political parties and view feminism as one aspect of a double militancy required of all politicized Spanish women.[1]

I would like to acknowledge Electa Arenal, Gabriela Mora, Elizabeth Starčevic, and Gloria Waldman for their critical reading of the manuscript and their many insightful comments, and JoAnne Engelbert for her helpful suggestions regarding the English translations.

1. For a complete listing and description of the various feminist groups in Spain, see the section "Mujeres del mundo" in the monthly issues of *Vindicación Feminista*, July 1976 to the present.

On several occasions since Franco's death, various groups representing different ideologies have joined together in public demonstrations, work stoppages, conferences, and symposia to demand a vindication of abortion facilities, legalized contraception, divorce, day care centers, the abolition of the adultery law concerning women and the *patria potestad paterna* clause,[2] equal pay for equal work, and amnesty for female prisoners convicted of crimes of a political or sex-related nature. If these activities have at times received insufficient coverage by the Spanish press, they have been continually documented and reported in Spain's only feminist magazine, *Vindicación Feminista* (Feminist Vindication), first published in the summer of 1976. Directed by Spain's leading feminist, the lawyer Lidia Falcón, and edited by the journalist Carmen Alcalde, this magazine has provided a consistently radical theoretical and activist approach toward Spanish feminism. Its monthly issues have included extensive coverage of such previously taboo areas of Spanish life as pornography, rape, prostitution, women's prisons, contraception, Basque women, and the role of women in the Spanish Civil War. Following its first year of success, *Vindicación Feminista* has expanded to include among its current publications several critical works on feminism. One of its first publications was Lidia Falcón's incisive exposé of women's prisons in Spain: *En el infierno: Ser mujer en las cárceles de España* (In Hell: To Be a Woman in Spanish Prisons) (1977).[3]

Falcón's writings, together with the works of Carmen Alcalde, María Aurelia Capmany, and María Campo Alange, constitute the core of recent nonfictional feminist literature that has sought to define and analyze the particular nature of Spanish feminism, Spanish machismo, the Spanish legal code, the family structure, and the contribution of women of the Second Republic to the development of the movement. The importance of these works cannot be overstated, for they represent a concerted effort to provide a link between Spanish feminism of the past and the present movement, a much needed step in the formulation of a uniquely Hispanic brand of feminism. As feminist Charo Ema stated:

> There have been women here who were feminists and no one knows about it. It's as if feminism were suddenly a new fashion

2. According to Article 154 of the Spanish Civil Code, the *patria potestad* clause states that "the father, and *in his absence*, the mother, has authority over legitimate children who are still minors." Feminist groups want parental authority to lie jointly with the father and mother.

3. Lidia Falcón, *En el infierno: Ser mujer en las cárceles de España* (Barcelona: Ediciones de Feminismo, S.A., 1977).

> that just arrived here like the "maxi-skirt," when what we really should do is look for the parallels between past and present, examine the feminism that existed here before, and see what its importance and relevance is to us now.[4]

The names of such Civil War intellectuals as Margarita Nelken, Victoria Kent, and Federica Montseny are essential in this rediscovery of Spanish feminism. The fact they have been largely neglected up to now is not merely a reflection of the low status of women in Spanish life but also a product of the Spanish political climate of the forties and fifties. Ana María Matute has spoken of the "suffocating environment"[5] of Spain in the forties, and Juan Goytisolo has referred to the "buffer zone"[6] which surrounded the country and made it impossible for young students to read the works of such politically unacceptable figures as Alberti and Lorca. As Montserrat Roig put it:

> They didn't tell us when we were growing up that there were poets like Antonio Machado and Rafael Alberti. They told us about Campoamor and Núñez de Arce. Then, suddenly, when we were twenty years old, we began to discover ourselves, and to realize that they have cheated us out of our childhood in the most base and despicable way. So, how can you expect them to tell us about Victoria Kent if they didn't even tell us about Alberti or Miguel Hernández?[7]

Many of the writings of Falcón, Alcalde, and the journalist Elisa Lamas, which analyze these and other aspects of feminism, have been adversely affected by Spanish censorship, especially during the Franco era. In accordance with this highly developed system, those works which reached the greatest public received the most stringent forms of censorship. Songs, television and radio programs, magazines, and newspapers have suffered the most from the rigid definition of good taste established by the regime. Therefore, it is not surprising that the

---

4. Interview with Charo Ema, conducted by Linda Gould Levine and Gloria Feiman Waldman, included in their book of interviews *Feminismo ante el franquismo: entrevistas con feministas de España* (Feminism in the Franco Years: Interviews with Feminists from Spain) (Miami: Ediciones Universal, 1980), p. 65. Hereafter, all references to interviews are taken from this book, unless otherwise indicated as "unpublished." The translations from the interviews and novels are by Levine.

5. Ana María Matute, "A Wounded Generation," trans. A. Gordon Ferguson, *Nation*, 29 November 1965, p. 422.

6. Juan Goytisolo, "La novela española contemporánea," *Libre* 2, December 1971–February 1972, p. 34.

7. Unpublished interview with Montserrat Roig, Barcelona, summer 1974.

special section on marriage and divorce published in a leading Spanish newspaper and written by seven women intellectuals—Lidia Falcón, Carmen Alcalde, María Aurelia Capmany, Susana March, Ana María Matute, Eva Forest, and Concha Alós—was suspended and its editors heavily fined. Similarly, it is not surprising that the public recitals of the feminist singer Julia León should have been subject to an even more stringent form of censorship, described by León in the following way:

> In order to have a recital, you have to present three copies with your lyrics to the Ministry of Information and Tourism. They return a few songs to you and keep the rest; then, they give you back one copy and you go with this copy and two more to the police. You have to do this for every recital, and when it's in Madrid, after all this, you also have to present a copy to the police station of the district and to the Bureau for the Protection of Minors. So, you waste two months preparing each recital. Aside from this previous censorship of your songs and the presence of the police the same night of the performance, someone has to be there at the rehearsal to check out everything you do, everything you think you are going to improvise.[8]

With reference to nonfictional feminist writings, countless examples have been offered by Falcón, Alcalde, and Lamas to substantiate this same view. Falcón describes the treatment given to her book *Mujer y sociedad* (Women in Society) (1969):

> *Mujer y sociedad* is a book with a thesis; it is a very harsh book, which, according to the censor's report, attacked all the basic institutions of the state, family and religion. There wasn't another book which stated things the way I did. When I first wrote it, the publishing house read it and thought that it wouldn't be released and they were right. The censors totally prohibited it. There weren't even corrections; they just didn't want to publish it. Later, some things were changed—sentences, adjectives; the language that was the harshest was toned down, and it was released. I finished writing it in 1968 and it was published in 1969. So, it was held up by censorship for one whole year.[9]

Similarly, Carmen Alcalde comments with reference to her book *La mujer en la guerra civil española* (Women in the Spanish Civil War) that "the difficulties I've had in publishing it have been tremendous,"[10] and Elisa Lamas' study, *Liberación femenina, control de la natalidad*

8. Levine and Waldman, *Feminismo ante el franquismo*, pp. 126, 129.
9. Ibid., p. 81.
10. Ibid., p. 38.

y aborto (Female Liberation: Birth Control and Abortion), "came out pretty distorted, because it seems it was too progressive the way it was."[11]

Works of fiction have been treated with more leniency primarily because they are least accessible to the public—due to price and to the degree of literary sophistication required to read them. This is not to say that censorship has not greatly affected the writings of many novelists and poets. Ana María Moix noted forty-five cuts in her novel *Walter, ¿por qué te fuiste?* (Walter, Why Did You Go Away?) (1973),[12] and countless statements by writers have attested to the self-censorship to which they themselves fall prey. Nevertheless, because of the allusive style that Spanish writers have learned to use, certain passages of their writings have escaped the censors, and thus the sexual freedom that characterizes certain sections of *Walter ¿por qué te fuiste?* would be totally inconceivable if visualized on television or sung about by Julia León.[13]

It is too soon to evaluate the impact that the feminist movement will have on contemporary Spanish letters and in particular on women authors. Nevertheless, even within the restrictions that censorship has imposed (externally and internally) on its writers and even within the context of the relative newness of the women's movement, one can point out a number of texts written by Spain's foremost women novelists that have attempted to explore and define the problems facing women in contemporary Spain. I will limit my discussion to the view of the upper-middle-class woman presented in the most recent novels of Carmen Martín Gaite, Ana María Matute, and Ana María Moix.

Both Martín Gaite and Matute form a part of the *generación del medio siglo* ("the generation of mid-century"), the group of young writers that were children during the Civil War, and were educated in the silent era of the forties and fifties. Accordingly, the female protagonists they describe in their most acclaimed novels—Martín Gaite's *Retahílas* (Links) (1974) and Matute's *La trampa* (The Trap) (1969)—are women in their forties, for whom the Spanish Civil War is a reality contained within the boundaries of their adolescent recollections. Moix, on the contrary, is a product of the sixties; at age thirty, she

11. Ibid., p. 121.

12. Unpublished interview with Ana María Moix, Barcelona, summer 1974.

13. In her interview with Levine and Waldman, Julia León commented that one of her songs dealing with a child's inquiry about "where children come from" was censored in Valladolid. See *Feminismo ante el franquismo*, p. 128.

forms part of *los novísimos* ("the newest ones"), the group of Spanish intellectuals weaned on the mass media, the crisis of realism in literature, the "coca-colazation" of Spain, student strikes, and the activism of the sixties. As in her well-known work *Julia* (1969), her female protagonists very much reflect this new social and political reality and provide a different view, both sexually and politically, from that seen in Martín Gaite and Matute.

Despite these differences there are a number of similarities in their works, especially in their narrative point of view. In *Retahílas*, *La trampa*, and *Julia* the reader immediately enters the consciousness of the protagonist, who seeks to recreate during the course of the novel certain key experiences that have shaped her life. In the case of *Retahílas* and *La trampa*, this process is facilitated by the central male character, who listens to the protagonist's story and in turn shares his tale with her. In both these novels, interior linear time has been suspended, and the events are retold as they surge in the characters' consciousness and apply at the moment. In Moix's novel, *Julia*, the external dialogue between an "I" and a "you" is replaced by an interior dialogue between two aspects of the character's self: the Julita of the past, a six-year-old child, and the Julia of the present, a twenty-year-old woman. Without falling into the trap of overidentifying the writer with her character, one can safely say that Eulalia of *Retahílas*, Matia of *La trampa*, and Julia, who appears in both *Julia* and *Walter*, bear some autobiographical resemblance to their creators. They are upper-middle-class intellectuals; they are interested in literature; and they are involved in some attempt to understand the social conditions which shaped their female reality.

Retahílas,[14] published in 1974, clearly represents the crystallization of many themes which Martín Gaite had briefly dealt with in her previous works of fiction and nonfiction: the desire to break bonds and experience freedom. This theme is seen in *Las ataduras* (Bonds) (1960); in the search for the ideal listener described in *La búsqueda de un interlocutor* (The Search for an Interlocutor) (1973); and in the effect of social conventions on the individual in *Ritmo lento* (Slow Beat) (1963) and *Entre visillos* (Between the Curtains) (1958). In *Retahílas*, Martín Gaite makes her most eloquent and tight-knit comment on these themes to date. It is also her most profound exploration of a woman's consciousness. The questions she raises through her

14. Carmen Martín Gaite, *Retahílas* (Barcelona: Destino, 1974). All page references are to this edition.

forty-five-year-old protagonist, Eulalia, strike at the very core of the new social structure that the women's movement is trying to create: to what degree is it possible to discard the sex-role stereotyping to which women have been subject since childhood and to forge a different view of female reality? To what degree is it possible to reject the traditional family unit and motherhood without feeling a sense of loss at a later time? To what degree can a woman seek a man who will not dominate her without feeling the need to be dominated by him? During the course of the novel these questions are carefully analyzed and dissected in Eulalia's dialogue with her nephew Germán. It is only through this dialogue that she is able to recover a sense of her lost self and reach a lucid comprehension of the traps she created for herself in her search for freedom. She recreates herself as a young woman, determined not to fall into the pattern of submissiveness and passivity that she observes in her mother. Although as a young girl her favorite readings are sentimental novels filled with passionate heroines seeking love, as she matures and comes into contact with Choderlos de Laclos' *Les Liaisons dangereuses* (1782), she rejects the conventional romantic roles that women are expected to follow and fabricates a self-styled feminist philosophy based on freedom and independence:

> Laclos pulverizaba el concepto de amor arraigado en Occidente, su heroína lo era por revolverse contra lo sublime, contra aquellos modelos ancestrales de conducta amorosa, al atreverse a demostrar que la única verdad del amor radicaba en su trampa; hice mi catecismo de aquel libro y de allí en adelante la señora Merteuil cínica, descreída, artífice de su propio destino, destronó a las mujeres de la raza de Adriana, palpitantes de amor, luchando entre deseo y raciocinio. . . . Mamá ya estaba delicada por entonces y seguía pendiente de todos los caprichos de papá, sumisa, disculpándose siempre; yo eso no lo podía soportar, era una imagen de futuro que rechazaba, quería largarme de viaje, vivir sin ataduras, que nadie me mandara, tomar el amor como un juego divertido que se deja o se coge según cuadre . . . ceder al otro amor con mayúsculas, a ese que hace sufrir y que enajena, sería someterse, perder el albedrío, y sólo de uno mismo dependía el rechazo, simplemente de mantener la cabeza clara; yo, después de maduras reflexiones, había decidido no enamorarme nunca y estaba segura de lograrlo. (pp. 148–49)

> Laclos pulverized the concept of love rooted in the West. His heroine was a heroine precisely because she rebelled against the sublime, against those ancestral models of amorous behavior by daring to demonstrate that the only truth of love was in its trap. I

> did my catechism with that book and from that point on, the cynical, disbelieving Madame Merteuil, creator of her own destiny, dethroned the women of Adriana's stock, throbbing with love, struggling between desire and reason. . . . Mother was already sickly by then and always at Father's beck and call. I couldn't stand that; it was an image of the future that I rejected. I wanted to get out of there, live without ties, not let anyone dominate me, view love as an entertaining game that you take or leave according to how it suits you. . . . To give in to that other love with a capital L, the one that makes you suffer and go crazy, would be to submit, to lose your will. If I only kept my head clear I could reject all that. So, after these mature reflections, I decided never to fall in love and I was sure I could achieve it.

What follows is the logical pattern in the following rebellious context: rejection of the family; studies in France; cult of "la utópica gloria de ser libre" (p. 149) (the utopian glory of being free); scorn mixed with secret envy of those friends who have allowed themselves the freedom to fall in love, get married, and have children without condemning a priori such a conventional pattern. If during the course of the novel, Eulalia is able to confess that "tanto pregonar al albedrío puede ser una trampa, un producto del miedo, hojarasca verbal para cubrir el ego solitario" (pp. 140–41) (making such a point of free will can be a trap, a product of fear, a verbal disguise designed to cover a lonely self), the fact remains that her failure to live authentically the reality she wanted to create is not just a product of her own particular self-deception or lack of self-knowledge. It is also a result of the limitations placed on her by a society that has continually thwarted women in their attempt to break away from the conventions of the times. In the 1950s, when Eulalia was a young woman in her twenties, only 15 percent of the total university population was female,[15] and there were few options and role models for the woman who tried to combine family and career. The degree to which Eulalia herself has internalized this situation is best reflected in her comment to her friend: "En España, Lucía, no cabe compaginar, lo sabemos de sobra, o eres madre o te haces persona" (p. 145) (Lucía, in Spain, you can't win; we know that only too well. Either you're a mother or you're a person).

Through the course of the novel, Martín Gaite gives her character the opportunity to reevaluate such statements as these and to renege

---

15. María Campo Alange, *La mujer en España: Cien años de su historia* (Women in Spain: One Hundred Years of Their History) (Madrid: Aguilar, 1964), p. 301.

on her previous values. Her marriage to Andrés, a detached university professor, whose personality is somewhat inscrutable to both Eulalia and the reader, provides the initial setting for this introspective process. Although marrying Andrés may appear to be a definite lapse in Eulalia's previous rejection of love, she carefully tries to act out in her marriage the philosophy she developed when single, only now the first-person singular becomes a somewhat forced plural: "no queríamos compromisos ni proyectos ni porvenir estable, no queríamos hijos, por supuesto" (p. 208) (We didn't want commitments or plans or a fixed future, and, of course, we didn't want children). For reasons which are not totally clear to the reader, but seem to be due to Eulalia's self-absorption and need for continual activity and change of lifestyle, Andrés becomes increasingly critical of her rhetoric and decides to leave her. It is at this point in her life that Eulalia's plan for independence rapidly disintegrates. Devastated at the breakup of her marriage, she no longer finds solace in her books but instead joins the sorority of other betrayed heroines of film and literature:

> Se me quitaron las ganas de comer y de dormir y de leer, todo el día pegada como una lapa a la mesita del teléfono, horas y horas, mi única obsesión era llamarle . . . pena y rabia me daba haber caído tan bajo, pero lo peor era que cuanto más ridícula me veía, más ganas me entraban de echarle a él la culpa en plan de novela pasional; todo el veneno de esos folletines de los que tanto he renegado en la vida se me desbordaba de sus diques y la marea vengativa venía a incrementarse con imágenes de películas y lecturas posteriores, una procesión de heroínas pálidas con los ojos llorosos . . . esperando al amante que no viene, echándole en cara su perfidia, muchachas de los cancioneros galaico portugueses . . . esposas engañadas del teatro clásico, Ana Karenina después de su caída, los rostros de Joan Fontaine y de Ingrid Bergman . . . todas se me agolpaban en el recuerdo prestándome su idioma exaltado y divino, tentándome con él. (pp. 196–97)

> I lost all desire to eat and sleep and read. I spent the whole day, stuck like a leech to the telephone. For hours and hours, my only obsession was to call him. . . . I felt pain and anger at seeing myself fall so low, but the worst was that the more ridiculous I felt, the more I felt like blaming him in the style of those romantic novels. All the poison of those serials which I spent so much time refuting suddenly hit me and my desire for vengeance was nourished and intensified with images from movies and books—a whole procession of pale heroines with tearful eyes . . . waiting for the lover who doesn't come, blaming him for his betrayal, of

> girls from Galician-Portuguese ballads, of deceived wives from classical theater, of Anna Karenina after her fall, the faces of Joan Fontaine and Ingrid Bergman—all suddenly appeared in my memory lending me their passionate and divine language, tempting me with it.

It is at this moment of the novel that the character becomes most aware of the difference between intellectualism and experience. At no other point in the work is her sense of vulnerability greater; her fear of being rejected by a potential suitor more prominent; her feeling that children might have saved her marriage more apparent. Perhaps her seeming lack of a fixed profession also contributes to her emotional crisis at the end. The reader is not quite sure what she actually does. Brief allusions are made to a career in journalism following studies in literature, but Eulalia gives much more importance to Andrés' profession than to her own. In this sense, she has internalized society's view that the man's profession is more important than the woman's, but she does not seem to be totally aware of the impact that society has had in determining this view of herself and her work. She continually blames herself for the breakup of her marriage and does not make the connection between her own problems and the conflicts of other women in the Spanish culture. However, the links are definitely there, and thus, Eulalia's individual story may also be viewed as a study of the problems faced by many intellectual women trying to create a new lifestyle without sufficient societal support or role models.

Martín Gaite's subsequent novel, *Fragmentos de interior* (Fragments from Within) (1976), is a radical departure from the exploration presented in *Retahílas*. It is a superficial, schematic piece of writing, which presents several views of the female condition without sufficiently developing any one of them. Perhaps part of the difficulty lies in the multiple narrative perspectives that the author has attempted to convey here. Whereas in *Retahílas*, the text exclusively centers on the consciousness of Eulalia and Germán, in *Fragmentos de interior*, a much shorter work, the narrative overly fragments itself in its attempt to capture the thoughts of Luisa, Jaime, Diego, Agustina, and Isabel. With the possible exception of Luisa, the young girl who leaves her hometown to be with a lover, none of the other female characters is able to make her way out of the conventional, one-dimensional mold the author has placed her in. Gloria, Diego's mistress, is the vain and vacuous aspiring actress, who goes from bed to bed in her attempt to find a good role; Isabel, Diego's daughter, is the rational, intelligent student activist, involved in some kind of undefined political group; Agustina, Diego's wife, is the passionate, self-consumed romantic, whose desperation over the deterioration of her marriage and dreams leads her to commit suicide. Unfortunately, these are all variations of the same female characters who have been populating Spanish fiction for some time, but without the depth or development they have received in other works. Teresa Serrat, in Juan Marsé's *Ultimas tardes con Teresa* (Final Afternoons with Teresa) (1966) is certainly a much more complex presentation of the university student of bourgeois background involved in political struggle than is Martín Gaite's Isabel. It would appear that Martín Gaite does best when she concentrates on one or two characters, as in *Ritmo lento* or *Retahílas*, and allows herself the space to explore with leisure the contradictions of the human psyche.

Ana María Matute's *La trampa*,[16] published five years before *Retahílas*, in 1969, is, to date, the author's most interesting presentation of a woman's psychology. Curiously, there are a number of interesting parallels in the external structure of the two novels. In both, we find that the protagonists' self-examination is initially triggered by certain events in their grandmothers' lives. In *Retahílas*, Eulalia's dying grandmother wants to be transported back to her country estate; Eulalia accompanies her and finds in her escape from the city the emotional distance needed to begin her self-exploration. In *La trampa*, Matia's grandmother, a central character in *Primera memoria* (First Memory) (1960), willfully celebrates her one-hundredth birthday at age ninety-nine and requests that her family return to the island to spend it with her. Matia, like Eulalia, is suddenly submerged into a reality filled with childhood evocations and recreates during the course of three days the main events in her life from the termination of *Primera memoria* to the present time. In this novel, Matute has set out a difficult assignment for herself by picking up the loose threads of Matia's life, totally set aside in the second novel of her trilogy, *Los soldados lloran de noche* (The Soldiers Cry at Night) (1964). The jump from portraying a fourteen-year-old girl in *Primera memoria* to a woman in her forties in *La trampa* is not easy to master, and Matute has achieved it with a certain amount of success although there are still many questions which remain to be answered.

The view of the female condition presented in this work is a depressing one. From the very first pages of the work, Matia's diary con-

16. Ana María Matute, *La trampa* (Barcelona: Destino, 1969). All page references are to this edition.

tains a clear denunciation of the education and socialization process to which she, as a woman, has been subject:

> Casi siempre intenté engañarme sobre el verdadero motivo de mis actos. Este fue el gran truco sobre el que se edificó mi educación sentimental (mi educación intelectual no importó jamás, ya que una mujer no precisa de ciertos bagajes para instalarse dignamente en la sociedad que se me destinaba), mi formación de criatura nacida para entablar una lucha mezquina y dulzona contra el sexo masculino (al que, por otra parte, estaba inexorablemente destinada). Así pues, mis más importantes y permitidas armas fueron velos con que encubrir el egoísmo y la ambición, la ignorancia y el desamparo, la pereza y la sensualidad. (p. 25)

> I almost always tried to deceive myself about the real motive of my acts. This was the great trick that my sentimental education was based on (my intellectual education never mattered since a woman doesn't need such baggage to move with dignity into the society I was destined for). As a little girl I was trained to engage in a coy, half-hearted struggle against the male sex (for whom I was inexorably destined, anyway). Thus, my most important and acceptable weapons were veils with which to cover selfishness and ambition, ignorance and helplessness, laziness and sensuality.

Unfortunately, many of the details of this struggle are omitted from the novel, and when they are presented, they do not exactly conform to the vision described in this passage. David, Matia's husband, is a weaker, more docile character than Matia, and ultimately it is Beverly, David's mother, who seizes control of the situation and decides that they must be separated. This is not to say that the character's emotions lack credibility; Matute has been able to capture in the mature Matia the same feeling of solitude, lack of comprehension of the world, and estrangement that she portrayed in the young protagonist of *Primera memoria*. What is missing, however, is a more detailed view of how the other Matia of the first novel, the rebellious, defiant girl who sought to break out of the conventional world of her grandmother, was squashed so brutally as to allow her more "cowardly," passive side to predominate. Matute tries to justify this evolution in one key passage of the work, which has clear social implications for its critique of the Spanish education system. Yet despite the reader's familiarity with this process, clearly documented from a male point of view by Azorín in his *La voluntad* (Will) (1902) and *Las confesiones de un pequeño filósofo* (Confessions of a Little Philosopher) (1904),[17] it lacks the depth necessary to be totally convincing. Her words are:

> Los primeros años de mi vida fui de carácter díscolo y rebelde; pero en el segundo colegio (donde fui internada, apenas acabó la guerra) me transformé completamente. De niña mala pasé a adolescente respetuosa, tímida y pasable estudiante. La antigua charlatanería, el descaro y la mala educación que me caracterizaban se doblaron suavemente; y llegó el silencio, un gran silencio a mi vida. (p. 30)

> During the first years of my life, I was disobedient and rebellious, but I totally changed when I was in the second school they sent me to, right after the war. From a mischievous child, I turned into a respectful, timid and just passable student. The old talkativeness, impudence and naughtiness that had characterized me before gave in without a struggle, and a silence, a great silence closed in around my life.

It is perhaps because of this silence and because the character "has lost her voice" that her personality somewhat eludes the reader. This could also be a product of the fragmented narrative style of the novel, which is divided into four points of view, each one of which has corresponding chapters in the work, devoted to Matia, Isa, Bear, and Mario. To this degree, Eulalia of *Retahílas* is much more clearly defined than Matia, and in this sense, Mario's presence in *La trampa* and his vision of Matia is vital in providing the reader with another perspective of the female protagonist and her "calada hasta los huesos en una antiquísima pereza" (p. 159) (total immersion in an ancient indolence). Another crucial difference between *Retahílas* and *La trampa* is Matia's passive acceptance of her detachment from life and feminine role. The following words would be totally inconceivable if spoken by Eulalia:

> Yo sé perfectamente por qué he venido aquí. Yo sé muy bien por qué razón no puedo desprenderme, ni me sabré ya desprender de la tiranía. He nacido en la tiranía y en ella moriré. Tal vez, incluso, con cierta confortabilidad, suponiéndome exenta de toda culpa. (p. 21)

---

17. José Martínez Ruiz (Azorín), *La Voluntad* (Madrid: Clásicos Castellanos, 1968); Martínez Ruiz, *Las confesiones de un pequeño filósofo* (Madrid: Espasa-Calpe, 1970).

> I know perfectly well why I came here. I know very well why I can't break loose, nor will ever be able to break loose from this tyranny. I was born in slavery and I will die in it, perhaps even with a certain comfort, thinking that I'm free from all blame.

It is obvious that Matute does not view herself as a proselytizing feminist in this novel, nor does such a role correspond to her definition of the novelist's task. If, according to her theory, "el escritor enciende luces rojas. Porque el escritor no es un moralista, ni un sociólogo ni un doctrinario. El escritor es un hombre que duda, se pregunta a sí mismo y provoca en el lector un angustia, recelos y repulsa que pueden ser beneficiosos"[18] (the writer sends out red signals, the writer isn't a moralist or a sociologist or a doctrinarian. The writer is a person who doubts, questions himself, and provokes in the reader an anguish, distrust and sense of repulsion that can be beneficial), this is what she achieves in *La trampa.* Much of the section devoted to Matia's "Diario en desorden" (Diary in Disorder) seems to be a self-questioning examination of the experience of motherhood, which, according to some critics, bears a close autobiographical resemblance to Matute's own relationship with her son, with one essential difference. Matute has been quoted as saying: "Mi hijo es mi razón de vida; la literatura, mi razón a ser"[19] (My son is my reason for living; literature, my reason for being). In Matia's case, neither seems to define her as clearly as in her creator's life. There is some mention made of studies in comparative literature, "que aún hoy intento aplicar a algún aspecto de mi vida, sin acierto ostensible" (p. 215) (that I still try to apply to some aspect of my life, without any ostensible success), but, as in the case of Eulalia, Matia does not seem to have either a defined profession or deep involvement in her work. Similarly, her attitude toward her son, though emotionally described in terms of a fierce sense of possessiveness and "amor . . . atroz, sobrecogedor" (p. 77) (a savage, awesome love), is actually conveyed in the novel with a sense of distance and maximum autonomy of the two parties. Even Bear, in one of his meditations about his mother, comments: "En el fondo mamá es una buena persona; la madre más conveniente que se puede desear. No anda metiendo la nariz donde no debe como, por ejemplo, la intolerable madre de Luis" (p. 255) (Deep down, mother is a good person, the most convenient mother that anyone could want. She doesn't butt in where she shouldn't, like, for instance, Luis's intolerable mother).

---

18. Rosa Roma, *Ana María Matute* (Madrid: Epesa, 1971), p. 77.

19. Ibid., p. 123; and interview with Matute conducted by Del Arco, *Tele-Express*, 7 August 1968.

It is only through her relationship with Mario that Matia appears to be connected to someone, that her solitary island links up with another person's equally isolated and self-protective world. Just as Eulalia ultimately reaches a level of self-comprehension through her night-long verbal marathon with Germán, Matia, too, is able to explore with Mario "las raíces de la incertidumbre; la incapacidad de comprender; el gran estupor" (p. 190) (the roots of uncertainty; her inability to understand; her great stupor). The understanding that a sensitive man is able to provide the female character is not counterbalanced by the presence of a strong female support system. Lucía in *Retahílas* tries to fulfill, in some sense, such a role with Eulalia, but the two are ultimately too different to penetrate totally the other's world. In the context of these novels, women have yet to turn to other women as a means of finding solidarity and comprehension of their problems. Although one does not necessarily expect to find in literature the concept of sisterhood propagated by the women's movement, the traditional lack of association among upper-middle-class Spanish women is reflected to some degree in these works, together with the individual message of solitude that the writer is trying to communicate.

Extensive interviews with various women lawyers, writers, and intellectuals have corroborated this feeling of a lack of community among upper-class women in Spain. As the journalist Montserrat Roig said:

> People don't work in teams here at all, perhaps due to the political situation and to the fact that there isn't freedom here and we're afraid. This has created very individualistic approaches to work. Also, women have been taught to be suspicious and distrustful. This is the base of the education that we've all received here, and as a result, we've had to struggle pretty much alone, first against our families, then against what we were taught in school, then on the street and then at work. This society is very hostile to the woman who works. So, among ourselves, we've grown up in this competition—sexual competition and physical competition and this has then been transferred to professional competition.[20]

With the growth of the feminist movement in Spain and the existence of over fifty different women's groups, this social reality will inevitably change and may ultimately be reflected in literature. The concept of solidarity and sisterhood has become an increasingly im-

20. Unpublished interview with Montserrat Roig.

portant element in contemporary fiction written by women, but it is noticeably absent from the novels of Matute and Martín Gaite.

The relationship between women is, however, a central aspect of Ana María Moix's novel *Julia*,[21] in which the protagonist Julia has a deep involvement with her university literature professor, Eva. Eva's importance in the novel is not merely limited to her role as an intellectual model for Julia; she also represents the mother, friend, and lover that Julia actively seeks. To this degree, Moix radically deviates from the presentation of the female protagonist seen in Martín Gaite and Matute by introducing the tabu theme of lesbianism into the core of her work. By means of an interior monologue narrated exclusively in third person throughout the novel, Moix captures the anxieties of her twenty-year-old protagonist, whose continual nightmares center on her rape at the age of six by Victor, a friend of the family. As a result of this traumatic experience, together with the sense of emotional deprivation she experienced as a child, she develops an intense physical aversion to men and an obsessive need to find a strong female figure with whom to identify and in whom to find solace.[22] Her monologue is filled with multiple images reflecting her sense of guilt at wishing the death of her parents; her fixation with the past and her other self, the Julita of six, whose very existence in her mind is a continual evocation of her rape; Freudian metaphors of phallic symbols, which threaten to consume her; and ultimately a need for self-destruction as a means of freeing her from her divided self.

In the first reading of the novel, neither the rape itself nor the lesbian theme is apparent; Moix herself has spoken of "the sensitivity of the critics" in not mentioning the homosexual overtones of the novel.[23] Considered from within the context of Spanish culture and its cult of machismo, lesbianism is a difficult issue to deal with. As the journalist Carmen Alcalde said:

> Lesbianism isn't considered here at all. People believe that it isn't important, that it's a game. It's not taken at all seriously. If two women are caught in a lesbian act, I can assure you that nothing

---

21. Ana María Moix, *Julia* (Barcelona: Seix Barral, 1969). All page references are to this edition.

22. For an in-depth analysis of Julia's psychology, see Sara E. Schyfter, "Rites Without Passage: The Adolescent World of *Julia*" in *The Analysis of Literary Texts: Current Trends in Methodology*, Third and Fourth York College Colloquia, ed. Randolph Pope (Ypsilanti, Mich.: Bilingual Press/Editorial Bilingue, 1980), pp. 41–50.

23. Unpublished interview with Ana María Moix.

> will happen to them because the first thing that will occur to anyone is to say that they just didn't have a man around. Lesbianism has no identity here. You can walk along in the street with your arm around a woman and the worst thing that will happen is that some foul-minded person will insult you. But if they report you to the police, the police won't know what to do. They don't understand that a woman could like another woman. It just doesn't fit in their concept of themselves, in the narcissism.[24]

With the growth of the feminist movement in Spain, this topic will no doubt be treated with increasing openness. There are presently two declared homosexual groups in Spain, the Colectivo de Lesbianas País Valencia (Lesbian Collective of Valencia), and the Frente de Liberación Homosexual del Estado Español (Homosexual Liberation Front of the Spanish State).[25] Also, Alcalde and Moix are preparing a book on the topic called *La otra opción amorosa* (The Other Option in Love). From a purely literary point of view, relatively few mentions have been made of this topic in comparison to the treatment of male homosexuality.[26] In *Fragmentos de interior*, Jaime is implicitly described as a homosexual, as is Ernesto in *Julia* and in *Walter, ¿por qué te fuiste?* On a more intense note, Juan Goytisolo's recent novels, *Señas de identidad* (Marks of Identity) (1966), *Don Julián* (Count Julian) (1970), and *Juan sin tierra* (Juan the Landless) (1975), are explicit glorifications of the homosexual, whose sexual preference marks a clear rejection of Hispanic social norms.

In Moix's novel, lesbianism finally emerges as a theme treated with sensitivity and care, although definitely with a somewhat guarded allusiveness. Several of the following passages regarding Julia's relationship with Eva can be considered within this context:

---

24. Levine and Waldman, *Feminismo ante el franquismo*, p. 36.

25. See *Vindicación Feminista*, October 1976, p. 44, for a detailed description of the ideology of the Frente de Liberación Homosexual del Estado Español.

26. In her novel, *El último verano en el espejo* (The Last Summer in the Mirror) (Barcelona: Destino, 1967), Teresa Barbero explores the sexual feeling that Elena has for her friend Marta. In an unpublished interview with Barbero conducted by Levine and Waldman in Madrid during the summer of 1974, Barbero commented that the lesbianism described in her novel is

> unconscious, as in the majority of similar cases. The educative molds are too great here for a Spanish woman to be able to face such a problem. On the other hand, this problem has arisen precisely because our society has tried to indoctrinate women, making them believe that man is a monster dangerous to their physical and moral integrity.

> Empezaba por despertarse, sobresaltada, en medio de una pesadilla. Sentía miedo. Se acogía a la imagen de Eva, a la extraña pasión que sentía por Eva. (p. 27)
>
> Durante aquellas últimas horas de insomnio, se esforzó por rechazar la imagen de Eva. Pensar en Eva le producía un dolor insoportable. Desesperaba. Sentía deseos de rasgar las sábanas, destrozar las mantas, agarrar un hacha y destruir los muebles de la habitación. . . . Anhelaba la presencia de Eva más que nada en el mundo; oír su voz, ver cómo movía las manos al hablar. Se daba cuenta de cuán pobres e insignificantes eran sus deseos: ver a Eva, escuchar palabras amables de sus labios y nada más. Se preguntaba una y mil veces por qué había de sufrir por algo tan sencillo, tan fácil para los otros. Aquel único deseo, absurdo a su edad, la desesperaba. Ponía en evidencia la natural ausencia de Eva y al mismo tiempo la absoluta soledad que la envolvía. (pp. 185–86)

> She began by waking up, startled, in the middle of the night. She felt afraid. She sought refuge in Eva's image, in the strange passion she felt for Eva.
>
> During those last hours of sleeplessness, she tried to reject Eva's image. Thinking about Eva gave her an unbearable pain. She was desperate. She felt like ripping up her sheets, tearing her blankets to shreds, grabbing an axe and destroying the furniture in her room. . . . She longed for Eva's presence more than anything in the world; to hear her voice, see how she moved her hands. She realized how modest and insignificant her desires were: just to see Eva, listen to kind words from her lips and nothing else. She asked herself one and a thousand times why she had to suffer over something so simple, so easy for others. That one wish, absurd at her age, made her desperate. It made her acutely aware of Eva's natural absence and at the same time of the absolute solitude that enveloped her.

As these passages indicate, Julia does not totally come to terms with her lesbianism. She merely perceives herself as different and observes that she feels physically sick when she is kissed by her friend Carlos, but she does not make the connection between such feelings and her obsession for Eva. It is interesting to note that she acts out with Eva the same love-sick pattern that Eulalia enacted with Andrés: a neurotic fixation with the telephone, anticipation of the phone call that either never comes or comes too late, followed by intense feelings of desperation and rejection, which in Julia's case, lead her to a suicide attempt. Her failure to end her life and the conclusion of the novel are depressing. By thwarting the success of Julia's attempt to kill herself, Moix not only condemns her character to an existence filled with the torment of her other self, Julita, "un dios martirizador" (p. 63) (a tormenting God), but also to an alienated life in a bourgeois, sexist society.

Throughout the novel, Moix continually satirizes the stereotyped view of women ardently defended by Julia's mother and grandmother. Her mother is clearly a victim of the feminine mystique. Her daily activities consist of visits to the beauty parlor and a fixation with the radio melodramas. As such, her vision of women conforms to this mold: "Una chica debe ser coqueta y presumida, de lo contrario parece un hombre" (p. 145) (A girl should be flirtatious and conceited. Otherwise, she seems like a man). In the figure of Julia's grandmother, Moix has brought together the most intolerant clichés that have been voiced about Spanish politics, literature, sexuality, and women. To this degree, she follows in the long tradition of the Doña Perfectas and Bernarda Albas who have populated Spanish fiction for the past one hundred years. Consistent with this personality is her attitude that "una mujer que no va a misa y no reza, no es una mujer decente, y eso, naturalmente, se nota en la apariencia" (p. 161) (a woman who doesn't go to mass and pray isn't a decent woman, and that, of course, can be seen in her appearance).

Significantly, the stifling atmosphere that Moix describes in *Julia* corresponds in great part to her own family life and upbringing. In her "Poética" (Poetics), the author writes about her two brothers, Miguel and Ramón, who are recreated in *Julia* in the characters of Rafael and Ernesto, and about her father, Don Jesús, "monárquico y sentimental . . . quien aseguraba que Sartre era la reencarnación del demonio y que sus lectores quedaban inmediatamente esclavizados al servicio de Satan"[27] (monarchical and sentimental . . . who was sure that Sartre was the reincarnation of the devil, and that all his readers would immediately be trapped into serving Satan). In *Julia* it is her grandmother who ultimately voices these views, for her father assumes a much more passive role and seeks only "peace and tranquility." In this sense, it is interesting to note how, with slight modifications, Moix has transferred to *Julia* many of the external details of her own life but with a vengefulness and desire for destruction that few writers have exercised

27. Ana María Moix, "Poética," in *Nueve novísimos poetas españoles* (Nine Very New Spanish Poets), ed. José María Castellet (Barcelona: Barral Editores, 1970), pp. 221–22.

on their characters. If Moix herself was able to break out of the mold of conventionality imposed by her family, she does not permit her literary alter ego to achieve this freedom. Unable—or unwilling—to kill Julia off in her first novel, she reintroduces her in her second novel, *Walter, ¿por qué te fuiste?*, only to exorcise her finally from her life at the end of the work. It is important to observe that Julia is a minor figure in *Walter*; Moix briefly refers to events in her life that the reader of *Julia* is already familiar with, but without delving into them in detailed fashion, for example, her relationship with "so and so, the literature prof," her minor participation in a student strike, the death of her brother Rafael, her suicide attempt. In this sense, when Moix does kill her at the end of *Walter*, the reader does not perceive her death in a real or painful way, for her very presence in the work has been too elusive to grasp fully. Such is the nature of her death itself; allusions are made to Julia's last months in a sanitarium, to her sadness and withdrawal from life, and then to her death, but the reader is not exactly sure what she dies of, for Moix is not interested in revealing the details.

Significantly, when she returns to the theme of the young woman surrounded by a stratified society in her monthly pieces, "Diario de una hija de familia" (Diary of a Daughter), published in *Vindicación Feminista*, it is without the pathos and morbidity revealed in *Julia* and *Walter*. Rather, she chooses to capitalize on the ironic sense of humor displayed in these novels, combined with a heightened feminist consciousness and clear-cut defense of the women's movement. The external pattern is the same one observed in her novels: she portrays a young woman, with two "radicalized" brothers, Ernesto and Rafael, and a staunchly conservative father, who believes that "el español debe ser, para empezar, un caballero, sobre todo con las damas, seres desvalidos a quienes debe protección. . . digan lo que digan ciertas revistas"[28] (a Spaniard, should be, first and foremost, a gentleman, especially with ladies, helpless creatures whom he should protect . . . regardless of what certain magazines say). However, a new, extremely well-executed element is now added. The vain, self-absorbed mother in *Julia* has become so totally politicized in *Vindicación* that she nearly gives her husband a heart attack by marching in feminist demonstrations and fighting for women's rights. Moix's feminist consciousness has never been greater than in these delightfully irreverent passages that satirize sexism, male chauvinism, tradition, and progres-

28. Ana María Moix, "Diario de una hija de familia," *Vindicación Feminista*, December 1976, p. 15.

sive leftists. Consistent with her other works, though, the daughter, whom one could identify with Julia, is still outshadowed by Florentina, her feminist Dutch cousin, whose countless pranks and ideas initiate the social revolution in the household.

If one can speak then of a definite sense of continuity in Moix's recent prose works, it is also apparent that her demythification of conventionality and her audacity in dealing with sexual topics become much more pronounced in her second novel. If *Julia* provides a guarded treatment of the theme of lesbianism, together with clear references to "the anti-baby pill," male homosexuality, and rape, *Walter, ¿por qué te fuiste?*[29] represents a more daring and inclusive view of several other sexual themes, previously taboo in Spanish literature: male and female masturbation, bisexuality, sodomy, and menstruation. Within this context, it is not surprising that forty-five cuts were made in the novel by the censors prior to its publication, although many were also of a political nature.[30] As previously stated, *Walter* is technically a much more difficult novel to approach than *Julia*. The connection with outside reality maintained in *Julia* through the external unities of time, place, and action is much less apparent in *Walter*, and what is left is a narrative discourse presented from various perspectives in which the voice of Ismael, the central character, and that of his cousins, María Antonia, Lea, and Ricardo, simultaneously appear on the page, in the first, second, and third persons. The concept of linear time is completely suspended; the distance between past and present is obliterated; and the only concrete reality that the reader can hold on to is Ismael's seven-year search for his cousin Lea, whom he needs to find both for himself and in order to give her the packet of letters that Julia left her upon her death.

When one considers that Moix completed this novel in one and a half months, after having thought about it for four years, the intensity and facility of her narrative skills is awesome.[31] Alternately using a lyrical and satirical style, she both captures the inner fragmentation of

29. Ana María Moix, *Walter, ¿por qué te fuiste?* (Barcelona: Barral Editores, 1973). All page references are to this edition.

30. In an unpublished interview conducted by Levine and Waldman, Moix indicated that one of the parts that was censored in the novel had to do with María Antonia's inquiry about sexual relationships between adults. When María Antonia realizes that her "mother did it with her father," her next conclusion was that Franco must also do "it" with his wife. The censors eliminated this section, for obvious reasons.

31. Moix also indicated in our interview that it took her twenty-five days to write *Julia*.

Ismael, the male alter ego of Julia herself, and unmasks anew the bourgeois society of the Barcelona of the sixties.

The vision of women presented in the work is somewhat confusing and disturbing. As stated before, Julia herself is a marginal character, passive, silent, and totally fixated as is Ismael with her older cousin Lea. Lea herself is a difficult character to comprehend in great part because she is primarily seen through Ismael's eyes and never totally emerges as a figure with discernible motives. In Lea, Moix has created the vision of a young woman determined to reject the values of her family and class; thus, when her cousin Maite tells her that everyone gets married, she replies: "Sí, una mierda, y trabajar y tener hijos y aburrirse y volverse viejo y feo y gordo" (p. 120) (Yes, it's shit, work and have kids and be bored and turn old and ugly and fat). Her deviation from the conventional pattern is most apparent in her sexual activities, which include having several lovers, seducing Ismael when he is nine years old, and ultimately having an alternately bisexual relationship with Ismael and Julia. This latter aspect is alluded to somewhat cryptically at the end of the work, when Ismael speaks of how Lea "a veces te dejaba a ti primero y lo sabías: era Julia quien bajaba la persiana aquella noche, corría las cortinas. ¿Y qué más? Te daba igual, con Julia te daba igual" (p. 228) (at times dropped you off first and you knew it; then it was Julia who lowered the blinds that night and drew the curtains. So what? It was the same to you; when it was Julia, it was the same), and, subsequently, when Lea herself describes her sexual relationship with Julia: "Julia, las manos tan pequeñas como torpes, viajando, temblorosas, por mi cuerpo reposado, tranquilo junto al suyo tan agitado, trémulo, pegándose en busca de algo que lo apaciguara" (p. 231) (Julia, with her hands so small and clumsy, nervously exploring my calm body lying tranquilly next to her excited and tremulous one, clinging to me in search of something that might soothe it).

Despite this sexually liberated attitude, Lea is depicted as a cynical, dissatisfied individual whose one moment of authentic revelation to Ismael manifests her level of self-hatred and contempt: "Os los advertí, que no me amarais, porque es fácil odiar a quien nos ama con la misma intensidad con que uno se odia a sí mismo" (p. 229) (I warned you two not to love me because it's easy to hate someone who loves you with the same intensity with which you hate yourself). In this way she joins the sisterhood of female characters that we have previously observed in Martín Gaite and Matute, who continually travel from one place to the next in an obsessive attempt at self-avoidance.

The other central female character, whose presence in the novel gives Moix even greater freedom to explore the theme of female sexuality, is María Antonia, another of Ismael's cousins, whose evolution throughout the novel includes a period of ardent Catholicism followed by stages of equally ardent Falangism and Marxism. Each stage has its corresponding sexual rhythm, which is treated somewhat ironically by the author.[32] In her first stage, she is presented as being simultaneously obsessed with sin and guilt and passionately attracted toward the other sex. It is within this context that Moix provides a highly comical view of masturbation, and the traumas that inadequate sex education can produce in an innocent girl. María Antonia says:

> ¡Recorrer el mundo, rozándole casi con el cuerpo, los árboles, las piedras, el pavimento de las grandes avenidas, los rótulos luminosos, el mar! ¿Lloraba, emocionada, por esa sensación o porque mentalmente recitaba algún poema amoroso o pensaba en la trágica existencia de Julien Sorel y Mathilde de la Môle? En el amor, en Francisco, en Pablo, la cabaña del bosque, cuanto hacíamos allí y ahora hacía yo sola, a veces, por la noche, qué vergüenza después, sin atreverme a mirar a nadie a la cara, a la mañana siguiente. Me lo había hecho aquella noche y por eso lloraba: por vergüenza y temor, porque sabía que los hijos se tienen con hombres, pero si yo me hacía lo mismo, ¿acaso no podía embarazarme yo misma? Cada mes, antes de tener la regla, temblaba. ¿Por qué la llamaban así? Menstruación nunca me gustó, la palabra sonaba a monstruo, monstruosidad, monstruación, menstruación. Lo había leído: una embarazada no tiene la regla. Por eso tanto miedo, los días antes de venirme. (p. 196)
>
> To roam the world, almost grazing the trees, stones, pavements of the long avenues, bright signs, and sea with her body! Was she

32. One of the most humorous sections dealing with María Antonia's political beliefs involves her attempt to convert a truck driver to Falangism by means of sexual persuasion. When he discovers that she's still a virgin, he becomes furious with her. She declares in retrospect:

> Qué guapo estaría, con la camisa negra, pronunciando discursos. ¿Por qué se había enfadado? Sólo intentaba iniciarle en el camino de la verdad y él me lo agradecía arrojándome por la cabeza el libro verde de José Antonio que le regalé antes de bajar del camión. (p. 201)
>
> How handsome he would be, with a black shirt on, giving speeches. Why had he gotten mad? I was only trying to initiate him on the path of truth, and he acknowledged this by throwing at my head José Antonio's green book that I had given him before I left his truck.

> crying, moved by that feeling or because she was mentally reciting some love poem or was thinking about the tragic existence of Julien Sorel or Mathilde de la Môle? And about love, Francisco, Pablo, the cabin in the woods, and what we did there and what I now did alone at times at night. What shame, afterwards, not daring to look at anyone in the face the next morning. I had done it that very night and that's why I was crying: out of shame and fear, because I knew that you have kids with men, but if I did the same thing to myself, couldn't I make myself pregnant? Every month, before I got my period, I trembled. Why did they call it that? I never liked menstruation. The word sounded like monster, monstrosity, monstruation, menstruation. I had read it somewhere: a pregnant woman doesn't get her period. That was why I was afraid the days before I got it.

With the same biting irony, Moix pokes irreverent fun at the myths about menstruation that are instilled in young girls by superstitious mothers. María Antonia's mother indoctrinates her into the rites of womanhood with the following decree: "Boba, ya eres mujer, lo serás una vez al mes, no comas helados, no te duches con agua ni demasiado fría ni demasiado caliente" (p. 190) (Silly, you're a woman now, you'll be one once a month. Don't eat ice cream, don't shower with water that's either too cold or too hot). This demythification of stereotyped views concerning female sexuality is combined with an even more satirical view of both machismo and the misogynist attitude propagated by the Catholic church. Recreated in Moix's text, as in the most critical parts of Joyce's *Portrait of the Artist* and Goytisolo's *Señas de identidad* and *Don Julián* is the classic Church view of unlawful sexuality, hell, and the dangers that women can bring upon the male sex. With her accustomed humor, Moix describes how Ricardo is forced into repentance after having spent his class hours dreaming of Marisa's breasts:

> Era horroroso el infierno y lo que hacías y pensabas hacer con Marisa. De haber continuado viéndola y entregándote a tus pensamientos, te hubieran caído las uñas, el pelo, salido manchas en la piel, eczemas pestilentes, pústulas, se pierde la vista, uno se queda ciego y se va paralizando poco a poco. Las mujeres producen tales enfermedades; caen los dientes, se pierde la memoria, uno sufre convulsiones nerviosas, a veces los médicos lo internan en un manicomio. . . . (pp. 154–55)

> Hell was horrible and so was what you had done and were thinking of doing with Marisa. If you had continued to see her and given in to your thoughts, your nails and hair would have fallen

off, you would have gotten blemishes on your skin, stinking eczemas, pustules. You would lose your sight, turn blind and slowly become paralyzed. Women are the cause of such diseases. Your teeth fall out, you lose your memory, you suffer nervous convulsions; at times, doctors even lock you up in insane asylums. . . .

Similarly, she satirizes the sexist notion that "en el extranjero las mujeres quieren trabajar, para poder salir más de sus casas, abandonando a sus hijos y, fuera de la vigilancia del esposo a quien deben fidelidad y obediencia, prostituirse" (p. 155) (in other countries, women want to work, in order to get out of their houses more, abandoning their children, prostituting themselves, staying out of the watch of their husbands to whom they owe fidelity and obedience); and ironically she describes Ricardo's indignation when María Antonia wants to make love to him without being married:

> ¿Eres una puta? ¿Crees que quiero casarme con una puta? ¡Si hoy deseas acostarte conmigo, mañana lo harás con otro y será el cuento de nunca acabar, y si ya estamos casados, ¿qué? ¡un cornudo! Quieres convertirme en un cornudo, ¿verdad? Pues no, no estoy dispuesto. ¡Puta, descarada, desvergonzada! (p. 202)
>
> You're a whore! Do you really believe that I want to marry a whore? If you want to go to bed with me today, tomorrow, you'll do it with someone else, and then you'll never stop and if we're already married, then what? A cuckold! You want to make a cuckold out of me, right? Well, no sir, not for me. Whore, hussy, shameless!

If all these examples fall within the sphere of a conventional reality continually criticized and demythified by the author, at other points in the novel Moix's imagination departs from the realm of reality as she creates for the reader a surrealistic sexuality based on the relationship between Ismael and his woman-horse companion, Albina. According to Moix, the inspiration for this section of the novel came to her from a friend who told her of a woman who played the role of a horse in a circus because of her resemblance to one.[33] Moix bases one of the most poignant and sexually daring sections of the novel on this tale, as she describes the difficulties that Albina and Ismael have while making love:

> Los senos, pequeños; el tronco, largo, delgado; el vientre cálido, el sexo sin pelo, infantil. Sin embargo, la cola resultaba ser un

33. The author indicated this in her interview with Levine and Waldman.

estorbo para hacer el amor: al experimentar placer, sin poder evitarlo, la movía y me azotaba la espalda. Una incomodidad: la cola y la desproporción entre el tamaño de sus cuerpos. En la cama, enorme, al besarla en la boca, las manos de Yeibo [Ismael] apenas alcanzaban el pecho de ella, mientras los pies llegan sólo al vientre de la mujer caballo. Para acariciarla debe levantarse, avanzar algunos pasos, a gatas, y cuando por fin va a penetrarla, está agotado debido a los continuos paseos arriba y abajo del cuerpo caballuno que él desea satisfacer en todas sus partes. . . . Hay otro modo más cómodo de hacer el amor: montarla. Pero a ella le ilusiona realizar el acto en la postura normal, y él intenta complacerla. Mientras la penetra, prefiere no mirar el rostro de Albina: la cabeza, medio oculta por las patas delanteras, en alto, ¡queda tan alejada de la suya! Un par de metros separan sus bocas. ¡Qué desolación! Se siente solo allí abajo, como ella arriba. (p. 45)

Her breasts were small; her trunk, long and thin; her stomach, warm; her vagina, hairless and childlike. Nonetheless, her tail was an impediment in making love. Whenever she felt pleasure, without being able to avoid it, she moved and hit me in the back. What an inconvenience: her tail and the disproportion between the size of the two bodies. When they were in bed, and he kissed her on the mouth, Yeibo's [Ismael's] hands were scarcely able to reach her chest, while his feet only reach the stomach of this woman horse. In order to caress her, he has to stand up, take a few steps on all fours and when he finally is going to enter her, he's exhausted due to the continual trips up and down this horselike body that he wants to satisfy all over. . . . There's another more comfortable way of making love by mounting her. But she has such hopes of realizing the act in a normal position that he tries to please her. While he enters her, he prefers not to look at Albina's face. His head, half hidden by her front legs, raised up, is so far away from hers that a few meters separate their mouths. What despair! He feels as alone down there as she does up there.

In this sense, Moix intensifies the treatment of illicit sexuality in the novel. Although the entire work is laden with irony and satire, her defense of a free sexuality for women is clear. It is disturbing that none of her female characters achieves a state of fulfillment or satisfaction and that all either die or disappear at the end of the work. However, the options for a new social reality for women are at least presented and explored, if not affirmed.

The critics have yet to confront the female consciousness presented in these and other works. Too often they have chosen to characterize the fiction written by women as "poetic," "lyrical," "sensitive," and "melodramatic" instead of delving into the social messages that the authors attempt to communicate or recognizing the literary values of the text. Too often, women writers with a feminist perspective have also been given a low priority by Spanish publishing houses. As Carmen Alcalde noted: "The publishers themselves publish a feminist book because they think they should publish everything, including feminist works, but they don't do anything to promote them."[34] No doubt this situation has changed somewhat because feminist groups have continually confronted the press and media with their demands and ideologies and have demonstrated that "we're conjugating in the street the verb 'to vindicate.'"[35]

The writings of Matute, Martín Gaite, and Moix represent an important step in the attempt to express in fiction this feminist consciousness. The ambiguities, conflicts, and doubts they portray in their novels reflect the difficult process of coming to terms with a new female reality still not accepted or sanctioned by Spanish society. The degree to which it will be accepted in the future will depend in great part on the continued activism of the Spanish woman and society's willingness to incorporate into its structure her goals, demands, and vision of the future.

---

34. Levine and Waldman, *Feminismo ante el franquismo*, pp. 26–27.
35. Cover of *Vindicación Feminista*, January 1977.

Sexual Politics and the Theme of Sexuality in Chicana Poetry

Elizabeth Ordóñez

Chicana feminism has been a natural consequence of the overall Chicano struggle for justice, equality, and freedom.[1] Chicanas active in the Chicano movement soon came to realize that the oppression they suffered was even more complex than that borne by their brothers, that sexual oppression was indeed as real as racial and ethnic oppression, and that internal oppression (within the Chicano community or la Raza itself) could exist along with external oppression in the dominant society. So the Chicana began to organize and militate, the majority within the Chicano movement, a few outside or in solidarity with the overall women's movement. In the early seventies articles poured out on both sides of the polemic about possible strategies vis-à-vis the Chicano, with most Chicana feminists expressing a desire to stand by their men and to avoid dividing the movement at all costs. But many were outspoken in their criticism, pointing

1. The term *Chicana* will be understood throughout this essay to mean the female variant of the Webster's dictionary definition: "American of Mexican descent." A Chicano or Chicana (word derived from the Spanish *mejicano*, "Mexican") may be born in the United States or in Mexico and may write in English, Spanish, or a combination of the two languages called code-switching by linguists. Usually the choice of language depends on whether the writer is English or Spanish dominant or whether he/she wishes to create a certain effect or mood by using one language or the other or a combination of the two. Similarly, a Chicano surname may or may not appear in Anglicized form (e.g., a writer may use Ordonez or Ordóñez, or both).

out the secondary status of women within the *movimiento chicano*, the very real and often personally experienced possibility that Chicano activists could exploit the *movimiento* for their own sexual self-interest, and that many Chicana activists were indeed allowed full freedom to go out into the streets provided that the frijoles were on the table in time for supper. The Chicana feminist has thus been constantly challenged to continue her struggle while at the same time never ceasing to love and dress the wounds of battle along the way.[2]

Within the context of the overall feminist polemic about strategies relevant to the sexual politics of the *movimiento chicano*, this study will explore some of the ways this theme affects and informs poetry written by Chicanas. One may see some of the poetry focusing upon

---

2. Key figures in the feminist polemic are activists and writers Enriqueta Longauez y Vasquez and Martha Cotera, who have made significant contributions to an understanding of Chicana feminism in the following works. Vasquez: "The Women of La Raza," *Sisterhood Is Powerful*, ed. Robin Morgan (New York: Vintage, 1970), pp. 379–84; reprinted in *Aztlan*, ed. Luis Valdez and Stan Steiner (New York: Vintage, 1972), pp. 272–78, and in *Chicano Voices*, ed. Carlota Cardenas de Dwyer (Boston: Houghton Mifflin, 1975), pp. 167–72. Cotera: *Profile of the Mexican American Woman* (Austin, Tex.: National Educational Laboratory Publishers, 1976), *Diosa y Hembra* (Austin, Tex.: Information Systems Development, 1976), and *The Chicana Feminist* (Austin, Tex.: Information Systems Development, 1977). In *Hijas de Cuahtemoc/Encuentro Femenil* and *Regeneración* such writers as Adelaida del Castillo—("Encuentro Femenil: La Vision Chicana," *La Gente*, 4[4] [March 1974]: 8)—and Bernice Rincón—("La Chicana: Her Role in the Past and Her Search for a New Role in the Future," *Regeneración*, 1[10] [1971]: 15–18)—argued that men and women should work together against oppression; others, such as Sylvia Delgado—("Chicana: The Forgotten Woman," *Regeneración*, 2[1] [1971]: 2–4)—and Nancy Nieto—("Macho Attitudes," *Hijas de Cuahtemoc*, no. 1, April 1971, p. 9)—chastized the Chicano male for self-serving attitudes and sexual exploitation; and Anna Nieto-Gómez—("Chicanas Identify," *Regeneración* 1[10] [1971]: 9)—called for Chicanas to unite and reject the statement of the Chicana Caucus of the First National Youth Conference in Denver, 1969, which maintained that the role of the Chicana in the *movimiento* was to "stand behind her man." In 1974, Guadalupe Valdés Fallís dared to say: "Chicano women's liberation will only come about when she frees herself from the domination of the Chicano male"; "The Liberated Chicana—Struggle Against Tradition," *Women: A Journal of Liberation*, 3(4) (1974): 20–21. The term "sexual politics" was, of course, introduced by Kate Millett in her book by the same name. Her use of the term *politics* to refer to "power-structured relationships, arrangements whereby one group of persons is controlled by another," and her theory that "sex is a status category with political implications" provide an implicit and underlying theoretical construct for this study: Kate Millett, *Sexual Politics* (New York: Avon Books, 1971), pp. 43–44.

the nature of the male-female relationship simply as versified forms of the feminist polemic. Other poetry incarnates the complexity and contradictions of the erotic experience in more subtle and lyrical forms. But in all its variations, the theme of sexuality consistently serves as a poetic vehicle whereby the Chicana comes to the authentic core of her being and creativity.

In our survey we shall see a wide range of poetry, from praise to denunciation, from analysis to redefinition. We shall hear the poetry in all the nuances of its tones: bold and angry poetry unafraid to criticize where criticism is due, contemplative poetry confronting and embracing the paradoxes inherent in the male-female relationship, and funny and joyous poetry spontaneously shouting the essence of woman as she really is. Each voice joins the chorus to celebrate the ultimately transformative power of women's poetry. Sylvia Gonzales' goal that "the Chicana must engage herself in her own battle for the liberation of her sisters"[3] becomes a reality for those poets whose work we shall share in the following pages.

The Chicana poet, though new, has antecedents and contemporary models from whom she can draw inspiration. The well-known and widely anthologized denunciation of male hypocrisy and the double standard by the seventeenth-century Mexican poet Sor Juana Inés de la Cruz ("hombres necios que acusáis . . .") (stupid men who accuse . . .) is a prototype of frank and open poetic feminism which expresses its legacy in such outspoken Chicanas as Lorna Dee Cervantes, Evangelina Vigil, and Bernice Zamora. Contemporary Mexican poet Rosario Castellanos provides a possible model for numerous vindications of the Malinche figure by Chicana poets by restoring to this indigenous foremother her power of speech and self-definition in the poem "Malinche."[4] As the Chicana is a synthesis of North American as well as Mexican culture, Anglo feminist poets, such as Sylvia Plath, Anne Sexton, and Adrienne Rich, provide indirect models of an or-

3. Sylvia Gonzales, "The Chicana in Literature," *La Luz* 1(9) (January 1973): 52.

4. Malinche, Malintzin Tenépal (by her indigenous names), Doña Marina (by her Spanish name), has long—too long—been considered the Eve of Mexican history. As interpreter, guide, and mistress of the Spanish conqueror, Hernán Cortés, she symbolizes the mother of the mestizo people. But misogynistic historicism has also viewed her as the willing victim of violation, even as a slut. Mexican poet Octavio Paz shapes her into a symbol of the violated native woman, "la Chingada" or the passive woman open to sexual violence. To another Mexican writer, Carlos Fuentes, Malinche generates betrayal and corruption in woman.

ganic synthesis between feminism and aesthetics, a fusion of personal, social, and aesthetic transformation. Finally, Chicana poets often turn to sisters of other ethnic minorities for the identification of political and aesthetic goals. For example, the Chicana poet Ana Castillo identifies with many of the processes and goals of black women's literature;[5] others, such as half-Nez Perce Inés Hernández Tovar, display the simplicity of American Indian poetic rhythms and forms in their verse. Thus, situated at a unique confluence of aesthetic and social currents, the Chicana poet cannot but be enriched by her personal and collective contact with them.

The Chicana, as poet, has produced a multidimensional portrait of her male counterpart and her relationship to him. Perhaps the more widely known and accepted side of the picture is her expression of support for and solidarity with the Chicano male. Particularly when the *movimiento* was searching for its collective indigenous roots, no individual artist felt justified in sowing the seeds of internal dissent. This position produced such proud expressions of female unity with the Chicano as Gloria Perez' "mi hombre":

like the sumptuous
pyramids of tenochtitlán
mi hombre
you stand in my mind
y en mi corazón
erect
. . .
como la adelita
siempre al lado
del guerrillero
i'll live with you
i'll hunger with you
i'll bleed with you
and i'll die with you

("Tenochtitlán" is the indigenous word for Mexico; "mi hombre" means my man; "y en mi corazón," and in my heart; "como la adelita / siempre al lado / del guerrillero," like Adelita [a heroine of the Mexican revolution] / always at the side / of the warrior.)

5. Carol Maier, in "The Poetry of Ana Castillo," *Letras femeninas*, 6(1) (Spring 1980): 52, cites the influence of Toni Morrison's conception of the growth of black literature on Castillo's view of her own development as a Chicana poet.

and Adaljiza Sosa Riddell's "A uno de más antes ahora" (To One from Before Now):

> Together we
> should disappear
> into the past,
> where we belong.[6]

Both these poets stress the strength to be derived by the conjoining of male and female in a common search for the powerful treasures of a likewise common past. In verbal murals, they paint the beauty, glory, and even suffering which is to be shared by the pair—in partnership—their faces turned proudly to the future, their spirits filled with the wisdom of the past. This position is echoed by many Chicana poets who add their voices to a common struggle. Dorinda Moreno shouts with unmistakable simplicity:

> Today the Chicana will shout her freedom
> . . .
> Her man at her side
> Their strength be their guide
> Their togetherness in stride;

Inés Hernández Tovar, in "Chicano-hermano" (Chicano Brother), offers her hand in brother/sisterhood:

> Hombre
> Hermano, Chicano-hermano
> Me alegra haberte conocido
> . . .
> Me alegra saber que hay hombres como tú
>
> Man
> Brother, Chicano-brother
> I'm pleased to have known you
> . . .
> I'm pleased to know there are men like you

and in "Mujer sin nombre" (Woman with No Name) Angela de Hoyos pleads for a bit of the Chicano's strength in her defiance of the damaging effects of time:

6. Gloria Perez, "mi hombre," in *Voices of Aztlan*, ed. Dorothy E. Harth and Lewis M. Baldwin (New York: Mentor, 1974), pp. 183–84; Adaljiza Sosa Riddell, "A uno de más antes ahora," *El Grito*, 7(1) (September 1973): 77. English translations in these and all subsequent poems are mine.

Chicano, amigo mío,
dame de tu aliento
para llevar conmigo
algo de tí
cuando me devore el tiempo.

Chicano, my friend,
give me of your breath
to take along with me
something of you
when I'm devoured by time.[7]

Even when the man is less than noble, the Chicana poet is capable of realizing and verbalizing that his bravado is often thinly disguised vulnerability and that this desperate creature called man is more in need of support than defiance, as another de Hoyos poem ironically reveals:

You may boast that in your prison
you have locked me for no reason
save the fact that in your house
there shouts a man

and I'll stay—NOT to add glory,
O my conquerer, to your story—
but because my instinct tells me
that perhaps

underneath all that bravado
quakes a hopeless desperado
who longs to win a battle
now and then.[8]

However, unlike the many essays on Chicana feminism—in which more or less definable and predictable positions can be attributed to each writer—the perspective of poetry is not fixed but rather responds honestly to the reality and contradictions of experience. Many of the same poets, such as Bernice Zamora and Inés Hernández Tovar, pay homage to the Chicano when homage is due, but when the situation warrants criticism, they are also capable of viewing truth from another perspective. This critical and frank view of the Chicano vis-à-vis

7. Dorinda Moreno, "Untitled," in her *La mujer es la tierra: La tierra de vida* (Berkeley, Ca.: Casa Editorial, 1975), n.p.n.; Inés Hernández Tovar, "Chicano-hermano," in her *Con Razón Corazón* (San Antonio, Tex.: Caracol, n.d.), p. 29; Angela de Hoyos, "Mujer sin nombre," in her *Chicano Poems for the Barrio* (Bloomington, Ind.: Backstage Books, 1975), n.p.n.

8. Angela de Hoyos, "Words Unspoken," *Hojas poéticas* 1(2) (May 1977): 3.

his female counterpart is perhaps the lesser-known side of the Chicana's portrayal of her *compañero*, and the audacity of many of these poems indicates a new willingness, and even necessity, to explore openly the internal contradictions of the *movimiento* if authentic human liberation is ever to take place. For if the Chicana accepts her political responsibility without reservations and is still made to occupy second place, unheeded and unheard (as one poem by Gonzales poignantly reveals: "She still cried, let me in. / And they replied with indifference. / . . . His eyes flashed past hers and said, / and now let's hear from the man at your left"),[9] then she must use the power of her pen for her own cause.

Bernice Zamora is one such poet capable of singing in praise of "José el revolucionario" (José the Revolutionary), whose "kisses arm as no other weapon,"[10] and of roundly denouncing the Chicano student activist's exploitation of woman from his safe hiding place behind the banners and slogans of the *movimiento*. In no uncertain terms she decries the Chicano's contradictory use of political rhetoric ("The gringo [white man] is oppressing you, Babe!") as he enjoys the benefits of a Ford fellowship, the sexual favors of *gabacha guisas* (Anglo "chicks") as well as a Chicana lover, and the domestic pleasures of a wife and five kids. When he demands to define her poetics, pointing out that she must "write about social reality," she ironically proves that for her and other Chicana poets, to write of "pájaros, mariposas [birds, butterflies], and the fragrance / of oppressing perfume I smell somewhere" *is* to write about social reality, woman's shared reality of being exploited in the name of the *movimiento*.[11]

Hernández Tovar is also able to affirm the existence of an ideal, as in the previously cited "Chicano-hermano," even if it becomes necessary to admit that the ideal is not always the only component of reality. In "Untitled" and "Chiflazones" (Crazy Things), she views the other side of Chicano-Chicana interrelationships, rejecting the male's self-righteous confidence, daring to say no if she cannot meet her lover halfway as an equal ("Untitled"), and succinctly and ironically repudiating male-defined, polarized requirements for female equality ("Chiflazones"):

---

9. Sylvia Gonzales, "On an Untitled Theme," unpublished poem cited by Eliana Rivero in "La Mujer y la Raza: Latinas y Chicanas," *Caracol*, 4(4) (December 1977): 7.

10. Bernice Zamora, "José el Revolucionario," *Mango*, 1(3–4) (1977): 20.

11. Bernice Zamora, "Notes from a Chicana 'Coed,'" *Caracol*, 3(9) (May 1977): 19.

He: The day you beat me
at a game of pool
I'll know we're equal.

She: The day you choose
to wash the dishes
I'll know we are.[12]

Numerous other Chicana poets have come out to denounce, through their verse, the Chicano's use of *la mujer* ("woman") and even the *movimiento* for his own ends. Evangelina Vigil, a heady, outspoken *poeta-feminista*, borrows the unrefined, often crude language which once had been exclusively male territory, shifting perspectives through reversal, as the title "Puto" suggests.[13] In her prize-winning poem, "Ay qué ritmo" (Oh what rhythm), Vigil exposes the game playing of the Latino disco in which "el ritmo del sexismo / da asco" (the rhythm of sexism / is sickening).[14] And in "Para los que piensan con la verga" (For Those Who Think with Their Cocks) Vigil again borrows from the male lexicon in order to blast those who think with their balls rather than their brains. Vigil uses this poem, like the others, to shock the male into a recognition of the limiting consequences of his behavior; it is not only woman who loses, but man himself:

se trata de viejos repulsivos
tapados con cobijas
de ascoso sexismo
agarrándose los huevos
a las escondidas
with brain cells
displaced
replaced
by sperm cells
concentrating:
pumping away
ya no queda
energía mental.[15]

---

12. Hernández Tovar, "Chiflazones," in *Con Razón Corazón*, p. 18.

13. Evangelina Vigil, "Puto," *Caracol*, 3(1) (September 1976): 5.

14. Evangelina Vigil, "Ay qué ritmo," *Caracol*, 3(1) (September 1976): 5. This poem won one of the top five prizes in the annual poetry contest sponsored by the Coordinating Council of Literary Magazines.

15. Evangelina Vigil, "Para los que piensan con la verga," *El Fuego de Aztlan*, 1(4) (Summer 1977): 56.

it's a question of repulsive old guys
hidden beneath covers
of sickening sexism
grabbing their balls
on the sly
. . . . .
now there's no more
mental energy.

A similar point of view is expressed through the rhythm of popular song in Anna Montes' "Bus Stop Macho":

Hey you, macho
Where's your head?
Times have changed
And your sweet words are dead.
I'm a thinking woman
With things to do,
In case you're interested,
I've got brains too![16]

In a direct, five-part cycle poem, "Old Lady—New Woman," tracing the development of one Chicana from subjugation to independence, Mary Ann Montanez echoes what we have seen in others, daring to tell it as it actually may be: "perhaps you are not working for 'la causa' [the cause] / but only for el chicano."[17] Finally, in a recent contribution to this polemical issue, Lorna Dee Cervantes angrily denounces the sexual exploitation of woman—glorified by tradition and disguised by political rhetoric—in her directly imagistic and ironic "You Cramp My Style, Baby":

You cramp my style, baby
when you roll on top of me
shouting, "Viva La Raza"
at the top of your prick.

You want me como un taco,
dripping grease,
or squeezing masa through my legs,
making tamales for you out of my daughters.

---

16. Anna Montes, "Bus Stop Macho," *Comadre*, no. 1, Summer 1977, p. 24.

17. Mary Ann Montanez, "Old Lady—New Woman," *Comadre*, no. 1, Summer 1977, p. 22.

You "mija"
"mija" "mija" me
until I can scream

and then you tell me,
"Esa, I LOVE
this revolution!
Come on Malinche,
gimme some more!"[18]

What is the truth about la Malinche, and how are Chicana poets involved in disseminating this truth in their poetry? Recent research has shown us that la Malinche was sold into slavery by her own family.[19] At the same time, the Aztecs had become a cruel, imperialistic nation attacking and pillaging other Indian settlements and exacting heavy taxes and bloody sacrifices from those conquered peoples. Having suffered personally at the hands of her own people and having been extraordinarily bright and perceptive (she was fluent in many Indian dialects and learned Spanish very quickly), la Malinche saw Cortés and the Spaniards not only as purveyors of political hope but as the fulfillment of religious prophecy: the return of Quetzalcoatl. Thus, motivated by political and religious concerns even more than by personal suffering, la Malinche considered the Spaniards as liberators from the yoke of Aztec dominance and their religion as a much needed reform for a native religion which had gone awry with abuses. In a sense, la Malinche made the blind leap of faith in a Kierkegaardian sense, as Del Castillo suggests,[20] but being a woman, history has largely attributed to her much baser, physical motives for her acts. Margaret Shedd has even gone so far as to characterize la Malinche as a nymphomaniac![21] So it is left to the Mexicana-Chicana to restore la Malinche's good name and to reveal to the world the truth about this important woman in history, for only in so doing can today's woman arrive at the truth about herself.

---

18. Lorna Dee Cervantes, "You Cramp My Style, Baby," *El Fuego de Aztlan*, 1(4) (Summer 1977): 39.

19. The following include important new perspectives on the Malinche theme: Juana Armanda Alegría, *Psícología de las mexicanas* (Mexico: Editorial Samo, 1975), pp. 65–79; and Cotera, *Diosa y Hembra*, pp. 31–35.

20. See Adelaida R. del Castillo, "Malintzin Tenépal: A Preliminary Look into a New Perspective," in *Essays on la Mujer*, ed. Rosaura Sanchez and Rosa Martinez Cruz (Los Angeles, Ca.: Chicano Studies Center, University of California, 1977), pp. 124–49.

21. Margaret Shedd, *Malinche and Cortés* (Garden City, N.Y.: Doubleday, 1971).

The Chicana poet could not immediately make that blind leap of faith either. She had to go through stages, stages of feeling uncomfortable with the burden of being called Malinche, of being cast in the role of traitor, stages in which little by little she divested herself of that burden and dressed herself with a new and restored image. Lorenza Calvillo Schmidt and Adaljiza Sosa Riddell are two poets who share a common burden: that of moving freely between two worlds (as did la Malinche), of loving men outside la Raza, of changing their names "por la ley" (by law),[22] and of thus having to carry the label of Malinche (with its outworn, negative connotations). Each poet addresses the Chicano in rediscovery, after having been estranged from him through assimilation, and in the poems of both women is the painful consciousness that they are somehow being blamed for something which is not entirely their fault ("Pinche, como duele ser Malinche") (Darn, it sure hurts to be Malinche), for as Sosa Riddell ironically concludes her poem: "sometimes, / you are muy gringo, too."[23]

From the consciousness of shared guilt and the consequent realization that the negative Malinche label is unjustly borne by woman, writers like Gonzales move toward a further reassessment of the Malinche figure, as she does in "Chicana Evolution." In this poem the writer portrays la Malinche as a feminine Messiah who must return to redeem her forsaken daughters; she becomes transformed into a spiritual mother of the Mexicana/Chicana.[24] Hernández Tovar also approaches la Malinche from a spiritual perspective, asking the Indian goddesses to pray for la Malinche, "acusada abusada / por la historia y / la gente," (accused abused / by history and / the people) when in fact, "ella sólo / supo querer" (she only / knew how to love).[25] Hernández Tovar thus stresses la Malinche's unselfish capacity to love, showing succinctly through a few short verses how her virtue was transformed into vice by the perverted perspective of history. Finally, the most extensive and dramatic reworking of the Malinche figure has been done by Carmen Tafolla in her poem "La Malinche."

Tafolla's Malinche speaks for herself: "Yo soy la Malinche" (I am

---

22. Adaljiza Sosa Riddell, "My Name Was Changed, por la ley," *El Grito*, 7(1) (September 1973): 76.

23. Lorenza Calvillo Schmidt, "Como Duele," and Sosa Riddell, "My Name Was Changed," *El Grito*, 7(1) (September 1973): 61, 76.

24. See Marcella Trujillo Gaitan, "The Dilemma of the Modern Chicana Artist and Critic," *De Colores*, 3(3) (1977): 44, for an analysis of this unpublished Gonzales poem.

25. Hernández Tovar, "Rezo," in *Con Razón Corazón* p. 25.

Malinche).[26] She explains what she has been called and then she begins her dramatic self-defense. With three verbs, the poet restores to Malinche her integrity and her decisiveness; in short, she is transformed from object into subject when she declares:

And you came.
    My dear Hernán Cortés, to share your "civilization"—to play a
  god, . . . and I began to dream . . .
    I saw,
        and I acted:

I saw our world
  And I saw yours
    And I saw—
                another.

She thus characterizes herself as a visionary who, upon being confronted with an opportunity of monumental potential, reaches out to take it. But history was unable to accept this, as she goes on to show: "They could not imagine me dealing on a level with you— / so they said I was raped, used, / chingada / Chingada!" That is what history said, but that is not what Malinche could say for herself when given the opportunity to do so by one of her descendants. And so in the conclusion to the poem, Malinche's cry issues from gut level to replace the violated, passive flesh of the old Malinche with the visionary and prophetic greatness of the new:

But Chingada, I was not.
  Not tricked, not screwed, not traitor.
For I was not traitor to myself—
  I saw a dream
    and I reached it.
        Another world. . . . .
                        la raza.
                                la raaaaaaa-zaaaaa . . .

Tafolla's Malinche succeeds in making the leap of faith and thus in not only redeeming herself but also rendering herself a collective model of female strength for future generations of Mexicanas and Chicanas.

But the shadow of Malinche as violated female—*la mujer chingada*—is not so easy to dispel, as we saw in Cervantes' poem "You

26. Carmen Tafolla, "La Malinche," *Tejidos*, 4(4) (Winter 1977): 1–2; reprinted in *Canto al Pueblo: An Anthology of Experiences*, ed. Leonardo Carrillo et al. (San Antonio, Tex.: Penca Books, 1978), pp. 38–39.

Cramp My Style, Baby." For if rape has become a powerful image of woman's helplessness and subjugation before the sheer brute force of the male, then that universal trauma for all women becomes exacerbated in the Chicana experience by those remnants of the collective physical and cultural rape which she carries buried within her collective unconscious. The Chicana's attitudes toward her own sexuality must be colored by that original rape by European culture, as well as by the sexual violence which often exists in her immediate personal environment. Several Chicana poets have captured these feelings of anger and vengeance, as well as the strength and integrity that this act of sexual violence engenders in *la mujer*.

On a personal level, Norma Cantu curses her assailant in "Violación" (Rape)[27] ("que te lleve el diablo / por ser tan inhumano" [May the devil take you / for being so inhuman]) for having raped her as a child, leaving her unable to love, with a scar of hatred in her heart. In "19 Años" (Nineteen Years Old) Tafolla tells the story of a valiant young girl whose life took that too familiar course from being a school dropout to pregnancy, miscarriage, rape by her former boyfriend, and then prostitution. In the language of the barrio, Tafolla captures the realism of a young girl trying to make the best of her circumstances, hiding her vulnerability under the hard shell of integrity and self-worth:

Porque ellos chinguichingui
ya a pesar de todo, saben que yo tengo el control final.
Por tanto que me chingan de afuera, no me pueden chingar el corazón.[28]

Because they fuckyfucky
and in spite of everything, they know I have the final say.
No matter how much they fuck from the outside, they can't fuck my innermost soul.

Tafolla's nineteen-year-old heroine defies rape and violation by maintaining her spirit intact.

Rita Mendoza has humorously made full use of the rape image to threaten collective female vengeance against the assailant in "The Rapist"[29] and to develop the theme of cultural violation through rape

27. Norma Cantu, "Violación," *Metamorfosis*, 1(2) (1978): 10.

28. Carmen Tafolla, "19 Años," in *Canto al Pueblo*, pp. 61–62.

29. Rita Mendoza, "The Rapist," *First Chicano Literary Prize* (Irvine: Department of Spanish and Portuguese, University of California, 1975), p. 85:

There's a rapist loose in town
trying to pull our panties down

as metaphor in "Rape Report." Mendoza thus develops the image of a horrifying female experience into a metaphor of cultural and collective significance:

> He pushed down and tried to force me to give in.
> When I told him he couldn't have what was mine,
> he used strong-arm tactics on me.
> I fought back, I clawed and screamed
> and for fighting for my honor,
> I was punished even more.
> He said, "I am doing you a favor, if you
> submit, it will be easier on you."
> I knew I was losing ground and then knew
> it would be less painful for me if I quit fighting.
> He received praise for what he did to me.
> He took something that was sacred and beautiful
> to me and replaced it with four-letter words.
> I am making this report in English, you see,
> I've been raped of my native tongue.[30]

Mendoza's style may be considered prosaic, but who can be rhapsodic about rape? Besides, her poem doubles as a "rape report" (to society's enforcers of justice) and as a denunciation of the cultural violation perpetrated on the speaker by that same society. It is poetic in the succinctness of that denunciation, proselike in the no nonsense directness of its double message.[31]

The Chicana poet's overall treatment of the theme of her sexuality is at times bold and defiant, but more often it is subtle with the bittersweet wisdom of the contradictions and paradoxes inherent in the male-female relationship. For even if the woman is fortunate not to have experienced physical violence—that is, rape—there is often a much more subtle hostility and tension which flows between the sexes: a distancing, a lack of communication, an alienation which even phys-

---

> Twelve attempts, and 3 completed
> Is that a terrific fete? [*sic*]
> He'll get his we'll see to that
> when we chop-off his bumbling bat
> After we destroy him,
> we'll laugh, we'll jeer
> Bastard, can you hear?

30. Rita Mendoza, "Rape Report," *First Chicano Literary Prize*, pp. 81–82.

31. See Marvin A. Lewis, "Rita Mendoza: Chicana Poetess," *Latin American Literary Review*, 5(10) (Spring–Summer 1977): 79–85, for a study sensitive to Mendoza's Chicana perspective.

ical intimacy cannot bridge. Poetry, with its own peculiar challenge to communicate intensely through a highly selective verbal process, is an especially apt medium for grappling with that paradox so germane to male-female relationships: that of communicating the seemingly incommunicable.

Gloria Anzaldúa and Marcella Meraz choose simplicity and directness to verbalize their desperation before the gap in communication between man and woman. Meraz, in "I Want to Say . . . ," simply states a fact: "There are so many things I want to say to you, / and you don't want to listen . . .";[32] Anzaldúa, in "Helpless," contrasts the desperation of woman before the indifference of man to her intense need to communicate: "I shake him / I hit him with words / spit his insults back into his mouth / He swallows them / grinning."[33] For another poet, Sylvia Chacón, the question is simply that of refusing to play man's game on his terms, as she communicates through her rejection of his behavior that she will not have their relationship reduced to its lowest carnal denominator: "I / refused / to be knifed / and forked along / in your eagerness / to get / the / meat."[34] Through this compact eating metaphor, Chacón implicitly demands communication on a level beyond that of physical appetite.

By far the most interesting, complex, and beautiful Chicana poetry on the theme of sexuality and male-female relationships is that which contemplates the inherent contradictions of such relationships and the welter of confusing emotions which they often engender. The poets may write in English or Spanish, may possess varying degrees of sophistication in their craft, but the message is always similar: what I feel is a paradox and yet feel it I must; I desire in spite of all reason which tells me I should not, so take heed, man, I am vulnerable.

Rina Rocha, in "To the Penetrator," uses a clearly sexual image to go beyond woman's purely physical relationship with man, to communicate her consciousness of being verbally manipulated, and, finally, to decry the paradoxical nature of her feelings in spite of all she knows:

> your eyes bite
> and your words cut
>   But I like the pain . . .

---

32. Marcella Meraz, "I Want to Say . . . ," *Tejidos*, 4(2) (Winter 1977): 12.
33. Gloria Anzaldúa, "Helpless," *Tejidos*, 4(1) (Spring 1977): 17.
34. Sylvia Chacón, "I Am the Jealously Entangled," in *Tejidos*, 3(4) (Winter 1976): 7; and in *Capirotada*, Spring 1977, p. 24.

you tease me
  on to the edges of my brain
then
you soothe me with
your hands
      and I uncoil
        my thoughts
resting
with you now I stare
    in your eyes again
and they
    bite
    bite
    bite
deeper in me
and
the words
    cut
    cut
    cut
towards my heart
and
I hate the love
i feel for you[35]

In the final verses, the "I" that hates the love is capitalized, the "i" that feels the love is lowercased; perhaps the differentiation of graphemes is insignificant, but more likely it encodes the way the speaker finally comes to judge herself and the contradictory nature of her feelings. Perhaps the capital "I" symbolizes subject, the lowercase "i" object, and the speaker concludes by viewing herself as a paradoxical amalgam of the two.

The archetypal "penetrator" is of course Don Juan, the seducer who seeks his own pleasure without commitments or consequences. The theories surrounding the Don Juan figure, from literary, psychological, and even sociopolitical perspectives, would require more analysis than is possible at this juncture. However, we may say that the figure is a symbol of attraction and repulsion, of hostility and desire, both on the part of the male and the female. Don Juan himself is too rich a character to dismiss as an entirely negative figure from a female

35. Rina Rocha, "To the Penetrator," *Revista Chicano-Riqueña*, 3(2) (Spring 1975): 5.

perspective, and his victims are too varied in their motives and impulses merely to inspire sympathy and pity. Perhaps Don Juan is more than just a despicable rake and has earned his power to fascinate precisely because of his inherent mystery and complexity.[36]

In two related poems structured around the theme of Don Juan, Margarita Cota Cárdenas has attempted to pierce beyond the level of stereotype to the inescapable paradox of woman's attraction to the *burlador* ("seducer" or Don Juan). Woman is characterized in her poems "Parábola del Tenorio" (Parable of [Don Juan] Tenorio) and "Tisbea se define" (Tisbea Defines Herself) as a subject just as desirous and erotically curious as the don himself. And he is portrayed in the first poem as a multidimensional creature with hidden, complementary attributes:

Parábola del Tenorio

Burlador,
no sé, todavía
que onda eres.
Sí, que sé, que te gustan las mujeres;
pero a la vez,
tal vez don que te salva,
te presiento incierto, sensible,
dulce y fino.

Mientras amar-y-burlar no es estimable,
nada apreciable, ningún hecho pristino,
como deseo extasiados placeres,
inolvidables amores, significando destino,
para conocerte a fondo,
saborearte hondo,
y sólo después, mucho más y muy tarde,
reprocharte con tu:
"¡tan largo me lo fiáis!"[37]

Parable of Don Juan Tenorio

Seducer,
I don't know, even now,
where you're coming from.

36. The Chicana poet, whose verses offer a new vision of the Don Juan figure from a female/feminist perspective, may have found as a source of her inspiration the playfully ironic stanzas on the same theme by the Argentine poet Alfonsina Storni: "Divertidas estancias a don Juan" (Joyful Stanzas to Don Juan).

37. Margarita Cota Cárdenas, "Parábola del Tenorio," in her *Noches Despertando Inconciencias* (Tucson, Ariz.: Scorpion Press, 1977), n.p.n.

Yes, I know that you enjoy women;
but at the same time,
perhaps your saving grace,
I sense you're uncertain, sensitive,
sweet and fine.

While love-and-leave is not estimable,
nothing admirable, no pristine act,
as I desire ecstatic pleasures,
unforgettable loves, hearkening destiny,
to know you perfectly,
taste you deeply,
and only afterwards, much, much later,
reproach you with your:
"there's plenty of time to repent!"

Tisbea se define

HOMBRE
no me quieras como hermana
mariposa soy
no lirio
vengo a gozar de ti
cantidad opuesta
sin misterios
un hombre una mujer
macho hembra
ay
consciente mariposa soy
AY SI SI SI SI SIIIIIIIIIII
me inciensa tu cirio
nos reconocemos tus llamas
en mis alas vuelan
dos egoístas
jugándole al sino[38]

Tisbea Defines Herself

MAN
don't love me as a sister
I'm a butterfly
not a lily
I come to take my pleasure of you
quantity opposite
without mysteries

38. Margarita Cota Cárdenas, "Tisbea se define," in *Noches*, n.p.n.

a man a woman
male female
oh
I am a conscious butterfly
OH YES YES YES YEEEEEEESSSSSS
your candle inflames me
we examine each other closely your flames
fly on my wings
two egoists
playing with fate

In spite of her feelings, woman is conscious of the significance of her acts, choosing to follow her instinct for pleasure yet knowing—unlike the moth who seeks the flame—that destiny may not be kind. If anyone is guilty of exploiting the other, it is both of them for having been motivated by purely selfish desires. Finally, though, we sense an overriding acceptance of the ambiguity inherent in the attraction between male and female. The lines between victim and victimizer, subject and object, are purposefully blurred so that both poems conclude with similar perspectives: sexuality is a blind and paradoxical force which drives women, as well as men, to seek their pleasure—in spite of the well-meaning lessons of reason and the potentially lamentable consequences of destiny.

Two poems in Spanish that contemplate the paradox of woman's need for man are "Realidad" (Reality) and "Hombre!!!!" (Man!!!!) by Emy López. "Realidad" restates an ancient aphorism from a fresh perspective:

Odio el licor
y lo bebo:
Me enferma
la tristeza
y la siento.
Detesto al hombre
por ser distinto
pero. . . .
lo sigo buscando. . . . . .[39]

I hate liquor
and I drink it:
Sadness
makes me sick
and I feel it.

39. Emy López, "Realidad," *El Fuego de Aztlan*, 1(4) (Summer 1977): 36.

I detest man
for being different
but. . . .
I keep on seeking him. . . . . . .

"Hombre!!!!" is a longer, more complex poem, which emanates from the same perspective as "Realidad" but which is able to touch upon many of the same problems as other poems we have discussed: no communication between man and woman, the betrayal and deception of woman by man, his silence or inconsequential words, his cynicism and indifference. Through extended erotic imagery, López effectively links the physical with the aesthetic, establishing her need for man not only for physical satisfaction but implicitly for the very creation of her art. The paradox of repulsion-attraction is transformed into the metaphor of man as muse, as fountainhead for woman's poetry:

Eres el perfume incierto
Que ronda habitaciones
De ciudades enteras.
Guardas en tu epidermis
El recuerdo femenino
Engendrado desde el génesis.
Tu pigmentación es Hombre
Y el sudor de tus orgasmos
Es inagotable en el engaño.

Delineo tus perfiles
Con dedos temblorosos;
Bebo tu silencio masculino
Desde la frente a los pies;
Y en cada extremidad
Encuentro el sueño traicionado.
Me disfruto al compás de tus controles
Y acepto la ronda
Del comienzo y final
De tus amores.

Juego con tu vientre
Tus emociones temporales;
Tu pelo es mensaje de traiciones
Que se enredan
En la pelvis de mis dolores.
Tu olor a selva enigmática
Atrae mis entrañas
Y necesito de tu forma
Pero rechazo tu cinismo de juerga.

El estanque de mi cuerpo
Como esponja busca empaparse
De tus gérmenes.
Sufro la realidad de tus espacios,
Pero te necesito Hombre . . .
Flor de mis desiertos,
Manantial de mis llantos poéticos
Y te amo con engaño
De besos, de caricias
Y palabras sin mañana.[40]

You are the unknown perfume
That hovers about chambers
Of cities entire.
You store upon your skin
The feminine memory
Begot since genesis.
Your pigmentation is Man
And the sweat of your orgasms
Is inexhaustibly deceptive.

I trace your profiles
With fingers trembling;
I drink your masculine silence
From your brow to your toes;
And in every limb
I find dreams betrayed.
My joy keeps time with your beat
And I accept the rounds
Of beginnings and endings
Of your loves.

I sport with your belly
Your fleeting emotions;
Your hairs are bearers of betrayal
Which weave themselves
On the pelvis of my sorrow.
Your wild, enigmatic smell
Inflames my blood
And I need your form
But I reject your cynical sprees.

My body, like a pool
A sponge seeks to saturate itself
With your seed.

---

40. Emy López, "Hombre!!!!," in *Canto al Pueblo*, p. 57.

I suffer the reality of your spaces,
But I need you Man . . .
Bloom of my deserts,
Spring of my poetic plaints
And I love you with the lure
Of kisses, of caresses
And words without tomorrow.

Finally, there are those few who do find a resolution to the sexual dichotomy through humor, lyricism, or defiance of convention. In so doing, they create the new Eve from the old, the new woman proud of her self-defined sexuality, frankly expressing it on her own terms. In "Of/To Man," Alma Villanueva laughingly waves her vibrant sexuality like a banner, seeming to mock man in derision—until the final, generous irony:

you, man, are the snake in
my garden—
yeah,
a snake in the grass.
everyone since Eve & Adam's
been blaming ME
for The First Fuck— and it was
ME who got knocked up! well,
hell, I'm not sorry.
I can come over & over (spiritual orgasms count, too)
and
you're limited to one
at a time: Is that the
main bitch?
well man, my man—
let's get herstory
straight. I come IN my cunt
IN my clit, you might say
my whole body is IN the
act: maybe you feel gypped and
someone dubbed me a
mystery.

some snakes are dark and fluid
and compelling— and for the life of me
I just can't resist them.
now, there's a mystery.[41]

---

41. Alma Villaneuva, "Of/To Man," *Third Chicano Literary Prize* (Irvine: Department of Spanish and Portuguese, University of California, 1977), p. 115.

Isabel Barraza, in "Sacrificios," affirms her freedom to take chances like a man and is willing to take the consequences: "Boredom . . . / too high a price to pay / for your regular lay / or let's just say / I'd rather be surprised . . . / Cold some nights, / quemosa / sabrosa on others."[42] In an unpublished poem, Ana Castillo expresses this new identity through a poetic voice that reveals a heretofore repressed and forbidden erotic desire: "Once / the moon fell / on you / the stifling air cooled / against you / the whole room was / eden / taking a taste / of you . . . / and i wanted to taste you / just Once." Purposefully maintaining a level of poetic ambiguity, the poet is able to suggest subtly the hesitant love of one woman for another. Veronica Cunningham, who proudly accepts her lesbianism as a legitimate and authentic option, an honest expression of her own sexuality, directly and openly defies convention. Even though she knows "that love / with lesbians / is / hard love / hard love / to live with / and / hard love / to deny," she freely chooses it—accepting the social ostracism which often accompanies it—as "righteous love / the kind / you kant / keep / under the covers."[43] For Cunningham, her sexuality—lesbianism—is implicitly essential to her muse, and to write authentically she had to learn to tap a likewise essential aspect of her being:

> when all the yous
> of my poetry
> were really
> she or her
> and
> i could never
> no
> i would never
> write them
> because
> of some fears
> i never even wanted
> to see.
> how could i have been
> that frightened
> of sharing
> the being
>   and
>   me.[44]

42. Isabel Barraza, "Sacrificios," *Mango*, 1(3–4) (1977): 21.

43. Veronica Cunningham, "Untitled," *Mango*, 1(3–4) (1977): 16.

44. Veronica Cunningham, "Untitled," *Festival de flor y canto*, ed. Alurista et al. (Los Angeles, Ca.: University of Southern California Press, 1976), p. 55.

In what Chicana poets are saying about the sexual politics of the *movimiento* and about the nature of their own sexuality, we can observe themes which range from solidarity with man to lesbianism or complete separation from him—with subtle nuances in between. Likewise, we encounter a variety of verse forms ranging from a proselike directness and simplicity to a more sophisticated and controlled lyricism. But although these Chicana voices are varied, they are also one. They sound a voice which is overcoming a previously externally and self-imposed silence. With this poetry the Chicana is beginning to speak for herself and her sisters, is beginning to expose the contradictions of her condition as social activist, poet, and woman. With these verses, the way of the Chicana word is being paved so that this and future generations of *mujeres* can continue to grow as artists and women with the freedom to speak their own language of truth.

It has been unfortunate that the Chicana's double oppression has often affected the dissemination of her work, as well as the themes and forms of her poetry. If the Chicano has been forced to found alternative presses, the Chicana has had to resort to alternatives of the alternatives, founding her own presses and journals and funding her own fledgling collections. This often makes the task of the interested reader and researcher difficult indeed. But the rewards of perseverance can be manifold, offering pleasure and inspiration to those readers who discover that uncommon burst of creative and political energy which characterizes much of recent Chicana poetry.

From Mistress to Murderess

The Metamorphosis of Buñuel's Tristana[1]

Beth Miller

The image of woman in Luis Buñuel's film *Tristana* is difficult to conceptualize with any precision because the character changes so much during the course of the drama. Tristana's characterization develops through the film's tripartite structure and depends primarily on her behavior and dynamic development in her social relationships with her guardian, Don Lope; her lover, Horacio; the maid, Saturna; the deaf-mute, Saturno; and her confessor. Although Tristana is perhaps the greatest of Buñuel's female creations, she seems, paradoxically, to be the one least understood by critics.[2] On

---

1. This chapter was originally written in English in 1973–1974; it appeared in a Spanish version in *Diálogos*, no. 60, 1974, pp. 16–20, and was reprinted in Beth Miller, *Mujeres en la literatura* (Mexico: Fleischer, 1978). It appears here in English in a revised and expanded version for the first time. *Tristana* was filmed in 1970 in Toledo and Estudios de Madrid; produced by Epoca Film and Talía Film (Madrid), Selenia Cinematografica (Rome), and Les Films Corona (Paris); and distributed by Mercurio Films; the screenplay is by Luis Buñuel and Julio Alejandro. The script is accessible in *Tristana de Luis Buñuel*, ed. Arnau Olivar and Enric Ripoll-Freixes (Barcelona: Aymá Editora, Col. Voz Imagen, Serie Cine 24, 1971); all page references to "script" are from this edition. The English translations are my own.

2. For a partial bibliography of articles on the film, mainly in relation to the novel, see Theodore A. Sackett, "Creation and Destruction of Personality in *Tristana*: Galdós and Buñuel," in *Anales Galdosianos* (Anejo, 1978), p. 89, notes 3 and 4. This was a commissioned volume based on the University of Southern California symposium on Benito Pérez Galdós, April 1–3, 1976.

the whole, the film has been similarly underrated, in large part owing to a consistent failure to apprehend its political and, especially, its socialist-feminist statement.[3] The relationship of the two is perhaps nowhere clearer than in Buñuel's cut from the scene in which Lope and Tristana go to bed for the first time to a scene of Spanish police hassling dissident workers in the street.

Buñuel's film, first screened in 1970, is based on the 1892 novel of the same title by Benito Pérez Galdós.[4] One of the significant differences between the two works lies in the temporal and geographic settings: the book's background is late nineteenth-century Madrid; the film's is provincial Toledo between 1929 and 1935. Both Tristanas are very literary characters, and both embody feminist themes. In this essay I will explore the complexities and implications of Buñuel's Tristana (played by Catherine Deneuve) with only occasional references to the character created by Galdós.[5] The film character Tristana is fascinating because of the multiple stock images of women which she combines and the subtle nuances (social and political, psychological and ideological) of these images in their cinematic and sociohistorical contexts. Buñuel's subversive irony, fine detailing, thematic richness, and probing of archetypes contribute to the character's depth and particularity.

---

3. Socialist (or Marxist) feminist theory is varied. One position is illustrated by Sheila Rowbotham in *Woman's Consciousness, Man's World* (Harmondsworth, Middlesex: Pelican Books, 1973), as well as in her earlier *Women, Resistance, and Revolution* (1972; rpt. New York: Vintage, 1974); also by Herbert Marcuse in his speech, "Marxism and Feminism," presented at Stanford University, 1974. It is a position endorsed by a large number of Latin American feminists. See references to nineteenth-century essays below.

4. Benito Pérez Galdós, *Tristana* (Madrid: Imprenta de la Guirnalda, 1892). All documentation from the novel comes from this edition, cited parenthetically in the text. See Beth Miller, "Imagen e ideología en *Tristana* de Galdós" (1975) in Miller, *Mujeres en la literatura.*

5. Most of the literary critics who have discussed the film have done so in relation to the novel. On balance, it is useful to adopt a cinematic view of the relationship: "La cinta se basó en una novela poco conocida de Benito Pérez Galdós, de quien Buñuel ya había adaptado *Nazarín* y al que el cineasta había rendido homenaje con *Viridiana*. . . . La verdad es que la película es Galdós de la misma manera que es Toledo y de la misma manera que es España" (The movie was based on a little-known novel by Benito Pérez Galdós, from whose work Buñuel had already adapted *Nazarín* and to whom the filmmaker had already paid homage with *Viridiana*. . . . The truth is that the film is Galdós in the same way as it is Toledo and in the same way as it is Spain); Francisco Sánchez, *Todo Buñuel* (Mexico: Cineteca Nacional, 1978), p. 195.

The main plot of the film, as of the novel, concerns an innocent young girl who is seduced by her guardian. She elopes from his house with a handsome young painter who wishes to marry her. Two years later, ill and still unmarried, she returns to the house of the guardian. As a result of a tumor, her leg is amputated. Soon afterwards, she marries her guardian and—in a departure from the novel, which ends more or less "happily ever after"—murders him by allowing him to die one snowy winter evening when he apparently suffers a heart attack. She refuses to call the doctor and instead opens the windows to allow the cold air to invade her husband's bedroom.

Tristana projects successively a half-dozen familiar stock images, nearly all of which possess a high degree of literary allusion. We see her at first through Don Lope's chivalrous and chauvinistic eyes as a helpless orphan in need of a protector: "Tú no puedes vivir sola" (script p. 28) (You cannot live alone). She is, for him, a pure and innocent virgin—"Eres un ángel" (script p. 31) (you're an angel)—but also an inferior. Although saddened by the death of her mother, Tristana exudes passivity and serenity. At play with the boys, she is childlike and carefree; with Don Lope, she is submissive, coquettish, and obedient. She fetches his slippers when he returns home from leisurely conversations at the café and kneels to place them on his feet. As her relationship with Lope progresses, we see her in a traditional old man/young girl situation (at the outset, she about nineteen, he past fifty-five). She learns to play multiple subordinate roles: obedient daughter, malleable pupil, kept woman. When she tells Lope—who calls her *hija* ("daughter") and whom she addresses as *tío* ("uncle") and refers to as her "tutor"—that she would like to buy him new slippers, he knows that it is the moment to pounce. She says "sí," as did hosts of literary maidens before her, including Galdós' Tristana, but since Lope is a liberal who preaches free love, the question is sex instead of marriage.[6]

6. In general, the characterization of Don Lope by Buñuel follows Galdós more closely than does Buñuel's characterization of Tristana, especially in terms of the central archetype of the *hidalgo* ("nobleman") whose traditional values are bankrupt and whose political views are suspect since they are held hypocritically and repeated in the form of clichés. Galdós comments that Lope "aborrecía el matrimonio; teníalo por la más espantosa fórmula de esclavitud que idearon los poderes de la tierra para meter en un puño a la pobrecita humanidad" (p. 29) (hated marriage; he considered it the most frightful formula for slavery invented by earthly powers to subject poor humankind) and that Lope maintained that "en las relaciones de hombre y mujer no hay más ley que la anarquía si la anarquía es ley" (p. 27) (in relations between men and women the only law is anarchy, if anarchy is a law); see also Miller, *Mujeres en la literatura*, pp. 46–50.

In the second part of the film, predictably Tristana takes up with an attractive young artist, Horacio, cuckolding her fatherly seducer. Her image is double: she becomes a young woman searching for sex, experience, and freedom—at that point synonymous—and a rebellious daughter. She now finds Lope's slippers repulsive and tosses them into the garbage among the kitchen scraps. Particularly after her encounter with Horacio, Tristana begins to achieve some understanding of her relationship with Lope and some consciousness of herself and her life as a woman, without which no decision to change would be possible. This understanding and the seeds of her long rebellion actually begin to develop in the first part of the film, prior to the affair with Horacio, as in Galdós' novel also. Later, Tristana explains her ambivalent feelings for Lope to Horacio: "Yo sólo le engaño a él, que no tiene ningún derecho sobre mí. Porque se lo merece. . . . A veces le odio por todo el daño que me ha hecho. Y otras, lo confieso, sentía cariño por él, como un padre" (script p. 76) (I am unfaithful to him since he has no just claim on me, and because he deserves it. Sometimes I hate him for all the harm he's done me. But sometimes, I confess, I have felt affection for him, as for a father). And, she laments, Lope "cambia de cara como de camisa" (script p. 76) (changes his attitude as though he were changing his shirt).

The third part of the action begins with her return to Don Lope's house after a two-year absence, during which she lived and traveled with Horacio. Her fatalistic attitude throughout this portion of the film recalls Galdós' Tristana, a more romantic heroine. Other nineteenth-century heroines, more active women's rightists, exhibited a similar attitude, perhaps less influenced by contemporary literary ideals than by their own experience. As Lucy Stone put it: "In education, in marriage, in everything, disappointment is the lot of women."[7] The pervasive fatalism is not so much inherent in the character of Tristana as in her environment. Buñuel consistently employs techniques—foreshadowing (the vision of the bell), repetition (the slippers, her dream), parallelism (Tristana's choices), prediction (in the case of Tristana's return to Lope)—to heighten dramatic tension, irony, and melodrama. By his use of these, he points to the repressive and fatal influence of provincial Spanish society and the inevitability of Tristana's disillusionment.

After the amputation of her leg, in 1932, Tristana ages rapidly and

7. Lucy Stone, "Disappointment Is the Lot of Woman" (1855), in *Voices from Women's Liberation*, ed. Leslie B. Tanner (New York: New American Library, 1971), p. 75.

exhibits drastic personality changes, undergoing what Galdós had termed a metamorphosis. Although crippled, she becomes progressively stronger, more domineering, independent, and austere. She no longer works at pleasing; she does not fear being repulsive. She becomes careless in her dress, wears her make-up as a mask, and declines to use the uncomfortable false leg. In the end, Buñuel suggests a final, multiple image of the self-sufficient woman Tristana will be after Lope's death, and the film ends with a series of flashbacks, earlier images from her past which she recalls in reverse chronological order: her recurrent dreaming of the bell tolling while Don Lope's head swings before her eyes; Tristana leaving the church with her cane, on the arm of Don Lope, after their wedding; Tristana seated at her dressing table in the country house, Saturno, the deaf-mute behind her caressing her neck and stroking her just-brushed hair; Tristana and Horacio standing with their arms around each other in the artist's studio; Don Lope in his bathrobe seizing Tristana by the waist and dragging her to bed for the first time; the final (corny) Buñuelian image of Saturno eating the apple which Tristana has brought to him at the institution for deaf-mutes.[8]

After her marriage to Lope, Tristana again presents a dual image whose face depends on the perceiver: a bride who will not leave her own room to share a marriage bed on her wedding night, for the domesticated Don Lope she is both a cold wife and a pitiable cripple. From a psychological or feminist perspective, however, her vindictive behavior is understandable. As Otto Rank said to Anaïs Nin about the latter's relationship to her father: "Revenge is necessary. To reestablish equilibrium in the emotional life. It rules us, deep down. It is at the root of Greek tragedies." As Nin herself says in a dream: "You can see

---

8. Por su imaginación pasan vertiginosamente las imágenes que la torturan desde hace años: tañido de la campana mayor (primer plano de ella, con la cabeza de don LOPE colgando como badajo). TRISTANA, sobresaltada, se incorpora en la cama. En su rostro se lee la angustia que la agobia. Otra imagen que se inmiscuye en su imaginación: final de la ceremonia de la boda, con TRISTANA apoyándose en un bastón abandonando la iglesia del brazo de don LOPE; TRISTANA sentada ante el tocador, en la casa de campo, y SATURNO a sus espaldas acariciándole la nuca y el cabello que ella se estaba cepillando; TRISTANA y HORACIO, de pie y abrazados, en el taller de este último, besándose apasionadamente; don LOPE, en bata, arrastrando a la jovencita TRISTANA hacia su cuarto, la primera vez, cogiéndola por la cintura; TRISTANA y SATURNA, en las afueras de la ciudad, dirigiéndose hacia el establecimiento para sordomudos; y, finalmente, en esta 'vuelta hacia atrás' imaginada por TRISTANA, ésta frente a SATURNO comiendo la manzana que ella le ha regalado" (script p. 134).

I was brought up in Spanish Catholicism, that my actions later are not evil; just a struggle to react against a prison."[9] Tristana's passive revenge on Don Lope at the climax of the film is presented by Buñuel from a similar ideological perspective and also incorporates dream analysis. The difference is that Buñuel, somewhat in the manner characteristic of Galdós, maintains a stance of apparent objectivity, which allows him to sympathize with Lope as well as with Tristana. He condemns, rather than justifies, the evil actions perpetrated by each of the characters on the others.

Even though after her marriage Tristana is legally a chattel (and a physical cripple), she struggles for independence. She insists on the right to her own bed and room and rejects Lope's anticlericalism and his hypocritical disdain for money. The feminist implications in her actions recall Virginia Woolf's 1928 analysis: "Intellectual freedom depends upon material things. . . . And women have always been poor. . . . Women have had less intellectual freedom than the sons of Athenian slaves. . . . That is why I have laid so much stress on money and a room of one's own."[10] Although Buñuel omits (because of the anachronism in Spain) the suffragist piano teacher who appears briefly in the novel, he has two other minor female characters exert a measure of feminist influence, by example, on Tristana, although neither provides any theoretical antidote for Spanish Catholicism, and neither can serve as a useful role model. Lope's wealthy sister's power and his maid's lack of power in their relationships with him and the relative ability of each woman to effect the decisions which determine her own life teach Tristana a practical lesson about the world and function as an antidote for the idealistic illusions on which she had been nurtured by Lope.

From a distance, the married Tristana, at the end of the film, in 1935, resembles the black-clad Spanish *viudas* ("widows")—churchgoing, respected, charitable, virtuous. Because she is a woman in Spain, her life is ingrown and cloistered: "Mujer honrada, pierna quebrada y en casa." A woman must be kept at home, according to the old saying, even if you have to break her leg, in order to safeguard her husband's honor, which depends on his wife's virtue, meaning marital fidelity. But Tristana becomes freer, ironically, after her illness than she had been before it, despite and because of her physical handi-

9. Anaïs Nin, *The Diary of Anaïs Nin: 1931–1934*, ed. Gunther Stuhlmann (New York: Harcourt, Brace & World, 1966), pp. 307, 254.

10. Virginia Woolf, *A Room of One's Own* (1929; rpt. New York: Harcourt, Brace & World, 1957), p. 112.

cap and its effect on Lope and as a result of her rebellious affair and subsequent loss of romantic illusions. She sacrifices old dreams as she is forced to focus on material realities, particularly on the fact of her physical abnormality. One-legged, she stands tall on the balcony above the appreciative deaf-mute Saturno and smilingly, nonchalantly, yet somewhat triumphantly, opens her robe to uncover her naked body. Buñuel contrasts this impressive visual image, in the following scene, with multiple shots of an icon of the Virgin Mary, heavily ornamented and clothed, as if shrouded in mystery and illusion. Tristana on the balcony has nothing to hide and unveils herself serenely.

Although the Virgin Mother is, especially in Spanish Catholicism, the model of all women, Tristana is obviously able to reject the model. She does not, however, reject the Church, to which she turned, in part, in rebellion against her anticlerical "father," whom she married on the advice of her confessor. Why does Tristana turn to the Catholic church when, as Mary Daly points out, there is "in the documents of Scripture, church fathers, popes, and theologians throughout the centuries . . . an all-pervasive misogynism and downgrading of women as persons?"[11] She does so not only to rebel against Lope's hypocritical iconoclasm—in a somewhat counterrevolutionary manner—but also, literally and figuratively, to get out of the house; the Church becomes a useful crutch for the crippled Tristana. It is, after all, an important center of social life, as Buñuel indicates with heavy-handed symbolism in the scene in which Lope converses with his new priest-friends in the kitchen. The men's relationship is fundamentally based on a cultural pattern of male friendship and bonding, and it excludes Tristana, as was the case earlier with the more worldly masculine fraternity of the habitués at the café. Tristana does not have similar relationships with women and never roams freely outside the house. In fact, she did not even go unescorted to see her lover before her first rebellion. After the amputation she travels in her wheelchair accompanied by Saturna, Saturno, or Lope, but she has no place to go except to church.

Also, Tristana's turning to the Church is a symbol and element of her metamorphosis and should be interpreted in the context of time and place. After the elections of 1933, a new Catholic party, the CEDA, became the most powerful in Spain, one indication of the swing to the right which was commencing after two years of Republican rule. Perhaps then, in her religiosity, Tristana is, after all, typical. Although women in Spain did not get the vote until the new constitu-

---

11. Mary Daly, "Women and the Catholic Church," in *Sisterhood Is Powerful*, ed. Robin Morgan (New York: Vintage Books, 1970), p. 125.

tion passed the Cortes in 1931, it is believed by many analysts that it was the female vote which two years later gave power to the CEDA since Spanish women voted "as their confessors instructed them,"[12] and the Church openly supported the CEDA.

Viewed economically and sociologically, the widow Tristana is a childless, single woman, belonging to a group which, in Germany, was punished by taxation for their uselessness to the state after Hitler came to power in 1933. Buñuel reminds us of the historical background, both Spanish and European, in brief scenes with Fascist police or soldiers and in Lope's reading of the newspaper. The widow Tristana, free of family responsibilities and financial worries, enjoys her new status as a propertied bourgeoise. She is not inclined—as she told her confessor before her marriage—to celibacy. Having outgrown narcissism and masochism and having disposed of her talkative, tiresome spouse, Tristana looks forward to a long-term sexual relationship with the handsome deaf-mute, assured not only of Saturno's silence but also of his faithfulness, gratitude, obedience, and willingness to please. The relationship recalls that of young Tristana and Don Lope, but now it is the male who is wholly subservient and financially dependent. Tristana, sexually and intellectually liberated from Lope, replaces her erstwhile father/lover with two men: a virile virgin youth and a safe, benign confessor.

Overall, Tristana represents woman in her search for liberty. The way to liberty is through choice and rebellion. Initially her field of choice is so restricted that the exercise may seem futile, pathetic, or ridiculous. But Tristana makes progress in choosing, gradually builds her will, and becomes acquainted with her own power and the limits of her determination. Buñuel contrasts her with Saturna, less free and less aggressive. What street to take, she asks the maid, at a fork in the thoroughfare. They're both the same, the maid doesn't care. I like this one, Tristana says decisively, indicating one of the two nearly identical alleys (which turns out to be Horacio's street). Half a block later, Saturna, in the tones of a child, says to no avail that, well, really, she liked the other one better.

Eventually, Tristana is able to decide between men, between courses of action, between life and death. The theme of personal freedom is obsessive in her character and central to her story. Her search for liberty in the film brings into play major questions about sexuality, patriarchy, and social class. As ideological vehicles, Buñuel employs his

12. Hugh Thomas, *The Spanish Civil War* (New York: Harper & Row, 1963), p. 46.

favorite symbolism (Freudian-sexual, especially phallic; archetypal; biblical) from the beginning of the film, notably in the visual images of castration and loss of innocence (apple eating) in Tristana's first, playful contact with the opposite sex. Buñuel, viewing pre-Civil War Toledo with hindsight that Tristana could not possess, involves her in dramatic irony and allows her tragic moments. When she leaves on the train with Horacio, Lope is sure of her return; when she arrives, Lope predicts: "Si entra en mi casa, ya no volverá a salir de ella" (script p. 102) (Once she enters my house, she'll never leave it again). Tristana's dream of freedom was as doomed as Lope's of liberalization; these were impossible individually because they were impossible in Spain after the demise of the Second Republic. Lope's head tolls in Tristana's vision, sounding doom.[13]

Lope is at once father, lover, and teacher for Tristana, the major influence in her intellectual formation and maturation. It is he, under the influence of Bakunin especially, who teaches her about freedom. From the beginning of their affair, Lope preaches sexual liberation and ridicules marriage. He criticizes capitalism, materialism, the police, and the bourgeois family. Tristana proves to be an apt pupil, internalizing Lope's values, ideology, and even his language, as is evidenced at the start of her affair with Horacio when she declares: "Sé que estoy deshonrada, pero libre para quererte" (script p. 75) (I realize I am dishonored, but free to love you). Her use of such expressions clearly recalls Lope's adherence to the code of honor and the contradictions inherent in the views he professes (for example, about free love and fidelity or about the work ethic). During her liaison with Horacio, she stalwartly refuses each proposal of marriage. But sexuality, she finds, is not enough to end effective serfdom. She illustrates, at first unknowingly, what many critics have observed, that "sexual freedom is the first freedom a woman is awarded and she thinks it is very important because it's all she has; compared to the dullness and restrictiveness of the rest of her life it glows very brightly."[14]

The most tangible freedom Tristana actually achieves is economic. In order to insure financial independence, she first must follow the law and marry Lope, knowing that as long as her husband lives, she remains his legal dependent. Even after the revolt against authority and

13. "The history of Spain during the two and a half years after the general elections of November 1933 was marked by a steady decline into chaos, violence, murder and, finally, war"; ibid., p. 74.

14. Dana Densmore, "On Celibacy," in *Voices from Women's Liberation*, p. 265.

subsequent role reversals of victim and victimizer in the third segment of the film, Tristana's physical handicap is a constant reminder and emblem of her psychological burden, of the damage done. And so she goes beyond the law, which, as Lope's sister says, "is made by men, little one." Tristana's vindictive murder of Lope is metaphorically suited to his crime and to his country's. She opens the windows in the sick old man's bedroom on a cold, snowy night, allowing a breath from outside to invade his house, engulf him, and hasten his demise.

Lope's conception of liberty is aristocratic and anachronistic. Buñuel has him repeat a variation of a marvelous speech by Galdós' Lope: "Los verdaderos sacerdotes somos nosotros, los que regulamos el honor y la moral, los que combatimos en pro del inocente, los enemigos de la maldad, de la hipocresía, de la injusticia y del vil metal"[15] (We are the true priests, we who uphold honor and morality, who do battle on behalf of the innocent; we who are the enemies of evil, hypocrisy, injustice, and base money). Most important, it was, like his chivalry, less a motivating force than a habit, and especially a habit of conversation. His liberalism, like Spain's earlier, was fraught with contradictions. Buñuel emphasizes its rhetorical nature. And when Lope reads aloud from the newspaper editorial about the Spanish Republic, there is ironical comment both on Spain and on Lope, for although he disagrees vehemently with the newspaper's political analysis, he is a representative of the weakness; in fact, it is his own: "El pecado original de la Primera República del pueblo español ha sido siempre, mientras estuvo en el poder, el querer curar con empirismos, y sólo con empirismos, la gangrena de las instituciones" (script p. 44) (The original sin of the First Republic of the Spanish people was always, while it was in power, the desire to cure with quackery, and only with quackery, the gangrene in the institutions).

Like Spain's, Lope's liberty slips away under a dictatorial oppression. When Tristana returns ill, in danger of death, and the doctor suggests a priest, Lope bellows: "¿Curas en mi casa? ¡Nunca!" (script p. 108) (Priests in my house? Never!). But after his marriage, he con-

15. Galdós, *Tristana*, p. 16. Galdós emphasizes the hypocrisy of Lope's idealism, especially in regard to Tristana: "D. Lope le cultivaba con esmero la imaginación, sembrando en ella ideas que fomentaron la conformidad con semejante vida; estimulaba la fácil disposición de la joven para idealizar las cosas, para verlo todo como no es, o como nos conviene o nos gusta que sea" (p. 30) (Don Lope cultivated her imagination with care, sowing ideas in her that fomented conformity with such a life; he stimulated the young girl's natural inclination to idealize things, to see things as they are not—as it pleases one to see them, or as one wishes they were).

vivially sips chocolate with them in his kitchen (while Tristana paces back and forth outside the door on pounding crutches). It is Tristana's ascendancy which has wrought the transformation, for if at the outset Lope vowed to get those ideas out of her head (script p. 27), referring to religious ones, she in short order gets those other ideas, moral ones, out of Lope's. By denying Lope attention, affection, and respect, she gradually makes him dependent and submissive. One terse scene from the third reel illustrates this situation. Tristana and Lope encounter a uniformed "Comandante" of the Guardia Civil after church; the latter approaches Tristana to thank her for her generous contribution to the orphans:

Tristana (*primer plano*). Es usted muy amable. Dale las gracias, Lope.
Don Lope. Gracias, comandante. (script p. 118)

Thus, she orders Lope to thank the comandante for his courtesy, and Lope does so submissively.

From the first, Tristana's dream of an impossible and idealized individual liberty is destined to bring her disappointment both because of Lope's hypocrisies and contradictions and because of the setting in which her search takes place. And if Lope could give her freedom, he could not do so without losing Tristana and, probably, his own identity. On the one hand, Lope tells her: "No trato de imponerte mi voluntad. Por esto somos felices. Porque ni tú ni yo hemos perdido el sentido de la libertad" (script pp. 57–58) (I don't attempt to impose my will on you. That's why we're happy, because neither of us has lost our sense of freedom). On the other hand, he threatens: "Si te sorprendo en algún mal paso, te mato" (script p. 69) (If I catch you fooling around, I'll kill you). Tristana is trapped in Lope's house, first of all, because she is a woman and he her psychological father-figure. The father-figure theme is constant from the beginning of the film, more pronounced than in the book (even though Buñuel bases much of his dialogue on the Galdós text). One Buñuelian symbol of Tristana's psychological need occurs in the cathedral scene, in which he has her lean over to kiss the prone statue of a dead archbishop and lie down on top of it.[16]

16. "Plano medio cercano, tomado ligeramente desde lo alto, de la cabeza de la escultura yacente de un sepulcro. Plano medio del mismo sepulcro: TRISTANA se inclina sobre la escultura de mármol o de alabastro, con intención de besarla en los labios. Otro plano de TRISTANA, poco menos que tendida sobre la estatua como una dócil amante" (script pp. 51–52) (Close middle-distance shot taken slightly from above, of the head of the recumbent statue on a tomb.

Don Lope is of course the patriarchal head of the house, and he governs as a despot, in the tradition of the Spanish Catholic monarchs. Although Lope claims to be a political liberal, he is wholly authoritarian in his relationship to Tristana until she ceases to permit his exercise of control. Early in their relationship he tells her: "Soy tu padre y tu marido. Y hago de uno o de otro según me conviene" (script, p. 69) (I am your father and your husband. I play one role or the other as it suits me). Here, as in John Stuart Mill's analysis, the system of sexual domination may be viewed as the prototype of other abuses of power and other forms of egotism.[17] Lope, self-professed defender of the weak and anticlerical freethinker, does not perceive his internal contradictions nor the inevitable connections between authoritarianism in church and state, which he believes he loathes, and authoritarianism in male-female relations, which he takes for granted. He is able to tell Saturna, "Tú a tus cacerolas" (script p. 48) (Attend to your pots and pans) because she is his inferior, socially, economically, and sexually. He tells his friends at the café that he respects the Ten Commandments except those which refer to sex because the latter, he is certain, were appended by Moses to the truly divine ones "for political reasons" which, of course, do not concern him, Lope (script p. 41).

But it is precisely this political relationship and this lack of concern which provide the film's major metaphor: Tristana's mutilated leg. The old Spanish saying, which Lope quotes, makes the tenor clear—"La mujer honrada, pierna quebrada y en casa" (script p. 46) (If you want to have a faithful wife, break her leg and keep her at home)—referring to the feudal sequestration of women in the home and to the traditional male honor theme. As Wilhelm Reich wrote in *The Mass Psychology of Fascism* in 1933: "The authoritarian state has a representative in every family, the father; in this way he becomes the state's most valuable tool."[18] In Buñuel's multileveled handling, the mutilation comes to suggest the common handicap of them all (Tristana, Horacio, Lope, Saturna, Saturno), for all the characters are virtually impris-

---

Middle-distance shot of same tomb: TRISTANA leans over the marble or alabaster statue, as if to kiss it on the lips. Another shot of TRISTANA, nearly stretched out on top of the statue, like a docile lover).

17. See Mill's essay, "The Subjection of Women" (1869), reprinted in *Three Essays by J. S. Mill* (London: Oxford University Press, 1966). Also see the discussion of Mill's feminism in Kate Millett, *Sexual Politics* (New York: Doubleday, 1970), Chap. 3, and of Engels and Millett in Charnie Guettel, *Marxism and Feminism* (Toronto: The Women's Press, 1974), pp. 3–62.

18. Wilhelm Reich, *The Mass Psychology of Fascism* (1933), trans. Theodore Wolfe (New York: Orgone Institute, 1946), p. 44.

oned, enclosed at home, while outside people make revolution and counterrevolution, and Spain approaches its disastrous Civil War.

Buñuel said not long ago in an interview with Carlos Fuentes:

> My ideas have not changed since I was twenty. Basically, I agree with Engels: An artist describes real social relationships with the purpose of destroying the conventional ideas about those relationships, undermining bourgeois optimism and forcing the public to doubt the tenets of the established order.[19]

The image of woman which emerges from this film illustrates the disparity between one woman's social relationships and sentimentalized visions of them, between the woman herself and sentimentalized visions of her. Critics have complained that *Tristana* is, of all Buñuel's later films, the most innocuous, even fashionable. With discreet charm, Buñuel comments on the problem of politics for the contemporary artist:

> Forty years ago, everything was very clear-cut. . . . The enemies were capitalism, the bourgeoisie, private property, chauvinism, religion, the police, institutional violence coated with middle-class sentimentality. . . . Now that's all changed. Publicity, the media, absorb everything, make everything innocuous, fashionable. (p. 91)

He adds: "I believe that the class struggle is no longer the central social problem. . . . The real issue is survival" (p. 93).

Tristana is best understood within her world—structurally her life is bounded by the panoramic shots of Toledo which open and close the film—but it is a world which was breaking apart. As Joan Mellen points out: "Toledo's narrow winding medieval streets provide a real labyrinth to echo Tristana's unconscious imprisonment."[20] Despite the circularity and repetition in the visual imagery, however, the total image of woman in Buñuel's film inevitably carries the old revolutionary message of necessary changes, necessary rebellion, necessary hope: Tristana is a product of her choices as well as of her background. The real issue for her is individual freedom. Although crippled in its pur-

19. Carlos Fuentes, "The Discreet Charm of Luis Buñuel," *New York Times Magazine*, 11 March 1973, p. 93; page numbers following quotations in the text refer to this article.

20. Joan Mellen, "Buñuel's *Tristana*," in *Women and Their Sexuality in the New Film* (New York: Horizon Press, 1974), p. 196. I wish to thank Julianne Burton for bringing this article to my attention. Mellen's interpretation differs from my own in many respects.

suit, she survives. She has refused to continue to serve, honor, and obey Lope or any other man, but her feminist victory is tinged by the director's stubborn pessimism about all social problems and social change (about which he seems to profess a thorough *plus ça change* cynicism). His heroine's quest leads her to suffer personal disfigurement and to choose the remedy of violence and results in her adopting the characteristics of her oppressor. She has successfully broken out of the traditional cultural conceptions of proper sex role behavior only to become more domineering, strong-minded, egoistic, spiteful, hostile, manipulative, and tough than Lope had been in his prime. The psychological damage she suffers in the process of her development is less severe than that of two other Buñuel heroines, Séverine in *Belle de Jour* or Viridiana, and I do not agree with those who interpret her as a freak or pervert (although hardly any of Buñuel's characters can wholly escape those epithets).

Buñuel's attitude toward this character, then, is highly ambivalent. Even though she is a victor individualistically, she is morally a villain, no better a human being than Lope. Would it, perhaps, be accurate to describe her in her maturity in the film's final segment as a bitch? From a radical-feminist perspective, the endpoint of Tristana's development in Buñuel's characterization—into an archetypal bitch—has political significance:

> The mere existence of Bitches negates the idea that a woman's reality must come through her relationship to a man and defies the belief that women are perpetual children who must always be under the guidance of another. . . . [The Bitch] is living testimony that woman's oppression does not have to be. . . .[21]

The metamorphosis is iconoclastic, in the sense that traditional institutions and established beliefs (both of the right and of the left) have been probed and ridiculed in the process of the character's development. Tristana, in the end, as "bitch," has become androgynous, incorporating qualities traditionally defined as masculine as well as those considered feminine. A most Buñuelian visual image of her emerges in the sequence in which she opens her robe on the balcony for Saturno; the Buñuelian other side of the coin is Lope's comment to the shopgirl as Tristana models a dress for his approval: "Perdone que se lo diga, señorita, pero se la podría tomar por un hombre visto de espaldas" (script p. 49) (Pardon me for saying so, madam, but she could be taken for a man viewed from behind).

---

21. Joreen, "The Bitch Manifesto," in *Radical Feminism*, ed. Anne Koedt, Ellen Levine, and Anita Rapone (New York: Quadrangle, 1973), p. 52.

Andrew Sarris, in an essay on Buñuel's film *Belle de Jour* (1967), accepts the Buñuelian ambiguities as part of a Buñuelian statement: "There are several possible interpretations of Buñuel's ending, but the formal symmetry of the film makes the debate academic. Buñuel is ultimately ambiguous so as not to moralize about his subject."[22] Following Buñuel's own statements about his art, many critics have pointed to the characteristically pregnant quality of Buñuel's image making. David Grossvogel defines Buñuelian ambiguity as the attempt to reveal the "monstrous disparity between what surfaces actually are and what they claim to be."[23] And Buñuel himself has said of his work: "I strive for a cinema that will give me an integral vision of reality; it will increase my knowledge of things and beings, and will open to me the marvelous world of the unknown, which I can neither read about in the daily press nor find in the street."[24] As Carlos Fuentes sees it: "Buñuel the artist knows that, in art, the solution to the enigma is another enigma."[25]

Although the ambiguities in Buñuel's characterization of Tristana and in the film cannot be resolved easily—because of the contradictions inherent in feminism as well as those that derive from the *auteur*'s own poetic, ideology, and conflictive surrealist and Spanish-Catholic legacies—there is nothing to be lost by approaching some of the difficult questions suggested. Katherine Singer Kovács, in her comparative study of Pierre Louÿs' novel *La Femme et le Pantin* (1898) and Luis Buñuel's *Cet obscur objet du désir* (1977), examines Buñuel's use of ambiguous elements and agrees that the use of menacing objects and the intimations of violence found here are typical both of surrealism in general and of Buñuel in particular.[26] Many critics have studied the surrealistic elements in Buñuel's films. Jean Claude Carrière points out that the influence of dreams is as important in *The Discreet Charm of the Bourgeoisie* (1972) as it was in Buñuel's first film, *Un Chien An-*

---

22. Andrew Sarris, "*Belle de Jour*," in Luis Buñuel, *Belle de Jour*, trans. Robert Adkinson (New York: Simon & Schuster, 1971), p. 27; reprinted from *The Village Voice, Confessions of a Cultist*, and *Film 68/69*.

23. David I. Grossvogel, "Buñuel's Obsessed Camera: *Tristana* Dismembered," *Diacritics*, 2 (Spring 1972): 51–56.

24. Luis Buñuel, "Cinema: An Instrument of Poetry," *Theatre Arts*, July 1962; quoted in *The Movies as Medium*, ed. Lewis Jacobs (New York: Farrar, Straus & Giroux, 1970), p. 4.

25. Carlos Fuentes, "Luis Buñuel," *El Sol de México en la Cultura*, no. 168, 18 December 1977, p. 11.

26. Katherine Singer Kovács, "Pierre Louÿs and Luis Buñuel: Two Visions of Obscure Objects," *Cinema Journal*, 19(1) (Fall 1979): 86–98.

dalou (1928).[27] The power of the dream sequences in *Tristana* recalls the horror of those in *Los olvidados* (1950).

The influence of surrealism on Buñuel is not limited to technique alone but affects the underlying thought as well. To believe, as Sarris does, that "formal symmetry" makes content "academic" is to misunderstand Buñuel and to diminish the depth of his art. In an interview with Beatriz Reyes Nevares, for example, when Buñuel was asked about his formal techniques, he responded that the form should never distract the spectator from a film's content and that "a film's moral should be in plain sight, without the covering of ornamental details. Without content, cinema is impossible."[28] Further, Buñuel has been widely quoted and is fond of saying that surrealism taught him that man is never free, yet fights for what he can never be.[29] So, too, in *Tristana*, the protagonist is ultimately unfree and in the end is forced to come to terms with the society in which she lives.

Catherine Deneuve, the beautiful actress who plays Tristana, also played the protagonist Séverine in Buñuel's *Belle de Jour*, and in both films her masklike, generally placid countenance hides her emotions and thought. What Molly Haskell says of Deneuve as Séverine is relevant to a discussion of Deneuve as Tristana, for Buñuel enables us to see both female characters from several points of view. Haskell writes of Séverine:

> As a spectator, a man luxuriates in the peculiarly erotic tension between the fashionable young bourgeoise and the masochistic voluptuary that emerges each afternoon; for the female spectator, she embraces all women who have ever fantasized such anonymous degradation, which is to say, all women. She is both an art-and-sex object and a subject who willingly surrenders herself. Once again, it is from the pedestal of purity on which her husband has raised her that she needs to fall so far and so precipitously. In the end, a tragedy must occur because society (husband, lover, friend) cannot tolerate her dual nature.[30]

---

27. Jean Claude Carrière, "Buñuel y las imágenes del sueño," *El Sol de México en la Cultura*, no. 168, 18 December 1977, p. 6.

28. Beatriz Reyes Nevares, *Trece directores del cine mexicano* (Mexico: SepSetentas 154, 1974), p. 73.

29. In answer to the question "¿Qué importancia tiene el surrealismo en el cine de nuestros días?" (What is the importance of surrealism in today's cinema?), Buñuel replied: "El surrealismo se ha fundido con la vida" (Surrealism has merged with life), ibid., pp. 72–73.

30. Molly Haskell, *From Reverence to Rape: The Treatment of Women in the Movies* (New York: Holt, Rinehart and Winston, 1974), p. 305.

On the other hand, in films and books, dual natures, like fallen idols, are tolerable and interesting. Buñuel's cinema thrives on duality, contradiction, and artistic images capable of reflecting complexity. The image of Tristana, as we have seen, is difficult to pin down and label because the changes in the character allow for a combination of archetypes and statements, much like an extended and multileveled metaphor. One could say, therefore, that although Tristana's surface as a vehicle is reflexive and enigmatic, the tenor—the drift of thought in relation to the vehicle—is discursive, tentative, shifting. At the film's end, Tristana looks toward the future; but the film's closure (the series of flashbacks) warns simultaneously that despite the liberating effect of focusing on the future, the future is never wholly free of the past.

A feminist critic may respond ambivalently to this openness and apparent lack of resolution, for it could be thought to suggest merely an otherness, a mirror. As we have seen, Tristana *is* often mirrorlike (one recalls the scenes at her dressing table in which the camera captures Deneuve's reflection). On the whole, this quality makes Buñuel's Tristana quite different from the Galdós original, and her elusiveness is precisely the most significant difference between the book and the picture, outweighing all the similarities in plot outline and dialogue. Of course, even if every word in the screenplay and every word in the book coincided exactly, the film would still be Buñuel's—Borges' parable about Pierre Menard (author in the twentieth century of Cervantes' *Don Quixote*) notwithstanding. As Jean Franco remarks of the Latin American novel: "The process by which topic, myth, and character are torn out of the European novel and subtly perverted often borders on parody."[31] Indeed, the relation between the film and Galdós' novel may also be summarized as parodic.

It is Buñuel's consciousness that shapes the film, which is why Catherine Deneuve/Tristana is essentially his creation. Buñuel is sympathetic to Lope, with whom he sometimes identifies. The actor who plays lecherous Lope in *Tristana*, Fernando del Rey, plays roles not very different from this one in other Buñuel films. Hispanist scholars have discussed at great length, in articles and at colloquia, the literary prototypes for Lope (Don Juan, Don Quixote, etc.). One non-Hispanist critic believes Don Lope stands for "the impotence and historical amnesia of Spain, a role depicted as well by Carlos Saura in *The Garden of Delights* through the character of Antonio."[32] An exile

31. Jean Franco, *Criticism and Literature Within the Context of a Dependent Culture* (New York University, Occasional Papers no. 16, 1975), p. 10.

32. Joan Mellen, "Buñuel's *Tristana*," p. 181.

from Spain living in Mexico City, Buñuel had had problems with Spanish censorship regarding *Viridiana*, the first film he did in Spain in decades. When asked in an interview in 1967 whether he had any plans to make a film in Spain, Buñuel responded: "I haven't planned anything since they refused to allow the shooting of *Tristana*."[33] Franco's government, in the summer of 1963, did refuse the authorization Buñuel had requested.

If we approach Tristana's complexity from an archetypal perspective, the perspective employed in the essay on female characters in Mexican literature (see pp. 227–42), we can see Buñuel's ambivalence toward his protagonist as arising from cultural sources which have become so much a part of his individual vision of the world that there is no way to erase the archetypes of good girl or bad, immoral or new-moral, no way for his heroine to escape echoes of clichés and stereotypes. One could even find echoes of the amazon myth in the character of Tristana (see pp. 53–66); she is certainly a far stronger woman than the Tristana of the Galdós novel (a trivialized "new woman," according to Emilia Pardo Bazán and others).[34]

There is sexual humor in the Buñuel film, often black humor and sardonic wit. If we apply Harriet Goldberg's humanistic and social-psychological criteria (see pp. 67–83), Tristana may be seen as a creation of man. Like Sor Juana and la Malinche, Tristana has few options and choices. Although it is not the convent that serves as a catalyst for her autonomy, the Church is, in the end, one of the institutions which, ironically, helps her in her conservative independence.

On another level, Tristana as a character is a creation of male authors (whether Galdós or Buñuel), and she is, like the historical figure Marina/Malinche, a character who presents two faces, in mask and in shadow (see pp. 97–114). But even in an interior view, behind her impassive face she embodies conflict between the masculine and feminine in herself; her resolution is in favor of the first. She presents, in the modern twentieth-century way, a multifaceted self, thus incorporating many of the various possibilities present in the different female characters in the medieval *Book of Good Love* (see pp. 84–96). On the other

33. Buñuel, *Belle de Jour*, trans. Adkinson, p. 11. See also the remarks by Buñuel, J. F. Aranda, and François Gergeley on this history in Luis Buñuel, *Viridiana* (Mexico: Era, 1962), pp. 149–58.

34. Emilia Pardo Bazán, "Tristana," *Nuevo Teatro Crítico*, 2(17) (May 1892): 76–90. See also Leon Livingstone, "The Law of Nature and Women's Liberation in *Tristana*," *Anales Galdosianos*, 7 (1972): 93–100; Ruth A. Schmidt, "*Tristana* and the Importance of Opportunity," *Anales Galdosianos*, 9 (1974): 135–44.

hand, precisely because she is a modern woman, she displays, like Sara de Etcheverts (see pp. 243–58) or Gabriela Mistral (see pp. 215–26), the contradictions and ambiguities of the modernist and postmodernist periods. From a political perspective, she is, in the end, a representative of the "censored sex" in Spain (see pp. 289–315).

Tristana, in her reluctance to marry Horacio, and then Lope, recalls the *mujer esquiva* of the seventeenth-century Spanish theater (see pp. 115–46). Nevertheless, like the female characters in eighteenth-century Hispanic drama (see pp. 184–200), she eventually consents. Less akin to the original Tristana of the Galdós novel than to the strong-willed protagonist in Gertrudis Gómez de Avellaneda's nineteenth-century play *La aventurera* (The Adventuress), the young woman seeks to humiliate her seducer and succeeds in doing so (Natalia, p. 207). In fact, she does more than that; she murders him. In her study of case histories of murder cases involving women perpetrators (which span the period from the 1840s to the 1890s, a critical time when middle-class women were undergoing a process of modernization), Mary Hartman writes that especially in the latter part of the century, "women murder not merely to escape what they perceive as hopeless or desperate circumstances, but also to achieve or retrieve some imagined happier state." She adds: "It is clear that by the end of the century many middle-class women were unwilling to accept the same sorts of legal and social inferiority as they had earlier."[35]

Although we can see the character in the light of centuries of literary history, Buñuel's Tristana is a woman of our century. Her face, like those of the women in Latin American literature (see pp. 280–88), changes as the film unfolds. These changes are significant ones that concern far more than psychological process in an individual personality. No less than the women in the tragedies of Federico García Lorca (see pp. 259–79), Tristana is portrayed as a product of historical forces and of a society and a culture in which women have suffered oppression for hundreds of years. She carries the burden of centuries of a Hispanic literary tradition as well as of Hispanic women's history—the *peso ancestral* ("ancestral weight") of which Alfonsina Storni wrote in her famous poem.

But, again, whether or not one judges that Tristana makes the right choices will depend on one's view of society as well as of women in society. Buñuel, in *The Discreet Charm of the Bourgeoisie* and in gen-

35. Mary S. Hartman, *Victorian Murderesses: A True History of Thirteen Respectable French and English Women Accused of Unspeakable Crimes* (New York: Schocken Books, 1977), p. 340.

eral, questions the status quo through symbols that heighten the reality of the action as it moves back and forth from the particular (the chickpeas, the slippers) to the general so that it is clear that the personal is also political. Although never without ambivalence, in *Viridiana* and *Belle de Jour*, as well as in *Tristana*, Buñuel expressly condemns the victimization of women by the bourgeois patriarchy. And in *Cet obscur objet du désir* not only is the elusive heroine notably mysterious, but she is played by two actresses whose appearances on the screen alternate with no apparent logic. For me, Tristana (especially Catherine Deneuve as Tristana) brings to mind love and revolution, as in the prologue to Buñuel's *L'Age d'Or* (1930),[36] and recalls Julio Cortázar's surrealistic la Maga in the 1963 novel *Rayuela* (Hopscotch).[37]

Buñuel's *Tristana* is, then, a creation that permits multiple interpretations, some of which are contradictory, even mutually exclusive. Buñuel is deliberate in his resistance to facile paraphrase. Like a number of other contemporary artists, he has recognized, to quote Fredric Jameson's remark about modern literature, "the profound vocation of the work of art in a commodity society," which is "*not* to be a commodity, *not* to be consumed, to be unpleasurable in the commodity sense."[38] For, in Buñuel's words, "Publicity, the media, absorb everything, make everything innocuous, fashionable."

Ultimately, Buñuel's *Tristana* is cultural artifact and mirror, work of art and commodity, the creation of Galdós and Buñuel, as well as of critics and the public. The character Tristana, like the image of the Mona Lisa in Rosario Castellanos' poem "Mirando a la Gioconda" (Looking at the Mona Lisa), will smile mysteriously through the centuries and be endlessly interpreted.[39]

---

36. Luis Buñuel, *"L'Age d'Or" and "Un Chien Andalou,"* trans. Marianne Alexandre (New York: Simon & Schuster, 1963), pp. 7–8; also see José de la Colina, "El díptico surrealista de Luis Buñuel," in Luis Buñuel, *Un perro andaluz [y] La edad de oro* (Mexico: Era, 1971), pp. 7–20.

37. See Gloria Orenstein, *The Theater of the Marvelous: Surrealism and the Contemporary Stage* (New York: New York University Press, 1975), Chap. 5 ("Surrealism and Women").

38. Fredric Jameson, *The Prison-House of Language* (Princeton, N.J.: Princeton University Press, 1972), pp. 175–76.

39. Rosario Castellanos, *Poesía no eres tú* (Mexico: Fondo de Cultura Económica, 1972), pp. 335–36.

Contributors

FERNANDO ALEGRÍA is professor of Latin American literature at Stanford University. Besides several novels and books of poetry, he has published *Walt Whitman en Hispanoamérica* (1954), *La poesía chilena* (1954), *Historia de la novela hispanoamericana* (1959), and *Literatura y revolución* (1971).

ELECTA ARENAL is an associate professor at the College of Staten Island, CUNY, and was an NEH Fellow at the Bunting Institute at Radcliffe College in 1978–1979. She is writing a book on the autobiographical and creative writings of seventeenth-century Hispanic nuns.

JULIANNE BURTON received the Ph. D. from Yale University and is assistant professor of Latin American literature at the University of California, Santa Cruz. She has published widely in this country and abroad on contemporary Latin American cinema.

ALAN DEYERMOND studied at Oxford University and is professor of Spanish at Westfield College, University of London (combining this with a professorship at Princeton, 1978–81). His recent books include *A Literary History of Spain: The Middle Ages* (1971; Spanish translation, 1973) and *Lazarillo de Tormes: A Critical Guide* (1975). He has published articles on the epic, the *Libro de Buen Amor*, *La Celestina*, and medieval romances and is compiling a catalogue of the lost literature of medieval Spain.

ROSALIE GIMENO received the Ph.D. from Case Western Reserve University and has been a lecturer at the University of California, Los Angeles, and at the University of Southern California. She has published studies and editions of Juan del Encina's theater.

HARRIET GOLDBERG is an associate professor of Spanish at Villanova University. She has published the *Jardín de nobles donzellas, Fray Martín de Córdoba: A Critical Edition and Study* (1974). She is a corresponding editor of *Allegorica* .

ESTELLE IRIZARRY is professor of Spanish at Georgetown University and the author of, among others, *Teoría y creación literaria en Francisco Ayala* (1971), an annotated critical edition of Ayala's *El rapto, Fragancia de jazmines y Diálogo entre el amor y un viejo* (1974), a scholarly edition of *Martín Fierro* (1975), *La inventiva surrealista de E. F. Granell* (1976), a critical edition of César Tiempo's *Versos de una . . .* (1977), and *Francisco Ayala* (1977). She writes a monthly section on Hispanic culture in the United States for the Mexican magazine *Nivel.*

KATHLEEN KISH is an associate professor at the University of North Carolina at Greensboro. She has published *An Edition of the First Italian Translation of the* CELESTINA (1973) and articles on *La Celestina* and Spanish ballads.

LUIS LEAL retired in 1976 from the University of Illinois and has been Visiting Professor of Spanish-American literature at the University of California at Santa Barbara and at Los Angeles. He has published *Mariano Azuela, vida y obra* (1961), *Historia del cuento hispanoamericano* (1966; 2nd ed., 1971), *Panorama de la literatura mexicana actual* (1968), and *Breve historia de la literatura hispanoamericana* (1971). He has published over a hundred articles in leading journals, both in the United States and Spanish America.

LINDA GOULD LEVINE is an associate professor of Spanish at Montclair State College and has also taught courses in Women's Studies. She has published *Juan Goytisolo: La destrucción creadora* (1976) and has coauthored with Gloria Feiman Waldman *Feminismo ante el franquismo* (1980).

MELVEENA McKENDRICK graduated from King's College, London, with a First Class Honours Degree in Spanish and received her Ph.D. from the University of Cambridge, England. She is a lecturer in Spanish at the University of Cambridge and a Fellow, Senior Tutor, and Lecturer in Spanish at Girton College, Cambridge. She has published *Ferdinand and Isabella* (1968), *A Concise History of Spain* (1972), *Woman and Society in the Spanish Drama of the Golden Age* (1974), and *Cervantes* (1980), together with articles on the Spanish

Golden Age drama. A composite edition of Calderón's *El mágico prodigioso*, in collaboration with A. A. Parker, is in the final stages of preparation. She is working at present on a book on the Spanish stage in the sixteenth and seventeenth centuries.

FRANCINE MASIELLO is an assistant professor of Latin American literature in the departments of Spanish and Portuguese and Comparative Literature at the University of California, Berkeley. She has written articles on Julio Cortázar, Oliverio Girondo, Norah Lange, and Manuel Puig.

BETH MILLER is an associate professor at the University of Southern California, where she has served as chair of the Department of Spanish and Portuguese. She has published *La poesía constructiva de Jaime Torres Bodet* (1974) and *Mujeres en la literatura* (1978), edited *Ensayos contemporáneos sobre Jaime Torres Bodet* (1976), translated seven American women poets—*Siete poetas norteamericanas contemporáneas* (1977)—and coauthored *26 Autoras del México actual* (1978).

ELIZABETH ORDÓÑEZ is an assistant professor at the University of Texas at Arlington. She has published articles on Clarice Lispector, Ana María Matute, Carmen Laforet, Elena Quiroga, and on women in Spain and in the contemporary Chicano film. She is on the editorial board of *Letras Femeninas* and has published poetry in *Primipara*.

RACHEL PHILLIPS taught for six years and received tenure at Vassar College. She is now an officer in the Trust Division of the First National Bank of Boston. She has published *The Poetic Modes of Octavio Paz* (1972) and *Alfonsina Storni: From Poetess to Poet* (1975).

MARCIA L. WELLES is an associate professor at Barnard College. She has published *Style and Structure in Gracián's "El Criticón"* (1976). Her articles include studies on Gracián, García Lorca, María de Zayas y Sotomayor, and contemporary Latin American women writers.

Index

This is an index of writers and other artists, anonymous works, historical characters, and major themes. Works by a known author are indexed under the author's name, even where that name is not mentioned in the text. Scholars and critics are indexed only where there is substantial discussion of their work. Themes implicit in the whole volume (e.g. feminist criticism, patriarchy) are indexed only where they are explicitly mentioned. The alphabetical order is English, not Spanish.

abbeys, double, 183
Abella Caprile, Margarita, 247n
Acuña, Manuel, 233–34
adab, 70
Adler, Raquel, 246–47
adultery, of wife, 195
Aguilar, Jerónimo de, 103n, 105
Agustín, José, 242
Agustini, Delmira, 19–20, 23
Alberti, Rafael, 291
Album Cubano, 212
Alcalde, Carmen, 290, 291, 292, 304–305, 315
Alegría, Fernando, 7–8
Alessandri Palma, Arturo, 216
Alexander the Great, 55–56, 57, 68, 82n
Alfonso VI, King of Castile, 54
Alfonso X (el Sabio), 53, 56–57, 58, 75n
alienation, 6, 215, 249, 252, 255, 270, 281, 282, 284–85, 288, 329–30
allegory, 38
Alós, Concha, 292
Álvarez de Cienfuegos, Nicasio, 196–97
Alvear, Marcelo de, 248n, 251
Amadís de Gaula, 104
amazons, 53–66, 115, 138, 140, 141, 185, 210, 357
ambiguity, 178, 354, 359
ambivalence, 247, 356, 357, 359
Amor, Guadalupe, 22
amplification, 40
ancien régime, 188
Andalusia, 271, 275, 277
androgyny, 21, 135–36, 155n, 173, 353, 357
anthologies, 9–10, 14, 15, 21, 22–23, 203
Anthony, Susan B., 212
Anzaldúa, Gloria, 330
Aquinas, St. Thomas, 71
archetypes, 227–42, 280, 342n, 353, 357
archpriests, lecherous, 59, 86
Argentina, 243–49, 251, 255, 258
Aristotle, 68, 71, 82, 85, 117, 118, 131, 170
Arroyo, Anita, 167
Arsamasseva, Margarita, 247n
art and psychological injury, 51–52
arte mayor, 40
Astell, Mary, 175n
Atalanta, 61
Atarazanas prison, 33, 37, 52
Atlantis, 54
Auden, W. H., 51
Augustine, St., 40, 43, 161
Augustinians, 158
Austen, Jane, 12n
autobiography, 29–37, 151–64, 165, 166, 168–70, 171, 172, 174, 176, 204
autonomy, 264
Ave Maria, 53
Avilés Fabila, René, 242
Aztecs, 99, 101, 103n, 107, 229, 230–31, 232, 325
Azuela, Mariano, 232–33

Baena, Juan Alfonso de, 36n
Bakunin, Mikhail Alexandrovich, 348
ballads, 63–64, 163, 195n

Banda Farfán, Raquel, 235–36
bandits, female, 115, 138, 139
Barbero, Teresa, 305
Barnes, Djuna, 12
Barraza, Isabel, 338
Barrios, Eduardo, 216, 217
Bazán de Cámera, Rosa, 247n
beatas, 236–38
Beauvoir, Simone de, 12, 21–22, 183, 278, 284, 287
Becerra Tanco, Luis, 231n
Behn, Aphra, 4
belle dame sans merci, 139
Bello, Andrés, 222
Berceo, Gonzalo de, 50n
bereavement, 267
Bergson, Henri, 219
Bernard of Clairvaux, St., 40
bestiary, 47, 49, 50n
Bible, 39, 40, 179, 180; Matthew, 88n; Acts, 43; Hebrews, 43
bisexuality, 310
Bishop, Elizabeth, 20
bitch, 353
Blake, William, 49n
Blancaniña, 195–96n
Bloomsbury, 23
Bocados de oro, 69n
Boedo movement, 247
Boethius, 39, 40
Böhl de Faber, Cecilia, 201, 202n
Bombal, María Luisa, 6, 20n, 280–88
"Boom" of Latin American novels, 13
Borges, Jorge Luis, 254, 356
Borges, Norah, 20n
Bosch, Hieronymus, 156
Bradstreet, Anne, 17, 42, 52
Bramón, Francisco, 230
Bravo Adams, Caridad, 20
Bretón de los Herreros, Manuel, 202n
Bridget of Sweden, St., 155n, 156n
Brontë, Emily, 20n
Brown, Rita Mae, 12n
Browning, Elizabeth Barrett, 20
Buenos Aires, 2, 248, 249, 251, 253–54, 257
Bullrich, Silvina, 6, 280–88
Buñuel, Luis, 8, 340–59
Bustamante, Cecilia, 21n

Caballero, Fernán, 201, 202n
Calderón de la Barca, Pedro, 124, 129–30, 131, 139, 164, 196n
Calvillo Schmidt, Lorenza, 326
Cambaceres, Eugenio, 250
Campo Alange, María, 290
Cáncer y Velasco, Jéronimo, 125
Cancionero de Baena, 36
Cancionero de Herberay des Essarts, 45n
Cancionero de Martínez de Burgos, 45n
Cancionero general, 44
Cantar de los siete infantes de Lara, 59–60, 63, 64
Cantar del cereo de Zamora (de Sancho II), 60
cantigas de amigo, 28
Cantu, Norma, 328
Capmany, María Aurelia, 290, 292
Carlos I, King of Spain, 100
Carmona, 31–32
Caro, Ana, 144
Carrera, Julieta, 14
Carrillo, Sancha, 30–31, 34
Carrillo, Santiago, 289
Cartagena, Alfonso de, 37, 43
Cartagena, Pedro de, 37, 44n
Cartagena, Teresa de, 4, 28, 29, 37–44, 50–52
Cassiodorus, 180
Castaño, Rosa de, 233
Castellanos, Rosario, 7, 12n, 13, 17, 18, 20, 21, 22, 229, 241, 318, 359
Castillo, Ana, 319, 338
Castillo, Hernando del, 44
Castillo Ledón, Amalia, 20
Catalina, Queen of Castile, 36
catechisms, 40n
Catherine, St., of Alexandria, 171, 172
Catherine, of Siena, 155n, 161
celibacy, 207, 237
celibate, temptation of, 69, 72, 75, 78, 79–81, 83
censorship, 169, 291–93, 309
Cepeda y Alcalde, Ignacio de, 204, 207, 208
Cervantes, Lorna Dee, 318, 324–25, 327–28
Cervantes Saavedra, Miguel de, 118, 137, 151, 164, 356
Chacón, Sylvia, 330
Châtillon, Gautier de, 55
Chicanas/os, 316–39
Chile, 215–17
Chingada, la, 97–98, 112, 228–29, 327
Choderlos de Laclos, Pierre, 295
choice, 198–99, 207, 347
Cholula, 99, 106
Christ, 3, 85, 86, 89, 90, 152, 153–56, 158, 159, 161, 167, 180, 220
Christie, Agatha, 20n
Christine de Pisan (Pizzan), 182
Cicero, 37
Cid, el, 54, 57
Cihuacoatl, 107, 108
Cinderella, 189
Circe, 63
Civil War, Spanish, 259–60, 291, 293, 348n, 352
Clark, William, 112–13
Clemente Orozco, José, 228

cliché, 202
Clytemnestra, 25
Coatlicue, 228, 232
code-switching (use of two languages in a literary work), 316n
Colectivo de Lesbianas País Valencia, 305
Colette, Sidonie Gabrielle, 12, 257n
Colonna, Vittoria, 213
Compton-Burnett, Ivy, 20n
Condesa traidora, la, 60
confessors, 159, 161, 162, 175, 177, 179; manuals for, 40n
confidantes, 198
consolatory treatises, 39
Contemporáneos, 12–13
convents, 39, 147–83, 186, 190, 191, 198, 208, 236, 269
conversos, 37, 41, 43, 44
Córdoba, 35, 36
Cornaro, Elena, 4n
Coronado, Carolina, 203, 213
Cortázar, Julio, 359
Cortés: Hernán, 97–112, 227, 231, 325; Leonor (illegitimate daughter), 110; Martín (illegitimate son of Hernán), 105, 110, 111, 227; Martín (legitimate son), 111
Cota Cárdenas, Margarita, 332–34
Cotarelo y Mori, Emilio, 205n, 208
Cotera, Martha, 317n
Council of the Indies, 113
Counter-Reformation, 174, 176
courtly love, 86, 94
creative process, reflections on, 42
criollos, 113
Cruz, Ramón de la, 8, 184–85, 186
Cruz, Sor Juana Inés de la, 2, 12, 17–18, 20n, 21, 22, 148–50, 151n, 157n, 164–83, 241, 318, 357
cuaderna vía, 61
Cuauhtémoc, 100
Cuba, 205, 209
Cunningham, Veronica, 338
Cyprian, St., 180
Cyrene, 61

Dadaism, 3
Daltón, Margarita, 242
Dança general de la Muerte, 49
D'Annunzio, Gabriele, 247, 250, 251
Darío, Rubén, 223
deafness, 38–39, 44, 52
Del Castillo, Adelaida, 317n, 325
Delgado, Sylvia, 317n
De los contrarios de amor, 124n, 128
demythification, 312–13
Deneuve, Catherine, 341, 355, 356, 359
De regimine principum, 68n
Dewey, John, 218
Deyermond, Alan, 60
Dial, The, 23, 208
dialogue, interior, 294
Diana, 140–41, 230
Díaz Arrieta, Hernán, 217
Díaz del Castillo, Bernal, 103–108, 109, 227
Díaz de Toledo, Fernán, 43
Dickinson, Emily, 20
dictation, 29, 51, 150, 151, 161, 162, 164
didacticism, 186–87
Diego, Juan, 229
Diez, Los, 217
Dinesen, Isak, 20n
dissociation, 285
Disticha Catonis, 70–71
doctorate won by woman, first, 4n
Domitila (Domitila Barrios de Chungara), 16
Doncella guerrera, la, 63–64
Don Juan, 129, 331–34, 356
Doolittle, Hilda, 12
double standard, 42, 146, 207, 273–75, 318
drama: Golden-Age, 115–46; 18th-century, 184–200; 20th-century, 259–79
dream, 35, 343, 344, 354–55
Du Guesclin, Bertrand, 32
Duncan, Isadora, 20n

editor, first Hispanic woman (Gertrudis Gómez de Avellaneda), 204
education, 4n, 142, 168, 176, 177, 179, 180, 181, 192, 197–99, 217–18, 296, 300
Elizabeth I, Queen of England, 141
Ema, Charo, 290
Engels, Friedrich, 282
Enlightenment, 184, 187
Enrique II, King of Castile, 31, 32, 33
Enrique III, 36
Enrique IV, 45n
Erasmus, Desiderius, 141, 143
Etcheverts, Sara de, 6, 243–58, 358
Eve, 53, 111, 228, 337
exegesis, Christian, 88n, 94n
exempla, 8, 31, 67–83, 148, 161, 177

Fadrique, Prince of Castile, 76n
fairy tales, 168
Falcon, Lidia, 290, 291, 292
family, 190, 192, 260
father, 190, 206, 342–43, 344, 350–51
feminist criticism, 4, 14, 182–83, 356. *See also* socialist-feminist theory
feminist debate in Middle Ages, 67n, 139–40, 141, 143
feminist history, 4–5
feminist writing, first Spanish, 42
femme fatale, 250

Fernán González, 57–59, 60
Fernández de Castillejo, Federico, 111n
Fernández de Hinestrosa: Juan, 31; Ruy, 31, 33, 34
Fernández de Moratín: Leandro, 184, 186, 187, 189, 190, 192, 194–95, 197, 198–200; Nicolás, 188–89, 190–91, 192, 193n, 194, 195–96, 197
Fernández de Santa Cruz, Manuel, 175, 179
Fernández Pecha, Fray Pedro, 35n
film, 252–54, 340–59
Finch, Anne, 16–17
first-person narrative, 281, 288. *See also* autobiography
flashback, 31, 35n, 257, 344
flirts, 238–39
Floresta de philósophos, 69n
Florida movement, 247
Foix, Leonor de, 45n
folklore, 60, 61, 72, 74
Forest, Eva, 292
formulas, 162
Fraire, Isable, 22
Franciscans, 38, 158
Franco, Francisco, 10, 259, 289, 290, 309n, 357
free will, 123–24
Frente de Liberación Homosexual del Estado Español, 305
Freud, Sigmund, 51, 69, 181n, 182, 281, 304
Friedan, Betty, 20n
Fuentes, Carlos, 98, 112, 235, 236, 352, 354
Fuller, Margaret, 208, 213
futurism, 247, 249, 255

Gaceta de las Mujeres, 204
Galindo, Sergio, 235, 236
Gallego, Juan Nicasio, 202n, 203, 212
Gallegos, Rómulo, 8, 229
Gambaro, Griselda, 21n
Gandhi, Mohandas Karamchand, 218, 219
García, King of Navarre, 58, 59
García de la Huerta, Vicente, 184, 185, 189, 192
García de Santa María, Álvar, 36, 37
García Lorca, Federico, 259–79, 291, 307, 358
García Márquez, Gabriel, 13
García Ponce, Juan, 242
García Tassara, Gabriel, 203, 204, 207
Garcilaso de la Vega, 140
Gargarians, 54
Garro, Elena, 13, 235
Gatín, Enrique de la, 247
Gauguin, Paul, 183n
Gertrude the Great, St., 157n
Gilliatt, Penelope, 20n
Ginzburg, Natalie, 20n
Girondo, Oliverio, 247n, 254
go-between, 87, 88, 90–91, 92, 93
Gómez de Avellaneda, Gertrudis, 7, 20, 21, 22, 201–14, 358
Gómez de la Serna, Ramón, 247n
Góngora y Argote, Luis de, 164
Gonzales, Sylvia, 318, 322, 326
González, Felipe, 289
González, Teresa, 246n
González Ruiz, Felipe, 111n
González Tuñón: Enrique, 247n; Raúl, 247n
González Vera, J. S., 217
gossip, 265–66
Goytisolo, Juan, 291, 305, 312
Gracián y Morales, Baltasar, 164, 179
Great Crash, 259
Greer, Germaine, 12
Gregory the Great, Pope, 40
Guillot, Víctor Juan, 244n
Güiraldes, Ricardo, 248n, 251, 252n

hagiography, 35, 151, 163
H. D., 12
hegemony, 11, 18
Helfta, convent of, 157n
Hellman, Lillian, 20n
Heracles, 54
hermits, 79–80
Hernández Puertocarrero, Alonso, 105
Hernández Tovar, Inés, 319, 320, 321, 322–23, 326
Herrera, Fernando de, 140
Hidalgo y Costilla, Miguel, 231
hierarchy, 144–45, 271n
Historia de proeliis, 55
Hitler, Adolf, 347
Hittites, 64
hombre esquivo, 122, 124, 145
Honduras, 100, 107, 109
Honegger, Arthur, 248n, 250
Hoover, Herbert, 222, 224, 225, 226
Hostos, Eugenio María de, 222
house, 34–35, 263, 264, 274, 351
Hoyos, Angela de, 320–21
Hugo, Victor, 210
Huidobro, Vicente, 216
humor, 67–83, 357
husband, cuckolded, 69, 72, 73, 74–79, 81–82, 83, 195

Ibáñez del Campo, Carlos, 215n, 216
Ibarbourou, Juana de, 20, 23
idealization, 8, 230
ideal landscape, 35, 38
ideology, 215–26, 258, 260, 348
imagery, 39–40, 41, 43–44, 45, 52,

155–58, 160–61, 253, 277n, 284, 335, 347–48, 351, 359; animal, 46–50, 155–56; city, 43; fire, 270; hunting, 47, 92; illness, 48, 50; landscape, 38; phallic, 49, 50, 270, 304; water, 270, 277
imprisonment, 52, 351–52. *See also* Atarazanas prison
Inés del Santísimo Sacramento, Madre, 152, 161–64
Inquisition, 176–77
insecurity, 2, 43
intertextuality, 17
Iriarte, Tomás de, 187–88, 189–90, 191–92, 194, 197–98
irony, 2, 41, 62, 180
Isaacs, Jorge, 8
Isabel (daughter of Moctezuma), 110
Isabel de Jesús, Madre, 4, 147–64, 167, 183
Isabel de Santa Mónica, Madre, 163
Isabel I (la Católica), Queen of Spain, 68n, 178n
Isabel II, 205
isolation, 38, 42, 44, 154, 165, 168, 169, 264, 266, 272–73, 274, 279, 283–84, 303

Jaramillo, Juan, 109
Jerome, St., 40, 167, 174, 180
Jesuits, 175, 177, 180
Jicotencal, 227–28, 231, 233
Jiménez, Juan Ramón, 217
Johannes Hispalensis, 68n
Jong, Erica, 12, 21, 201
Joseph, St., 154
Jovellanos, Gaspar Melchor de, 193n, 195
Joyce, James, 312
Juana de Portugal, 45n
Juan Manuel, 30
Judith and Holofernes, 41, 57
Julian of Norwich, 155n
Jurado, Alicia, 21n

Kempe, Margery, 155n, 161
Kent, Victoria, 291
kharjas, 27–28
Kierkegaard, Søren, 325
Krishna, 255

Lagerlöf, Selma, 20n
Lamas, Elisa, 291, 292–93
Lamias, 56
lament, 57
Lange, Norah, 13, 244, 254
language, 98, 102, 103, 109, 110, 114, 171
Larreta, Enrique, 251
Lars, Claudia, 20
Las Casas, Fray Bartolomé de, 109, 110
Lawrence, D. H., 247, 255
Leduc, Violette, 20n
León, Julia, 292, 293
lesbianism, 116, 181, 304–306, 338–39
Lessing, Doris, 5, 12, 20n
Lewis, Meriwether, 112–13
Libre de Alexandre, 55–56, 57, 58
Libro de Calila e Digna, 75–76
Libro de los buenos proverbios, 68–69
Libro de los engaños, 69n, 76–78
Libro de los gatos, 49n
Libro del infante don Pedro, 55n
Lienzo de Tlaxcala, 101
life expectancy, 4n
Lispector, Clarice, 12, 20n
Lista y Aragón, Alberto, 203
literacy, 4, 51, 159–60
Literatura Argentina, La, 246–47
Llorona, La, 107
London, 4n
Longauez y Vasquez, Enriqueta, 317n
López, Emy, 334–37
López de Ayala, Ignacio, 192–93
López de Córdoba: Leonor, 4, 28, 29–37, 44, 50–52; Lope (brother), 33; Martín (father), 30–32
López de Gómara, Francisco, 104, 108–109
López Portillo, Margarita, 229
López Velarde, Ramón, 234
Louÿs, Pierre, 354
love melancholy, 48n
Lowell, Amy, 20
Lugones, Leopoldo, 244n, 251
Lynch, Marta, 6, 280–88
lyric, oral, 27–28

McCarthy, Mary, 20n
machismo, 21, 323–24
Macías, 50
Magallanes Moure, Manuel, 217
Mailer, Norman, 201
Malinche. *See* Marina
Mancera, Marquesa de, 166, 168
Mandelstam, Nadezhda (widow of Osip), 34
Manrique, Catalina, 44n, 45n
Manrique, Gómez, 37
Mansfield, Katherine, 12
Manuel, Marina, 44n, 45n
March, Susana, 292
María de San José, Sor, 147n
Marichal, Juan, 40
Marina (la Malinche, Malintzín Tenépal), 97–114, 227–28, 229, 231, 318, 325–28, 357
Marina (mistress of Martín Cortés), 111
Marinetti, Filippo Tommaso, 247, 250, 258

Maritain, Jacques, 219
marriage, 282, 297; choice in, 198–99, 207; open, 191; rejection of, 115–46, 169, 358
Married Women's Property Act, 213
Marsé, Juan, 299
Marshall, Edison, 111n
Martial, 179
Martín de Córdoba, Fray, 68n, 83n
Martín Gaite, Carmen, 10, 293, 294–99, 301, 302, 303, 304, 305, 310, 315
Martínez de Castro, Manuel, 228–29
Martínez de Toledo, Alfonso, 64–65, 66, 81–83
Martínez Ruiz, José, 300–301
Marx, Karl, 183n
Mary, Blessed Virgin, 31, 35, 53, 85, 86, 89–90, 91, 97, 154–55, 161, 229–32, 234, 346
masturbation, 311
Matos Fragoso, Juan de, 125
matriarchy, 261, 278
Matulka, Barbara, 139, 143
Matute, Ana María, 10, 291, 292, 293, 294, 299–303, 304, 310, 315
Mauries, Blanca B., 238
Mayas, 101, 103
Meldiú, Lázara, 18–19
Melián Lafinur, Álvaro, 251
memoirs, 29–37
memory, 288
Mendoza, María Luisa, 20n, 21n
Mendoza, Rita, 328–29
menstruation, 312
Meraz, Marcella, 330
Merino de Carvallo, Nelly, 245
Mesonero Romanos, Ramón de, 203
mester de clerecía, 55, 57
mestizos, 113, 114
Meun, Jean de, 182n
Mexican Revolution, 113
Mexico, 97–114, 227–42
Mexico City, 108, 150, 164, 168
Michel, Concha, 16
Mill, John Stuart, 183, 351
Millett, Kate, 213n, 317n
Mira de Amescua, Antonio, 132–33, 134, 140
mirror, 285, 287, 356
misogyny, 8, 64–65, 67–83, 95, 145, 172, 179, 248, 257
Mistral, Gabriela, 6–8, 20, 23, 200, 215–26, 358
mobility, social, 188
Moctezuma, 99, 101, 102, 103n, 105–107, 110, 112
Moix, Ana María, 10, 293–94, 304–15
Molina, Luisa, 213
Mondragón, Magdalena, 233
Montanez, Mary Ann, 324
Montes, Anna, 324
Montessori, Maria, 218
Montherlant, Henry de, 247, 257, 258
Montseny, Victoria, 291
Moore, Marianne, 12, 20, 23
Morell, Juliana, 147n
Moreno, Dorinda, 320
Moreto y Cabaña, Agustín, 121–24, 125, 139
Morrison, Toni, 319n
mote, 44n
motherhood, 262–63, 302
Mujueres de América, 245–46
mujer esquiva, 115–46, 358
Muse, Tenth, 165
mysticism, 151–64, 165, 181, 183

Nahuatl, 101, 103n, 171
narcissism, 136–37
Nelken, Margarita, 291
Neoplatonism, 144
Neruda, Pablo, 216, 225
Neustat, Betty, 151n
Nevares Santoyo, Marta de, 141
Nibelungenlied, 61
Nicaragua, 222–26
Nidos, Mencía de, 133
Nieto, Nancy, 317n
Nieto-Gómez, Anna, 317n
Nietzsche, Friedrich, 251–52
Nin, Anaïs, 344–45
Nobel Prize, 7
Noche triste, 99, 101
Norris, John, 175n
notary, 29, 30, 31, 51
Novo, Salvador, 12
Núñez de Miranda, Antonio, 175, 179
nuns, 38–39, 41, 88, 93, 147–83, 187

Ocampo, María Luisa, 239
Ocampo, Silvina, 20n
Ocampo, Victoria, 20n, 23, 244–45
O'Connor, Flannery, 20n
Olid, Cristóbal de, 100
Oliveros de Castilla, 104
O'Neill, Carlota, 21n
Onís, Federico de, 218
Ortega y Gasset, José, 221
Orto do Esposo, 38
Ovid, 140, 180, 182n

Pacheco, José Emilio, 242
Pacheco de Haedo, Carmelinda, 239–40
pacifism, 220
Pacini, Regina, 251
palinode, 65
Pamphilus, 88
Panchatantra, 75n
Pardo Bazán, Emilia, 357
Paredes, Condesa de, 166

parody, 61, 89, 356
Parra, Teresa de la, 20n
pastorela, 57
pastourelle, 60
patriarchal poetry, 3–4, 18
patriarchy, 4, 16, 18, 20, 166, 181n, 189–92, 199–200, 207, 258, 263–65, 268, 282, 290, 316–17, 351, 359
Paul, St., 180
Paz, Ireneo (grandfather of Octavio), 98
Paz, Octavio, 97–98, 112, 181n, 228, 240–41
Pedro I, King of Castile, 30, 31, 32, 36
Pedro Alfonso, 71, 74–75, 77n, 78n
Penthesilea, 57, 140
Perez, Gloria, 319–20
Pérez de Guzmán, Fernán, 36
Pérez de Zambrana, Luisa, 203, 213
Pérez Galdós, Benito, 8, 307, 341–45, 349–50, 356–59
Pérez Patiño, Gómez, 36n
Peter, St., 161, 167
Petrarch, Francesco, 50n, 141
Petrarchan lyric, 140
Philoctetes, 51
picaresque, 156
Piercy, Marge, 18
Pinar, Florencia, 4, 28, 29, 44–52; brother of, 45
plagiarism, 41–42, 212
Plath, Sylvia, 12n, 318
Plato, 131, 145
Pocahontas, 59
Poema de Fernán González, 57–59
Poema de Mio Cid, 54
poetisa, 9, 20, 214
pogroms, 35, 43
poison damsel, 68
politics, sexual, 316–39, 345, 351
Poniatowska, Elena, 6
Poridat de las poridades, 68
Portal, Magda, 22
Prado, Pedro, 216, 217
prayer, 35
precocity, 168, 176
pregunta, 45n
Prescott, William, 110, 112
pride, 188, 189
Primo de Rivera y Orbaneja, Miguel, 259
property, 213, 264
prostitutes, 79–80, 240

Quetzalcoatl, 101, 107, 325
Quevedo y Villegas, Francisco Gómez de, 164
Quintana, Manuel José, 192, 193–94, 195, 203
Quintilian, 178, 180
Quiroga, Horacio, 244n

racial prejudice, 18, 35, 316–17
Ramírez, Ignacio, 111
Rank, Otto, 344
rape, 195, 304, 328
Real Academia Española, 204, 210–12
rebellion, 2, 24, 65–66, 92, 93, 116, 140, 142–43, 188, 190, 200, 207, 269, 272, 276–77, 278, 284, 287, 296, 343, 346, 347
Recabarren, Luis E., 216
refrains, 28
reification, 285–87, 288
respuesta, 45n
revision, literary, 204–206
Rey, Fernando del, 356
rhetoric, 40, 56
Rhys, Jean, 12
Rich, Adrienne, 16, 20, 52n, 318
Rico, Dina, 238
Rico González, Víctor, 111n
Rimbaud, Arthur, 51
Rincón, Bernice, 317n
Riva Palacio, Vicente, 236
Rivas, Duque de, 8
Rivas Mercado, Antonieta, 17n
Rocha, Rina, 330–31
Rodoreda, Mercedes, 20n
Rodríguez, Gustavo, 107
Rodríguez del Padrón, Juan, 57
Roig, Montserrat, 291, 303
Rojas, Fernando de, 49n, 50n
Rojas, Ricardo, 251
Rojas González, Francisco, 229, 230, 239
Rojas Zorrilla, Francisco de, 125–26, 138–39
Rokha, Pablo de, 216
role reversal in literature, example, 186
romance, medieval, 29n, 40, 104, 140
Romanz del infant García, 60
Rose, Ernestine Potowski, 212
Rubín de Celís, Carmen, 242
Rudel, Jaufre, 50
Ruiz, Juan, 8, 60–62, 70–71, 72, 82, 84–96, 357
Rukeyser, Muriel, 2
Rulfo, Juan, 237–38
Ruskin, John, 221

Sacajawea, 112–13
sacrifice, 194, 208
Sahagún, Fray Bernardino de, 101–102, 232
sainete, 184, 186
Sainz, Gustavo, 242
Salic law, 130
Sancha, Countess of Castile, 57–59, 60
Sánchez de Arévalo, Rodrigo, 39
Sánchez de Vercial, Clemente, 67–68, 69, 77n, 78–81

Sand, George, 20, 203, 208, 210
Sandino, César Augusto, 220, 222–26
Sandoval, Capt., 108
San Pedro, Diego de, 44n, 83n
Santa María, Pablo de, 37
Santiago de Chile, 217
Santillana, Marquis of, 62
Sappho, 21, 213
Sarmiento, María, 45n
Sartre, Jean-Paul, 284
satire, 64–65
Saura, Carlos, 356
Seligson, Esther, 242
Seneca, 37, 69n, 178; pseudo-, 69n
sensibility, feminine, 16, 21
sermons, 64, 67, 68n, 70, 71, 153, 175
Serrana, Elisa, 6, 280–88
Serrana de la Vera, la, 63
serranillas, 60–62
Sevilla, Diego de, 45n
Sexton, Anne, 21, 201, 318
sexual desire, 47–48, 50, 52
sexuality, 50, 318, 329, 330, 334, 337–39, 348
Shakespeare, William, 73, 146
shame, 271–72, 273
Sigüenza y Góngora, Carlos de, 170, 231
Sindbad, 76n
sisterhood, 303–304
slavery, 171, 209–10
Sleeping Beauty, 144
socialist-feminist theory, 341n
Socrates, 69n
Sontag, Susan, 12n
Soria (poet), 44n
Sosa Riddell, Adaljiza, 320, 326
sources, 40, 41, 55, 88, 178, 180
spinsters, 235–36, 238, 263–64, 283
Sponsler, Lucy A., 59–60, 65
Staël, Mme. de, 203
Stanton, Elizabeth Cady, 212
Stein, Gertrude, 3, 18, 214
stereotypes, 24, 235, 242, 280, 295, 307
sterility, 261, 268, 272
Stone, Lucy, 212, 343
Storni, Alfonsina, 2–4, 6, 13, 17, 19–20, 21, 23, 244, 249n, 332n, 358
Stowe, Harriet Beecher, 209
structure, 40; interlace, 40; tripartite, 340
style: conversational, 30, 31; feminine, 15, 18; oral, 162–63, 164
Suárez, Adolfo, 289
Suárez de Peralta, Juan, 110–11
submissiveness, 196, 200
suicide, 208, 244n, 273, 279
Sur, 23, 245, 246
surrealism, 354–55

Tabasco, 100, 103n, 104
Tafolla, Carmen, 326–27, 328
Tapia, Andrés de, 102–103, 104
Teatro de la Cruz, 202n
Tecuichpo, 110
Teilhard de Chardin, Pierre, 219
Tellado, Corín, 20n
Tenochtitlán, 99, 101
Teresa de Jesús, St., 4, 147, 151, 152, 161, 162, 163n, 165, 167, 177n, 213
Tetepanquetzal, 100
Thomas, St., 161
Tirso de Molina, 128–29, 135–37, 139, 140, 144
Tlaxcala, 101
Toledo, 43, 44, 352
Tolosa, Martín de, 110
Tolstoy, Lev Nikolayevich, 104, 217
Tonantzín, 229
topoi, 41
Torquemada, Juan de, 228
Torres Bodet, Jaime, 13
Tovar, Juan, 242
tradition, feminine literary, 14–21, 23–24
Trastámarans, 31, 32, 33, 34, 36
Triolet, Elsa, 20n
Tristan, Flora, 183
Turia, Ricardo de, 133–34, 139, 144
typology, 111

ultraism, 244, 247n, 249, 253
Unamuno, Miguel de, 217
universities: Cambridge, 4n, 15; Columbia, 259; Mexico, 168; Oxford, 4n; Puerto Rico, 220–22; Salamanca, 38
Uriburu, José Félix, 243, 244n

Valdés Fallís, Guadalupe, 317n
Valenzuela, Luisa, 21n
Valera, Juan, 203, 207, 208
Valéry, Paul, 218
Vasconcelos, José, 218
Vásquez, Ramón, 111n
Vayona (poet), 45n
Vega Carpio, Lope Félix de, 63, 117–21, 122, 124, 126–28, 129, 130–33, 134–35, 137, 138, 139, 140, 141–142, 143, 144
Vélez de Guevara, Juan, 124n, 139
Vélez de Guevara, Luis, 63
Venus, 89–90, 91
Vergel de consolación, 38
Vieira, António, 175, 177, 180
Vigil, Evangelina, 318, 323–24
Vignale, Pedro Juan, 247n
villancicos, 28, 171
Villanueva, Alma, 337
Villarreal, Concha de, 233

Villaurrutia, Xavier, 12
Villon, François, 50
Vindicación Feminista, 290, 308
Virgil, 82, 83
visions, 155–58, 159, 160–61

Wardropper, Bruce W., 123–24
warrior maiden, 63–64
Washington, George, 205
Weil, Simone, 20n
Welty, Eudora, 20n
Wertmüller, Lina, 201
widowhood, 264, 279
wild women, 62, 88, 94–95
Wilson, Edmund, 51
wisdom literature, 68
Wollstonecraft, Mary, 183
woman, masculine, 63–64, 115, 127, 133, 135–36, 140, 141, 168, 173, 181, 182
woman's poetry reworked by man, 28
woman's right to literary activity, 42, 148, 176, 177
Women's Rights Conventions, 213, 214
Woolf, Virginia, 5n, 12, 21, 183, 345
writing, dangers of, 180

Yáñez, Agustín, 237
Yrigoyen, Hipólito, 255

Zaid, Gabriel, 13
Zambrano, Esperanza, 20
Zamora, Bernice, 318, 321, 322
Zayas Sotomayor, María de, 4, 142
Zorrilla, José, 8, 203
Zúñiga, Juana de, 111

Designer: Dave Comstock
Compositor: G & S Typesetters, Inc.
Printer: Vail-Ballou Press
Binder: Vail-Ballou Press
Text: 10/13 Sabon
Display: Bernhard Modern and Cochin